New Kittredge Sh.....,

MW01380160

William Shakespeare

KING JOHN
AND
HENRY VIII

William Shakespeare

KING JOHN

AND

HENRY VIII

King John Editors
James H. Lake
Louisiana State University, Shreveport

Courtney Lehmann
University of the Pacific

Henry VIII Editor
Jane Wells
Muskingum University

Series Editor
James H. Lake

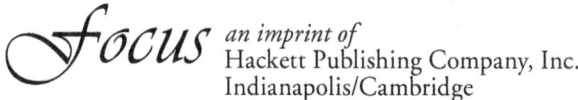 *an imprint of*
Hackett Publishing Company, Inc.
Indianapolis/Cambridge

A Focus Book

Focus an imprint of
    Hackett Publishing Company

Copyright © 2015 by Hackett Publishing Company, Inc.

All rights reserved
Printed in the United States of America

18 17 16 15   1 2 3 4 5 6 7

For further information, please address
    Hackett Publishing Company, Inc.
    P.O. Box 44937
    Indianapolis, Indiana 46244-0937

    www.hackettpublishing.com

Cover image: "Herbert Beerbohm Tree as King John in *King John* by William
Shakespeare" by Charles Buchel, 1900. © Victoria and Albert Museum, London.
Reprinted by permission of the Victoria and Albert Museum.

Cover design adapted from design by Guy Wetherbee | Elk Amino Design,
New England | elkaminodesign@yahoo.com

Composition by William Hartman

Library of Congress Cataloging-in-Publication Data

Shakespeare, William, 1564–1616.
    King John / William Shakespeare ; editors, James H. Lake, Louisiana State
University, Shreveport ; Courtney Lehmann, University of the Pacific ;
and, Henry VIII / editor, Jane Wells, Muskingum University.
        pages cm. — (New Kittredge Shakespeare)
        Includes bibliographical references.
        ISBN 978-1-58510-756-8 (pbk.)
        1. John, King of England, 1167–1216—Drama. 2. Great Britain—History—
John, 1199–1216—Drama. 3. Henry VIII, King of England, 1491–1547—Drama.
4. Great Britain—History—Henry VIII, 1509-1547—Drama. 5. Shakespeare,
William, 1564–1616—Histories. 6. Shakespeare, William, 1564–1616 King John.
7. Shakespeare, William, 1564–1616 Henry VIII. 8. Shakespeare, William,
1564–1616—Dramatic production. I. Lake, James H., editor. II. Lehmann,
Courtney, 1969– editor. III. Wells, Jane W., editor. IV. Shakespeare, William,
1564–1616. Henry VIII. V. Title.
    PR2762.L46 2015
    822.3'3—dc23   2015012431

Table of Contents

Publisher's Note   vi
In Memoriam   vi
Acknowledgments   vi

Preface to *King John* and *Henry VIII*   vii

Introduction to the Kittredge Edition of *King John*   3
Introduction to the Focus Edition of *King John*   7
The Life and Death of King John   45
Plot Outline of *King John*   129
Genealogy of *King John*   133
How to Read *King John* as Performance   135
Topics for Discussion and Further Study of *King John*   141
King John Bibliography and Filmography   145

Introduction to the Kittredge Edition of *Henry VIII*   151
Introduction to the Focus Edition of *Henry VIII*   155
The Famous History of the Life of King Henry the Eighth   173
Plot Outline of *Henry VIII*   283
Genealogy of *Henry VIII*   287
How to Read *Henry VIII* as Performance   289
Topics for Discussion and Further Study of *Henry VIII*   293
Henry VIII Bibliography and Filmography   297

Timeline for *King John* and *Henry VIII*   303

Publisher's Note

George Lyman Kittredge was one of the foremost American Shakespeare scholars of the 20th century. *New Kittredge Shakespeare* builds on his celebrated scholarship and extensive notes. Each edition contains a new, updated introduction, with comments on contemporary film versions of the play, an essay on reading the play as performance, and topics for discussion, with an annotated bibliography and filmography. For this, an accomplished Shakespeare and film scholar has been commissioned to modernize each volume.

The series focuses on understanding the language and allusions in the play, as well as encountering Shakespeare as performance. The audience ranges from students at all levels to readers interested in encountering the text in the context of its performance on stage or on film.

Ron Pullins, Founding publisher of
New Kittredge Shakespeare
Newburyport, 2009

In Memoriam

In memory of our friends and fellow editors
Bernice W. Kliman
Kenneth S. Rothwell
Thomas Pendleton

Acknowledgments

The Editors owe a debt of gratitude to the outstanding staff of Hackett Publishing, especially to Laura Clark, Brian Rak, and Rick Todhunter, and also to those at Focus Publishing who so patiently oversaw the publication of NKS series from its inception: Ron Pullins, Cythia Zawalich, Kerri and Guy Wetherbee, Linda Diering, and Haily Klein. James H. Lake wishes to personally acknowledge the sustained support of Larry Anderson, LSUS Dean of Arts and Sciences, English Department secretary Deloris Agbonkhese, Noel Librarian Susan Davison and Special Collections Curator Robert Leitz and Assistant Curator Martha Lawler. Special thanks are due to colleagues Sam Crowl, John Ford, Gayle Gaskill, Russell Jackson, Courtney Lehmann, Patricia Lennox, Laury Magnus, John Mahon, Jane Wells, and the many New Kittredge editors whose participation has ensured the success of the series.

PREFACE TO *KING JOHN* AND *HENRY VIII*

Although written at different times in Shakespeare's career and about kings who reigned four hundred years apart, *King John* and *Henry VIII* are often paired and seem to deserve each other.[1] In terms of chronology and composition, however, the two plays might appear not to match. Yet there are important connections that do indeed bind them together. Historically, King John's rule was the earliest of all of Shakespeare's English kings and Henry VIII's the latest, King Henry's daughter Queen Elizabeth having died less than a decade before Shakespeare wrote the play. Also the two plays are naturally paired as outliers, since their two kings both fall respectively outside the sequence of monarchies Shakespeare covered in his other eight history plays, which showcase the reigns of six successive kings (from Richard II through Richard III), divided into two groups of four, called *tetralogies*. And thus *King John* and *Henry VIII* serve as historical bookends to these tetralogies and as such naturally fit together.

It is also important to note that from alternative points of view, the *characters* of King John and Henry VIII might be paired as outliers, since both are types of tyrants, both defy the authority of the historically established Catholic Church, and both have problematic dealings in domestic affairs. It is true that the two kings experience radically different fates: John withers away and is allegedly poisoned by monks, while Henry triumphantly overcomes the machinations of his council. Yet, in both instances, taking on the Catholic Church was a surefire way of appealing to largely Protestant audiences. And also in each instance, both plays are daring experiments in evoking audience sympathy for marginal characters, presenting the voices of injured women (Constance in *King John* and Catherine in *Henry VIII*) who are among the most powerful in all of Shakespeare, indeed characters whose grievances detract from the audience's potential sympathy for the two eponymous kings.

---

1. See Frances A. Shirley, ed. *King John and Henry VIII: Critical Essays*. New York and London: Garland Publishing, Inc., 1988.

Placing together two history plays written so far apart but concerning many of the same themes and issues of the age has another advantage: it allows readers and audiences to see in consolidated form not only how Shakespeare's artistry developed, but also how his religious and political perspectives evolved over time.

William Shakespeare

THE LIFE AND DEATH OF
KING JOHN

Editors

James H. Lake
Louisiana State University, Shreveport

Courtney Lehmann
University of the Pacific

INTRODUCTION TO THE
KITTREDGE EDITION OF *KING JOHN*

Editor's Note: During his many years at Harvard College (1888–1936), George Lyman Kittredge (1860–1941) was famous as one of America's greatest and most popular teachers; he wrote books on Chaucer, *Beowulf, Sir Gawain and the Green Knight*, and *Witchcraft in Old and New England*, and published over 400 essays on a variety of subjects; but Kittredge's reputation as a Shakespearean rests upon his fame as a teacher and as an editor of Shakespeare's plays, sixteen of which were fully annotated and published posthumously, in 1945. It is in the introductions and notes to these plays that one realizes Kittredge's great learning and unique ability to make Shakespeare accessible to a broad range of readers. Thus Kittredge's introduction has been only slightly edited for this edition.

The Troublesome Raigne of Iohn King of England. . . . As it was (sundry times) publikely acted by the Queenes Maiesties Players and *The Second part of the troublesome Raigne of King Iohn. . . . As it was (sundry times) publikely acted by the same* were both published in 1591 as distinct quartos and republished together in 1611 and 1622. The title page of the 1611 publication asserts that the whole was "Written by W. Sh.," and that of 1622 spells the surname at full length. This ascription is unquestionably false. The author must remain anonymous. George Peele is a possible candidate, but the evidence in his favor is purely internal and not very impressive. The date of composition may be conjecturally put back two or three years before the publication in 1591. The short address in verse "To the Gentlemen Readers," prefixed to part 1, mentions *Tamburlaine* as having been received with applause. It sounds like a prologue, but may or may not have been written at the same time as the play. *Tamburlaine* dates from about 1587.

Shakespeare's play *The Life and Death of King John* was first printed in the Folio of 1623, which is therefore our only authority for the text. Meres mentions it in 1598 among Shakespeare's tragedies [in his *Palladis Tamia: Wits Treasury*]. How much earlier it [*King John*] was written cannot be exactly determined. Shakespeare's son

Hamnet died in August 1596, and biographers are tempted to read his father's own grief in the passionate laments of Constance for Arthur. But that is reasoning in a circle, for nobody doubts that the greatest of all dramatists could have written these passages if he had never had a son. Still, 1596 is a reasonable date for *King John*. In any case, it is more likely to have preceded *Richard II* than to have followed it.

For his material Shakespeare went to *The Troublesome Reign* instead of working up a plot from Holinshed's *Chronicle*; but *King John* is a new play, not a revision. Like its predecessor it covers the whole of John's reign (1199–1216), and the order of events is the same, with a modicum of readjustment. That order quite warrantably sacrifices historical preciseness to dramatic effect. Chatillon's embassy is the invention of the older playwright. So is the episode of the Faulconbridge brothers, for which he may have taken a hint from the case of Dunois, the famous Bastard of Orleans, as recorded by Holinshed. Austria (in both plays) is a fusion (accidental or deliberate) of Duke Leopold, Richard Cœur-de-Lion's captor, who died in 1195, with Widomar Viscount of Limoges, killed, Holinshed says, by a bastard son of Richard to avenge his father, who met his death while besieging the viscount's castle.

Many incidents or whole episodes of *The Troublesome Reign* are dropped by Shakespeare. His omissions are: Philip Faulconbridge's fruitless attempt to arrange for a duel with the Duke of Austria; his tearing the lion's skin from Austria's shoulders; his killing Austria in battle *coram populo*; the long scene in which he ransacks the chests of a monk and a nun and arrests Peter the prophet; the interview between Peter and King John in which the prophet interprets the omen of the five moons and tells the king that he shall lose his crown before high noon on Ascension Day; the very long scene on Ascension Day in which the king hears Peter reiterate his prophecy, is informed by Hubert of Arthur's fatal fall, orders him to hang Peter forthwith, is told by Faulconbridge that the sentence has been carried out and also that Lewis (having been elected King of England by the peers) is expected to land at any moment, submits to Pandulph, and learns that the French fleet has actually been sighted off the coast of Kent; the scene at St. Edmondsbury, in which the English peers, despite the efforts of Faulconbridge, swear fealty to Lewis, and Lewis and the French nobles take an oath to put their English allies to death when the victory is won; the soliloquy of Thomas, a monk of Swinstead, in which he resolves to murder King John, and the interview between him and the Abbot, in which he discloses his purpose and is absolved; the poisoning of the king in a wassail cup and the death of the monk, who must, as "taster," drink first from the cup that he offers; and the coronation of Henry III.

In most instances nothing is lost by these omissions, for the facts are made known to the audience in the course of the dialogue. Shakespeare has been censured, however, for nowhere revealing the poisoner's motive. Surely no such explanation was requisite. We have King John's orders to Faulconbridge (3.3.7–11):

> . . . see thou shake the bags
> Of hoarding abbots; set at liberty
> Imprison'd angels. The fat ribs of peace
> Must by the hungry now be fed upon.
> Use our commission in his utmost force.

And Faulconbridge has duly rendered his account (4.2.144–145):

> How I have sped among the clergymen
> The sums I have collected shall express.

After that, the monk's motive might reasonably be taken for granted.

Most of the old play is in sonorous blank verse with occasional bits of competent prose. One scene exhibits a riotous mingle-mangle of rhyming measures—fourteeners, octosyllabics, and Skeltonical short lines—as well as a bit of prose dialogue. This is the comic scene (omitted by Shakespeare) in which Faulconbridge plunders the clergy.

In *King John* the language is Shakespeare's throughout, with occasional slight echoes of the older phraseology. He rewrites completely even those passages of which he keeps the substance. Compare with Faulconbridge's concluding speech in *King John* the similar valediction in the old play, which runs as follows:

> Thus England's peace begins in Henry's reign,
> And bloody wars are clos'd with happy league.
> Let England live but true within itself,
> And all the world can never wrong her state;
> Lewis, thou shalt be bravely shipp'd to France,
> For never Frenchman got of English ground
> The twentieth part that thou hast conquered.
> Dauphin, thy hand! To Worcester we will march.
> Lords all, lay hands to bear your sovereign
> With obsequies of honour to his grave.
> If England's peers and people join in one,
> Nor Pope, nor France, nor Spain can do them wrong.

—George Lyman Kittredge

INTRODUCTION TO THE
FOCUS EDITION OF *KING JOHN*

Do you have a secret wish? Is it for power? For wealth? Or for something less ambitious but still important to your happiness? How far would you go to achieve it? Would you do something dishonest or betray friends or family? Have you ever known or suspected someone who would? These are disturbing questions. But they are nevertheless as riveting for us today as they were for audiences over four hundred years ago, when William Shakespeare wrote *The Life and Death of King John*, a play that mirrors not only the temptations, anxieties, and fears of Shakespeare's time, but also of ours. Indeed, just shortly before Shakespeare wrote *King John*, Christopher Marlowe had written *Tamburlaine* and *Doctor Faustus,* two hugely popular plays about men whose ambitions drive them to sacrifice everything, even their souls, for power and knowledge. Shakespeare's *King John* is about this same sort of driving ambition; and though set in a world that existed many hundreds of years ago, it is still familiar to all of us because it is one wherein the key players must make hard archetypal choices, must choose between public or private interests, between what is legitimate and what is not. And in every instance, the decisions have a spiraling effect on the action. But let's begin with some history.

The time in which Shakespeare wrote *King John* was both exciting and dangerous. It was a time of discovery and adventure, of war and the threat of war, of political intrigue and religious discord, and of a population explosion—from 2.5 million in 1525 to 5 million by 1680—despite heavy mortality, years of bad weather, bad harvests, and endemic plague. Yet it was also a time of rising literacy, stemming from the New Learning, which emphasized rhetoric, the powerful art of persuasion, and showed from the classics and history how to apply the past to current situations, thereby offering a formula for professional success to the ambitious students in Oxford and Cambridge and in the three hundred free schools famously built all across England by Tudor monarchs. And by Elizabeth's time, those monarchs had also become famous for their support of the plays of Shakespeare and his contemporaries, whose works were staged regularly at court and in the public play-houses first appearing in London's suburbs in the 1570s.

The theater soon became big business, and the acting companies established in London also toured throughout the countryside, especially during plague season, bringing plays to audiences in small towns all across England. But regardless of venue, Elizabethan audiences were always excited by two essential topics: politics and religion, dangerous and inextricably linked subjects, the popularity of which was such that despite the inherent risk, they were integral to most of the plays of the time. And knowing the risks, playwrights and performing companies carefully guarded themselves as a matter of course by situating their plays in foreign lands or by choosing an historical source from the distant past, as in the case of *King John*.

Besides this, everyone knew that religion linked to politics was a topic of long-standing interest, traceable to the Church–State disputes in the reigns of King Henry II (1154–1189) and his son King John (1199–1216). These disputes did not explode, however, until King Henry VIII (1509–1547) renounced the Pope, created his own brand of Catholicism, and named himself "Supreme Head" of Church and State—thereby inadvertently launching the Protestant Reformation in England. King Henry VIII's son Edward VI (1547–1553) furthered the Protestant cause but died young and was succeeded by his Catholic half-sister Mary (1553–1558), who immediately restored the Old Faith. Thus by the time Elizabeth became queen (1558–1603), England's religion had changed four times in just over a decade.[1] And the "compromise" Elizabeth thrust upon her people was not merely unpopular but distasteful to religious conservatives and radicals alike. Yet since the queen, like her father, governed both State and Church, those who failed to support her religion could be branded as traitors and punished accordingly.[2]

It is for this reason especially that Elizabethans would have related to the religio-political struggles portrayed in *King John*; however dangerous, they reflected England's greatest worries, exacerbated by growing fears for the royal succession.[3] Queen

1. See Eamon Duffy, *The Stripping of the Altars: Traditional Religion in England, 1400–1580*, 2nd edition (New Haven, CT: Yale University Press, 2005).

2. According to Robert S. Miola, "Elizabeth herself oversaw the execution of at least 183 Catholics . . . (thousands more were fined, imprisoned, tortured, and forced into exile)." "'An Alien People Clutching Their Gods': Shakespeare's Ancient Religions," *Shakespeare Survey* 54 (2001): 35. Records show also that following the Catholic Uprising of 1569, the government executed between 450 and 900 persons. See Richard Rex, *Elizabeth I: Fortune's Bastard* (Stroud, Gloucestershire: Tempus, 2003), 8. See also Alan Dures, *English Catholicism: 1558–1642* (London: Longman, 1983).

3. Several scholars have noted analogs between the reigns of King John and Queen Elizabeth—for example, both sovereigns were at some point accused of being usurpers and bastards; both claimed to be the "supreme head" of Church and State, both were excommunicated for defying the Pope and in both instances the Pope promised to forgive regicide; both had rivals, Prince Arthur and Mary Queen of Scots, respectively, who were later put to death; both endured uprisings; and both withstood foreign sea invasions that were thwarted by providential storms. See Lily B. Campbell, *Shakespeare's Histories: Mirrors of Elizabethan Policy* (1947) (San Marino, CA: The Huntington Library, 1978), 126–167, and E. A. J. Honigmann, ed., *King John: The Arden Edition* (London: Methuen, 1954), xxvii–xxx. For

Elizabeth had been on the throne for thirty years, was in fragile health, was childless, and would not live another decade; Mary Queen of Scots had already been executed (1587) and her son King James VI stood ready to be called, but Elizabeth refused to name an heir, and it appeared that she would never do so. Indeed, though the crown went peacefully to King James after all (1603–1625), political and religious unrest persisted, as did the nation's engagement with conflicting ideas of governance, leadership, and monarchy—closely knit ideas all mirrored in *King John* and in the other history plays of the 1590s.

There were at this time two opposing views of history and of monarchy, both of which Shakespeare interrogates in his plays.[4] The still-popular medieval view of history held that all of the past and future is providential, that ultimately God directs all that happens. The other view—from classic writers such as Cicero, Livy, and Plutarch, and much later from Machiavelli—taught that history is cyclical, repeats itself, and, that by studying the mistakes of the past, one can have some control over the future.[5] Contiguous with this view was a debate regarding whether historical events occur because the time is precisely right or because the appropriate person steps forward or is sent by God. Needless to say, Queen Elizabeth's government supported the idea that God providentially sent her grandfather Henry Tudor, Earl of Richmond, to end the Wars of the Roses (1455–1485) and establish the Tudor dynasty.[6]

The two views of monarchy both derived from the 12th century. One view, from John of Salisbury's *Policraticus* (*The Statesman's Handbook*, c. 1159), says that a king is the head of the "body politic," a metaphorical body that must always be guarded from illness; thus if the head is the source of contamination, it must be excised to protect or heal the body. Simply put, in some cases a king may be removed for the sake of the nation, especially in the case of tyrants, such as Richard III or Macbeth.[7] The second view, from a nameless French document, sometimes called *The Norman*

---

other analogies, see Virginia Mason Vaughn, "*King John:* A Study in Subversion and Containment," in *King John: New Perspectives,* ed. Deborah T. Curren-Aquino (Newark: University of Delaware Press, 1989), 62–75.

4. See Peter Burke, *The Renaissance Sense of the Past* (New York: St. Martin's Press, 1969). See also F. J. Levy, *Tudor Historical Thought* (1967) (Toronto: University of Toronto Press, 2004).

5. The idea was in fact proverbial: "Like time bringeth forth like examples." See F. P. Wilson, "The English History Play," in *Shakespeare and Other Studies,* ed. Helen Gardner (Oxford: Clarendon Press, 1969), 5. For other examples, see George William Smith, *The Oxford Dictionary of English Proverbs,* 3rd edition, ed. F. P. Wilson (Oxford: Clarendon Press, 1980), and also Morris Palmer Tilley, *A Dictionary of Proverbs in English in the Sixteenth and Seventeenth Centuries* (Ann Arbor: University of Michigan Press, 1950).

6. This idea has come to be known as the Tudor Myth, a term coined by E. M. W. Tillyard in *Shakespeare's History Plays* (London: Chatto & Windus, 1944). For a recent interpretation of the idea, see Robin Headlam Wells, *Shakespeare's Politics: A Conceptual Introduction,* 2nd edition (London and New York: Continuum, 2009).

7. For example, when King John's barons saw him becoming a tyrant, they asked Prince Lewis of France to use his army to remove their king.

Anonymous (c. 1100), holds that the king actually has two bodies or personae, one natural and the other sacred;[8] and it is this idea that led to the Tudor "doctrine of passive obedience," which taught that the king in his sacred body is "God's substitute" (*Richard II*, 1.2.37) and thus can be removed only by God. From this perspective, monarchy is unopposable, and so *how* one gains the crown is far less important than its actual possession. In other words, whoever holds the title has the prerogative, which is the point King John makes when he says early in the play that his "strong possession" gives him the "right" to be king (1.1.39).[9]

Yet this may not be Shakespeare's point. And some in his audience might well have noted that in the opening of the play, Queen Elinor, John's mother, strongly questions her son's "right" (1.1.40–41), and that subsequent action "depicts a king without a second body, whose physical presence alone proves inadequate to maintain loyalty in his subjects and order in his kingdom."[10] Indeed many of Shakespeare's plays, especially his histories, interrogate this topic, and in so doing imply that the ideal monarch must in fact integrate the king's two bodies, must merge public and private values, as does Prince Hal, for example, when he finally reveals himself as a monarch who is both publically and privately good, thus being "the mirror of all Christian kings" (*Henry V*, 2, Chorus 6). This ancient debate about monarchy, interesting to our ancestors, may not engage us now, but we should be aware that it anticipates our own equally profound concerns about ethical leadership and the limits and responsibilities of government today.

There is more. England's religio-political predicament was compounded by crippling monetary inflation, which began in the middle of the 16th century and extended well into the next, causing rising members of the gentry and courtier classes to become much more competitive than their parents. Anthony Elser writes that the younger generation had such "intense personal ambition" that there was a "change in the quality and tempo of Elizabethan life."[11] Yet upward mobility was "a fact of life in the period," and it was ambition that spurred Elizabethan students

---

8. See Ernst Kantorowicz, *The King's Two Bodies: A Study in Medieval Political Theology* (Princeton, NJ: Princeton University Press, 1957).

9. Lily B. Campbell points out that "[t]he Tudors upheld the principle that 'the crown once possessed cleareth and purifies all manner of defaults or imperfections.'" See Campbell, *Shakespeare's Histories: Mirrors of Elizabethan Policy*, 156.

10. Barbara Traister, "The King's One Body: Unceremonial Kingship in *King John*," in ed., Deborah T. Curren-Aquino, *King John: New Perspectives* (Cranberry, NJ: Associated Presses, Inc., 1989), 98.

11. See Anthony Elser, *The Aspiring Mind of the Elizabeth Younger Generation*, 2nd edition (Durham, NC: Duke University Press, 1993), xviii. It is this "intense personal ambition" linked to the religio-political unrest of the age that Shakespeare focuses on in *King John*, where the phenomenon is called "commodity," the extreme self-interest we see in all the main characters, except Prince Arthur, who employs self-interest but once and then only to safeguard his life; and Philip the Bastard, who after extolling "commodity" early on (2.1.571–608), steadily disengages himself from it. See also James L. Calderwood, "Commodity and Honour in *King John*," *University of Toronto Quarterly* 29 (1960): 341–356.

to learn the rhetorical strategies necessary for promotion to the queen's court.[12] Indeed, students were magnetically drawn to rhetoric, the art of persuasion, through which one learns to defend contradictory arguments with equal persuasiveness. Much of what students learned in school was also available in popular "courtesy books" or "behavior manuals," self-help tomes on how to write, talk, act, and dress like a gentleman—and thus hopefully to gain advancement at court, either without formal schooling or in addition to it. Castiglione's *Book of the Courtier*, Erasmus' *The Education of a Christian Prince*, Elyot's *The Governor*, and even Machiavelli's *The Prince* were such books—they all taught one how to act nobly and they all gave good advice on getting ahead in a competitive world. And indeed Shakespeare's plays, especially his history plays, often work toward this same goal, showcasing and interrogating the ideas of greatness and leadership delineated in these self-help manuals, so that from his plays Shakespeare's audiences might learn to become better citizens.[13] In *King John*, for example, theatergoers gained a moral exemplum as the play traces the education of a young nobleman in a coming-of-age story, wherein Philip the Bastard, already of royal lineage and fast gaining the qualities of leadership, gradually learns to relinquish destructive self-interest (commodity) in exchange for civic pride and selfless public service, thereby providing a salutary lesson in ethics.

Shakespeare's audience also learned, just as we do, about his remarkable ability to manipulate audience response, for Shakespeare drew not only upon the many books he read but also upon the rhetorical strategies he absorbed in school, and thus in the course of his plays we often find the playwright subtly shifting us from one perspective to its opposite. Consequently, we discover ourselves loving or pitying a character we hated earlier in the action or hating one we had earlier respected[14]—or even *simultaneously* absorbing multiple perspectives, as we do through characters such as Falstaff or Shylock. This is the case in *King John* when we come to internalize the shifting perspective of Philip the Bastard—or of King John himself.[15] Shakespeare heightens the effect, moreover, by giving the key characters in this play approximately the same percentage of lines, in a fairly evenly divided number of speeches in swiftly shifting scenes that span ten different

12. Jean Howard, *The State and Social Struggle in Early Modern England* (London and New York: Routledge, 1994), 10.

13. In response to the Puritan complaint that the theater corrupted society, Sir Philip Sidney wrote his *Apology for Poetry* (1595), in which he argued that tragedies made kings fear to be tyrants and that comedies made audiences avoid the human foibles exposed on stage and thereby improved everyone.

14. Elder Olson applies this idea to *King Lear*, in *Tragedy and the Theory of Drama* (Detroit: Wayne State University Press, 1966), 213. And the idea is applicable also to *Richard II*.

15. Though named Philip the Bastard in the Dramatis Personae, his name is changed to Sir Richard, when he is knighted by King John (1.1.161–163), so that we are to recall his natural father, Richard the Lionhearted, as we trace the Bastard's slow disengagement from a political world; while at the same time we follow John through rapid mood swings until at last we see his "scribbled form . . . shrink up" (5.7.33–35).

settings, not only to emphasize "the broad sweep of events" but also to show that by rapidly jostling us through a barrage of perspectives he can demonstrate the power of his medium to control audience response, just as film directors today use their cameras to the same end.[16]

From another perspective, of course, the play is the tragedy of the eponymous hero, what Elizabethans would have perceived as a *de casibus* tragedy,[17] though the title character is certainly not "a good and great king," despite at least one argument to the contrary.[18] King John is in fact a "villain-hero," akin to Richard III or Macbeth, both of whom, like John, are destroyed by their obsession with "commodity."[19] Also in his "natural body" King John does not have the strength of character necessary for a true hero; it is only in his "sacred body" that he can project this role and that only through the embassy of Philip the Bastard, who serves as England's de facto king[20] while John, in tacit absence, slowly disintegrates.[21] But more on this later.

The Backstory

For now, let's accept an important premise: earlier audiences and those living today, though coming from different environments and with different expectations, are still alike in that every audience brings to the theater a "backstory," distilled from prior information or misinformation already received. And accepting this, let's consider what audiences today might already think about the historical King John; then what Elizabethan audiences would have thought; and finally, what current historians generally say.

As a prompt, let's see if these lines from this childhood poem are familiar:

16. See Champion, Larry S., "'Confound Their Skill in Couvetousness': The Ambivalent Perspective of Shakespeare's *King John*," *Tennessee Studies in Literature* 24 (1979): 35–55. Champion gives the following line percentages: Philip the Bastard: 21%, King John: 17%, Constance: 10%, Hubert: 8%, King Philip: 8%, Cardinal Pandulph: 6%, and Prince Arthur: 5%.

17. *De casibus* (of the fall): From Giovanni Boccaccio's *De casibus virorum illustrium*: *Of the fall of illustrious Men* (c. 1358), stories of the great and famous who fell because of ambition and selfish pride. Boccaccio's work inspired John Lydgate's *Fall of Princes* (c. 1431–1438) and William Baldwin's *A Mirror for Magistrates* (1559), which went through five editions.

18. Irving Ribner, *Patterns in Shakespearean Tragedy* (London: Methuen, 1960), 40ff.

19. See Carole Levin, *Propaganda in the English Reformation: Heroic and Villainous Images of King John* (Lewiston and Queenstown: Mellen, 1988). See also Clarence Valentine Boyer, *The Villain as Hero in Elizabethan Tragedy* (1914) (New York: Russell and Russell, 1964).

20. Just as John had served as de facto king in his brother King Richard's absence. And we are also reminded of the bastard's similarity in his appearance and deeds to his natural father, Richard the Lionhearted.

21. In Shakespeare's primary source, *The Troublesome Reign of King John*, King John's dying words are, "Shameless my life, and shamefully it ends." See Geoffrey Bullough, *Narrative and Dramatic Sources of Shakespeare*, Volume 4 (8 Vols.) (New York: Columbia University Press, 1966), 148.

John, John, bad King John,
Shamed the throne that he sat on;
Not a scruple, not a straw,
Cared this monarch for the law;
Promises he daily broke;
None could trust a word he spoke. . . .

—Eleanor and Herbert Farjeon,
Kings and Queens (1932)
(London: J. W. Dent, 1953)

If you don't recall these lines, what about the old Disney movies, when Robin Hood and Friar Tuck outwitted bad King John and the Sheriff of Nottingham? In the 1973 Disney film *Robin Hood*, John's subjects sing the following song, which may ring a bell:

Oh the world will sing of an English King
A thousand years from now
And not because he passed some laws
Or had that lofty brow
While bonny good King Richard leads
The great crusade he's on
We'll all have to slave away
For that good-for-nothin' John. . . .

—*Robin Hood* (Disney, 1973)

Or do you remember, perhaps from history classes, that King John was a medieval tyrant in a family of tyrants, some braver and more popular than others, but all much braver and better liked than he? Bad press that only gets worse: in fact, a recent BBC documentary, "The Most Evil Men and Women in History," places King John in the company of Hitler, Attila the Hun, Ivan the Terrible, and Vlad the Impaler.[22]

On the other hand, a once-popular children's history book, still in print, which characteristically reduces John to "a bad son, a bad brother, a bad king and a bad man," nevertheless concludes that "out of his wicked reign great good came to the English nation."[23] This of course was the *Magna Carta*, England's first bill of rights, a key document in the history of democracy, which King John's subjects pressed upon him a couple of years before he died while fighting a losing battle with France.

These negative images are arresting and some, we shall see, are close to the truth. But they are not images of King John that Shakespeare's audiences would have

---

22. See http://documentaryaddict.com/The+Most+Evil+Men+and+Women+in+Histroy+Bad+King +John-7220-doc.html, accessed September 26, 2014.

23. H. E. Marshall, *Our Island Story* (1905) (London: Civitas, 2005), 103.

brought with them to the theater—though the legend of Robin Hood was even more popular back then than it is now. Nor would Shakespeare's audiences have been impressed by the *Magna Carta*. For England was a totalitarian state, not a democracy, and Queen Elizabeth, though fabulously popular, was an autocratic ruler. Documents like the *Magna Carta* were politically dangerous. And so Shakespeare omitted it from his play, and it was not until late in the next century that anyone thought to resurrect the document.[24]

Yet unlike the *Magna Carta*, King John was a famous and popular topic. He was in fact, for many Elizabethans, a heroic figure, an early defender of national unity against foreign aggressors and the first English king before Henry VIII to defy Rome and to be excommunicated, just as Queen Elizabeth had been excommunicated in 1570, when she refused to renounce her new church and return her country to the Old Faith. Thus while King John's contemporaries, the medieval churchmen who chronicled his reign, describe him as a cruel tyrant, a despoiler of monasteries, later Protestant reformers as early as William Tyndale, in The *Obedience of a Christian Man* (1528), praise King John. He is included as a martyr in John Foxe's *Book of Martyrs* (1583), treated sympathetically in Raphael Holinshed's *Chronicles* (1587), and also in the two King John plays that precede Shakespeare's: John Bale's *King Johan* (c. 1547–1561) and the anonymous *The Troublesome Reign of King John* (1591), widely accepted as the chief source for Shakespeare's play, as Kittredge says in his introduction.

What then is the truth about King John? What do historians now say? The first important fact is that John was descended from a line of legendary kings,[25] all warriors, from William the Conqueror to Geffrey of Anjou, the first Plantagenet,[26] then Henry II, who had subdued half of France, to Richard I (Cœur de Lion), the crusader, plus John's mother, Elinor of Aquitaine, a legend in her own time and also a great warrior queen.[27] The second fact is simply that John was neither a warrior nor much of a conqueror. He had possessed so little in his youth that he had been called John Lack-land, and in order to console him, his father, King Henry II, had made him Lord of Ireland.

King Henry died in 1189 and was succeeded by his son Richard the Lionhearted—who reigned for a decade, though most of his time was spent not in England but in the Holy Land or in France, where he died on April 6, 1199, with his brother John being crowned hardly two months later, on May 27, despite a cloud on John's claim.[28] For though Richard had on his deathbed named John as his heir,

24. The document was first used politically, when the jurist Edward Coke found among its many freedoms a prohibition against taxation without Parliamentary consent, which he used to negate King Charles I's war tax. For commentary on why Shakespeare did not include Robin Hood as a character in the play, see pages 41–42.

25. See Genealogy of King John.

26. So named because he wore in his cap a spring of broom plant (Lat. *Planta* + *genista*).

27. In fact she says "I am a soldier" (1.1.151).

28. Richard was fighting in the Third Crusade (1189–1192) in an effort to regain Jerusalem.

he had done so in spite of the fact that the rightful king was their young nephew Prince Arthur, whom he had previously named as his heir and whose deceased father Geffrey would have followed Richard in the hereditary line of succession. But because Arthur was just a teenager and John was already de facto king, governing England while Richard was out of the country, John managed, with the support of his powerful mother Queen Elinor, to elbow himself to the throne.[29]

No would-be king ever wanted to reign more than King John, yet while he possessed intelligence, ability, and charm when it was useful, John lacked the three keys for a king's success in the Middle Ages: valor, honor, and largess. Thus while King Richard was famous for bravery, chivalry, and generosity, John had a reputation for cowardice, treachery, and churlishness. For example, when it served his purposes John had sided with the enemies of his family and had betrayed both his father and his brother Richard when they most needed him. Then soon after his coronation, John divorced his childless first wife, Queen Isabella of Gloucester, to make a strategically advantageous marriage with Isabella of Angouleme, with whom he had become enchanted, ignoring the fact that she was already engaged. That he did not try to make amends or to soften the breech with his new bride's family or with the intended groom was typical of John. He always took what he wanted as his right, without any concern for the rights or feelings of others. And when his coffers were low, John taxed merchants and nobles alike, wreaking harsh vengeance on those who failed to oblige him. It was because of such meanness of spirit that John grew increasingly unpopular; yet his reign was troubled from the start, not just because of his character flaws but also because of specific conflicts with three particular adversaries: the French monarchy, the Roman Pope, and John's own English barons.

The French monarchy had supported Prince Arthur's claim from the beginning, as did most of Europe, so that throughout his reign John was frequently at war with King Philip of France or his son, Prince Lewis the Dauphin. At first there was hope for lasting peace. And in 1200, as part of a treaty, John relinquished some of his continental claims and was acknowledged as the King of England, Lord of Ireland, and Duke of Normandy and Aquitaine, while Arthur was named Duke of Brittany, among sundry other titles. To seal the treaty, King John's niece, Blanch of Castile, was pledged to marry Prince Lewis. Three years later, however, the hostilities were hotly resumed. Prince Arthur, now sixteen years old, captured and imprisoned Queen Elinor. Then in a surprise attack, John freed his mother and captured Arthur,

---

29. Raphael Holinshed writes in his *Chronicles* (1587) that on his deathbed King Richard had "Unto his brother John . . . assigned the crowne of England, and all other his lands and dominions, causing the nobles there present to sweare fealtie unto him," but that many in Europe preferred "to be under the governance of Arthur . . . considering that he seemed by most right to be their chief lord, forsomuch as he was sonne to Geoffrey elder brother to John." See Bullough, *Narrative and Dramatic Sources*, 4.25. In Shakespeare's play, however, John appears as a usurper and Prince Arthur as a child manipulated by rival factions.

who was spirited away to Normandy, never to be heard of again.[30] King John's brilliant victory was a fluke, however, for thereafter the wars seldom went well for him, so that by 1204, John had lost almost all of his continental holdings and was called not only "lack-land" but also "soft-sword." Plus public suspicion growing to certainty that Prince Arthur was dead and that the king was responsible did much to discredit John in the eyes of his people.

King John's vexation with the royal succession and the battle to defend it were compounded by conflicts with the Roman Pope and with the English barons, with whom John was repeatedly thoughtless and discourteous. The problems with the Catholic Church began in 1205, when Pope Innocent III ignored all other nominations for a new archbishop of Canterbury and gave the post to Stephen Langton, despite John's strong objections to the candidate. Then when the king remained obstinate and continued to refuse Langton as archbishop, the Pope placed England and Wales under an interdict (March 23, 1208), whereby no one was allowed to attend mass, receive the last rites, or bury their dead in consecrated ground.[31] When King John retaliated by plundering the wealth of the monasteries, as King Henry VIII would do three centuries later, the Pope excommunicated him, absolved his subjects of allegiance to their king, and invited King Philip of France to drive John from his throne. The war was avoided, however, when John suddenly and prudently gave in and submitted himself to the papal legate, Cardinal Pandulph, so that in the summer of 1214, Pope Innocent III lifted the interdict, welcomed John back into the Church, and returned his kingdom to him as a papal fiefdom.

Also in the summer of 1214, following his peace with Rome, John took the initiative, invaded France, and was then roundly beaten in the Battle of Bovines on July 27. The cost of war and rising inflation prompted John to raise new taxes. And the aggrieved English barons, especially those in the north who were now in rebellion, responded with the *Magna Carta*, a bill of rights, which they compelled the King to sign on June 15, 1215, at Runnymede, a meadow along the River Thames. Yet having signed, John reversed himself, recanted and sought revenge upon his barons, who in turn entreated Prince Lewis to come to their aide. And though Pope Innocent III protested and took John's part (since the English king had returned to the Church), Lewis nevertheless raised an army against John, was joined by most of the English barons, and captured both London and Winchester, while King John was forced eastward to Lincoln and Norfolk.[32]

The war continued with losses on both sides but without resolution. For King John, however, it was perilous. While crossing the Wash, a dangerous body of water

---

30. Shakespeare changes the setting, but it is likely that Prince Arthur was murdered, either by King John or by his order, though it is possible that he died attempting to escape. Still his fate remains an unsolved mystery, akin to the disappearance of the two young princes, in the Tower of London, centuries later during the time of King Richard III (1452–1485).

31. Allowances were made for infant baptism and confession for the dying.

32. See n. 7.

in northeastern England, John lost most of his soldiers and supplies and even the crown jewels. Physically weakened, probably by dysentery, he sought refuge in Swinstead Abbey on October 12, 1216. It is unlikely that John was poisoned there, as legends say, but his condition deteriorated, after an evening of heavy eating and drinking, and he had to be removed to Lincoln, where he died in the Bishop's Castle, at Newark, on October 18, and was buried at Worcester Cathedral. The fighting lagged on for some months, but in the end King John's nine-year-old son Henry gained the support of the English barons. The French withdrew and peace was made on September 17, 1217. And though not without troubles, King Henry III reigned for fifty-six years. King John had reigned for seventeen, which Shakespeare compresses into what seems a matter of weeks.

Historians today have different opinions about King John. No one sees him now as a hero or a martyr. All admit to his shortcomings, though some have tried to rehabilitate his reputation and have suggested that his faults were typical of the age.[33] Ralph Turner compares King John to "some twentieth-century US presidents, who had important goals and some great achievements, but whose psychological make-up cost them popular support and limited their successes."[34] But there are many who say that the old image of "Bad King John" is not far from the truth. W. L. Warren claims, for example, that John "had the mental abilities of a great king," that he also had "the inclinations of a petty tyrant," and that his reign, which "could have been an epic struggle," was "marred by flaws of the protagonist."[35] Frank McLynn gives vivid examples of John's tyranny but his succinct conclusion serves well: "John was distrusted by his fellow princes, despised by his barons, and deeply unpopular with the common people" and "was widely regarded as cruel, treacherous, cowardly and politically inept."[36] Indeed, John Gillingham believes that the medieval chroniclers, because they were John's contemporaries, actually knew him best and were probably more accurate than was previously thought.[37]

Contexts

If both medieval chroniclers and modern historians would differ with Elizabethans about the historical King John, then how do today's audiences view the eponymous "hero" and the other compelling characters in Shakespeare's play? To what degree

---

33. See G. E. Seel., *King John: An Underrated King* (London and New York: Anthem Press, 2012).

34. Ralph V. Turner, *King John* (London and New York: Longman, 1994), 264.

35. W. L. Warren, *King John* (Berkley: University of California Press, 1961), 258–259.

36. Frank McLynn, *Richard & John: Kings at War* (Philadelphia: Da Capo Press, 2007), 287.

37. See http://documentaryaddict.com/The+Most+Evil+Men+and+Women+in+History+Bad+King +John-7220-doc.html. See also Danny Danzign and John Gillingham, *1215: The Year of Magna Carta* (New York: Touchstone, 2004). For a balanced discussion of current scholarship, see Ferdinand Mount, "Back to Runnymede," *The London Review of Books* 37.8 (23 April 2005): 15–18.

might our reception of these characters compare with that of Shakespeare's audiences? Let's begin by noting a difference between our postmodern view and the early-modern xenophobic view of an important segment of society: those members thought by the "majority" to be "other" than themselves and who used to be relegated to its margins: women, children, bastards, fools, Moors, Jews, and other racial and religious minorities, including Catholics, most foreigners, and even actors.[38] Leslie Fiedler grouped them all together under the title "the stranger in our midst," who "by virtue of his strangeness . . . can sometimes see the silliness of the games we play in deadly earnest."[39] And these marginal characters, one notes quickly, are often the most interesting and perceptive in Shakespeare's plays.

In *King John* they are the most important, as becomes increasing clear if we recall the two lenses, noted above, through which Shakespeare's audience might have viewed both King John and Philip the Bastard, the two characters with the most lines in the play.[40] We suggested that for John the responses were largely polarized—Protestants in favor, Catholics, not—but that all were in probable agreement that he is a villain-hero, akin to Richard III, Claudius, or Macbeth, but lacking their vigor and sense of commitment. In this context, it is also important to note that Shakespeare follows a repetitive mimetic pattern in his plays, often retesting ideas, tropes, scenes, or characters in new and different loci, and that King John's character falls squarely within this mimetic pattern.[41] As a tyrant and accused infanticide he is reminiscent of Richard III and looks forward to Macbeth but lacks their demonic charm; as a weak and vacillating ruler, he anticipates Richard II and King Lear. But the evolution of his character is the reverse of theirs, for while Richard and Lear begin badly but then win our sympathy in the end,[42] King John starts off well enough, but then later fades away in failure if not in disgrace. Finally, one might argue for John's inclusion among the play's liminal characters, since he is a younger son whose claim to the throne is illegitimate—an argument that might apply as well to the other villain-heroes referenced above.

Yet Shakespeare's audiences could have gone further, as have some modern critics, by noting that, legitimate or not, King John starts out as a strong character, mediating between the Faulconbridge brothers and defying both the French ambassador and the Papal legate, but that he is soon upstaged by the Bastard, whose

38. On the complexity of "the status of foreigners" in early-modern England see Richard Marienstras, *New Perspectives on Shakespeare's World*, trans. Janet Lloyd (Paris and Cambridge: Cambridge University Press, 1985), 99–125. Actors not attached to a licensed company or to a noble household were considered unemployed and could be imprisoned.

39. Leslie A. Fiedler, *The Stranger in Shakespeare* (London: Croom Helm, 1972), 57.

40. See n. 16.

41. Mark Taylor, *Shakespeare's Imitations* (Newark: University of Delaware Press, 2002), 60–75. See also Paul V. Kreider, *Repetition in Shakespeare's Plays* (1941) (New York: Octagon, 1975).

42. See n. 14.

presence overshadows and then eclipses him.[43] Others might have noted that at first
John is indeed "a powerful and aggressive leader" but that his "every act is tainted
by his false position,"[44] or that while *potentially* heroic, he commits a "tragic error"
by causing Arthur's death, yet still manages to win salvation by his "remorse."[45]
Perhaps John gains some sympathy when we see "the nobles group once more around
the dying king" and are persuaded that "his prestige is largely restored in the perception of those around him."[46] These are indeed possible interpretations.

Yet isn't it also possible that some in the original audiences, unaware of the
anachronism, would have seen, with David Giles, that "John is a true psychopath . . . [and that] there *is* nothing consistent about him—the only consistent thing
is his inconsistency"?[47] Or at least that John is "foolish, vicious, frightened, and
paranoid. . . . Neither flawed tragic hero nor out-and-out villain," just as Guy Henry
found him, when he played the title role in Gregory Doran's 2002 production at
the Swan Theatre in Stratford-upon-Avon?[48] Or is it perhaps even more likely that
some in the audience, then as now, would have seen King John's character as simply
too ambiguous to define: "a figure whose every triumph conceals a fresh defeat, a
victim eliciting neither sympathy nor pity"?[49] Yet what is important here is not that
John's character can or cannot be agreed upon or precisely discerned, but rather that
Shakespeare has encoded that character so that it *must* be seen from multiple, shifting, and contradictory perspectives.

According to Aristotle, playwrights "imitate men involved in action and these
must either be noble or base . . . all of us being different in character because of some
quality of goodness or evil."[50] In other words, one's actions determine the charac-

43. John W. Blanpied, *Time and the Artist in Shakespeare's Histories* (Newark: University of Delware
Press, 1983), 98.

44. Edward Berry, *Patterns of Decay: Shakespeare's Early Histories* (Charlottesville: University of Virginia Press, 1956), 115.

45. Ribner, *Patterns in Shakespearean Tragedy*, 40–44. This is also implied when Faulconbridge promises to serve King John in heaven, as he has done on earth (5.7.74–75). His responsibility for the death
of Arthur would remind the audience of other tyrannical infanticides, such as Richard III and Macbeth,
as well as biblical murderers, such as Cain and Herod.

46. John Roe, *Shakespeare and Machiavelli* (Cambridge: D. S. Brewer, 2002), 127.

47. David Giles, director of the 1984 televised BBC production of *King John*, quoted by Henry Fen-
wick, "The Production," in *The BBC TV Shakespeare: King John*, ed. John Wilders and David Giles
(London: BBC, 1986), 29.

48. Guy Henry, "King John," *Players of Shakespeare 6: Essays in the Performance of Shakespeare's History
Plays*, ed. Robert Smallwood (Cambridge: Cambridge University Press, 2004), 33.

49. Michael Egan, "King John," in *The Greenwood Companion to Shakespeare*, Vol. 1, ed. Joseph Rosen-
bloom (London and Westport, CT: Greenwood Press, 2005), 175.

50. *Aristotle's Poetics: A Translation and Commentary for Students of Literature*, ed. Leon Golden and O.
B. Hardison, Jr. (Englewood Cliffs, NJ: Prentice Hall, 1968), 4–5. We do not know if Shakespeare read
Artistotle's *Poetics* but he would have been familiar with it, and his friend Ben Jonson owned a copy.
See Elizabeth Woodbridge, *Studies in Jonson's Comedy* (New York: Gordian Press, 1966), 10–11. See
also D. Heyward Brock, *A Ben Jonson Companion* (Bloomington: Indiana University Press, 1983), 13.

ter—or as a great poet was to write centuries later, "What I do is me: for that I came."[51] King John's actions, seldom noble, become so base that he commands the murder of a child, his nephew Arthur (3.3), in a pivotal moment that marks the decline of his fortunes and the loss of his audience.[52] Thus our focus is redirected from the tyrannical king to the three women, the child Arthur, the Bastard, and even the Catholic cardinal—those characters whose liminal status allows them freedom of expression and whose observations are so often penetrating and to the point.

Women

Simply put, in Shakespeare's time women were believed to be inferior to men, the logic being that "the male was active and formative, the female material and passive,"[53] and that therefore they should be "powerless in the male world."[54] The fact that many women were intelligent and well-educated made no difference. That two noble ladies lead the philosophical discussion in Castiglione's *Courtier*[55] or that Queen Elizabeth at age sixty had translated Boethius' *Consolation of Philosophy* would have been taken as exceptions that only proved the rule.[56] Shakespeare's "well-ordered patriarchal world" was one in which women were supposed to be either "silent or invisible."[57] Yet, though they are indeed "never the central actors" in Shakespeare history plays, they come close to stealing the show in *King John*.[58] And while the three women still have fewer lines than any male character, they are more engaging than anyone except Arthur and the Bastard.

51. Gerard Manley Hopkins (1844–1889), "As King Fishers Catch Fire, Dragon Flies Draw Flame."

52. Roy Battenhouse notes that this event is momentarily reinforced by John's ordering the death of Peter the prophet simply because he foresees that John will lose the crown on Ascension Day (4.2). "Religion in *King John*: Shakespeare's View," *Connotations* 1.2 (1999): 142.

53. Ralph Houlbrook, *The English Family: 1450–1700* (London and New York: Longman, 1984), 97. See also Ian Maclean, *The Renaissance Notion of Woman* (1980) (Cambridge: Cambridge University Press, 1995).

54. Philip Kolin, *Shakespeare and Feminist Criticism: An Annotated Bibliography and Commentary* (New York and London: Garland, 1991), 352.

55. Baldassare Castiglione, *The Book of the Courtier*, trans. Sir Thomas Hoby (1561) (London: Dent, 1928). The book is cast as a philosophical symposium presided over by Elisabetta Gonzago and her sister-in-law, Emilia Pia, who is first to speak.

56. When it served her purposes, Queen Elizabeth referred to herself as a prince and in her famous Armada speech, she presumably said that she had "the heart and stomach of a king." See Carole Levin, *The Heart and Stomach of a King: Elizabeth I and the Politics of Sex and Power* (Philadelphia: University of Pennsylvania Press, 1994).

57. Phyllis Rankin, *Stages of History: Shakespeare's English Chronicles* (Ithaca, NY: Cornell University Press, 1990), 178.

58. Phyllis Rankin, "Anti-Historians: Women's Roles in Shakespeare's Histories," *Theatre Journal* 37 (1985): 343.

Phyllis Rankin notes that the sole purpose of the play's women, bereft as they are of husbands and fathers, is "to dispute the fathers' will and threaten their patriarchal legacies."[59] Thus they are "transgressive figures," perceived as dangerous because they are not only disruptive but also truthful. Alison Thorne says, in fact, that they are gender archetypes, "tell-tale women," whose "rhetorical figure of 'frank speech' was used to reveal the truth,"[60] and moreover that the dramatist knew that the pathos of their "potentially subversive" outbursts could effect "productive ends."[61] In other words, Shakespeare knew that while the characters on stage were appalled by the excess of female emotion, the theater audience would be deeply moved.

Elinor is arguably a stronger character than either Constance or Blanch—or anyone else on stage—considering her unmatchable backstory as warrior queen from Aquitaine and host to troubadours and poets, and as an octogenarian still commanding and silencing her son, as though he were her lackey, as is apparent just five lines into the play, when she intervenes between the King and the French ambassador, "immediately forc[ing] the monarch into a subservient role."[62] John assumes this role as long as his mother shares the stage. And though the old queen is diminished somewhat by her "bitter" quarrel with Constance when the two are scrapping, in 2.1, over who will control Prince Arthur, she still remains formidable.[63]

It is Constance's affective lamentations in the next act, however, that evoke empathy from the audience, as indeed does the fact of her widowhood,[64] enhanced by the extremity of Arthur's youth and his persona as a kind of sacrificial lamb,[65] so

59. Rankin, *Stages of History*, 178.

60. See Alison Thorne's essay "'O, lawful let it be / That I have room . . . to curse awhile': Voicing the Nation's Conscience in Female Complaint in *Richard III, King John*, and *Henry VIII*," in *This England, That Shakespeare*, ed. Willy Malley and Margaret Tudeau-Clayton (Burlington, VT: Ashgate, 2010), 108–109.

61. Thorne, "'O, lawful let it be / That I have room . . . to curse awhile': Voicing the Nation's Conscience in Female Complaint in *Richard III, King John*, and *Henry VIII*," 117.

62. Juliet Dusinberre, "King John and Embarrassing Women," *Shakespeare Survey* 42 (1990): 41.

63. Philip Kolin notes that their "bitter insults . . . actually undermine their interests" (353).

64. Historically, Constance was not a widow at this time but was married to her third husband, Guy Viscount of Thours. She died at Nantes, in 1201, three years before Queen Elinor.

65. Beatrice Groves draws attention to the lamb as "one of the most ubiquitous metaphors for Christ," and one is reminded also of Abraham's binding of Isaac. Arthur himself implies as much, when he promises to "sit as quiet as a lamb," if not "bound" by Hubert (4.1.77–80). See Groves' *Texts and Traditions: Religion in Shakespeare 1592–1604* (Oxford: Oxford University Press, 2007), 112–113. Harold C. Gardiner has shown, in fact, that the old biblical plays, such as those portraying the binding of Isaac, were performed in some places up to the reign of King James. See Gardiner's *Mysteries' End: An Investigation of the Last Days of the Medieval Stage* (New Haven, CT: Yale University Press, 1946), 87. See also Emrys Jones, *The Origins of Shakespeare* (Oxford: Clarendon Press, 1977), 233–262. For the numerous biblical allusions and analogues in *King John* and in Shakespeare's older plays, see Naseeb Shaheen, *Biblical References in Shakespeare's Plays* (Newark: University of Delaware Press, 1999).

that Constance's image is endowed with a tragic aura that moves us as much as do her words. And when she is unexpectedly "rebuked for her show of emotion: 'You are as fond of grief as of your child' (3.4.94)," as though "implying that her grief is selfish,"[66] the rebuke itself, coming from the French king who has just betrayed her, serves quite purposefully to intensify her pathos and hence our respect and regard.

Yet it must be noted that both Constance and Elinor are not entirely selfless and do in fact rely upon commodity to attempt their goals, while Blanch alone is consistently guileless and unselfish in an instinctive pursuit of her duty. Scarcely married an hour, she relinquishes all attachment to family and home for what "she is bound in honour still to do" (2.1.531), though assured that "Whoever wins, on that side shall I lose" (3.1.345). As good as her word, and her word is sterling, she stands as a silent model for the Bastard to follow and as a complement to what he must learn about loyalty, sacrifice, and political expedience.[67]

Children

Roughly 40% of the entire population of Elizabethan England was comprised of dependent children living at home—despite high infant mortality, a fact that may have strengthened parental attachment.[68] Indeed, "prolonged parental anxiety for the physical, material and moral well-being of children was by no means unique."[69] And Ben Jonson's eulogy upon the death of his seven-year-old son—"Farewell thou child of my right hand and joy"—is an example of parental devotion reminiscent of Constance's lament for Arthur (3.4.71–107) and is obviously also sincere.

The two children in Shakespeare's *King John*, Prince Arthur and Prince Henry, are about the same age, just under ten, the age when boys began wearing men's clothing; prior to this time they would have been dressed as girls and raised in the company of women.[70] The boys are so similar, in fact, that a single actor will often

66. Hattie Fletcher and Marianne Novy, "Father-Child Identification, Loss and Gender in Shakespeare's Plays," in *Shakespeare and Childhood*, ed. Kate Chedgzoy, Susanne Greenhalgh, and Robert Shaughnessy (Cambridge: Cambridge University Press, 2007), 61.

67. According to Lawrence Stone, "a man's honour depended on the reliability of his spoken word; a woman's honour on her reputation for chastity." *The Family, Sex and Marriage in England, 1500–1800*, abridged edition (New York and London: Harper, 1979), 316. Thus Shakespeare seems to have purposefully endowed Blanch with a sense of honor that goes far beyond this stereotype.

68. Keith Wrightson, *English Society: 1580–1680* (New Brunswick, NJ: Rutgers University Press, 1982), 106.

69. Wrightson, 111.

70. Philippe Aries says that boys wore cloaks or open cassocks, like those worn by priests. *Centuries of Childhood: A Social History of Family Life* (New York: Knopf, 1962), 51–52. Catherine Belsey shows, however, that boys wore girls' dresses, accompanying her essay with period pictures. "Shakespeare's Little Boys: Theatrical Apprenticeship and the Construction of Childhood," *Rematerializing Shakespeare: Authority and Representation on the Early Modern English Stage*, ed. Bryan Reynolds and William N. West (London and New York: Palgrave Macmillan, 2005), 53–71.

play both parts,[71] their costume signaling their alikeness and their innocence. And if Arthur represents a sacrificial lamb, as noted above, then he is resurrected as a savior figure in Prince Henry, who comes to bring order to England at the end of the play.[72]

Bastards

Richard Greaves contends that in the 1590s nearly 16% of the population were illegitimate, much higher than in Catholic France,[73] while Martin Ingram gives a conservative 3% but says that about one-fifth of the brides were pregnant at marriage.[74] Even Queen Elizabeth's supposed "bastardy was an open secret," yet "to mention it was treasonable."[75] With bastards everywhere in society, they would naturally find their way on stage. There were "dirty bastards," "monstrous bastards," "cheating bastards,"[76] and there were also "heroic bastards."[77] Alison Findlay lists seventy-one plays with bastards, performed between 1588 and 1652, at least eight of which were by Shakespeare.[78]

Most of Shakespeare's bastards are bad. The Bastard in *King John* is unquestionably good, a heroic figure whose "status as an outsider makes him particularly suitable to explore the paradoxical relationship between qualities of glorious individualism and service to society which make up the archetypal hero."[79] He is a protean character, witty and perceptive, like Touchstone in *As You Like It* or the Fool in *King Lear*, directing and then commenting upon the action, like Rosalind or Hamlet. At the beginning of the play, he is "prepared to concede his landed inheritance in exchange for a royal patronymic, in a sense exchanging one form of legitimate identity for another," and then by the end, he not only "demonstrates

---

71. Historically, Arthur was sixteen when he died, while Henry was nine when he inherited the throne.

72. See Roy Battenhouse's brief comment upon "Arthur resurrected as Prince Henry" (148), credited to Ernst Honigmann's Introduction to *King John: The Arden Edition* (London: Methuen, 1954), xiv.

73. Richard Greaves, *Society and Religion in Elizabethan England* (Minneapolis: University of Minnesota Press, 1981), 215.

74. Martin Ingram, *Church Court, Sex and Marriage in England, 1570–1640* (Cambridge: Cambridge University Press, 1990), 157.

75. Alison Findlay, *Illegitimate Power: Bastards in Renaissance Drama* (Manchester: Manchester University Press, 1994), 2.

76. Michael Neill, *Putting History to the Question* (New York: Columbia University Press, 2000), 128–147.

77. Findlay, *Illegitimate Power: Bastards in Renaissance Drama*, 171–212.

78. *King John, 1 and 2 Henry 6, King Lear, Much Ado About Nothing, Troilus and Cressida, The Tempest, The Winter's Tale, Pericles*. Findlay, *Illegitimate Power: Bastards in Renaissance Drama*, 253–257.

79. Findlay, *Illegitimate Power: Bastards in Renaissance Drama*, 170.

through his behavior that he is worthy of his father King Richard's name" but also proves the "potential mutability of Englishness."[80]

For Una Ellis-Feremor, the Bastard is "a positive, if simple, ideal of service, a . . . picture of kingly bearing and . . . certain attributes that will appear in all of Shakespeare's later successful kings: tenacity, resourcefulness, and shrewdness."[81] Having no living father, he gives his service to King John, who treats him as his heir, finally granting him "the ordering of this present time" (5.1.79). Yet it is transparent to the audience that Prince Henry, waiting in the tiring room, was the intended heir all along and that the Bastard would then dedicate himself to his new king, as he had done with the old. In this he is like Hubert, who pledged allegiance to both Prince Arthur and King John. And while Cardinal Pandulph is a master of Jesuitical equivocation, he and the Bastard are also alike, at least in their myopic devotion to a cause represented by a titanic figure: while the Bastard is faithful to an idealized England and the sacred body of its King, the Cardinal is devoted to advancing Rome and its Pope.

Performance History

> Rarely performed plays like *King John* with their peaks of fashion and troughs of deep neglect, are truer barometers of the time than age-old favorites which never leave the stage. When such plays are revived, it is for a reason.
>
> —Catherine Bates, "Commodity's Slaves,"
> *Times Literary Supplement*, April 12, 2001

King John is a true curiosity in the Shakespeare canon, since the first surviving record of a performance of the play does not appear until 1737. However, despite the missing paper trail, it is highly likely that *King John* was performed in the 1590s by The Lord Chamberlain's Men and, later, in the Blackfriars Theatre, by The King's Men—sometime between 1608 and the closing of the theater in 1642. Francis Meres includes Shakespeare's *King John* in his compendium of plays in *Palladis Tamia* (1598) and Shakespeare's contemporary, Anthony Munday, points to what is most certainly the Bard's version of *King John* in his 1598 Robin Hood play, *The Death of Robert, Earl of Huntington*. Following a dumb show featuring the central characters in *King John*, Munday invokes the character of Hubert as the "foul keeper of poor *babes*," a line that alludes quite directly to Shakespeare's play because only

---

80. Helen Vella Bonavita, "Staying True to England: Representing Patriotism in Sixteenth-Century Drama," in *Negotiating Identities: Constructing Selves and Others*, ed. Helen Vella Bonavita (New York: Rodopi, 2011), 61.

81. Una Ellis-Feremor, *Frontiers of Drama* (1945) (London: Methuen, 1964), 39.

in his adaptation is Arthur, Hubert's hostage, converted from an adolescent to a mere child, indeed, a "poor babe" awaiting his tragic destiny.

After nearly a century and a half of apparent neglect, Shakespeare's *King John* was staged by Colley Cibber in 1737 at Covent Garden, starring Dennis Delane in the title role. David Garrick, who started imagining his production when he heard a rumor that Cibber's interpretation would be aggressively anti-Catholic, brought his own version to Covent Garden in 1745. Hereafter *King John* was performed intermittently in London, the provinces, and even former British colonies like America. Attracting renowned actors and actresses, the play itself became associated with theatrical opportunism—an application of "tickling Commodity" (2.1.583)—so that established artists like Garrick, Edmund Keane, William Charles Macready, along with Susannah Cibber, Sara Siddons, and Helen Faucit cemented their reputations by performing *King John* as a star vehicle.

Though the play's popularity crested in the mid-19th century, *King John* was revived in 1899 by Sir Herbert Beerbohm Tree at Her Majesty's Theatre in London. More importantly, a filmed segment of the king in his death throes survived the theatrical run and, fortuitously, *King John* became the first Shakespeare play *ever* to appear on film. It is not an exaggeration to state that *King John* helped to begin a revolution in the arts, one in which Shakespeare continues to play an integral role in the age of new media. But aside from his appearances as the villain of

Sir Herbert Beerbohm Tree depicts King John in his death throes in a scene filmed in 1899.

20th-century *Robin Hood* films, King John is not the explicit subject of another motion picture until 2011—in Jonathan English's depiction of the tyrannical king's battles with his barons, *Ironclad*. But more on that later.

The fact that there is no record of a performance of the play until 1737 invites speculation. Is there something inherently subversive about Shakespeare's *King John*? Seditious might be a better word. Certainly King Charles I (1625–1649) provided fodder for the play's anti-monarchical and anti-Catholic sentiments, since he frequently ruled without Parliamentary approval and, together with his partner in crime, the Archbishop Laud, reintroduced religious practices that too closely resembled Catholicism, thus alienating England's Protestant majority. Staging *King John* at this time could not help but be interpreted as an attempt to discredit Charles and, therefore, could be considered treasonous and punishable, potentially, by death.

Why *King John* was not staged in the late 17th or early 18th century is a bit more curious. One possible explanation lies in the conflicts over the royal succession that plagued the Restoration era and beyond. In 1660, Charles II, son of Charles I, "restored" the throne to its monarchical line of succession. When the king died in 1685, he was peacefully replaced by James II. However, Protestant resentment began to grow as the king appointed prominent Catholics to key posts. Fearful that James II's intent was to create a Catholic dynasty after his second wife gave birth to a son, the king's own daughter, Mary II, deposed him together with her husband, the Protestant hero King William III of Orange, in 1688. Otherwise recognized as a period of relative peace and stability, the Glorious Revolution (1688–1702) would seem to have provided the perfect stage for *King John*. For instance, in 1689, William and Mary signed the Bill of Rights, which was, essentially, a "sequel" to John's signing of the *Magna Carta* in 1215. *King John* would also have played well at this time as trenchant, anti-Catholic propaganda, as supporters of James II's claim to the throne, referred to as Jacobites, continued to contest William and Mary's joint rule and ultimately attempted to overthrow them when James III (son of James II) attempted to restore—once again—the Stuart dynasty. It wasn't until the throne passed to the Hanovers, who ruled from 1714 to 1901, that the succession crisis ended. Early into their reign, in 1737, Colley Cibber found the conditions fit for staging *King John*.

A more practical explanation for the century-and-a-half gap that separates Shakespeare's writing of *King John* and its "first" performance in 1737 lies in the fact that this play requires strong women actresses playing strong female characters—a *coup de théâtre* that was not possible until the Restoration, when women were at last permitted to perform on the English stage. Colley Cibber had a particularly poignant take on the character of Constance, arguing that whereas much of *King John* is unworthy of its Shakespearean imprimatur, several speeches from the Bastard, and "the character of *Constance* intire [*sic*] . . . are truly *Shakespearean*."[82] Although Cib-

---

82. Qtd. in Brian Vickers, ed., *The Critical Heritage: 1774–1801*, Vol. 6 (6 Vols.) (London and New York: Routledge, 1981), 93.

ber's wife Susannah was acknowledged for her performance as Constance, Sarah Siddons set the precedent for the role, playing Arthur's bereaved mother from 1783 to 1812. In her essay "Constance: A Theatrical Trinity," Carol J. Carlisle explains that Constance has long been recognized as an unusually challenging part. To represent her ever-changing, ever-extreme emotions with "harmony and propriety," to keep from crossing the "boundary between poetry and frenzy," to avoid becoming "either too sentimental or too shrewish"—this is the difficult task that Shakespeare set for the actress who undertakes his most extravagantly depicted heroine.[83]

For some critics, Siddons remains the only actress who has successfully negotiated the challenges posed by the role. Indeed, Siddons "was ere long regarded as so consummate in the part of Constance, that it was not unusual for spectators to leave the house when her part in the tragedy of *King John* was over, as if they could no longer enjoy Shakespeare himself when she ceased to be his interpreter."[84] Confirmation of her ongoing popularity and the play's success comes from none other than Jane Austen, who wrote to her sister from London about "a very unlucky change of the Play for this very night—*Hamlet* instead of *King John*—and we are to go on Monday to *Macbeth* instead, but it is such a disappointment to us. . . ."[85]

In 1842, Siddons' Victorian successor, Helen Faucit, was working with William Charles Macready on what has been described as "not only one of his most splendid revivals but also one of the most notable productions of this play in theater history."[86] Both Macready and Faucit were the beneficiaries of the "new" fashion for antiquarianism, or the study of antiquity, which was chiefly concerned with the artifacts of an era, including its minutiae. Deeply intrigued by this trend, Charles Kemble, who played the Bastard in Macready's production, hired the antiquarian scholar James Planché to study the clothing and fashions of the early 13th century for the 1842 venture. Planché drew his inspiration from visiting English churches, viewing reliquaries, illuminated manuscripts, engravings, and funereal effigies. The quest for historical accuracy led to one of the dominant performance trends in *King John*: an emphasis on theatrical spectacle involving elaborate staging, elegant, high-period costuming, sophisticated choreography, an impressive array of "extras" (for battle scenes in particular), and powerful musical underscoring. In fact, Macready's production set the standard for the next one hundred years not only for *King John* but also for performing Shakespeare's plays in general.

The antiquarian tradition reached its summit with Beerbohm Tree's production of *King John* in Her Majesty's Theatre in 1899, perfectly in keeping with the

83. Carol J. Carlisle, "Constance: A Theatrical Trinity," in *King John: Changing Perspectives*, ed. Deborah T. Curren-Aquino (Newark: University of Delaware Press, 1989), 144.

84. Thomas Campbell. *The Life of Sarah Siddons* (1834), Vol. 1 (2 Vols.) (London: Effingham Wilson, Royal Exchange; Reprint: Ann Arbor: University of Michigan Library, 2007), 209.

85. See *Jane Austen's Letters*, 4th edition, ed. Deirdre Le Faye (Oxford: Oxford University Press, 2011), 189.

86. Carlisle, "Constance: A Theatrical Trinity," 149.

pageantry surrounding the eightieth birthday of Queen Victoria, which made her the longest-reigning British monarch of all time. Ironically, this 13th-century period piece coincided with the *newest* possible development in the long history of the arts: the dawning of cinema. Although the film of *King John*, ostensibly a series of moving tableau combined into a single reel (five to six minutes of screen time), is considered lost, one surviving segment reveals the convulsive king dying painfully and despairingly, as Pembroke, Prince Henry, and Bigot look on with fear and uncertainty. Robert Hamilton Ball speculates, based on the location shooting on the bank of the Thames, that Beerbohm Tree was attempting to simulate Runnymede, where King John signed the *Magna Carta*—a "tableau . . . [that] needed no words, only pantomime for its effects."[87] Given the time compression in a one-reel film, the action would have to leap from the signing of the great charter straight to King John's death, which could imply that imposing legislative checks on the monarchy actually "poisons" the king. On an extra-filmic level, the inclusion of the *Magna Carta* scene is ironic since, at the time, Britain was expanding its empire and, in the process, denying fundamental rights and privileges to its colonized citizens in the developing world.[88]

The first example of screened Shakespeare in history, *King John*, as Kenneth Rothwell brilliantly observes, is a play that "proleptically deals with the economic forces that would drive this fledgling art from its very beginnings. . . . The most cash-driven art form in history, film from the beginning has been enslaved to 'tickling commodity.'"[89] Beyond its predictive capacity as a proto-capitalistic play, *King John* is, in and of itself, highly cinematic—in its wild, almost proto-"Western" style battle scenes, in its strategic use of locations that only a camera can effectively bridge, and in its simulation of rapid-cutting between the characters' conflicting perspectives. Beerbohm Tree's truly spectacular theatrical adaptation (on which the film was based) made use of techniques such as visual and musical underscoring that would soon become staples of cinematic representation. In 3.2, for example, when John intimates to Hubert that Arthur must not live, Arthur is shown delicately plucking daisies, whereas John callously decapitates them with his sword; elsewhere, instrumentation is employed to enhance the emotional connection between the audience and the action. Beerbohm Tree also included the signing of the *Magna Carta* in his theatrical adaptation, and made extensive use of extras for the battle scenes and pageantry, employing more than three hundred individuals in this capacity. Ironically, the film segment, which runs for approximately seventy-seven seconds, offers none of these cinematic qualities. Indeed, it is demonstrative of a

87. See Robert Hamilton Ball's *Shakespeare on Silent Film: A Strange Eventful History* (New York: Routledge, 1968), 23.

88. Not coincidentally, Rudyard Kipling's famous apology for imperialism, "The White Man's Burden," also appeared in 1899.

89. Kenneth Rothwell, *A History of Shakespeare on Screen: A Century of Film and Television* (Cambridge: Cambridge University Press, 1999), 2–3.

"motion picture" only in its grainy texture and, at one point, slightly unsteady camera. All that the audience sees is a single, static, medium shot from a fixed, frontal point of view—a perspective far more circumscribed than in the theater. Curiously, Shakespeare's *King John* has never been made into a feature film.

Theatrical adaptations staged after Beerbohm Tree's landmark production tended to emerge in concert with the need for patriotism during World War I and World War II, focusing on the Bastard as the ironic spokesman for a nation. But there was a distinctive change in the reception of *King John* in the early 20th century. After being all the rage in the 19th century, the play, as one reviewer writes of F. R. Benson's productions (1901, 1909, 1913, 1916), became distasteful to audiences: "Amongst all the plays of Shakespeare this is, perhaps, one of the least acceptable to modern audiences. There are great scenes and tragic episodes, but the atmosphere is too satiated with medieval barbarism to appeal strongly to an audience of the twentieth century."[90] The irony of this statement—with the coming barbarism of the Holocaust—can be lost on no one.

In the World War Two era and beyond, *King John* has emerged as a reflection of a society disillusioned by war games. Hence, Tyrone Guthrie's production, staged before the blitzkrieg that savaged London, begins by substituting hobby-horses for the real ones used on stage by Beerbohm Tree, thus initiating a vision of the play as a political satire. At a time when Hitler was threatening world domination, the depiction of murderous boys with toys is a provocative one to say the least, bringing new meaning to the Bastard's lust for war—and its spoils—when he tells his serving man that "There's toys abroad" (1.1.236). Posing further contrast to the extravagant 19th-century performance tradition, Guthrie's minimalist stage reflects the exigencies of a wartime economy and marks the beginning of a trend in which the director, rather than a star actor, would adapt the play as a means of social commentary.

In 1970, Buzz Goodbody, the first woman director for the Royal Shakespeare Company, revived *King John* as a sardonic comedy and, in so doing, liberated future productions from sentimentalizing the king's death. Moreover, Goodbody produced this very big play for a very small space—the RSC's The Other Place—a venue that she played a significant part in creating, as a product of the alternative-theater movement of the late 1960s and early 1970s. As Alycia Smith-Howard maintains:

> Goodbody created a theater dedicated to minimalist and hard-hitting
> classical productions of Shakespeare that challenged then-current
> trends in the staging of his plays and fostered a production ethos that
> was driven by a collaborative process of theater-making. Within this
> dynamic working environment, actors and directors were released
> from the pressures of commercial success and set at liberty to

90. This reviewer from the *Birmingham Mail* is quoted in *The Internet Shakespeare King John: Performance History*, by Michael Best, http://internetshakespeare.uvic.ca/Annex/Texts/Jn/intro/StageHistory /section/The%20twentieth%20century, accessed September 26, 2014.

re-discover their crafts. More than a mere "small theater," The Other Place was a crucible, a politicized laboratory for social and artistic experimentation.[91]

"I would like to see good Shakespearean productions done by Marxists,"[92] Goodbody famously quipped, since it was her belief that theater belonged, first and foremost, to the people: "The Royal Shakespeare Company is financed by the whole of society. We know why we play to an audience largely drawn from the upper and middle classes. We have to broaden that audience for artistic as well as social reasons. We know it'll take years. Unless we make the attempt classical theatre will atrophy."[93]

The next major production of the play is also the only version of *King John* that is widely available for viewing: a made-for-television adaptation directed by David Giles for the BBC's complete Shakespeare series in 1984. Bearing in mind that, for the sake of continuity, the directors chosen for the series were not permitted to offer a personal interpretation of the play, it should come as no surprise that Giles' production makes little—if any—creative use of the camera. Indeed, the film's "vocabulary" is comprised of mostly medium shots and close-ups, as well as basic shot-reverse-shot sequences. In short, this televisual adaptation is neither fish nor fowl: although it is stagey, it lacks the dramatic immediacy of theater; although the camera is visible as a controlling presence, it rarely satisfies our voyeuristic desire to know more than the characters on stage do, taking care to circumscribe the more subversive aspects of the play.

Yet Giles takes advantage of the camera's ability to focus our attention in other ways. The most obvious example is the Bastard's use of direct address, a technique quite specifically associated with the news media and, therefore, with the cultivation of trust and "truth." As the play's principal interlocutor and commentator, Philip of Faulconbridge promises, as if savoring the taste, to administer "Sweet, sweet, sweet poison for the age's tooth" (1.1.215). Though the Bastard is, at the very beginning of the play, seductive in his speech, he is endowed neither with malice nor excessive ambition. His commitment to follow "Gain" is not a convincing source of motivation for his character, for the Bastard is nothing if not generous in his actions; the only mannerism that identifies him with self-interest is his tendency to lick his lips when opportunity knocks. Hence, when Elinor, who initially disapproves of the Bastard's saucy indictment of his mother, entices him to follow her to the war in France, he practically salivates.

91. Alycia Smith-Howard, "Knowing Her Place: Buzz Goodbody and The Other Place," *Early Modern Studies Journal* 5 (2013): 77–93 (82).

92. Qtd. in Catherine Stott, "Woman Director Buzz Goodbody Talks to Catherine Stott," *The Guardian*, October 27, 1971.

93. Buzz Goodbody, "Studio/2nd Auditorium Stratford 1974" (unpublished proposal, December 15, 1973).

The fact that the indomitable Elinor is attracted to her newfound grandson's charm and appetite for enterprise is evident in the matching colors they wear after the Bastard's knighting and renaming as Richard Plantagenet in act 1. When he reappears in act 2 in sumptuous gold, black, and gray, his royal parentage is recalled in the impressive manelike collar that adorns his neck and shoulders, denoting him as the son of King Richard, Cœur-de-Lion. After the Bastard returns with Austria's head in act 3, Elinor, the ancient, leather-faced soldier-queen, delights in his dirty deed and, rather than kissing his "grandam's" hand, the Bastard requites her affection by kissing her on the lips for five excruciatingly long seconds—sealing their mutual commitment to victory by any means necessary.

In contrast to the Bastard's appeal, John is a petulant, malice-streaked man played by Leonard Rossiter. Even Rossiter, who was admired both for his classic and comedic talent (he was famous for his leading role in *The Fall and Rise of Reginald Perrin*), confessed his own difficulties in discovering a compelling approach to the lackluster part. The fact that the opening scene shows John slumped in a chair admiring his rings, while his mother stands ramrod straight, ready to intercept all comers before his throne, immediately identifies Elinor as John's missing backbone—the figure who quite literally props up his power. Rossiter is therefore at his best when he isn't flanked by strong characters. His villainy is most compelling, for example, when he seduces Hubert, whom he courts like a lover in the

Leonard Rossiter plays the suspicious and self-indulgent King John in David Giles' 1984 BBC adaptation.

interest of killing Arthur. Softly sinister, John convinces Hubert to kill his ward after various protestations of love and promises of unspecified fortunes. At this juncture, Giles relies on shot-reverse-shot techniques to underscore the waxing of their cruel league, as the two forge a homoerotic compact christened by the blood of innocents.

Yet still more seductive are the words of Arthur, the blonde, Raphaelesque cherub with searing eyes. The antithesis of Cardinal Pandulph—who speaks with saccharine in his voice even as he stirs up lethal hostilities between France and England—Arthur uses his absolute innocence to charm Hubert out of blinding and killing him. Eloquent and irresistibly childlike, Arthur is a particularly intriguing character in this adaptation of *King John*, principally because he is the very portrait of a beautiful, Ganymede-like youth, whose milky white skin makes him appear as though he had scarcely been weaned. Indeed, Constance is always clutching him to her bosom like a prosthetic heart—a tableau that works perfectly with the infantilizing set construction that, prior to the death of Arthur, stresses a "toy-like" approach.[94] Dappled with small, cardboard-like tents, battlements, and pennants, the deliberately artificial staging conflates men and politics with boys on a playground.

Critics have taken issue with the fact that Arthur's deeply moving lines are radically reduced by Giles. In fact, Mark A. Heberle goes so far as to suggest that the BBC production, in cutting roughly 50% of the exchange between Arthur and Hubert—the longest dialogue involving a child in the entire Shakespeare canon—is symptomatic of "our own failure to take them [children] seriously."[95] Geraldine Cousin, however, offers what may be a more practical explanation: "The effectiveness of IV.i was limited by the difficulty the young Luc Owen had with Shakespeare's formalized language."[96] The cuts, according to Cousin, were intended so that "a complicated thought-process was made clear to the very end of each line and speech."[97] This micromanaging of Arthur's every word shows in Owen's performance when his frequently furrowed eyebrows betray his extreme concentration on his lines; yet the effect of his very deliberate delivery is not artificiality but rather earnestness. Using love rather than rank to persuade his would-be executioner to spare him, Arthur reveals his debt to his mother's nurture by replacing the rhetoric of authority with the rhetoric of care; he does not cajole Hubert into honoring his royal prerogative, but instead woos him away from John:

94. See Geraldine Cousin, King John: *Shakespeare in Performance Series*, ed. J. R. Mulryne and J. C. Bulman (Manchester and New York: Manchester University Press, 1994), 85.

95. See Mark A. Heberle, "'Innocent Prate': *King John* and Shakespeare's Children," in *"Infant Tongues": The Voice of the Child in Literature*, ed. Elizabeth Goodenough, Mark A. Heberle, and Naomi Sokoloff (Detroit: Wayne State University Press, 1994), 30.

96. See Cousin, King John: *Shakespeare in Performance Series*. Edited by J. R. Mulryne and J. C. Bulman. Manchester and New York: Manchester UP, 1994: 94.

97. Cousin, 94.

Constance (Claire Bloom) weeps with Arthur (Michael Croudson) before they part in Giles' production.

> . . . I would to heaven
> I were your son, so you would love me, Hubert. . . .
> Are you sick Hubert? You look pale to-day:
> In sooth I would you were a little sick,
> That I might sit all night and watch with you.
> I warrant I love you more than you do me. (4.1.25–26, 30–33)

The "accidental" death of Arthur soon makes children of men, as Hubert, Salisbury, Pembroke, and the Bastard bond in tears over the boy's dead body.

No one loves Arthur more than his mother, played by an intrepid Claire Bloom in the 1984 television movie. Bloom, as many critics have pointed out, does not have the luxury of fully indulging the depth of Constance's emotions because of the restraint demanded by television performances. Carol Carlisle was particularly critical of Bloom's decision to underplay the role, whose performance she likened—at its best—to an "animal at bay" that evoked "not Mrs. Siddons's tigress but a household cat. . . ."[98] If the hysteria of her predecessors is missing from Bloom's Constance, then it is revisited in her physical attachment to Arthur, whom she is always caressing with suffocating closeness. Her Madonna-like appearance in an all-white

---

98. Carlisle, "Constance: A Theatrical Trinity," 157.

dress—replete with a delicate gold coronet encircling her head—identifies her with Arthur's angelic qualities while cleverly anticipating the Pietà that she will soon come to personify. Disagreeing with critics like Carlisle, Cousin cites Bloom's performance as pioneering in that it "challenged the conventional view of the character by portraying Constance as eminently sane and reasonable."[99]

Indeed, though one scarcely recognizes Constance when she enters the "mad scene" with dark, unbraided tresses that bestrew her shoulders, her wild appearance belies her stonelike composure. The decision to replace her divine white costume with a dull gray one not only captures her despairing demeanor but also points proleptically to Arthur's final resting place on the stones outside the tower. It is only when France commands her to "Bind up your hairs" (3.3.70) that she becomes emotionally overwrought, fumbling to re-braid her long locks. But as a world-weary wisdom washes across her face, she saves her best words to upbraid the reptilian, war-brokering Cardinal for peddling false hopes of heaven:

> And, father Cardinal, I have heard you say
> That we shall see and know our friends in heaven.
> If that be true, I shall see my boy again. . . .
> But now will canker-sorrow eat my bud
> And chase the native beauty from his cheek,
> And he will look as hollow as a ghost,
> As dim and meagre as an ague's fit;
> And so he'll die; and rising so again,
> When I shall meet him in the court of heaven
> I shall not know him. Therefore never, never
> Must I behold my pretty Arthur more! (3.3.78–80, 84–91)

The sense of finality that Constance feels at this juncture leads her to fight for her sanity until the end, confessing, "I will not keep this form upon my head / When there is such disorder in my wit" (3.3.103–104). The fact that Constance no longer wears her gold coronet suggests that she is indeed referring to a diseased mind, making her words resonate with intimations of suicide. She concludes by indicting everyone on stage for their complicity, crying: "O Lord! my boy, my Arthur, my fair son! / My life, my joy, my food, my all the world! / My widow-comfort, and my sorrows' cure!" (3.3.105–107). When she exits, she tears the heart out of the play.

The other significant female characters, Elinor and Blanch, serve as natural foils to each other. In Giles' production, Elinor stands alone and stands her ground, even when Constance spits in her face. Hardly one to resist a challenge, Elinor reaches quickly for her long dagger and draws it halfway out of its sheath; there is little doubt that she would have used it, were it not for the intervention of the men who part the incensed women. Elinor is imperious, dignified, and stealthy; even more so than

---

99. Cousin, *King John: Shakespeare in Performance Series*, 91.

the Bastard, she understands the value of "commodity." Her upbraiding of Constance—"Out, insolent! Thy bastard shall be King / That thou mayst be a queen and check the world" (2.1.122–123)—draws knowing chuckles of approval from both the French and English sides, who scorn Constance's supposed ambition while letting Elinor's go unchecked.

Like Elinor and Constance, Blanch is a surprisingly strong figure in the BBC production. Her costuming—a white dress with a golden coronet—is identical to Constance's clothing and accessories, thus giving her the appearance of "a younger version of Constance."[100] In 3.1, Giles' use of blocking also implicitly aligns Blanch and Constance as both kneel simultaneously before the Dauphin to plead for their opposing causes. Cousin argues that "David Giles' production stressed the women's shared helplessness rather than their opposing claims," to the extent that Constance and Blanch "see[m] virtually a mirror-image of the other."[101] The only significant difference in their appearance is that whereas Constance initially wears her hair back behind a veil, Blanch wears her hair down. Though appropriate for a virgin bride, Blanch's imperfect, brunette curls nevertheless suggest an affinity with Constance's later appearance in her "mad scene." And indeed, Blanch becomes suddenly struck by the insanity of her predicament as a pawn in a political chess match played exclusively by men:

> Which is the side that I must go withal?
> I am with both; each army hath a hand,
> And in their rage, I having hold of both,
> They whirl asunder and dismember me.
> Husband, I cannot pray that thou mayst win;
> Uncle, I needs must pray that thou mayst lose;
> Father, I may not wish the fortune thine;
> Grandam, I will not wish thy wishes thrive.
> Whoever wins, on that side shall I lose:
> Assured loss before the match be play'd. (3.1.337–346)

With the precedent soon to be set by Constance and Elinor, whose deaths are telescoped by Shakespeare to within three days of each other (rather than the historical spate of three years), Blanch disappears from the play just barely ahead of them, assuring her husband, in response to his presumptuous claim "With me thy fortune lies," that "[t]here where my fortune lives, there my life dies" (3.1.347–348).

The Dauphin, meanwhile, seems not only diffident toward his bride's concerns, but also rather imbecile and too easily manipulated by the silver-tongued Pandulph. "How green you are and fresh in this old world!" (3.3.147) exclaims the Cardinal, rejoicing in the Dauphin's naïvete like the Big Bad Wolf of *Little Red Riding Hood*.

---

100. Cousin, King John: *Shakespeare in Performance Series*, 90.
101. Cousin, 90.

But when Pandulph returns in act 5 to end the war he began, he finds the Dauphin a changed man. Confident in battle, covetous of his privileges, and defiant toward Rome, the young Prince angrily replies to the unscrupulous Cardinal:

> Your grace shall pardon me, I will not back.
> I am too high-born to be propertied,
> To be a secondary at control. . . .
> Am I Rome's slave? What penny hath Rome borne,
> What men provided, what munition sent
> To underprop this action? Is't not I
> That undergo this charge? Who else but I,
> And such as to my claim are liable,
> Sweat in this business and maintain this war? . . .
> No, no! on my soul, it never shall be said! (5.2.79–81, 98–103, 109)

Unlike the Dauphin, who rages hot and cold, Cardinal Pandulph is consistently subtle and insidious throughout the production, scheming to advance the Church even if that means kindling a war of mutually assured destruction between England and France. His lengthy speeches in Giles' production take on the quality of a congressional filibuster; at once hawkish and glib, the Cardinal freezes John and France quite literally in their tracks. Poised hand to hand, palm to palm for more than eight minutes of screen time, the two enemy kings stare in amazement at the Cardinal as he waxes both poetic—and politic—in his effort to persuade the French king to wage a holy war against the heretical John. In what is his most "heroic" moment, John rebukes Pandulph as a "meddling priest" as he exclaims to France:

> Though you and all the kings of Christendom
> Are led so grossly by this meddling priest,
> Dreading the curse that money may buy out. . . .
> This juggling witchcraft with revenue cherish,
> Yet I alone, alone do me oppose
> Against the Pope and count his friends my foes.
> (3.1.165–167, 172–174)

Subsequent to David Giles' 1984 production, a flurry of adaptations directed by women have appeared at fairly consistent intervals after Buzz Goodbody's pioneering direction of *King John* in 1970, including productions by Deborah Warner (1988), Barbara Gaines (1991, 2004), Tina Packer (2005), Josie Rourke (2006), and Maria Aberg (2012). What, in a play that renders women so expendable to political exigency, would female directors find so attractive, so worthy of representation? Given the commentary that Buzz Goodbody received in 1970 from male reviewers—remarks such as "Buzz Goodbody certainly boasts an apt surname. She's leggy, curvy, well-endowed in the right places"—it is not surprising that it took eighteen years for another woman to take on *King John* for the RSC.[102] In 1988, when the repercussions of the Reagan–Thatcher years were sinking in, Deborah Warner produced the play in the RSC's The Other Place. Although it is unlikely that the sparse staging was intended as a critique of "trickle-down" economics, the timing of the adaptation can't help but comment on the "commodity-driven" society of its time. It is significant, then, that the Bastard is an unromanticized, plain-dealing guy in this production, whereas the king wears his crown attached to a chain at his waist; he is literally tethered to the trappings of his power. Rather than viewing The Other Place as limiting, Warner embraced the possibility of making the stage floor her principal prop, which she converts from a tennis court to a bull ring and, finally, to a chess board. Circus music is played during scene transitions, underlining the political games that turn kings into unlicensed fools in Shakespeare's history plays.

Parting ways with the more typical rendering of Constance as a white-garbed Madonna figure, Warner's *King John* approaches the character as a black-clad avenging angel. Interestingly, the actress herself, Susan Engle, likened her performance of the role to a political protester—"in Vietnam or in Westminster."[103] Taking protest for theme, Barbara Gaines staged *King John* for the Shakespeare Repertory Theater in Chicago in 1991 and 2004. Gaines was drawn to adapt the play at these two historical junctures in part because both periods were defined by wars in the Gulf: the 1990–1991 campaigns Operation Desert Shield and Operation Desert Storm, as well as the ongoing wars in Afghanistan and Iraq, known as Operation Enduring Freedom. However, in 1991, Gaines was equally keen on expressing her concerns about the events then occurring in the former Czechoslovakia, dedicating the production to the Czech writer Zebenek Urbanek, who was not only a famous translator of Shakespeare's plays, but also known for his political courage as a leader in the anti-Soviet movement.

In 2005, Tina Packer staged *King John* for Shakespeare & Company at the Founders' Theater in Massachusetts, establishing a dynamic in which "the show's perspective moves from the distanced overview of those for whom war seems like an abstract game to the immediate, brutal consequences of such strategizing."[104] One of the ways Packer drives home this vision is by casting girls in the roles of Arthur and Henry. From production stills one can see that Arthur wears a dress, a performance decision that positions him, age-wise, as a boy who has not quite reached the breeching age, when male children leave the company of women to learn the ways of men. In a clever reversal of Shakespearean stage conventions, Arthur is played by a female actor, Susannah Millonzi, whose tender years alone "strik[e] a

102. Reviewer Ian Woodward, qtd. in Michael Best, http://internetshakespeare.uvic.ca/Annex/Texts/Jn/intro/StageHistory/section/The%20twentieth%20century, accessed September 25, 2014.

103. Qtd. in Cousin, King John: *Shakespeare in Performance Series*, 116.

104. Ben Brantley, "The Powers That Be Play Chess with War," *The New York Times*, August 29, 2005. http://www.nytimes.com/2005/08/20/theater/reviews/20shak.html?_r=0, accessed September 26, 2014.

jolting note of pathos" in the audience.[105] In the very next year, Josie Rourke's RSC production was also distinguished by its treatment of Arthur—in this case, by the staging of his fall—which was so realistic that audiences cried out in horror on a nightly basis.

Of all the directors, male or female, who have attempted to stage *King John*, it is the RSC's Maria Aberg who has created the most radical adaptation of the play to date. Made in 2012 for the Swan Theatre in Stratford-upon-Avon, Aberg's production stars actress Pippa Nixon as the Bastard, and features Paola Dionisotti as the smooth-tongued Cardinal. "It started off," Aberg observes of her casting decisions, "with a curiosity about seeing a woman tackling what is, in a clichéd way, a very masculine part."[106] The added benefit of her nontraditional casting is that women, whose performances constitute only 20% of the stage time in Shakespeare's plays, don't just suddenly disappear from *King John* in act 3. In fact, posing marked contrast to the stage history of the play, the female characters in Aberg's production never completely drop out of view. Constance and Elinor return as ghosts in acts 4 and 5, and it is Blanch, as Jami Ranch explains, whose "quiet trajectory through the play . . . provided much of the pathos in Aberg's production."[107] Indeed, Blanch serves as a choral figure for Aberg, a silent witness to—and an example of—the collateral damage of war:

> Blanch was an overgrown schoolgirl in platform shoes, bobby socks, and a pink skirt. She was not so much an innocent as an extremely dim socialite, but her inability to object to her arranged marriage added extra depth to this thinly written character. . . . She was an extra-textual addition to Constance's final breakdown, sitting on the steps, glassy-eyed, in shock, and shivering, highlighting the powerlessness of spectators in the game of politics.[108]

Amidst rumors indicating that the RSC did not even have a woman on its shortlist when appointing Gregory Doran as its new artistic director in 2012, Aberg's decision to convert the Bastard to a female hero rendered the play even more topical and timely.

If it is controversial to create a female Bastard, then it is even more iconoclastic to create a female Cardinal—especially knowing that, to this day, women cannot be priests in the Catholic Church. Yet critics found Paola Dionisotti's performance of Cardinal Pandulph to be "a master class in Shakespearean acting."[109] Against a

105. Brantley.

106. Maria Aberg, "Director Q&A," http://www.rsc.org.uk/explore/king-john-maria-aberg-2012-director-q-and-a.aspxLast, accessed September 26, 2014.

107. Jami Rogers, "Review of *King John*," *Shakespeare Bulletin* 31.1 (2013): 95–99 (99).

108. Rogers, 99.

109. Rogers, "Review of *King John*," 96.

1980's-style backdrop of wild parties and self-indulgence, Dionisotti canvases the playing space, "walking slowly in her black pants suit and using her Sophia Loren sunglasses for emphasis—shifting them down on her nose to peer above them . . . it was a movement that held in it both power and determination."[110] One wonders how this gesture worked in Constance's exchange with the cold-hearted Cardinal who, in Aberg's production, is a fellow woman, ostensibly capable of bearing a child:

> *Pand.* You hold too heinous a respect of grief.
> *Const.* He talks to me that never had a son. (3.3.92–93)

Earlier in act 3, when Dionisotti coaxes the French king into war with John by commanding Philip to "Let go the hand of that arch-heretic, / And raise the power of France upon his head," Dionisotti pauses to peer above her sunglasses and adds slyly, "Unless he do submit himself to Rome" (3.1.196–198). Here, and throughout the production, the cardinal adopts the intonation of a spider speaking to the proverbial fly.

Although Dionisotti's performance has been universally praised, two aspects of the production have proved more problematic with critics: first, the awarding of all of Hubert's lines to the Bastard, thus conflating the two characters; and, second, the establishment of a sexual relationship between King John and the Bastard. The combination, as Rogers observes, "result[ed] in the near-rape of the Bastard (playing Hubert's lines) in the aftermath of Arthur's death. This placed John in a position of power at a moment that normally finds him weak while the Bastard is in the ascendancy."[111] Although this decision may not quite make sense in terms of the play's trajectory, it does make sense in the eyes of a director who knows that society is not quite ready to face a completely uncompromised female hero. Underscoring the Bastard's vulnerability at this juncture serves as a potent reminder that the world's longest-running and least prosecuted war crime is, in fact, rape. But despite the production's keen representation of female power and the injustices that continue to haunt women beyond the fourth wall, Aberg resists the notion that her production is wrapped up in gender politics. When asked what she brings to the production as a female director, Aberg asserts: "I will bring what I bring to it as a human being. It's impossible for me to say what I bring to this as a woman. I am also a lot of other things."[112]

By virtue of circumstances, Gregory Doran's RSC production of *King John* in 2001 is, perhaps, the ultimate reflection of a play inescapably engaged in its political moment. Doran recalls a matinee performance that drastically changed the meaning of the play for him. Despite the fact that the show opened during the summer months, Doran and his cast continued to question why the second half of the

---

110. Rogers, 96.
111. Rogers, 111.
112. Maria Aberg, "Director Q&A."

play was so different from the first and, he explains, "we didn't really understand that until one Tuesday matinee in September."[113] Twenty minutes into the performance, the first plane hit the World Trade Center; following intermission and unbeknownst to the audience, both towers had collapsed. Doran remembers the intense discussions backstage as they talked about informing the audience and canceling the rest of the performance. "And then," he explains, "the play itself started to articulate the situation."[114] Immediately, Arthur's leap from the tower resonated powerfully with the situation occurring in New York, where panicked employees of the World Trade Center were jumping to their deaths. The Bastard's lines, "I . . . lose my way / Among the thorns and dangers of this world. / . . . and vast confusion waits, / As doth a raven on a sick-fall'n beast" (4.3.147–148; 159–160), seemed to comment on lives that were suddenly reduced to rubble and a world locked in chaos. Kelly Hunter, who played Constance, recalls that by the evening performance, the cast, crew, and audience "were in that strange limbo-land of shock that everyone experienced in their own way. But there was a need for the play—as simple as that."[115]

The "need" that Hunter identifies refers more specifically to the characters of Constance, Hubert, and Arthur as examples of "the few voices of reason in a play peopled with irrational, unreasonable voices."[116] (Significantly, throughout the theatrical run, Hunter plays Constance dressed from head to toe in a black costume that uncannily resembles a birka.) Clearly, September 11, 2001, left an indelible mark on the production, as Doran observes:

I've never known a moment when Shakespeare actually at that point gave words to a situation where nobody could find the words to explain or articulate what was happening, but what we knew was that vast confusion now waited upon the world like a raven on a sick-fallen beast. And it was an astonishing coincidence that just heightened my sense that Shakespeare somehow just provides.[117]

The final three productions to be discussed here are cinematic spinoffs of Shakespeare's play that bring us full cycle from John's life as an adolescent to his death as a king. The critically acclaimed film *The Lion in Winter* (Anthony Harvey, 1968), starring Peter O'Toole as Henry II and Katherine Hepburn as Elinor of Aquitaine,

113. "Interpreting Shakespeare: An Interview with Gregory Doran," http://theoxfordculturereview.com/2013/02/13/interpreting-shakespeare-an-interview-with-gregory-doran/, accessed September 26, 2014.
114. "Interpreting Shakespeare."
115. Kelly Hunter, "Constance in *King John*," in *Players of Shakespeare*, Vol. 6, ed. Robert Smallwood (Cambridge and New York: Cambridge University Press, 2004), 37–49 (38).
116. Hunter, 38.
117. "Interpreting Shakespeare: An Interview with Gregory Doran."

Prince John (Nigel Terry) is a dunce in *The Lion in Winter* (1968).

offers a glimpse of the young John that is even less appealing than Shakespeare's vision of the "mature" John. Renata Adler describes Nigel Terry's Prince John as "a caricatured, spastic adolescent"[118]—a figure whose speeches serve only to reinforce this unflattering perspective, as his self-pitying rhetoric makes painfully clear: "Poor John. Who says poor John? Don't everybody sob at once! My God, if I went up in flames there's not a living soul who'd pee on me to put the fire out!" Similarly, in the animated Disney film *Robin Hood* (1973), John is a pure (if amusing) villain; he is depicted as a lion without a mane, who therefore looks quite like a lioness wearing an oversized crown. His further feminization at the hands of Disney animators is evident whenever John's chief counselor, a snake, brings up the subject of his mother; John responds instinctively by sucking his thumb and weeping. The question is: Whose role does the snake represent? On the one hand, the snake is always kissing and hissing up to John and offering him advice, not unlike the insidious, silver-tongued (or is it forked-tongued?) Cardinal Pandulph. On the other hand, the snake is also depicted as a faithful friend to John, sleeping at the foot of his bed and cheerleading for him as necessary, quite like the role of the Bastard in Shakespeare's play. Meanwhile, in this Disney classic, John spends most of his time delighting in levying heavy taxes on his people and reveling in heaps and piles of gold coins—precisely the loot that Robin Hood, the fox, will steal out from underneath him.

One has to wonder why Shakespeare eliminates Robin Hood from his play of *King John*. Robin Hood was an incredibly popular figure in the 16th century, and

118. Renata Adler, Movie Review: *The Lion in Winter* (1968). *The New York Times* 31 October 1968. http://www.nytimes.com/movie/review?res=9F00E6DF1630E034BC4950DFB6678383679EDE. Last accessed 26 September 2014.

everybody knew that he was King John's nemesis. As early as the 13th century, "Robehod" and "Rabunhod" (among other variations) were terms commonly used to designate criminals, so while a historical Robin Hood may be hard to pin down, it is clear that prototypes were already alive and well in the medieval imagination. As a representative of the "common man," the Bastard certainly shares some of Robin Hood's characteristics. After all, his birth alone renders him a kind of outlaw. However, while the Bastard does, in fact, rob the monasteries, he doesn't give the spoils to the people; rather, he uses the loot to ingratiate himself further with the king. The omission of Robin Hood from *King John* is almost too glaring not to be deliberate; perhaps Shakespeare resisted incorporating the legend into the play knowing that such a character could steal more than the king's money bags—he could steal the show.

In *Ironclad*, set in 1215–1216 at the end of John's life, the king fares no better than he does as an adolescent in *The Lion in Winter* or, for that matter, as a lion in *Robin Hood*. Set just after the signing of the *Magna Carta*, this siege film revolves around the rebels' stand against John at Rochester castle, when the king decided to fight against the barons who had forced him to sign the historic document. Predictably, the film is less focused on John than it is on a Templar Knight known as Thomas Marshall (James Purefoy), who collaborates with the historical rebel William d'Aubigny, Lord of Belvoir (Brian Cox), to defeat John and survives to become the film's romantic hero. Meanwhile, the arch-villainous king is habitually shown dismembering his enemies with a level of gore that would make even the director and star of *Braveheart* blush (Mel Gibson, 1995). For instance, when John captures William d'Aubigny he cuts the traitor's hands and feet off and then gives the order for (what remains of) him to be splattered against the castle walls with the help of

Paul Giamatti plays King John as a bloodthirsty tyrant in *Ironclad* (2011).

a trebuchet, or a medieval version of the catapult. (The real William d'Aubigny survived the siege and went on to fight for John's heir, Henry III.) The scene that has received the most critical attention by far is the "pig bomb" episode that, ironically, is actually closer to the truth than what the rest of the film presents as "history." Intent on burning the struts of Rochester castle and bringing his enemies to their knees, the real King John ordered that the foundation be larded with bacon fat; the film, however, shows live pigs being herded into the mine beneath the struts and then set on fire, squealing as they burn.

One can't help but wonder why, in our war-saturated world, we seem to long for the kind of spectacular violence that makes *King John* so disturbingly contemporary. Yet in the play, the Bastard duly warns us of the costs of complicity with this zeitgeist, when he exclaims that "he is but a bastard to the time / That doth not smack of observation" (1.1.209–210). Recalling Catherine Bates' claim that "[r]arely performed plays like *King John* . . . are truer barometers of the time than age old favorites which never leave the stage. When such plays are revived, it is for a reason," we must consider the possibility that *King John* is fast becoming a parable for our time.[119] If that is the case, then the play's striking revival on the 21st-century stage is a poignant reminder that, just as young Elizabethan scholars were taught, history *will* repeat itself if we fail to heed its lessons. We must, rather, "smack of observation," or our silence will indeed prove us bastards to the time.

Note on Annotations

George Lyman Kittredge's edition of *The Complete Works of Shakespeare* (1936) contains a comprehensive glossary, as well as brief introductions to each of the plays. Kittredge had originally planned to publish fully annotated editions of all of the plays but had completed only sixteen before he died in 1941. Unfortunately, *King John* was not one of these plays, and thus we have supplied all annotations, and in so doing have consulted Kittredge's glossary, as well as the *Oxford English Dictionary* (London: Penguin Books, 2009; http://www.oed.com/); David and Ben Crystal, *Shakespeare's Words: A Glossary and Language Companion* (London: 2004); Eugene F. Shewmaker, *Shakespeare's Language: A Glossary of Unfamiliar Words* (New York: Facts on File, 1999); C. T. Onions, *A Shakespeare Glossary*, rev. Robert D. Eagleson (Oxford: Clarendon Press, 1986); Gordon Williams, *A Glossary of Shakespeare's Sexual Language* (London: Athlone, 1997); and Eric Partridge, *Shakespeare's Bawdy* (London: E. P. Dutton, 1960).

119. See "Commodity's Slaves," *Times Literary Supplement*, April 12, 2001.

THE LIFE AND DEATH OF KING JOHN

DRAMATIS PERSONÆ.

King John.
Prince Henry, his son.
Arthur, Duke of Britain (Bretagne), son of the *King's* elder brother, Geffrey.
The Earl of Pembroke.
The Earl of Essex.
The Earl of Salisbury.
The Lord Bigot.
Hubert de Burgh.
Robert Faulconbridge, son to Sir Robert Faulconbridge.
Philip the Bastard, his half-brother.
James Gurney, servant to *Lady Faulconbridge.*
Peter of Pomfret, a prophet.
Philip, King of France.
Lewis, the Dauphin.
The Duke of Austria.
Cardinal Pandulph, the Pope's legate.
Melun, a French lord.
Chatillon, ambassador from France.

Queen Elinor, widow of King Henry II, and mother to *King John.*
Constance, mother to *Arthur.*
Blanch of Spain, daughter to the King of Castile and niece to *King John.*
Lady Faulconbridge, widow of Sir Robert Faulconbridge.

Lords, Citizens of Angiers, Sheriff, Heralds, Officers, Soldiers, Executioners,
    Messengers, Attendants.

SCENE.—*Sometimes in England, sometimes in France.*

ACT I

SCENE I. [*King John's Palace.*]

Enter King John, Queen Elinor, Pembroke,
Essex, and Salisbury, [and others,] with
Chatillon of France.

K. JOHN.	Now say, Chatillon, what would France with us?†	
CHAT.	Thus, after greeting, speaks the King of France In my behaviour to the majesty, The borrowed majesty, of England here.	
ELI.	A strange beginning! "Borrowed majesty?"	5
K. JOHN.	Silence, good mother; hear the embassy.	
CHAT.	Philip of France, in right and true behalf Of thy deceased brother Geffrey's son, Arthur Plantagenet, lays most lawful claim To this fair island and the territories, To Ireland, Poictiers, Anjou, Touraine, Maine, Desiring thee to lay aside the sword Which sways usurpingly these several titles And put the same into young Arthur's hand, Thy nephew and right royal sovereign.	10 15
K. JOHN.	What follows if we disallow of this?	
CHAT.	The proud control of fierce and bloody war, To enforce these rights so forcibly withheld.	
K. JOHN.	Here have we war for war and blood for blood, Controlment for controlment. So answer France.	20

ACT I, SCENE I
3. **behaviour**: conduct; manner; person. 5. **Borrowed**: pretended; usurped. 6. **embassy**: messages. 7. **right and true behalf**: supporting the claim. 13. **sways usurpingly**: wrongfully controls. 16. **disallow**: refuse. 17. **control**: compulsion. 20. **controlment**: strong censure.

---

† In David Giles' 1984 BBC production, the blocking of the opening scene is particularly noticeable in terms of how it establishes the relationship between John and his mother Elinor. Whereas John slouches in his chair with a goblet of wine, Elinor stands like a sentinel in front of the throne, prepared to intercept those who threaten her son's sovereignty. Positioned between the foreign ambassadors and John himself (who is literally relegated to the background), Elinor squares off with the French in this production even before any words are spoken. How would you position mother and son in this scene, before they deliver their opening lines? Consider what blocking tells us about power.

CHAT.	Then take my king's defiance from my mouth,
	The farthest limit of my embassy.
K. JOHN.	Bear mine to him, and so depart in peace.
	Be thou as lightning in the eyes of France;
	For ere thou canst report I will be there,	25
	The thunder of my cannon shall be heard.
	So hence! Be thou the trumpet of our wrath
	And sullen presage of your own decay.
	An honourable conduct let him have;
	Pembroke, look to't. Farewell, Chatillon.	30

Exeunt Chatillon and Pembroke.

ELI.	What now, my son? Have I not ever said
	How that ambitious Constance would not cease
	Till she had kindled France and all the world
	Upon the right and party of her son?
	This might have been prevented and made whole	35
	With very easy arguments of love,
	Which now the manage of two kingdoms must
	With fearful bloody issue arbitrate.
K. JOHN.	Our strong possession and our right for us!
ELI.	[*Aside to King John*] Your strong possession much more than
	your right,†	40
	Or else it must go wrong with you and me.
	So much my conscience whispers in your ear,
	Which none but heaven and you and I shall hear.

Enter a Sheriff.

ESSEX.	My liege, here is the strangest controversy
	Come from the country to be judg'd by you	45
	That e'er I heard. Shall I produce the men?
K. JOHN.	Let them approach.	[*Exit Sheriff.*]
	Our abbeys and our priories shall pay
	This expedition's charge.

---

28. **presage of your own decay**: herald as in signaling his own death. 29. **conduct**: escort. 36. **arguments of love**: friendly persuasion. 40–41: **strong possession . . . right**: Queen Elinor reminds John that his claim is unwarranted, thereby implying the legality of Arthur's. This is an innovation, since it is not in Shakespeare's sources. 49. **expedition's**: suggests a rapid change.

---

† What does this brief speech, designated as an aside, suggest about the relationship between King John and his mother? Does it imply any previous discussion between them? Does Elinor appear to be angry or controlling, or just concerned that her son is unpredictable? Or is she being merely maternal? What does the BBC film version suggest?

Enter Robert Faulconbridge and
Philip [his bastard brother].

What men are you?   50

PHIL.   Your faithful subject I, a gentleman,
Born in Northamptonshire, and eldest son,
As I suppose, to Robert Faulconbridge,
A soldier by the honour-giving hand
Of Cœur-de-lion knighted in the field.   55

K. JOHN.   What are thou?

ROB.   The son and heir to that same Faulconbridge.

K. JOHN.   Is that the elder, and art thou the heir?
You came not of one mother then, it seems.

PHIL.   Most certain of one mother, mighty king—   60
That is well known—and, as I think, one father;
But for the certain knowledge of that truth
I put you o'er to heaven and to my mother.
Of that I doubt, as all men's children may.

ELI.   Out on thee, rude man! Thou dost shame thy mother   65
And wound her honour with this diffidence.

PHIL.   I, madam? No, I have no reason for it.
That is my brother's plea, and none of mine;
The which if he can prove, 'a pops me out
At least from fair five hundred pound a year.   70
Heaven guard my mother's honour and my land!

K. JOHN.   A good blunt fellow. Why, being younger born,
Doth he lay claim to thine inheritance?

PHIL.   I know not why, except to get the land;
But once he slander'd me with bastardy.   75
But whe'r I be as true begot or no,
That still I lay upon my mother's head;
But that I am as well begot, my liege
(Fair fall the bones that took the pains for me!),
Compare our faces and be judge yourself.   80
If old Sir Robert did beget us both
And were our father, and this son like him—

---

55. **Cœur-de-lion**: King Richard I, called "Lionhearted" after drawing a lion's heart out of its mouth, according to legend. 63. **put you o'er**: refer you. 66. **diffidence**: distrust. 69. **'a**: he. 75. **once**: briefly put. 76. **whe'r**: whether. 77. **lay upon my mother's head**: leave to my mother's account. 79. **Fair fall**: good luck befall him.

	O old Sir Robert, father, on my knee	
	I give heaven thanks I was not like to thee!	
K. JOHN.	Why, what a madcap hath heaven lent us here!	85
ELI.	He hath a trick of Cœur-de-lion's face;	
	The accent of his tongue affecteth him.	
	Do you not read some tokens of my son	
	In the large composition of this man?	
K. JOHN.	Mine eye hath well examined his parts	90
	And finds them perfect Richard. Sirrah, speak,	
	What doth move you to claim your brother's land?	
PHIL.	Because he hath a half-face, like my father.	
	With half that face would he have all my land:	
	A half-fac'd groat, five hundred pound a year!	95
ROB.	My gracious liege, when that my father liv'd,	
	Your brother did employ my father much—	
PHIL.	Well, sir, by this you cannot get my land.	
	Your tale must be how he employ'd my mother.	
ROB.	And once dispatch'd him in an embassy	100
	To Germany, there with the Emperor	
	To treat of high affairs touching that time.	
	Th' advantage of his absence took the King	
	And in the meantime sojourn'd at my father's;	
	Where how he did prevail I shame to speak,	105
	But truth is truth. Large lengths of seas and shores	
	Between my father and my mother lay,	
	As I have heard my father speak himself,	
	When this same lusty gentleman was got.	
	Upon his deathbed he by will bequeath'd	110
	His lands to me, and took it on his death	
	That this, my mother's son, was none of his;	
	And if he were, he came into the world	
	Full fourteen weeks before the course of time.	
	Then, good my liege, let me have what is mine,	115
	My father's land, as was my father's will.	
K. JOHN.	Sirrah, your brother is legitimate.	
	Your father's wife did after wedlock bear him,	
	And if she did play false, the fault was hers;	

86. **trick**: distinguishing likeness. 87. **affecteth**: resembles. 93. **half-face**: profile. 95. **half-fac'd groat**: coin of slight value. 97. **brother**: King Richard. 99. **employ'd my mother**: sexually intimate. 109. **lusty**: robust.

Which fault lies on the hazards of all husbands 120
That marry wives. Tell me, how if my brother,
Who, as you say, took pains to get this son,
Had of your father claim'd this son for his?
In sooth, good friend, your father might have kept
This calf, bred from his cow, from all the world. 125
In sooth he might. Then, if he were my brother's,
My brother might not claim him; nor your father,
Being none of his, refuse him. This concludes:
My mother's son did get your father's heir;
Your father's heir must have your father's land. 130

ROB. Shall then my father's will be of no force
To dispossess that child which is not his?

PHIL. Of no more force to dispossess me, sir,
Than was his will to get me, as I think.

ELI. Whether hadst thou rather be a Faulconbridge, 135
And like thy brother, to enjoy thy land,
Or the reputed son of Cœur-de-lion,
Lord of thy presence and no land beside?

BAST.† Madam, and if my brother had my shape,
And I had his, Sir Robert his, like him; 140
And if my legs were two such riding rods,
My arms such eel-skins stuff'd, my face so thin
That in mine ear I durst not stick a rose
Lest men should say "Look where three-farthings goes!"
And, to his shape, were heir to all this land— 145
Would I might never stir from off this place,
I would give it every foot to have this face!
I would not be Sir Nob in any case.

ELI. I like thee well. Wilt thou forsake thy fortune,
Bequeath thy land to him, and follow me? 150
I am a soldier, and now bound to France.

BAST. Brother, take you my land, I'll take my chance.
Your face hath got five hundred pound a year;
Yet sell your face for fivepence, and 'tis dear.
Madam, I'll follow you unto the death. 155

126. **brother's**: Richard; Cœur-de-lion. 131. **will**: pun on lust. 138. **Lord . . . presence**: your own master. 141: **riding rods**: sexual pun. 142: **face**: appearance, effrontery, bravery. 143. **rose**: pun on coin and female genitalia. 148. **Nob**: Sir Robert. 153: **face**: continues monetary punning.

† (Lines 139–147) Hereafter Philip's character is called the Bastard.

ELI.	Nay, I would have you go before me thither.
BAST.	Our country manners give our betters way.
K. JOHN.	What is thy name?
BAST.	Philip, my liege, so is my name begun—
	Philip, good old Sir Robert's wive's eldest son. 160
K. JOHN.	From henceforth bear his name whose form thou bearest.
	Kneel thou down Philip, but arise more great;
	Arise Sir Richard and Plantagenet.
BAST.	Brother by th' mother's side, give me your hand!
	My father gave me honour, yours gave land. 165
	Now blessed be the hour, by night or day,
	When I was got, Sir Robert was away!
ELI.	The very spirit of Plantagenet!
	I am thy grandam, Richard. Call me so.
BAST.	Madam, by chance, but not by truth. 170
	What though?
	Something about, a little from the right,
	In at the window, or else o'er the hatch.
	Who dares not stir by day must walk by night;
	And have is have, however men do catch. 175
	Near or far off, well won is still well shot,
	And I am I, howe'er I was begot.
K. JOHN.	Go, Faulconbridge; now hast thou thy desire:
	A landless knight makes thee a landed squire.
	Come, madam, and come, Richard; we must speed 180
	For France, for France, for it is more than need.
BAST.	Brother, adieu. Good fortune come to thee!
	For thou wast got i' th' way of honesty.
	Exeunt all but Bastard [Philip].
	A foot of honour better than I was,
	But many a many foot of land the worse! 185
	Well, now can I make any Joan a lady.
	"Good den, Sir Richard!" "God-a-mercy, fellow!"
	And if his name be George, I'll call him Peter;
	For new-made honour doth forget men's names:

156. **go before me thither**: procession decorum. 157. **give our betters way**: the best goes first. 163. **Plantagenet**: Royalty descended from Geffrey of Anjou (d. 1151), King John's grandfather, who was known for wearing in his hat a sprig (*planta*) of the broom (*genesta*) shrub. 166. **hour**: pun, pronounced whore (homonym). 170. **truth**: pun, pronounced troth. 172–177. senses of proverbial expressions. 179. **landless**: irony (John was sometimes called "John Lackland").

'Tis too respective and too sociable   190
For your conversion. Now your traveller,
He and his toothpick at my worship's mess:
And when my knightly stomach is suffic'd,
Why, then I suck my teeth and catechize
My picked man of countries. "My dear sir,"   195
Thus, leaning on mine elbow, I begin,
"I shall beseech you." That is question now,
And then comes answer like an Absey-book:
"O sir," says answer, "at your best command,
At your employment, at your service, sir!"   200
"No, sir," says question. "I, sweet sir, at yours!"
And so, ere answer knows what question would—
Saving in dialogue of compliment,
And talking of the Alps and Apennines,
The Pyrenean and the river Po—   205
It draws toward supper in conclusion so.
But this is worshipful society
And fits the mounting spirit like myself;
For he is but a bastard to the time
That doth not smack of observation—   210
And so am I, whether I smack or no;
And not alone in habit and device,
Exterior form, outward accoutrement,
But from the inward motion to deliver
Sweet, sweet, sweet poison for the age's tooth;   215
Which, though I will not practice to deceive,
Yet, to avoid deceit, I mean to learn;
For it shall strew the footsteps of my rising.
But who comes in such haste in riding robes?
What woman post is this? Hath she no husband   220
That will take pains to blow a horn before her?

Enter Lady Faulconbridge and James Gurney.

O me! it is my mother. How now, good lady?
What brings you here to court so hastily?

---

190. **respective**: respectful. 191. **conversion**: change for the better. 192. **toothpick**: stylish affectation.
195. **picked man**: triple pun (refined, chosen, ironic reference to tooth picking). 198. **Absey-book**:
popular schoolbook structured as a dialogue. 212. **habit**: apparel, device, insignia 215. **age's tooth**:
popular taste. 216. **practice**: scheme. 221. **blow a horn**: 1. Herald announcement; 2. A cuckold wearing horns announcing his wife's infidelity.

LADY.	Where is that slave, thy brother?	
	Where is he,	225
	That holds in chase mine honour up and down?	
BAST.	My brother Robert? old Sir Robert's son?	
	Colbrand the giant, that same mighty man?	
	Is it Sir Robert's son that you seek so?	
LADY.	Sir Robert's son? Ay, thou unreverend boy,	230
	Sir Robert's son. Why scorn'st thou at Sir Robert?	
	He is Sir Robert's son, and so art thou.	
BAST.	James Gurney, wilt thou give us leave awhile?	
GUR.	Good leave, good Philip.	
BAST.	Philip?—sparrow!—James,	235
	There's toys abroad. Anon I'll tell thee more. *Exit James.*	
	Madam, I was not old Sir Robert's son;	
	Sir Robert might have eat his part in me	
	Upon Good Friday and ne'er broke his fast.	
	Sir Robert could do well: marry, to confess,	240
	Could he get me? Sir Robert could not do it;	
	We know his handiwork. Therefore, good mother,	
	To whom am I beholding for these limbs?	
	Sir Robert never holp to make this leg.	
LADY.	Hast thou conspired with thy brother too,	245
	That for thine own gain shouldst defend mine honour?	
	What means this scorn, thou most untoward knave?	
BAST.	Knight, knight, good mother, Basilisco-like!	
	What! I am dubb'd; I have it on my shoulder.	
	But, mother, I am not Sir Robert's son;	250
	I have disclaim'd Sir Robert and my land;	
	Legitimation, name, and all is gone.	
	Then, good my mother, let me know my father!	
	Some proper man, I hope. Who was it, mother?	
LADY.	Hast thou denied thyself a Faulconbridge?	255
BAST.	As faithfully as I deny the devil.	
LADY.	King Richard Cœur-de-lion was thy father.	
	By long and vehement suit I was seduc'd	
	To make room for him in my husband's bed.	

---

228. **Colbrand**: Danish giant in the romance *Guy of Warwick*. 235. **sparrow**: traditional name for Philip (it diminishes the character). 248. **Basilisco**: silly braggart in *Solomon and Persida* (an old anonymous play).

Heaven lay not my transgression to my charge!   260
Thou art the issue of my dear offence,
Which was so strongly urg'd past my defence.

BAST.   Now, by this light, were I to get again,
Madam, I would not wish a better father.
Some sins do bear their privilege on earth,   265
And so doth yours. Your fault was not your folly.
Needs must you lay your heart at his dispose,
Subjected tribute to commanding love,
Against whose fury and unmatched force
The awless lion could not wage the fight   270
Nor keep his princely heart from Richard's hand.
He that perforce robs lions of their hearts
May easily win a woman's. Ay, my mother,
With all my heart I thank thee for my father!
Who lives and dares but say thou didst not well   275
When I was got, I'll send his soul to hell.
Come, lady, I will show thee to my kin;
And they shall say, when Richard me begot,
If thou hadst said him nay, it had been sin.
Who says it was, he lies; I say 'twas not.   *Exeunt.*   280

ACT II

SCENE I. [*France. Before Angiers.*]

Enter, before Angiers, Philip,
King of France, Lewis [the] Dauphin,
Constance, Arthur, [with Forces, at one
door; at the other,] Austria [with Forces].

FRANCE.   Before Angiers well met, brave Austria.
Arthur, that great forerunner of thy blood,
Richard, that robb'd the lion of his heart
And fought the holy wars in Palestine,
By this brave duke came early to his grave;   5
And, for amends to his posterity,
At our importance hither is he come

ACT 2, SCENE I
5. **duke**: Leopold V, Duke of Austria. 7. **importance**: request.

To spread his colours, boy, in thy behalf,
And to rebuke the usurpation
Of thy unnatural uncle, English John.   10
Embrace him, love him, give him welcome hither.

ARTH.   God shall forgive you Cœur-de-lion's death
The rather that you give his offspring life,
Shadowing their right under your wings of war.
I give you welcome with a powerless hand,   15
But with a heart full of unstained love.
Welcome before the gates of Angiers, Duke.

FRANCE.   A noble boy! Who would not do thee right?

AUST.   Upon thy cheek lay I this zealous kiss
As seal to this indenture of my love: 20
That to my home I will no more return
Till Angiers and the right thou hast in France,
Together with that pale, that white-fac'd shore
Whose foot spurns back the ocean's roaring tides
And coops from other lands her islanders—   25
Even till that England, hedg'd in with the main,
That water-walled bulwark, still secure
And confident from foreign purposes—
Even till that utmost corner of the West
Salute thee for her king. Till then, fair boy,   30
Will I not think of home, but follow arms.

CONST.   O, take his mother's thanks, a widow's thanks,
Till your strong hand shall help to give him strength
To make a more requital to your love!

AUST.   The peace of heaven is theirs that lift their swords   35
In such a just and charitable war.

FRANCE.   Well then, to work! Our cannon shall be bent
Against the brows of this resisting town.
Call for our chiefest men of discipline,
To cull the plots of best advantages.   40
We'll lay before this town our royal bones,
Wade to the market place in Frenchmen's blood,
But we will make it subject to this boy.

10. **unnatural**: lacking feeling of kinship. 13. **offspring**: Richard's descendants. 14. **Shadowing**: sheltering; divine protection. 15. **powerless**: lacking an army. 20. **seal to this indenture**: the kiss (metaphorically seals the agreement). 25. **coops**: protects; encloses. 28. **confident**: safe. 34. **a more**: greater (pun amour).

CONST.   Stay for an answer to your embassy,
                Lest unadvis'd you stain your swords with blood.   45
                My Lord Chatillon may from England bring
                That right in peace which here we urge in war,
                And then we shall repent each drop of blood
                That hot rash haste so indirectly shed.

Enter Chatillon.

FRANCE.   A wonder, lady! Lo, upon thy wish   50
                Our messenger Chatillon is arriv'd!
                What England says, say briefly, gentle lord.
                We coldly pause for thee; Chatillon, speak.

CHAT.   Then turn your forces from this paltry siege
                And stir them up against a mightier task.   55
                England, impatient of your just demands,
                Hath put himself in arms. The adverse winds,
                Whose leisure I have stay'd, have given him time
                To land his legions all as soon as I.
                His marches are expedient to this town,   60
                His forces strong, his soldiers confident.
                With him along is come the mother queen,
                An Ate stirring him to blood and strife;
                With her, her niece, the Lady Blanch of Spain;
                With them a bastard of the King's deceas'd;   65
                And all th' unsettled humours of the land,
                Rash, inconsiderate, fiery voluntaries,
                With ladies' faces and fierce dragons' spleens,
                Have sold their fortunes at their native homes,
                Bearing their birthrights proudly on their backs,   70
                To make a hazard of new fortunes here.
                In brief, a braver choice of dauntless spirits
                Than now the English bottoms have waft o'er
                Did never float upon the swelling tide
                To do offence and scathe in Christendom.   *Drum beats.* 75
                The interruption of their churlish drums
                Cuts off more circumstance. They are at hand,
                To parley or to fight; therefore prepare.

---

45. **unadvis'd**: rashly. 49. **indirectly**: wrongfully; unjustly. 53. **coldly**: calmly; rationally. 55. **stir them up**: redirect them. 56. **impatient**: heedless. 58. **stay'd**: awaited. 60. **expedient**: quickly; directly. 62. **Mother Queen**: Queen Mother. 63. **Ate**: goddess of discord. 65. **King deceas'd**: King Richard. 66. **unsettled**: King John's discontented citizens. 69–70. **sold their fortunes . . . birthrights**: traded their inheritances for arms. 71. **hazard**: risked; gambled. 73. **bottoms**: nautical vessels; ships. 75. **scathe**: damage. 76. **churlish**: harsh. 77. **circumstance**: discussion.

FRANCE.	How much unlook'd for is this expedition!	
AUST.	By how much unexpected, by so much	80
	We must awake endeavour for defence;	
	For courage mounteth with occasion.	
	Let them be welcome then; we are prepar'd.	

Enter King of England, Bastard, Queen
[Elinor], Blanch, Pembroke, and others.

K. JOHN.	Peace be to France, if France in peace permit	
	Our just and lineal entrance to our own!	85
	If not, bleed France, and peace ascend to heaven,	
	Whiles we, God's wrathful agent, do correct	
	Their proud contempt that beats his peace to heaven!	
FRANCE.	Peace be to England, if that war return	
	From France to England, there to live in peace!	90
	England we love, and for that England's sake	
	With burden of our armour here we sweat.	
	This toil of ours should be a work of thine;	
	But thou from loving England art so far	
	That thou hast underwrought his lawful king,	95
	Cut off the sequence of posterity,	
	Outfaced infant state, and done a rape	
	Upon the maiden virtue of the crown.	
	Look here upon thy brother Geffrey's face!	
	These eyes, these brows, were moulded out of his;	100
	This little abstract doth contain that large	
	Which died in Geffrey, and the hand of time	
	Shall draw this brief into as huge a volume.	
	That Geffrey was thy elder brother born,	
	And this his son. England was Geffrey's right,	105
	And this is Geffrey's. In the name of God,	
	How comes it then that thou art call'd a king	
	When living blood doth in these temples beat	
	Which owe the crown that thou o'ermasterest?	
K. JOHN.	From whom hast thou this great commission, France,	110
	To draw my answer from thy articles?	

---

82. **mounteth**: implies Fortune's wheel. 82. **occasion**: implies Occasio the Latin goddess conflated with Fortune. 85. **lineal**: rightful descent. 91. **England's sake**: Arthur's sake. 93. **toil of ours should**: John, as Arthur's rightful subject, should fight for him. 95. **underwrought**: undermined. 96. **sequence of posterity**: royal succession. 97. **Outfaced infant state**: defied an infant king. 101. **little abstract**: embodiment of his faith. 103. **brief**: small version of his father will become as great. 109. **owe**: own. 109. **o'ermasterest**: seized; usurped. 110. **commission**: authority. 111. **draw my answer**: demand charges for accusations.

FRANCE.	From that supernal judge that stirs good thoughts
	In any breast of strong authority
	To look into the blots and stains of right.
	That judge hath made me guardian to this boy; 115
	Under whose warrant I impeach thy wrong,
	And by whose help I mean to chastise it.
K. JOHN.	Alack! thou dost usurp authority.
FRANCE.	Excuse—it is to beat usurping down.
ELI.	Who is it thou dost call usurper, France? 120
CONST.	Let me make answer: thy usurping son.
ELI.	Out, insolent! Thy bastard shall be King,
	That thou mayst be a queen and check the world!
CONST.	My bed was ever to thy son as true
	As thine was to thy husband; and this boy 125
	Liker in feature to his father Geffrey
	Than thou and John in manners, being as like
	As rain to water or devil to his dam.
	My boy a bastard? By my soul, I think
	His father never was so true begot! 130
	It cannot be, an if thou wert his mother.
ELI.	There's a good mother, boy, that blots thy father!
CONST.	There's a good grandam, boy, that would blot thee!
AUST.	Peace!
BAST.	Hear the crier. 135
AUST.	What the devil art thou?
BAST.	One that will play the devil, sir, with you†
	An 'a may catch your hide and you alone.
	You are the hare of whom the proverb goes,
	Whose valour plucks dead lions by the beard. 140

---

112. **supernal judge**: divine. 116. **impeach**: accuse. 123. **queen**: possible pun: queen bawd. 123. **check**: control. 132. **blots**: deforms. 136. **Play the devil**: cause disruption. 139. **proverb**: "hares may pull dead lions by their beards."

---

† The Bastard insults Austria throughout this and later scenes, but there is something rather unique about the tenor of this particular threat. Notice how the "monster" that the Bastard plans to make of the Austrian dignitary is, in fact, a cuckold. On the page, the Bastard's threat to Austria's wife is easily missed; what kind of visual or auditory underscoring would you employ on stage or screen to clarify the nature of the Bastard's words? Note also that the Bastard ends his insult by referring to himself as a lion roaring (299), in keeping with his (newly discovered) relationship to King Richard the Lionhearted.

	I'll smoke your skin-coat an I catch you right. Sirrah, look to't! I' faith I will, i' faith!	
BLANCH.	O, well did he become that lion's robe That did disrobe the lion of that robe!	
BAST.	It lies as sightly on the back of him As great Alcides' shows upon an ass. But, ass, I'll take that burthen from your back Or lay on that shall make your shoulders crack.	145
AUST.	What cracker is this same that deafs our ears With this abundance of superfluous breath? King Philip, determine what we shall do straight.	150
FRANCE.	Women and fools, break off your conference. King John, this is the very sum of all: England and Ireland, Anjou, Touraine, Maine, In right of Arthur do I claim of thee. Wilt thou resign them and lay down thy arms?	155
K. JOHN.	My life as soon. I do defy thee, France. Arthur of Britain, yield thee to my hand, And out of my dear love I'll give thee more Than e'er the coward hand of France can win. Submit thee, boy.	160
ELI.	Come to thy grandam, child.	
CONST.	Do, child! go to it grandam, child! Give grandam kingdom, and it grandam will Give it a plum, a cherry, and a fig. There's a good grandam!	165
ARTH.	Good my mother, peace! I would that I were low laid in my grave. I am not worth this coil that's made for me.	
ELI.	His mother shames him so, poor boy he weeps.	170
CONST.	Now shame upon you, whe'r she does or no! His grandam's wrongs, and not his mother's shames, Draws those heaven-moving pearls from his poor eyes, Which heaven shall take in nature of a fee.	

---

141. **smoke**: thrash. 143. **lion's robe**: the lion's hide taken by King Richard now worn by Austria. 144. **disrobe**: remove the lion's skin. 149. **cracker**: boaster. 152. **fools**: children. 165. **fig**: something worthless, contemptuous, poisonous. 169. **coil**: commotion; fuss. 170. **shames**: embarrasses. 171. **shame**: disgrace. 172. **shames**: sins. 173. **pearls from his poor eyes**: beads (Arthur's tears compared to prayers counted on a priceless rosary).

	Ay, with these crystal beads heaven shall be brib'd	175
	To do him justice and revenge on you.	
ELI.	Thou monstrous slanderer of heaven and earth!	
CONST.	Thou monstrous injurer of heaven and earth,	
	Call not me slanderer! Thou and thine usurp	
	The dominations, royalties, and rights	180
	Of this oppressed boy. This is thy eldest son's son,	
	Infortunate in nothing but in thee.	
	Thy sins are visited in this poor child;	
	The canon of the law is laid on him,	
	Being but the second generation	185
	Removed from thy sin-conceiving womb.	
K. JOHN.	Bedlam, have done!	
CONST.	I have but this to say,	
	That he is not only plagued for her sin,	
	But God hath made her sin and her the plague	190
	On this removed issue, plagu'd for her	
	And with her plague; her sin his injury,	
	Her injury the beadle to her sin;	
	All punish'd in the person of this child,	
	And all for her—a plague upon her!	195
ELI.	Thou unadvised scold, I can produce	
	A will that bars the title of thy son.	
CONST.	Ay, who doubts that? A will! a wicked will;	
	A woman's will; a cank'red grandam's will!	
FRANCE.	Peace, lady! pause, or be more temperate.	200
	It ill beseems this presence to cry aim	
	To these ill-tuned repetitions.	
	Some trumpet summon hither to the walls	
	These men of Angiers. Let us hear them speak	
	Whose title they admit, Arthur's or John's.	205

Trumpet sounds. Enter Citizens upon the walls.

CITIZEN.	Who is it that hath warn'd us to the walls?	
FRANCE.	'Tis France, for England.	

---

181. **eldest son's**: eldest grandson. 184. **canon of the law**: sacred law. 186. **sin-conceiving womb**: implies that Elinor committed adultery and her issue therefore is illegitimate. 187. **Bedlam**: lunatic. 193. **beadle**: punisher. 196–197. **produce / A will**: King Richard's will made John his heir. 196. **unadvised**: reckless. 196. **scold**: a quarrelsome woman. 199. **A woman's will**: invalid; cankered; rotten; corrupt. 206. **warn'd**: summoned.

K. JOHN.   England for itself.
           You men of Angiers, and my loving subjects—

FRANCE.   You loving men of Angiers, Arthur's subjects,   210
           Our trumpet call'd you to this gentle parle—

K. JOHN.   For our advantage; therefore hear us first.
           These flags of France that are advanced here
           Before the eye and prospect of your town
           Have hither march'd to your endamagement.   215
           The cannons have their bowels full of wrath,
           And ready mounted are they to spit forth
           Their iron indignation 'gainst your walls.
           All preparation for a bloody siege
           And merciless proceeding by these French   220
           Confronts your city's eyes, your winking gates;
           And but for our approach, those sleeping stones
           That as a waist doth girdle you about,
           By the compulsion of their ordinance
           By this time from their fixed beds of lime   225
           Had been dishabited, and wide havoc made
           For bloody power to rush upon your peace.
           But on the sight of us your lawful king,
           Who painfully with much expedient march
           Have brought a countercheck before your gates,   230
           To save unscratch'd your city's threat'ned cheeks—
           Behold, the French amaz'd vouchsafe a parle;
           And now, instead of bullets wrapp'd in fire
           To make a shaking fever in your walls,
           They shoot but calm words folded up in smoke,   235
           To make a faithless error in your ears;
           Which trust accordingly, kind citizens,
           And let us in, your king, whose labour'd spirits,
           Forwearied in this action of swift speed,
           Crave harbourage within your city walls.   240

FRANCE.   When I have said, make answer to us both.
           Lo, in this right hand, whose protection
           Is most divinely vow'd upon the right
           Of him it holds, stands young Plantagenet,
           Son to the elder brother of this man,   245
           And king o'er him and all that he enjoys.

---

211. **parle**: meeting. 213. **flags**: anachronism—flags were unknown until the late 15th century. 214. **prospect**: view. 240: **harbourage**: refuge. 244: **holds**: safeguards.

For this downtrodden equity we tread
In warlike march these greens before your town,
Being no further enemy to you
Than the constraint of hospitable zeal   250
In the relief of this oppressed child
Religiously provokes. Be pleased then
To pay that duty which you truly owe
To him that owes it, namely, this young prince;
And then our arms, like to a muzzled bear,   255
Save in aspect, hath all offence seal'd up;
Our cannons' malice vainly shall be spent
Against th' invulnerable clouds of heaven;
And with a blessed and unvex'd retire,
With unhack'd swords and helmets all unbruis'd,   260
We will bear home that lusty blood again
Which here we came to spout against your town,
And leave your children, wives, and you in peace.
But if you fondly pass our proffer'd offer,
'Tis not the roundure of your old-fac'd walls   265
Can hide you from our messengers of war,
Though all these English and their discipline
Were harbour'd in their rude circumference.
Then tell us, shall your city call us lord
In that behalf which we have challeng'd it?   270
Or shall we give the signal to our rage
And stalk in blood to our possession?

CITIZEN.   In brief, we are the King of England's subjects.
             For him, and in his right, we hold this town.

K. JOHN.   Acknowledge then the King, and let me in.   275

CITIZEN.   That can we not; but he that proves the King,
             To him will we prove loyal. Till that time
             Have we ramm'd up our gates against the world.

K. JOHN.   Doth not the crown of England prove the King?
             And if not that, I bring you witnesses,   280
             Twice fifteen thousand hearts of England's breed—

BAST.   Bastards and else.

K. JOHN.   To verify our title with their lives.

FRANCE.   As many and as well-born bloods as those—

---

259. **unvex'd retire**: unimpeded withdrawal. 264. **fondly**: foolishly. 264. **pass**: refuse. 265. **roundure**: round circumference. 266. **messengers of war**: cannon shot. 276. **proves**: is shown to the king.

| BAST. | Some bastards too. | 285 |

FRANCE.   Stand in his face to contradict his claim.

CITIZEN.   Till you compound whose right is worthiest,
We for the worthiest hold the right from both.

K. JOHN.   Then God forgive the sin of all those souls
That to their everlasting residence,   290
Before the dew of evening fall, shall fleet
In dreadful trial of our kingdom's king!

FRANCE.   Amen, amen! Mount, chevaliers! to arms!

BAST.   Saint George that swing'd the dragon, and e'er since
Sits on his horseback at mine hostess' door,   295
Teach us some fence! [To Austria] Sirrah, were I at home,
At your den, sirrah, with your lioness,
I would set an ox-head to your lion's hide
And make a monster of you.

AUST.   Peace, no more!   300

BAST.   O, tremble! for you hear the lion roar.

K. JOHN.   Up higher to the plain, where we'll set forth
In best appointment all our regiments.

BAST.   Speed then to take advantage of the field.

FRANCE.   It shall be so; and at the other hill   305
Command the rest to stand. God and our right!   Exeunt.

*Here, after excursions, enter the Herald of
France, with Trumpets, to the gates.*

F. HER.   You men of Angiers, open wide your gates
And let young Arthur, Duke of Britain, in,
Who by the hand of France this day hath made
Much work for tears in many an English mother   310
Whose sons lie scattered on the bleeding ground.
Many a widow's husband groveling lies.
Coldly embracing the discoloured earth;
And victory with little loss doth play
Upon the dancing banners of the French.   315
Who are at hand, triumphantly display'd,

---

287. **compound**: settle; agree. 294. **Saint George**: patron saint of England who famously killed a dragon. Elizabethan taverns sometimes had signs depicting St. George and the dragon. 296. **fence**: defense; swordplay. 296–299. **Sirrah . . . make a monster**: an ox's head is the sign of the cuckold, someone whose wife has betrayed him.

To enter conquerors and to proclaim
Arthur of Britain England's King and yours.

Enter English Herald, with Trumpet.

E. HER.   Rejoice, you men of Angiers, ring your bells!
King John, your king and England's, doth approach,   320
Commander of this hot malicious day.
Their armours that march'd hence so silver-bright
Hither return all gilt with Frenchmen's blood.
There stuck no plume in any English crest
That is removed by a staff of France.   325
Our colours do return in those same hands
That did display them when we first march'd forth;
And like a jolly troop of huntsmen come
Our lusty English, all with purpled hands,
Dy'd in the dying slaughter of their foes.   330
Open your gates, and give the victors way!

CITIZEN.   Heralds, from off our tow'rs we might behold
From first to last the onset and retire
Of both your armies, whose equality
By our best eyes cannot be censured.   335
Blood hath bought blood, and blows have answer'd blows;
Strength match'd with strength, and power confronted power.
Both are alike, and both alike we like.
One must prove greatest. While they weigh so even,
We hold our town for neither; yet for both.   340

*Enter the two Kings, with
their Powers, at several doors.*

K. JOHN.   France, hast thou yet more blood to cast away?
Say, shall the current of our right run on?
Whose passage, vex'd with thy impediment,
Shall leave his native channel and o'erswell
With course disturb'd even thy confining shores,   345
Unless thou let his silver water keep
A peaceful progress to the ocean.

FRANCE.   England, thou hast not sav'd one drop of blood
In this hot trial more than we of France;
Rather, lost more. And by this hand I swear,   350
That sways the earth this climate overlooks,
Before we will lay down our just-borne arms,

---

323. **gilt**: stained. 329. **purpled**: bloodstained. 337. **power**: army.

| | We'll put thee down, 'gainst whom these arms we bear,
Or add a royal number to the dead,
Gracing the scroll that tells of this war's loss
With slaughter coupled to the name of kings. | 355 |

BAST.   Ha, majesty! how high thy glory tow'rs
When the rich blood of kings is set on fire!
O, now doth Death line his dead chaps with steel;
The swords of soldiers are his teeth, his fangs;   360
And now he feasts, mousing the flesh of men,
In undetermin'd differences of kings.
Why stand these royal fronts amazèd thus?
Cry "havoc," kings. Back to the stainèd field,
You equal potents, fiery kindled spirits!   365
Then let confusion of one part confirm
The other's peace. Till then, blows, blood, and death!

K. JOHN.   Whose party do the townsmen yet admit?

FRANCE.   Speak, citizens, for England. Who's your king?

CITIZEN.   The King of England, when we know the King.   370

FRANCE.   Know him in us that here hold up his right.

K. JOHN.   In us that are our own great deputy
And bear possession of our person here,
Lord of our presence, Angiers, and of you.

CITIZEN.   A greater pow'r than we denies all this;   375
And till it be undoubted, we do lock
Our former scruple in our strong-barr'd gates;
King'd of our fears, until our fears, resolv'd,
Be by some certain king purg'd and depos'd.

BAST.   By heaven, these scroyles of Angiers flout you, kings,   380
And stand securely on their battlements,
As in a theatre, whence they gape and point
At your industrious scenes and acts of death.
Your royal presences be rul'd by me:
Do like the mutines of Jerusalem,   385
Be friends awhile, and both conjointly bend
Your sharpest deeds of malice on this town.

359. **chaps**: jaws. 361. **mousing**: biting and tearing; a cat with a mouse. 363. **amazed**: confused. 364. **Cry "havoc"**: spare none; give no quarter. 365. **potents**: powers. 366. **part**: party. 378. **King'd of our fears**: governed by our fears. 380. **scroyles**: wretches; scoundrels. 385. **mutines of Jerusalem**: separate factions in Jerusalem combining forces to defend the city against the emperor Titus around 70 CE. 386. **bend**: direct.

By east and west let France and England mount
Their battering cannon, charged to the mouths,
Till their soul-fearing clamours have brawl'd down   390
The flinty ribs of this contemptuous city.
I'd play incessantly upon these jades,
Even till unfenced desolation
Leave them as naked as the vulgar air.
That done, dissever your united strengths   395
And part your mingled colours once again,
Turn face to face and bloody point to point.
Then in a moment Fortune shall cull forth
Out of one side her happy minion,
To whom in favour she shall give the day   400
And kiss him with a glorious victory.
How like you this wild counsel, mighty states?
Smacks it not something of the policy?

K. JOHN.   Now, by the sky that hangs above our heads,
I like it well. France, shall we knit our pow'rs   405
And lay this Angiers even with the ground;
Then after fight who shall be king of it?

BAST.   An if thou hast the mettle of a king,
Being wrong'd as we are by this peevish town,
Turn thou the mouth of thy artillery,   410
As we will ours, against these saucy walls;
And when that we have dash'd them to the ground,
Why, then defy each other, and pell-mell
Make work upon ourselves, for heaven or hell.

FRANCE.   Let it be so. Say, where will you assault?   415

K. JOHN.   We from the west will send destruction
Into this city's bosom.

AUST.   I from the north.

FRANCE.   Our thunder from the south
Shall rain their drift of bullets on this town.   420

BAST.   [Aside] O prudent discipline! From north to south!
Austria and France shoot in each other's mouth.
I'll stir them to it.—Come, away, away!

---

390. **soul-fearing**: terrifying. 392. **jades**: worthless fellows. 394. **naked**: lacking weapons. 398. **Fortune**: Medieval Fortuna, often fickle. 399. **minion**: favorite. 402. **states**: rulers; kings. 403. **policy**: political maneuver associated with Niccolo Machiavelli's *The Prince*. 405. **pow'rs**: armies. 411. **saucy**: impudent. 421. **discipline**: skillful maneuvers.

CITIZEN.   Hear us, great kings. Vouchsafe awhile to stay,
             And I shall show you peace and fair-fac'd league,   425
             Win you this city without stroke or wound,
             Rescue those breathing lives to die in beds
             That here come sacrifices for the field.
             Persever not, but hear me, mighty kings!

K. JOHN.   Speak on with favour; we are bent to hear.   430

CITIZEN.   That daughter there of Spain, the Lady Blanch,
             Is niece to England. Look upon the years
             Of Lewis the Dauphin and that lovely maid.
             If lusty love should go in quest of beauty,
             Where should he find it fairer than in Blanch?   435
             If zealous love should go in search of virtue,
             Where should he find it purer than in Blanch?
             If love ambitious sought a match of birth,
             Whose veins bound richer blood than Lady Blanch?
             Such as she is, in beauty, virtue, birth,   440
             Is the young Dauphin every way complete:
             If not complete, I say, he is not she;
             And she again wants nothing to name want,
             If want it be not that she is not he.
             He is the half part of a blessed man,   445
             Left to be finished by such as she;
             And she a fair divided excellence,
             Whose fullness of perfection lies in him.
             O, two such silver currents, when they join,
             Do glorify the banks that bound them in;   450
             And two such shores to two such streams made one,
             Two such controlling bounds, shall you be, kings,
             To these two princes, if you marry them.
             This union shall do more than battery can
             To our fast-closed gates; for at this match,   455
             With swifter spleen than powder can enforce,
             The mouth of passage shall we fling wide ope
             And give you entrance; but without this match,
             The sea enraged is not half so deaf,
             Lions more confident, mountains and rocks   460

---

430. **bent**: ready. 432. **England**: John. 434. **lusty**: physical. 436. **zealous**: holy. 438. **ambitious**: aspiring. 438. **match of birth**: politically expedient. 439. **bound**: contained. 440–448. **Such as she is . . . perfection lies in him**: popular wordplay in Elizabethan love poetry (the two lovers complement each other to form a perfect whole). 448. **him**: not gender specific. 449–451. **two such silver currents . . . made one**: common metaphor used in love poetry. 453. **princes**: both sexes.

More free from motion—no, not Death himself
In mortal fury half so peremptory
As we to keep this city.

BAST.   Here's a "Stay!"
That shakes the rotten carcass of old Death   465
Out of his rags! Here's a large mouth indeed,
That spits forth death, and mountains, rocks, and seas;
Talks as familiarly of roaring lions
As maids of thirteen do of puppy-dogs!
What cannoneer begot this lusty blood?   470
He speaks plain cannon-fire and smoke and bounce;
He gives the bastinado with his tongue.
Our ears are cudgell'd; not a word of his
But buffets better than a fist of France.
Zounds! I was never so bethump'd with words   475
Since I first call'd my brother's father dad.

ELI.   Son, list to this conjunction, make this match,
Give with our niece a dowry large enough;
For by this knot thou shalt so surely tie
Thy now-unsur'd assurance to the crown   480
That yon green boy shall have no sun to ripe
The bloom that promiseth a mighty fruit.
I see a yielding in the looks of France.
Mark how they whisper. Urge them while their souls
Are capable of this ambition,   485
Lest zeal, now melted by the windy breath
Of soft petitions, pity, and remorse,
Cool and congeal again to what it was.

CITIZEN.   Why answer not the double Majesties
This friendly treaty of our threat'ned town?   490

FRANCE.   Speak England first, that hath been forward first
To speak unto this city. What say you?

K. JOHN.   If that the Dauphin there, thy princely son,
Can in this book of beauty read "I love,"
Her dowry shall weigh equal with a queen;   495
For Anjou, and fair Touraine, Maine, Poictiers,

---

462. **peremptory**: determined. 464. **"Stay!"**: obstacle. 465. **Death**: Death was often depicted as a
ragged skeleton mounted upon a horse as in the four horsemen of the Apocalypse. 472. **bastinado**: beat
with a stick. 475. **Zounds!**: God's wounds. 477. **list**: listen. 480. **now-unsur'd**: unsecured. 481. **green**:
immature. 487. **remorse**: compassion.

And all that we upon this side the sea
(Except this city now by us besieg'd)
Find liable to our crown and dignity,
Shall gild her bridal bed and make her rich   500
In titles, honours, and promotions,
As she in beauty, education, blood,
Holds hand with any princess of the world.

FRANCE.   What say'st thou, boy? Look in the lady's face.

DAU.   I do, my lord, and in her eye I find†   505
A wonder, or a wondrous miracle—
The shadow of myself form'd in her eye;
Which, being but the shadow of your son,
Becomes a sun and makes your son a shadow.
I do protest I never lov'd myself   510
Till now infixed I beheld myself
Drawn in the flattering table of her eye.

                                    Whispers with Blanch.

BAST.   [*Aside*] Drawn in the flattering table of her eye,
Hang'd in the frowning wrinkle of her brow,
And quarter'd in her heart! He doth espy   515
Himself love's traitor. This is pity now
That hang'd and drawn and quarter'd there should be
In such a love so vile a lout as he.

BLANCH.   My uncle's will in this respect is mine.
If he see aught in you that makes him like,   520
That anything he sees which moves his liking,
I can with ease translate it to my will;
Or if you will, to speak more properly,
I will enforce it eas'ly to my love.
Further I will not flatter you, my lord,   525
That all I see in you is worthy love
Than this—that nothing do I see in you,

---

499. **liable**: subject. 505–512. puns and wordplay common in Elizabethan love poetry in which lovers are reflected in each other's eyes. 507. **shadow**: likeness. 508. **shadow**: dark image cast by the sun (wordplay). 512. **Drawn**: pun on artistic sketch and disembowelment; as in "hang'd and drawn and quarter'd" (517).

---

†   Some audiences might believe that Shakespeare is lampooning Petrarchan love in this exchange between the Dauphin and Blanch, as the Bastard's asides might suggest. How would you stage this exchange to show otherwise? Do the Bastard's comments (513–518) imply anything about his own "romantic" feelings? How does the BBC version differ from your own impression of this scene?

	Though churlish thoughts themselves should be your judge,	
	That I can find should merit any hate.	
K. JOHN.	What say these young ones? What say you, my niece?	530
BLANCH.	That she is bound in honour still to do	
	What you in wisdom still vouchsafe to say.	
K. JOHN.	Speak then, Prince Dauphin. Can you love this lady?	
DAU.	Nay, ask me if I can refrain from love,	
	For I do love her most unfeignedly.	535
K. JOHN.	Then do I give Volquessen, Touraine, Maine,	
	Poictiers, and Anjou, these five provinces,	
	With her to thee; and this addition more,	
	Full thirty thousand marks of English coin.	
	Philip of France, if thou be pleas'd withal,	540
	Command thy son and daughter to join hands.	
FRANCE.	It likes us well. Young princes, close your hands.	
AUST.	And your lips too; for I am well assur'd	
	That I did so when I was first assur'd.	
FRANCE.	Now, citizens of Angiers, ope your gates,	545
	Let in that amity which you have made;	
	For at Saint Mary's Chapel presently	
	The rites of marriage shall be solemniz'd.	
	Is not the Lady Constance in this troop?	
	I know she is not; for this match made up	550
	Her presence would have interrupted much.	
	Where is she and her son? Tell me, who knows.	
DAU.	She is sad and passionate at your Highness' tent.	
FRANCE.	And, by my faith, this league that we have made	
	Will give her sadness very little cure.	555
	Brother of England, how may we content	
	This widow lady? In her right we came,	
	Which we, God knows, have turn'd another way,	
	To our own vantage.	
K. JOHN.	We will heal up all;	560
	For we'll create young Arthur Duke of Britain	
	And Earl of Richmond, and this rich fair town	
	We make him lord of. Call the Lady Constance.	

543. **assur'd**: certain. 544. **assur'd**: betrothed. 546. **amity**: friendships. 547. **presently**: immediately.
553. **passionate**: sorrowful; grieved.

Some speedy messenger bid her repair
To our solemnity. I trust we shall,   565
If not fill up the measure of her will,
Yet in some measure satisfy her so
That we shall stop her exclamation.
Go we as well as haste will suffer us
To this unlook'd-for, unprepar`ed` pomp.   570

Exeunt [all but the Bastard].

BAST.   Mad world! mad kings! mad composition!†
John, to stop Arthur's title in the whole,
Hath willingly departed with a part;
And France—whose armour conscience buckled on,
Whom zeal and charity brought to the field   575
As God's own soldier—rounded in the ear
With that same purpose-changer, that sly devil,
That broker that still breaks the pate of faith,
That daily break-vow, he that wins of all,
Of kings, of beggars, old men, young men, maids,   580
Who, having no external thing to lose
But the word "maid," cheats the poor maid of that—
That smooth-fac'd gentleman, tickling Commodity,
Commodity, the bias of the world—
The world, who of itself is peis`ed` well,   585
Made to run even upon even ground
Till this advantage, this vile drawing bias,
This sway of motion, this Commodity,
Makes it take head from all indifferency,
From all direction, purpose, course, intent—   590
And this same bias, this Commodity,
This bawd, this broker, this all-changing word,
Clapp'd on the outward eye of fickle France,
Hath drawn him from his own determin'd aid,
From a resolv'd and honourable war,   595
To a most base and vile-concluded peace.

---

565. **solemnity**: marriage ceremony. 566. **will**: wishes; desires. 571. **composition**: agreement; settlement. 575. **zeal**: religion (Arthur's claim had Papal sanction). 583. **Commodity**: advantage; expedience; opportunity; self-interest. 587. **bias**: in bowling the weight is placed in a ball to curve its course. 593. **fickle France**: France is now depicted as a weighted ball, inclined toward evil.

---

†   How do you feel about the Bastard's character in the immediate aftermath of his soliloquy on "tickling Commodity" (583)? Do you trust him? Can you see, in the BBC version, how effectively the Bastard ingratiates himself to us during this speech? Can you imagine accomplishing this through any means *other than* direct address?

The Bastard (George Costan) engages in direct address with the camera in the 1984 BBC film production.

And why rail I on this Commodity?
But for because he hath not woo'd me yet:
Not that I have the power to clutch my hand
When his fair angels would salute my palm,   600
But for my hand, as unattempted yet,
Like a poor beggar, raileth on the rich.
Well, whiles I am a beggar, I will rail
And say there is no sin but to be rich;
And being rich, my virtue then shall be   605
To say there is no vice but beggary.
Since kings break faith upon commodity,
Gain, be my lord, for I will worship thee!   *Exit.*

600. **angels**: coin.

ACT III

SCENE I. [*France. The French King's tent.*]

Enter Constance, Arthur, and Salisbury.

CONST.   Gone to be married? Gone to swear a peace?
           False blood to false blood join'd! Gone to be friends?
           Shall Lewis have Blanch, and Blanch those provinces?
           It is not so! thou hast misspoke, misheard.
           Be well advis'd, tell o'er thy tale again.   5
           It cannot be; thou dost but say 'tis so.
           I trust I may not trust thee, for thy word
           Is but the vain breath of a common man.
           Believe me, I do not believe thee, man;
           I have a king's oath to the contrary.   10
           Thou shalt be punish'd for thus frighting me,
           For I am sick, and capable of fears;
           Oppress'd with wrongs, and therefore full of fears;
           A widow, husbandless, subject to fears;
           A woman, naturally born to fears;   15
           And though thou now confess thou didst but jest,
           With my vex'd spirits I cannot take a truce,
           But they will quake and tremble all this day.
           What dost thou mean by shaking of thy head?
           Why dost thou look so sadly on my son?   20
           What means that hand upon that breast of thine?
           Why holds thine eye that lamentable rheum,
           Like a proud river peering o'er his bounds?
           Be these sad signs confirmers of thy words?
           Then speak again—not all thy former tale,   25
           But this one word, whether thy tale be true.

SAL.   As true as I believe you think them false
           That give you cause to prove my saying true.

CONST.   O, if thou teach me to believe this sorrow,
           Teach thou this sorrow how to make me die;   30
           And let belief and life encounter so
           As doth the fury of two desperate men

ACT 3, SCENE I
14. **husbandless**: Shakespeare draws more sympathy for Constance by making her a widow; historically, she was no longer a widow, but had married twice since Geffrey's death (1186). 17. **take a truce**: make peace. 22. **rheum**: tears. 23. **peering o'er**: flooding.

Which in the very meeting fall and die!
Lewis marry Blanch? O boy, then where art thou?
France friend with England? What becomes of me?   35
Fellow, be gone. I cannot brook thy sight;
This news hath made thee a most ugly man.

SAL.   What other harm have I, good lady, done
But spoke the harm that is by others done?

CONST.   Which harm within itself so heinous is   40
As it makes harmful all that speak of it.

ARTH.   I do beseech you, madam, be content.

CONST.   If thou that bid'st me be content wert grim,
Ugly, and sland'rous to thy mother's womb,
Full of unpleasing blots and sightless stains,   45
Lame, foolish, crooked, swart, prodigious,
Patch'd with foul moles and eye-offending marks,
I would not care, I then would be content,
For then I should not love thee—no, nor thou
Become thy great birth nor deserve a crown.   50
But thou art fair, and at thy birth, dear boy,
Nature and Fortune join'd to make thee great.
Of Nature's gifts thou mayst with lilies boast
And with the half-blown rose. But Fortune, O,
She is corrupted, chang'd, and won from thee!   55
Sh' adulterates hourly with thine uncle John,
And with her golden hand hath pluck'd on France
To tread down fair respect of sovereignty,
And made his majesty the bawd to theirs.
France is a bawd to Fortune and King John—   60
That strumpet Fortune! that usurping John!
Tell me, thou fellow, is not France forsworn?
Envenom him with words; or get thee gone
And leave those woes alone which I alone
Am bound to underbear.   65

SAL.   Pardon me, madam,
I may not go without you to the kings.

---

34. **boy**: servant (term of derision). 36. **Fellow**: a menial servant. 37. **ugly**: evoking horror. 44. **Ugly**: repugnant. 45. **blots**: disgraceful blemishes. 45. **sightless**: unsightly; offensive. 46. **prodigious**: monstrous; evil. 47. **Patch'd**: blotched 52. **Nature and Fortune**: Nature bestows the gifts with which one is born. Fortune bestows those one acquires. 60. **bawd**: pander. 62. **forsworn**: perjured; falsely sworn. 65. **underbear**: suffer; endure.

CONST.   Thou mayst! thou shalt! I will not go with thee.
           I will instruct my sorrows to be proud;
           For grief is proud, and makes his owner stoop.   70
           To me, and to the state of my great grief,
           Let kings assemble; for my grief's so great
           That no supporter but the huge firm earth
           Can hold it up.   [*Seats herself on the ground.*]
           Here I and sorrows sit;   75
           Here is my throne, bid kings come bow to it.

                      Enter King John, France, Dauphin,
                      Blanch, Elinor, Philip [*the Bastard*],
                      Austria, [*and Attendants*].

FRANCE.   'Tis true, fair daughter, and this blessed day
           Ever in France shall be kept festival.
           To solemnize this day the glorious sun
           Stays in his course and plays the alchymist,   80
           Turning with splendour of his precious eye
           The meagre cloddy earth to glittering gold.
           The yearly course that brings this day about
           Shall never see it but a holiday.

CONST.   [*Rises*] A wicked day, and not a holy day!   85
           What hath this day deserv'd? what hath it done
           That it in golden letters should be set
           Among the high tides in the calendar?
           Nay, rather turn this day out of the week,
           This day of shame, oppression, perjury.   90
           Or, if it must stand still, let wives with child
           Pray that their burthens may not fall this day,
           Lest that their hopes prodigiously be cross'd;
           But on this day, let seamen fear no wrack;
           No bargains break that are not this day made;   95
           This day all things begun, come to ill end,
           Yea, faith itself to hollow falsehood change!

FRANCE.   By heaven, lady, you shall have no cause
           To curse the fair proceedings of this day.
           Have I not pawn'd to you my majesty?   100

---

71. **state**: condition, regal court. 75. **Here**: the ground. 78. **festival**: national holiday. 82. **meagre**: barren. 93. **prodigiously be cross'd**: thwarted by the birth of a monster-child. 100. **pawn'd**: pledged; staked.

CONST.	You have beguil'd me with a counterfeit
	Resembling majesty, which, being touch'd and tried,
	Proves valueless. You are forsworn, forsworn!
	You came in arms to spill mine enemies' blood,
	But now in arms you strengthen it with yours. 105
	The grappling vigour and rough frown of war
	Is cold in amity and painted peace,
	And our oppression hath made up this league.
	Arm, arm, you heavens, against these perjur'd kings!
	A widow cries; be husband to me, heavens! 110
	Let not the hours of this ungodly day
	Wear out the day in peace; but ere sunset
	Set armed discord 'twixt these perjur'd kings!
	Hear me, O, hear me!
AUST.	Lady Constance, peace! 115
CONST.	War! war! no peace! Peace is to me a war.
	O Limoges! O Austria! thou dost shame
	That bloody spoil. Thou slave, thou wretch, thou coward!
	Thou little valiant, great in villainy!
	Thou ever strong upon the stronger side! 120
	Thou Fortune's champion, that dost never fight
	But when her humorous ladyship is by
	To teach thee safety! Thou art perjur'd too,
	And sooth'st up greatness. What a fool art thou,
	A ramping fool, to brag and stamp and swear 125
	Upon my party! Thou cold-blooded slave,
	Hast thou not spoke like thunder on my side?
	Been sworn my soldier, bidding me depend
	Upon thy stars, thy fortune, and thy strength?
	And dost thou now fall over to my foes? 130
	Thou wear a lion's hide? Doff it for shame,
	And hang a calve's-skin on those recreant limbs.
AUST.	O, that a man should speak those words to me!
BAST.	And hang a calve's-skin on those recreant limbs.
AUST.	Thou dar'st not say so, villain, for thy life. 135
BAST.	And hang a calve's-skin on those recreant limbs.

---

101. **counterfeit**: false coin. 102–103. **touch'd and tried / Proves valueless**: counterfeit coin proven fake when tested. 107. **painted**: false. 108. **oppression**: misfortune. 117. **O Limoges! O Austria!**: the two are treated as one. 118. **bloody spoil**: the lion skin stolen from King Richard. 122. **humorous**: fickle. 132. **calve's-skin**: fool's coat; a coward.

K. John.	We like not this; thou dost forget thyself.

Enter Pandulph.

France.	Here comes the holy legate of the Pope.
Pand.	Hail, you anointed deputies of heaven!

To thee, King John, my holy errand is.   140
I Pandulph, of fair Milan Cardinal,
And from Pope Innocent the legate here,
Do in his name religiously demand
Why thou against the Church, our holy mother,
So willfully dost spurn, and force perforce   145
Keep Stephen Langton, chosen Archbishop
Of Canterbury, from that holy see.
This, in our foresaid holy father's name,
Pope Innocent, I do demand of thee.

K. John.	What earthly name to interrogatories 150

Can task the free breath of a sacred king?
Thou canst not, Cardinal, devise a name
So slight, unworthy, and ridiculous
To charge me to an answer, as the Pope.
Tell him this tale, and from the mouth of England   155
Add thus much more, that no Italian priest
Shall tithe or toll in our dominions;
But as we, under heaven, are supreme head,
So, under Him that great supremacy,
Where we do reign, we will alone uphold,   160
Without th' assistance of a mortal hand.
So tell the Pope, all reverence set apart
To him and his usurp'd authority.

France.	Brother of England, you blaspheme in this.
K. John.	Though you and all the kings of Christendom 165

Are led so grossly by this meddling priest,
Dreading the curse that money may buy out,
And by the merit of vile gold, dross, dust,
Purchase corrupted pardon of a man,
Who in that sale sells pardon from himself—   170
Though you, and all the rest so grossly led,

---

138. **holy legate**: Pope's representative. 151. **task**: challenge. 154. **charge**: order. 157. **tithe or toll**: tax. 162. **set apart**: discarded. 166. **grossly**: foolishly. 168–169. **merit of vile gold . . . Purchase corrupted pardon**: buying the pardon of sins. 170: **sells pardon from himself**: damns himself by selling indulgences to sin (pardons).

This juggling witchcraft with revenue cherish,
Yet I alone, alone do me oppose
Against the Pope and count his friends my foes.

PAND.   Then by the lawful power that I have   175
That shalt stand curs'd and excommunicate,
And blessed shall he be that doth revolt
From his allegiance to an heretic,
And meritorious shall that hand be call'd,
Canonized, and worshipp'd as a saint,   180
That takes away by any secret course
Thy hateful life.

CONST.   O, lawful let it be
That I have room with Rome to curse awhile!
Good father Cardinal, cry thou amen   185
To my keen curses; for without my wrong
There is no tongue hath power to curse him right.

PAND.   There's law and warrant, lady, for my curse.

CONST.   And for mine too! When law can do no right,
Let it be lawful that law bar no wrong.   190
Law cannot give my child his kingdom here,
For he that holds his kingdom holds the law.
Therefore, since law itself is perfect wrong,
How can the law forbid my tongue to curse?

PAND.   Philip of France, on peril of a curse,   195
Let go the hand of that arch-heretic,
And raise the power of France upon his head
Unless he do submit himself to Rome.

ELI.   Look'st thou pale, France? Do not let go thy hand.

CONST.   Look to that, devil! lest that France repent,   200
And by disjoining hands hell lose a soul.

AUST.   King Philip, listen to the Cardinal.

BAST.   And hang a calve's-skin on his recreant limbs.

AUST.   Well, ruffian, I must pocket up these wrongs,
Because—   205

BAST.   Your breeches best may carry them.

K. JOHN. Philip, what say'st thou to the Cardinal?

---

179. **meritorious**: most worthy. 180. **Canonized**: exulted. 184. **room with Rome**: homonym (word-play). 200. **devil**: Elinor. 204. **pocket up**: endure. 206. **breeches**: knee-length trousers.

CONST.	What should he say, but as the Cardinal?
DAU.	Bethink you, father; for the difference
	Is purchase of a heavy curse from Rome 210
	Or the light loss of England for a friend.
	Forgo the easier.
BLANCH.	That's the curse of Rome.
CONST.	O Lewis, stand fast! The devil tempts thee here
	In likeness of a new untrimmèd bride. 215
BLANCH.	The Lady Constance speaks not from her faith,
	But from her need.
CONST.	O, if thou grant my need,
	Which only lives but by the death of faith,
	That need must needs infer this principle— 220
	That faith would live again by death of need!
	O, then tread down my need, and faith mounts up;
	Keep my need up, and faith is trodden down!
K. JOHN.	The King is mov'd and answers not to this.
CONST.	O, be remov'd from him, and answer well! 225
AUST.	Do so, King Philip; hang no more in doubt.
BAST.	Hang nothing but a calve's-skin, most sweet lout.
FRANCE.	I am perplex'd and know not what to say.
PAN.	What canst thou say but will perplex thee more,
	If thou stand excommunicate and curs'd? 230
FRANCE.	Good reverend father, make my person yours
	And tell me how you would bestow yourself.
	This royal hand and mine are newly knit,
	And the conjunction of our inward souls
	Married in league, coupled, and link'd together 235
	With all religious strength of sacred vows.
	The latest breath that gave the sound of words
	Was deep-sworn faith, peace, amity, true love
	Between our kingdoms and our royal selves;
	And even before this truce, but new before, 240
	No longer than we well could wash our hands
	To clap this royal bargain up of peace,

212. **Forgo the easier**: insignificant. 215. **untrimmed**: virgin. 217. **need**: request for help. 221. **faith ... need**: faith would be restored if my request were satisfied. 224. **mov'd**: confused. 225. **remov'd**: distracted. 225. **him**: King John. 227. **calve's-skin**: symbol of cowardice. 231. **make my person yours**: put yourself in my position. 232. **bestow yourself**: act. 242. **clap this royal bargain up**: seal; settle.

Heaven knows they were besmear'd and overstain'd
With slaughter's pencil, where revenge did paint
The fearful difference of incensed kings.   245
And shall these hands so lately purg'd of blood,
So newly join'd in love, so strong in both,
Unyoke this seizure and this kind regret?
Play fast and loose with faith? so jest with heaven,
Make such unconstant children of ourselves,   250
As now again to snatch our palm from palm,
Unswear faith sworn, and on the marriage bed
Of smiling peace to march a bloody host
And make a riot on the gentle brow
Of true sincerity? O holy sir,   255
My reverend father, let it not be so!
Out of your grace, devise, ordain, impose
Some gentle order, and then we shall be blest
To do your pleasure and continue friends.

PAND.   All form is formless, order orderless,†   260
Save what is opposite to England's love.
Therefore, to arms! be champion of our Church!
Or let the Church our mother breathe her curse,
A mother's curse, on her revolting son.
France, thou mayst hold a serpent by the tongue,   265
A chafed lion by the mortal paw,
A fasting tiger safer by the tooth,
Than keep in peace that hand which thou dost hold.

---

248. **Unyoke this seizure**: break the bonds of friendship. 250. **unconstant**: fickle. 266. **chafed lion**: enraged lion. 266. **mortal**: deadly.

---

† Cardinal Pandulph is Shakespeare's best version of an equivocating priest—a charge that was leveled at Jesuit clergy in the late 16th and early 17th centuries, particularly under James I. Equivocation (prevarication) is the use of ambiguity to conceal the truth; since Catholicism was outlawed in Elizabethan England, Catholics, especially Jesuits, equivocated to avoid denying their faith. Notice how the Cardinal uses sophisticated literary structures like chiasmus to confuse his audience, for example, by exclaiming:

> But thou hast sworn against religion,
> By what thou swear'st against the thing thou swear'st,
> And mak'st an oath the surety for thy truth
> Against an oath. The truth thou art unsure
> To swear, swears only not to be forsworn;
> Else what a mockery it should be to swear! (3.1.287–292)

In the BBC production, David Giles takes pains to represent Pandulph as a very measured and rational figure, even though what he speaks would be considered heresy among England's Protestant majority. There are many other approaches to the Cardinal's character that might bring out his more devious nature; how might your version do so?

FRANCE.	I may disjoin my hand, but not my faith.	
PAND.	So mak'st thou faith an enemy to faith,	270

And like a civil war set'st oath to oath,
Thy tongue against thy tongue. O, let thy vow
First made to heaven, first be to heaven perform'd,
That is, to be the champion of our Church!
What since thou swor'st is sworn against thyself   275
And may not be performèd by thyself;
For that which thou hast sworn to do amiss
Is not amiss when it is truly done;
And being not done where doing tends to ill,
The truth is then most done, not doing it.   280
The better act of purposes mistook
Is to mistake again. Though indirect,
Yet indirection thereby grows direct,
And falsehood falsehood cures, as fire cools fire
Within the scorched veins of one new burn'd.   285
It is religion that doth make vows kept;
But thou hast sworn against religion,
By what thou swear'st against the thing thou swear'st,
And mak'st an oath the surety for thy truth
Against an oath. The truth thou art unsure   290
To swear, swears only not to be forsworn;
Else what a mockery should it be to swear!
But thou dost swear, only to be forsworn,
And most forsworn to keep what thou dost swear.
Therefore thy later vows against thy first   295
Is in thyself rebellion to thyself;
And better conquest never canst thou make
Than arm thy constant and thy nobler parts
Against these giddy loose suggestions;
Upon which better part our pray'rs come in,   300
If thou vouchsafe them. But if not, then know
The peril of our curses light on thee
So heavy as thou shalt not shake them off,
But in despair die under their black weight.

270–304. Cardinal Pandulph's speech exemplifies equivocation: deceiving without technically lying.
277. **that which thou hast sworn**: A promised wrong is not wrong if the promise has not been fulfilled,
or if it is fulfilled in a just cause. 282: **indirect**: deceitful. 283: **indirection**: devious (having turned
away from the truth, another turning away might restore one to the right path). 287–294. the greatest
wrong is keeping an oath falsely sworn. 299. **giddy**: crazy. 299. **loose**: unrestrained. 299. **suggestions**:
temptations.

| AUST. | Rebellion, flat rebellion! | 305 |

| BAST. | Will't not be? |
| | Will not a calve's-skin stop that mouth of thine? |

| DAU. | Father, to arms! |

BLANCH.	Upon thy wedding day?
	Against the blood that thou hast married?	310
	What, shall our feast be kept with slaughtered men?
	Shall braying trumpets and loud churlish drums,
	Clamours of hell, be measures to our pomp?
	O husband, hear me (ay, alack, how new
	Is husband in my mouth!) even for that name	315
	Which till this time my tongue did ne'er pronounce!
	Upon my knee I beg, go not to arms
	Against mine uncle.

CONST.	O, upon my knee,
	Made hard with kneeling, I do pray to thee,	320
	Thou virtuous Dauphin, alter not the doom
	Forethought by heaven!

| BLANCH. | Now shall I see thy love. What motive may |
| | Be stronger with thee than the name of wife? |

| CONST. | That which upholdeth him that thee upholds, | 325 |
| | His honour. O, thine honour, Lewis, thine honour! |

| DAU. | I muse your Majesty doth seem so cold |
| | When such profound respects do pull you on. |

| PAND. | I will denounce a curse upon his head. |

| FRANCE. | Thou shalt not need. England, I will fall from thee. | 330 |

| CONST. | O fair return of banish'd majesty! |

| ELI. | O foul revolt of French inconstancy! |

| K. JOHN. | France, thou shalt rue this hour within this hour. |

| BAST. | Old Time the clock-setter, that bald sexton Time— |
| | Is it as he will? Well then, France shall rue. | 335 |

---

306. **Will't not be**: will nothing quiet you? 310. **blood**: kinship. 313. **measures**: dancing. 313. **pomp**: ceremony. 322. **Forethought**: ordained. 327. **muse**: wonder. 334. **Old Time**: Father Time, who was often depicted with a bald head and a single lock of hair. Time's female counterpart, Occasion, was also depicted bald with a single lock of hair to be seized for good fortune, and was thus conflated with the Latin goddess Fortuna. 334. **sexton**: he who sets the church clock and digs the graves.

BLANCH.	The sun's o'ercast with blood. Fair day, adieu!†
	Which is the side that I must go withal?
	I am with both; each army hath a hand,
	And in their rage, I having hold of both,
	They whirl asunder and dismember me.
	Husband, I cannot pray that thou mayst win;
	Uncle, I needs must pray that thou mayst lose;
	Father, I may not wish the fortune thine;
	Grandam, I will not wish thy wishes thrive.
	Whoever wins, on that side shall I lose:
	Assurèd loss before the match be play'd!
DAU.	Lady, with me! With me thy fortune lies.
BLANCH.	There where my fortune lives, there my life dies.
K. JOHN.	Cousin, go draw our puissance together. [Exit Bastard.]
	France, I am burn'd up with inflaming wrath,
	A rage whose heat hath this condition,
	That nothing can allay—nothing but blood,
	The blood, and dearest-valued blood, of France.
FRANCE.	Thy rage shall burn thee up, and thou shalt turn
	To ashes, ere our blood shall quench that fire.
	Look to thyself; thou art in jeopardy.
K. JOHN.	No more than he that threats. To arms let's hie! Exeunt.

340, 345, 350, 355

336. sun's . . . blood: harbingers, bad weather, ill omen. 349. Cousin: kinsman. 349. puissance: army.

† Blanch is often overshadowed by Constance and Elinor. But it is hard to deny, after reading her lines in 3.1 (her only scene in the play), that she, too, is a force to be reckoned with. Consider all of Blanch's lines in their broader context—war—alongside the ways in which she fights for respectability among her newfound friends and foes. Although she seems to know that she is, already, classified as "collateral damage," she also fights her convenient dismissal as such, demanding a hearing with every line she speaks. Yet her last spoken word is "dies," as if to acknowledge that there are no winners in war. What do you think of Blanch in the BBC version? As mentioned in the introduction, note that she, too, wears her hair down, just as Constance does in 3.4. This extratextual stage business raises a question that the play does not: Does this detail imply that Blanch is already driven to madness by the absurdity of her situation?

SCENE II. *[France. Plains near Angiers.]*

Alarums, excursions. Enter Bastard,
with Austria's head.

BAST.   Now, by my life, this day grows wondrous hot!
         Some airy devil hovers in the sky
         And pours down mischief. Austria's head lie there
         While Philip breathes.

Enter [King] John, Arthur, Hubert.

K. JOHN. Hubert, keep this boy. Philip, make up!   5
          My mother is assailed in our tent,
          And ta'en, I fear.

BAST.   My lord, I rescued her.
          Her Highness is in safety, fear you not.
          But on, my liege! for very little pains   10
          Will bring this labour to an happy end.   *Exeunt.*

SCENE III. *[France. Another part of the plains.]*

Alarums, excursions, retreat. Enter [King]
John, Elinor, Arthur, Bastard, Hubert, Lords.

K. JOHN. *[To Elinor]* So shall it be. Your Grace shall stay behind,
          So strongly guarded. *[To Arthur]* Cousin, look not sad.
          Thy grandam loves thee, and thy uncle will
          As dear be to thee as thy father was.

ARTH.   O, this will make my mother die with grief!   5

K. JOHN. *[To Bastard]* Cousin, away for England! Haste before;
          And ere our coming see thou shake the bags
          Of hoarding abbots; set at liberty
          Imprison'd angels. The fat ribs of peace
          Must by the hungry now be fed upon.   10
          Use our commission in his utmost force.

ACT 3, SCENE 2
2–3. **airy devil hovers . . . pours down mischief**: a storm. 4. **breathes**: catches his breath. 5. **make up**: move; get going.

ACT 3, SCENE 3
2. **Cousin**: kinsman. 9. **angels**: coins depicting an angel, Michael the Archangel.

BAST.	Bell, book, and candle shall not drive me back When gold and silver becks me to come on. I leave your Highness. Grandam, I will pray (If ever I remember to be holy) 15 For your fair safety. So I kiss your hand.
ELI.	Farewell, gentle cousin.
K. JOHN.	Coz, farewell. [*Exit Bastard.*]
ELI.	Come hither, little kinsman. Hark, a word. [*Takes Arthur aside.*]
K. JOHN.	Come hither, Hubert. O my gentle Hubert, 20 We owe thee much! Within this wall of flesh There is a soul counts thee her creditor And with advantage means to pay thy love; And, my good friend, thy voluntary oath Lives in this bosom, dearly cherished. 25 Give me thy hand. I had a thing to say, But I will fit it with some better time. By heaven, Hubert, I am almost asham'd To say what good respect I have of thee.
HUB.	I am much bounden to your Majesty. 30
K. JOHN.	Good friend, thou hast no cause to say so yet, But thou shalt have; and, creep time ne'er so slow, Yet it shall come for me to do thee good. I had a thing to say; but let it go. The sun is in the heaven, and the proud day, 35 Attended with the pleasures of the world, Is all too wanton and too full of gauds To give me audience. If the midnight bell Did with his iron tongue and brazen mouth Sound on into the drowsy ear of night; 40 If this same were a churchyard where we stand, And thou possessèd with a thousand wrongs; Or if that surly spirit, melancholy, Had bak'd thy blood and made it heavy, thick, Which else runs tickling up and down the veins, 45 Making that idiot, laughter, keep men's eyes And strain their cheeks to idle merriment,

12. **Bell, book, and candle**: combined tools of excommunication. 19. **little kinsman**: Historically Arthur was about seventeen at the time of his death (1203). Shakespeare draws sympathy for Arthur by making him a child in the play. 23. **advantage**: interest. 23. **pay**: repay. 24. **oath**: allegiance. 29. **respect**: opinion; regard. 37. **gauds**: showy trifles.

	A passion hateful to my purposes;	
	Or if that thou couldst see me without eyes,	
	Hear me without thine ears, and make reply	50
	Without a tongue, using conceit alone,	
	Without eyes, ears, and harmful sound of words:	
	Then, in despite of brooded watchful day,	
	I would into thy bosom pour my thoughts.	
	But, ah, I will not! Yet I love thee well,	55
	And, by my troth, I think thou lov'st me well.	

Hub.   So well that what you bid me undertake,
            Though that my death were adjunct to my act,
            By heaven, I would do it!

K. John.   Do not I know thou wouldst?[†]   60
            Good Hubert, Hubert, Hubert, throw thine eye
            On yon young boy. I'll tell thee what, my friend,
            He is a very serpent in my way;
            And wheresoe'er this foot of mine doth tread,
            He lies before me. Dost thou understand me?   65
            Thou art his keeper.

Hub.   And I'll keep him so
            That he shall not offend your Majesty.

K. John.   Death.

Hub.   My lord?   70

K. John.   A grave.

Hub.   He shall not live.

K. John.   Enough.
            I could be merry now. Hubert, I love thee.
            Well, I'll not say what I intend for thee.   75
            Remember.—Madam, fare you well.
            I'll send those powers o'er to your Majesty.

Eli.   My blessing go with thee!

---

58. **adjunct to**: resulted from. 77. **powers**: military forces; troops.

---

†   In this seduction scene, John talks the impressionable Hubert into ridding him of Arthur. When
     he succeeds in persuading Hubert, John offers an ambiguous reward: "Hubert, I love thee. /
     Well, I'll not say what I intended for thee. Remember" (74–76). What in the world is John saying?
     Should Hubert be puzzled or flattered? If you were to create a series of reaction shots involving
     John and Hubert, what kind of facial expressions/reaction shots would you privilege to indicate
     whether or not the two men see eye to eye in this scene?

K. John.	[*To Arthur*] For England, cousin! go.
	Hubert shall be your man, attend on you 80
	With all true duty.—On toward Calais, ho! *Exeunt.*

SCENE IV. [*France. The French King's tent.*]†

Enter France, Dauphin, Pandulph, Attendants.

France.	So by a roaring tempest on the flood
	A whole armado of convicted sail
	Is scattered and disjoin'd from fellowship.
Pand.	Courage and comfort! All shall yet go well.
France.	What can go well when we have run so ill? 5
	Are we not beaten? Is not Angiers lost?
	Arthur ta'en prisoner? divers dear friends slain?
	And bloody England into England gone,
	O'erbearing interruption, spite of France?
Dau.	What he hath won, that hath he fortified. 10
	So hot a speed with such advice dispos'd,
	Such temperate order in so fierce a course,
	Doth want example. Who hath read or heard
	Of any kindred action like to this?
France.	Well could I bear that England had this praise, 15
	So we could find some pattern of our shame.

Enter Constance.

---

80. **man**: servant.
Act 3, Scene 4
1. **flood**: sea. 2. **armado**: fleet. 2. **convicted**: defeated; doomed. 5. **run**: done; proceeded. 9. **O'erbearing**: overwhelming. 9. **spite**: despite. 11. **advice**: judgment. 13. **want example**: need precedent. 16. **pattern**: precedent.

---

† Consider Constance's "mad scene." Is it fair to call it so? Isn't it a kind of madness to outlive one's own children? Although Constance insists on her sanity, she is rarely believed to be anything other than crazy. Perhaps this has to do more with the internal cues that Shakespeare provides the audience, rather than Constance's words. Notice how, for example, Cardinal Pandulph frames our own expectations when he exclaims: "Lady, you utter madness and not sorrow" (3.4.44). Second, it is hard to ignore King Philip's direction to Constance to "[b]ind up [her] hairs" (3.4.70) knowing that, in the Renaissance, mature women with unbound hair were considered to be wanton, mad, or both. Think about these cues and the extent to which the scene's internal directors—Pandulph and King Philip—influence our perception of the truth in this scene.

Look who comes here! a grave unto a soul,
Holding th' eternal spirit against her will
In the vile prison of afflicted breath.
I prithee, lady, go away with me.   20

CONST.   Lo now! now see the issue of your peace!

FRANCE.   Patience, good lady! comfort, gentle Constance!

CONST.   No, I defy all counsel, all redress,
But that which ends all counsel, true redress.
Death, death, O amiable lovely death!   25
Thou odoriferous stench! sound rottenness!
Arise forth from the couch of lasting night,
Thou hate and terror to prosperity,
And I will kiss thy detestable bones,
And put my eyeballs in thy vaulty brows,   30
And ring these fingers with thy household worms,
And stop this gap of breath with fulsome dust,
And be a carrion monster like thyself.
Come, grin on me, and I will think thou smil'st
And buss thee as thy wife. Misery's love,   35
O, come to me!

FRANCE.   O fair affliction, peace!

CONST.   No, no, I will not, having breath to cry.
O that my tongue were in the thunder's mouth!
Then with a passion would I shake the world   40
And rouse from sleep that fell anatomy
Which cannot hear a lady's feeble voice,
Which scorns a modern invocation.

PAND.   Lady, you utter madness and not sorrow.

CONST.   Thou art not holy to belie me so.   45
I am not mad. This hair I tear is mine;
My name is Constance; I was Geffrey's wife;
Young Arthur is my son, and he is lost.
I am not mad. I would to heaven I were!
For then 'tis like I should forget myself.   50
O, if I could, what grief should I forget!
Preach some philosophy to make me mad,
And thou shalt be canoniz'd, Cardinal;
For, being not mad, but sensible of grief,

---

23. **defy**: reject. 27. **lasting**: eternal. 32. **fulsome**: repulsive. 35. **buss**: kiss. 41. **fell**: fierce; terrible. 41.
anatomy: corpse; skeleton. 46–49. **hair . . . mad**: disarrayed hair was a sign of madness. 50. **like**: likely.

	My reasonable part produces reason	55
	How I may be deliver'd of these woes	
	And teaches me to kill or hang myself.	
	If I were mad, I should forget my son,	
	Or madly think a babe of clouts were he.	
	I am not mad. Too well, too well I feel	60
	The different plague of each calamity.	

FRANCE. Bind up those tresses. O, what love I note
In the fair multitude of those her hairs!
Where but by chance a silver drop hath fall'n,
Even to that drop ten thousand wiry friends   65
Do glue themselves in sociable grief,
Like true, inseparable, faithful loves,
Sticking together in calamity.

CONST. To England, if you will.

FRANCE. Bind up your hairs.   70

CONST. Yes, that I will! and wherefore will I do it?
I tore them from their bonds and cried aloud
"O that these hands could so redeem my son
As they have given these hairs their liberty!"
But now I envy at their liberty   75
And will again commit them to their bonds,
Because my poor child is a prisoner.
And, father Cardinal, I have heard you say
That we shall see and know our friends in heaven.
If that be true, I shall see my boy again;   80
For since the birth of Cain, the first male child,
To him that did but yesterday suspire,
There was not such a gracious creature born.
But now will canker-sorrow eat my bud
And chase the native beauty from his cheek,   85
And he will look as hollow as a ghost,
As dim and meagre as an ague's fit;
And so he'll die; and rising so again,
When I shall meet him in the court of heaven
I shall not know him. Therefore never, never   90
Must I behold my pretty Arthur more!

---

59. **babe of clouts**: ragdoll. 65. **wiry friends**: hairs. 66. **sociable**: sensitive; sympathetic. 81. **Cain**: the first murderer, killed his brother. 82. **suspire**: breathe. 83. **gracious**: meriting grace. 84. **canker-sorrow**: all-consuming grief. 84. **my bud**: her son Arthur.

PAND.   You hold too heinous a respect of grief.

CONST.   He talks to me that never had a son.

FRANCE.   You are as fond of grief as of your child.

CONST.   Grief fills the room up of my absent child: 95
            Lies in his bed, walks up and down with me,
            Puts on his pretty looks, repeats his words,
            Remembers me of all his gracious parts,
            Stuffs out his vacant garments with his form.
            Then have I reason to be fond of grief?   100
            Fare you well. Had you such a loss as I,
            I could give better comfort than you do.
            I will not keep this form upon my head   [*Tears her hair.*]
            When there is such disorder in my wit.
            O Lord! my boy, my Arthur, my fair son!   105
            My life, my joy, my food, my all the world!
            My widow-comfort, and my sorrows' cure!   *Exit.*

FRANCE.   I fear some outrage, and I'll follow her.   *Exit.*

DAU.   There's nothing in this world can make me joy.
            Life is as tedious as a twice-told tale   110
            Vexing the dull ear of a drowsy man;
            And bitter shame hath spoil'd the sweet world's taste,
            That it yields naught but shame and bitterness.

PAND.   Before the curing of a strong disease,
            Even in the instant of repair and health,   115
            The fit is strongest. Evils that take leave
            On their departure most of all show evil.
            What have you lost by losing of this day?

DAU.   All days of glory, joy, and happiness.

PAND.   If you had won it, certainly you had.   120
            No, no! When Fortune means to men most good,
            She looks upon them with a threat'ning eye.
            'Tis strange to think how much King John hath lost
            In this which he accounts so clearly won.
            Are not you griev'd that Arthur is his prisoner?   125

DAU.   As heartily as he is glad he hath him.

---

92. **heinous respect**: bad regard. 94. **fond**: foolishly attached. 103. ***Tears her hair***: s.d. see n. 46 above (the stage direction confirms her mental state). 104. **disorder in my wit**: disturbed mind. 108. **outrage**: violence. 115. **repair**: recovery. 118. **day**: day of battle.

PAND.	Your mind is all as youthful as your blood.

PAND.   Your mind is all as youthful as your blood.
Now hear me speak with a prophetic spirit;
For even the breath of what I mean to speak
Shall blow each dust, each straw, each little rub,   130
Out of the path which shall directly lead
Thy foot to England's throne; and therefore mark.
John hath seiz'd Arthur; and it cannot be
That, whiles warm life plays in that infant's veins,
The misplac'd John should entertain an hour,   135
One minute, nay, one quiet breath of rest.
A sceptre snatch'd with an unruly hand
Must be as boisterously maintain'd as gain'd;
And he that stands upon a slipp'ry place
Makes nice of no vile hold to stay him up.   140
That John may stand, then Arthur needs must fall.
So be it, for it cannot be but so.

DAU.   But what shall I gain by young Arthur's fall?

PAND.   You, in the right of Lady Blanch your wife,
May then make all the claim that Arthur did.   145

DAU.   And lose it, life and all, as Arthur did.

PAND.   How green you are and fresh in this old world!
John lays you plots; the times conspire with you;
For he that steeps his safety in true blood
Shall find but bloody safety and untrue.   150
This act so evilly borne shall cool the hearts
Of all his people and freeze up their zeal,
That none so small advantage shall step forth
To check his reign but they will cherish it;
No natural exhalation in the sky,   155
No scope of nature, no distemper'd day,
No common wind, no customed event,
But they will pluck away his natural cause
And call them meteors, prodigies, and signs,
Abortives, presages, and tongues of heaven,   160
Plainly denouncing vengeance upon John.

---

130. **rub**: obstacle. 135. **misplac'd**: usurping. 140. **Makes...up**: uses unscrupulous methods. 147. **green**: inexperienced. 148. **lays you plots**: provides the way. 149. **steeps . . . true blood**: he who kills a rightful king will also bleed. 155. **exaltation**: shooting star; comet. 159. **prodigies**: omens. 160. **Abortives**: abnormalities.

Cardinal Pandulph (Richard Wordsworth) in Giles' BBC production: "How green you are and fresh in this old world!"

DAU.	May be he will not touch young Arthur's life,
	But hold himself safe in his prisonment.
PAND.	O, sir, when he shall hear of your approach,

PAND. O, sir, when he shall hear of your approach,
      If that young Arthur be not gone already,   165
      Even at that news he dies; and then the hearts
      Of all his people shall revolt from him,
      And kiss the lips of unacquainted change,
      And pick strong matter of revolt and wrath
      Out of the bloody fingers' ends of John.   170
      Methinks I see this hurly all on foot.
      And O, what better matter breeds for you
      Than I have nam'd! The bastard Faulconbridge
      Is now in England ransacking the Church,
      Offending charity. If but a dozen French   175
      Were there in arms, they would be as a call
      To train ten thousand English to their side,

---

168. **unacquainted**: strange. 172. **matter**: 1) evidence; 2) discharge from a wound. 171. **hurly**: tumult. 172. **matter**: evidence. 176. **call**: decoy.

Or as a little snow, tumbled about,
Anon becomes a mountain. O noble Dauphin,
Go with me to the King. 'Tis wonderful   180
What may be wrought out of their discontent
Now that their souls are topful of offence.
For England go! I will whet on the King.

DAU.   Strong reasons make strange actions. Let us go.
If you say ay, the King will not say no.   *Exeunt.*   185

ACT IV

SCENE I. [*England. A room in a castle.*]

Enter Hubert and Executioners.

HUB.   Heat me these irons hot, and look you stand
Within the arras. When I strike my foot
Upon the bosom of the ground, rush forth
And bind the boy which you shall find with me
Fast to the chair. Be heedful. Hence, and watch.   5

EXEC.   I hope your warrant will bear out the deed.

HUB.   Uncleanly scruples! Fear not you. Look to't.
[*Exeunt Executioners.*]
Young lad, come forth; I have to say with you.

Enter Arthur.

ARTH.   Good morrow, Hubert.

HUB.   Good morrow, little Prince.   10

ARTH.   As little Prince, having so great a title
To be more prince, as may be. You are sad.

HUB.   Indeed I have been merrier.

ARTH.   Mercy on me!
Methinks nobody should be sad but I.   15
Yet I remember, when I was in France,

---

182. **topful**: overflowing with offense. 183. **whet**: encourage.
ACT 4, SCENE 1
2. **Within**: inside; behind. 2. **arras**: tapestry; wall-hanging. 7. **Uncleanly**: unbecoming. 8. **to say with**: to speak with. 11–12. **As little . . . as may be**: smaller in stature than my princely title or my rightful claim to the throne of England.

Young gentlemen would be as sad as night
Only for wantonness. By my Christendom,
So I were out of prison and kept sheep,
I should be as merry as the day is long!   20
And so I would be here but that I doubt
My uncle practices more harm to me.
He is afraid of me, and I of him.
Is it my fault that I was Geffrey's son?
No indeed is't not! and I would to heaven   25
I were your son, so you would love me, Hubert.

HUB.   [*Aside*] If I talk to him, with his innocent prate
             He will awake my mercy, which lies dead.
             Therefore I will be sudden and dispatch.

ARTH.   Are you sick, Hubert? You look pale to-day.   30
             In sooth I would you were a little sick,
             That I might sit all night and watch with you.
             I warrant I love you more than you do me.

HUB.   [*Aside*] His words do take possession of my bosom.—
             Read here, young Arthur: [*Shows a paper.*]   35
             [*Aside*] How now, foolish rheum?
             Turning dispiteous torture out of door?
             I must be brief, lest resolution drop
             Out at mine eyes in tender womanish tears.—
             Can you not read it? Is it not fair writ?   40

ARTH.   Too fairly, Hubert, for so foul effect!
             Must you with hot irons burn out both mine eyes?

HUB.   Young boy, I must.

ARTH.   And will you?

HUB.   And I will.   45

ARTH.   Have you the heart? When your head did but ache,
             I knit my handkercher about your brows
             (The best I had; a princess wrought it me)
             And I did never ask it you again;
             And with my hand at midnight held your head;   50
             And like the watchful minutes to the hour
             Still and anon cheer'd up the heavy time,
             Saying "What lack you?" and "Where lies your grief?"

---

18. **wantonness**: caprice; affection. 18. **Christendom**: baptism; christening. 21. **doubt**: suspect; fear.
22. **practices**: plots; schemes. 27. **prate**: prattle. 29. **dispatch**: act quickly. 36. **rheum**: tears. 40. **fair writ**: clearly. 41. **effect**: end. 48. **wrought**: embroidered.

Or "What good love may I perform for you?"
Many a poor man's son would have lien still   55
And ne'er have spoke a loving word to you;
But you at your sick service had a prince.
Nay, you may think my love was crafty love
And call it cunning. Do, an if you will.
If heaven be pleas'd that you must use me ill,   60
Why, then you must. Will you put out mine eyes?
These eyes that never did nor never shall
So much as frown on you?

HUB.   I have sworn to do it;
And with hot irons must I burn them out.   65

ARTH.   Ah, none but in this iron age would do it!
The iron of itself, though heat redhot,
Approaching near these eyes, would drink my tears
And quench his fiery indignation
Even in the water of mine innocence;   70
Nay, after that, consume away in rust
But for containing fire to harm mine eyes.
Are you more stubborn-hard than hammer'd iron?
An if an angel should have come to me
And told me Hubert should put out mine eyes,   75
I would not have believ'd him—no tongue but Hubert's.

HUB.   [Stamps] Come forth!

         [Enter Executioners, with cord, irons & etc.]

Do as I bid you do.

ARTH.   O, save me, Hubert, save me! My eyes are out
Even with the fierce looks of these bloody men.   80

HUB.   Give me the iron, I say, and bind him here.

ARTH.   Alas, what need you be so boist'rous-rough?
I will not struggle, I will stand stone-still.
For heaven sake, Hubert, let me not be bound!
Nay, hear me, Hubert! Drive these men away,   85
And I will sit as quiet as a lamb;
I will not stir nor winch nor speak a word,
Nor look upon the iron angerly.

54. love: favor; kindness. 57. at... prince: you had a prince as your nurse. 66. iron age: last and most
corrupt of the four ages (golden, silver, bronze, and iron). 67. heat: heated. 71. But: simply; merely. 87.
winch: flinch.

	Thrust but these men away, and I'll forgive you,	
	Whatever torment you do put me to.	90
HUB.	Go stand within; let me alone with him.	
EXEC.	I am best pleas'd to be from such a deed.	

[Exeunt Executioners.]

ARTH.	Alas, I then have chid away my friend!	
	He hath a stern look, but a gentle heart.	
	Let him come back, that his compassion may	95
	Give life to yours.	
HUB.	Come, boy, prepare yourself.	
ARTH.	Is there no remedy?	
HUB.	None, but to lose your eyes.	
ARTH.	O heaven! that there were but a mote in yours,	100
	A grain, a dust, a gnat, a wandering hair,	
	Any annoyance in that precious sense!	
	Then, feeling what small things are boisterous there,	
	Your vile intent must needs seem horrible.	
HUB.	Is this your promise? Go to, hold your tongue.	105
ARTH.	Hubert, the utterance of a brace of tongues	
	Must needs want pleading for a pair of eyes.	
	Let me not hold my tongue; let me not, Hubert!	
	Or, Hubert, if you will, cut out my tongue,	
	So I may keep mine eyes. O, spare mine eyes,	110
	Though to no use but still to look on you!	
	Lo, by my troth, the instrument is cold	
	And would not harm me.	
HUB.	I can heat it, boy.	
ARTH.	No, in good sooth! The fire is dead with grief,	115
	Being create for comfort, to be us'd	
	In undeserv'd extremes. See else yourself!	
	There is no malice in this burning coal;	
	The breath of heaven hath blown his spirit out	
	And strew'd repentant ashes on his head.	120
HUB.	But with my breath I can revive it, boy.	
ARTH.	And if you do, you will but make it blush	
	And glow with shame of your proceedings, Hubert.	

93. **friend**: the executioner. 100. **mote**: speck. 102. **sense**: sight. 103. **boisterous**: painful. 106. **brace**: two; a pair. 112. **troth**: faithfulness. 115. **sooth**: truth. 116. **create**: created.

Nay, it perchance will sparkle in your eyes,
And, like a dog that is compell'd to fight,   125
Snatch at his master that doth tarre him on.
All things that you should use to do me wrong
Deny their office. Only you do lack
That mercy which fierce fire and iron extends,
Creatures of note for mercy-lacking uses.   130

HUB.   Well, see to live! I will not touch thine eyes
For all the treasure that thine uncle owes.
Yet am I sworn, and I did purpose, boy,
With this same very iron to burn them out.

ARTH.   O, now you look like Hubert! All this while   135
You were disguised.

HUB.   Peace! no more! Adieu.
Your uncle must not know but you are dead.
I'll fill these dogged spies with false reports;
And, pretty child, sleep doubtless and secure   140
That Hubert, for the wealth of all the world,
Will not offend thee.

ARTH.   O heaven! I thank you, Hubert.

HUB.   Silence! no more! Go closely in with me.
Much danger do I undergo for thee.   *Exeunt.*   145

SCENE II. [*King John's Palace.*]

*Enter [King] John, Pembroke, Salisbury,
and other Lords. [The King takes his state.]*

K. JOHN.   Here once again we sit, once again crown'd,
And look'd upon, I hope, with cheerful eyes.

PEM.   This once again, but that your Highness pleas'd,
Was once superfluous. You were crown'd before,
And that high royalty was ne'er pluck'd off,   5
The faiths of men ne'er stained with revolt;
Fresh expectation troubled not the land
With any long'd-for change or better state.

124. **sparkle**: give off sparks. 126. **tarre**: provoke. 128. **Deny their office**: refuse to fulfill their purpose. 130. **Creatures . . . mercy-lacking uses**: creations (fire and iron) needed for causing pain. 132. **owes**: owns. 139. **dogged spies**: cruel; dangerous.

ACT 4, SCENE 2
1. **once again**: refers to John's second coronation. 7. **expectation**: anticipation.

SAL. Therefore, to be possess'd with double pomp,
   To guard a title that was rich before,   10
   To gild refinèd gold, to paint the lily,
   To throw a perfume on the violet,
   To smooth the ice, or add another hue
   Unto the rainbow, or with taper light
   To seek the beauteous eye of heaven to garnish, 15
   Is wasteful and ridiculous excess.

PEM. But that your royal pleasure must be done,
   This act is as an ancient tale new told
   And, in the last repeating, troublesome,
   Being urged at a time unseasonable.   20

SAL. In this the antique and well-noted face
   Of plain old form is much disfigurèd,
   And, like a shifted wind unto a sail,
   It makes the course of thoughts to fetch about,
   Startles and frights consideration,   25
   Makes sound opinion sick, and truth suspected
   For putting on so new a fashion'd robe.

PEM. When workmen strive to do better than well,
   They do confound their skill in covetousness;
   And oftentimes excusing of a fault   30
   Doth make the fault the worse by the excuse,
   As patches set upon a little breach
   Discredit more in hiding of the fault
   Than did the fault before it was so patch'd.

SAL. To this effect, before you were new crown'd, 35
   We breath'd our counsel; but it pleas'd your Highness
   To overbear it, and we are all well pleas'd,
   Since all and every part of what we would
   Doth make a stand at what your Highness will.

K. JOHN. Some reasons of this double coronation 40
   I have possess'd you with, and think them strong;
   And more, more strong (then lesser is my fear),
   I shall indue you with. Meantime but ask
   What you would have reform'd that is not well,

---

10. **guard**: adorn; protect. 14. **taper light**: candlelight. 19. **troublesome**: annoyance. 21. **antique**: ancient; familiar (pun on antic: bizarre or jester-like). 24. **fetch about**: change. 29. **confound their skill in covetousness**: ruin what is well done by trying to better. 32. **breach**: hole. 36. **breath'd**: spoke; gave. 37. **overbear**: overrule. 38–39. **what we would / Doth make a stand at what your Highness will**: we can do only what you command. 41. **possess'd you**: told you. 43. **indue**: provide.

	And well shall you perceive how willingly	45
	I will both hear and grant you your requests.	
PEM.	Then I—as one that am the tongue of these	
	To sound the purposes of all their hearts,	
	Both for myself and them, but chief of all,	
	Your safety, for the which myself and them	50
	Bend their best studies—heartily request	
	Th' enfranchisement of Arthur, whose restraint	

PEM.

And well shall you perceive how willingly   45
I will both hear and grant you your requests.

PEM. Then I—as one that am the tongue of these
To sound the purposes of all their hearts,
Both for myself and them, but chief of all,
Your safety, for the which myself and them   50
Bend their best studies—heartily request
Th' enfranchisement of Arthur, whose restraint
Doth move the murmuring lips of discontent
To break into this dangerous argument:—
If what in rest you have in right you hold,   55
Why then your fears, which (as they say) attend
The steps of wrong, should move you to mew up
Your tender kinsman, and to choke his days
With barbarous ignorance and deny his youth
The rich advantage of good exercise.   60
That the time's enemies may not have this
To grace occasions, let it be our suit
That you have bid us ask his liberty;
Which for our goods we do no further ask
Than whereupon our weal, on you depending,   65
Counts it your weal he have his liberty.

Enter Hubert.

K. JOHN. Let it be so. I do commit his youth
To your direction.   *[Talks with Hubert aside.]*
Hubert, what news with you?

PEM. This is the man should do the bloody deed;   70
He show'd his warrant to a friend of mine.
The image of a wicked heinous fault
Lives in his eye; that close aspect of his
Does show the mood of a much-troubled breast;
And I do fearfully believe 'tis done,   75
What we so fear'd he had a charge to do.

SAL. The colour of the King doth come and go
Between his purpose and his conscience,
Like heralds 'twixt two dreadful battles set.
His passion is so ripe it needs must break.   80

---

52. **enfranchisement**: release. 55. **rest**: peacetime. 55. **in right**: rightfully hold. 57. **mew up**: imprison. 58. **tender**: young. 60. **exercise**: primary education and training. 61. **time's enemies**: those opposing the present government. 73. **close**: secretive. 73. **aspect**: expression. 76. **charge to do**: to murder Prince Arthur.

PEM.	And when it breaks, I fear will issue thence
	The foul corruption of a sweet child's death.
K. JOHN.	We cannot hold mortality's strong hand.
	Good lords, although my will to give is living,
	The suit which you demand is gone and dead. 85
	He tells us Arthur is deceas'd to-night.
SAL.	Indeed we fear'd his sickness was past cure.
PEM.	Indeed we heard how near his death he was
	Before the child himself felt he was sick.
	This must be answer'd, either here or hence. 90
K. JOHN.	Why do you bend such solemn brows on me?
	Think you I bear the shears of destiny?
	Have I commandment on the pulse of life?
SAL.	It is apparent foul play, and 'tis shame
	That greatness should so grossly offer it. 95
	So thrive it in your game! and so farewell.
PEM.	Stay yet, Lord Salisbury. I'll go with thee
	And find th' inheritance of this poor child,
	His little kingdom of a forcèd grave.
	That blood which ow'd the breadth of all this isle 100
	Three foot of it doth hold—bad world the while!
	This must not be thus borne; this will break out
	To all our sorrows, and ere long I doubt. *Exeunt [Lords].*
K. JOHN.	They burn in indignation. I repent.

Enter Messenger.

	There is no sure foundation set on blood, 105
	No certain life achiev'd by others' death.—
	A fearful eye thou hast. Where is that blood
	That I have seen inhabit in those cheeks?
	So foul a sky clears not without a storm.
	Pour down thy weather. How goes all in France? 110
MESS.	From France to England. Never such a pow'r
	For any foreign preparation
	Was levied in the body of a land.
	The copy of your speed is learn'd by them;

---

90. **answer'd**: atoned for either now or in the next life. 92. **shears of destiny**: held by Atropos, one of the three fates. 95. **grossly**: openly. 96. **So . . . game**: bad luck unto you. 99. **forced**: enforced. 100. **ow'd**: owned. 103. **doubt**: suspect. 107. **fearful**: frightened. 111. **pow'r**: army; force. 114. **copy**: example.

	For when you should be told they do prepare,	115
	The tidings comes that they are all arriv'd.	
K. John.	O, where hath our intelligence been drunk?	
	Where hath it slept? Where is my mother's care,	
	That such an army could be drawn in France	
	And she not hear of it?	120
Mess.	My liege, her ear	
	Is stopp'd with dust. The first of April died	
	Your noble mother; and, as I hear, my lord,	
	The Lady Constance in a frenzy died	
	Three days before. But this from rumour's tongue	125
	I idly heard; if true or false I know not.	
K. John.	Withhold thy speed, dreadful Occasion!	
	O, make a league with me, till I have pleas'd	
	My discontented peers! What? mother dead?	
	How wildly then walks my estate in France!	130
	Under whose conduct came those pow'rs of France	
	That thou for truth giv'st out are landed here?	
Mess.	Under the Dauphin.	

Enter Bastard and Peter of Pomfret.

K. John.	Thou hast made me giddy	
	With these ill tidings.—Now? What says the world	135
	To your proceedings? Do not seek to stuff	
	My head with more ill news; for it is full.	
Bast.	But if you be afeard to hear the worst,	
	Then let the worst, unheard, fall on your head!	
K. John.	Bear with me, cousin, for I was amaz'd	140
	Under the tide; but now I breathe again	
	Aloft the flood, and can give audience	
	To any tongue, speak it of what it will.	
Bast.	How I have sped among the clergymen	
	The sums I have collected shall express.	145
	But as I travell'd hither through the land,	
	I find the people strangely fantasied,	

---

117. **intelligence**: secret service. 119. **drawn**: raised. 124. **Constance**: she died in 1201, three years before Queen Elinor. 127. **Occasion**: Latin goddess conflating Fortune and Time. 129. **mother dead**: Queen Elinor died in April 1204. 130. **wildly**: disorderly. 130. **walks**: proceeds. 134. **giddy**: confused. 140. **amaz'd**: bewildered; overwhelmed. 144. **sped**: fared; succeeded. 147. **fantasied**: filled with fantasies; weird ideas.

Possess'd with rumours, full of idle dreams,
Not knowing what they fear, but full of fear.
And here's a prophet that I brought with me   150
From forth the streets of Pomfret, whom I found
With many hundreds treading on his heels;
To whom he sung in rude harsh-sounding rhymes
That, ere the next Ascension Day at noon,
Your Highness should deliver up your crown.   155

K. JOHN.   Thou idle dreamer, wherefore didst thou so?

PETER.   Foreknowing that the truth will fall out so.

K. JOHN.   Hubert, away with him! imprison him,
And on that day at noon whereon he says
I shall yield up my crown, let him be hang'd.   160
Deliver him to safety, and return,
For I must use thee.   [Exit Hubert with Peter.]
O my gentle cousin,
Hear'st thou the news abroad, who are arriv'd?

BAST.   The French, my lord. Men's mouths are full of it. 165
Besides, I met Lord Bigot and Lord Salisbury
With eyes as red as new-enkindled fire,
And others more, going to seek the grave
Of Arthur, whom they say is kill'd to-night
On your suggestion.   170

K. JOHN.   Gentle kinsman, go
And thrust thyself into their companies.
I have a way to win their loves again.
Bring them before me.

BAST.   I will seek them out.   175

K. JOHN.   Nay, but make haste! the better foot before.
O, let me have no subject enemies
When adverse foreigners affright my towns
With dreadful pomp of stout invasion!
Be Mercury, set feathers to thy heels,   180
And fly (like thought) from them to me again.

BAST.   The spirit of the time shall teach me speed.   *Exit.*

K. JOHN.   Spoke like a sprightful noble gentleman.
Go after him; for he perhaps shall need

---

156. **idle**: foolish. 161. **safety**: custody. 163. **gentle**: noble. 172. **thrust**: place. 176. **better foot before**: quickly. 178. **adverse**: hostile. 179. **stout**: bold; arrogant. 183. **sprightful**: high-spirited.

	Some messenger betwixt me and the peers,	185
	And be thou he.	
MESS.	With all my heart, my liege. [*Exit.*]	
K. JOHN.	My mother dead?	

Enter Hubert.

HUB.	My lord, they say five moons were seen to-night;	
	Four fixed, and the fifth did whirl about	190
	The other four in wondrous motion.	
K. JOHN.	Five moons?	
HUB.	Old men and beldames in the streets	
	Do prophesy upon it dangerously.	
	Young Arthur's death is common in their mouths;	195
	And when they talk of him, they shake their heads	
	And whisper one another in the ear;	
	And he that speaks doth gripe the hearer's wrist,	
	Whilst he that hears makes fearful action	
	With wrinkled brows, with nods, with rolling eyes.	200
	I saw a smith stand with his hammer, thus,	
	The whilst his iron did on the anvil cool,	
	With open mouth swallowing a tailor's news,	
	Who, with his shears and measure in his hand,	
	Standing on slippers, which his nimble haste	205
	Had falsely thrust upon contrary feet,	
	Told of a many thousand warlike French	
	That were embattled and rank'd in Kent.	
	Another lean unwash'd artificer	
	Cuts off his tale and talks of Arthur's death.	210
K. JOHN.	Why seek'st thou to possess me with these fears?	
	Why urgest thou so oft young Arthur's death?	
	Thy hand hath murd'red him. I had a mighty cause	
	To wish him dead, but thou hadst none to kill him.	
HUB.	No had, my lord? Why, did you not provoke me?	215
K. JOHN.	It is the curse of kings to be attended	
	By slaves that take their humours for a warrant	
	To break within the bloody house of life,	
	And on the winking of authority	

---

189. **five moons**: astrologically ominous. 193. **beldames**: crones. 194. **prophesy**: find danger in it. 195. **common . . . mouths**: commonly discuss. 199. **action**: movements. 205. **slippers**: tailors usually worked barefooted. 208. **embattled**: deployed; ready to fight. 208. **rank'd**: assembled in order. 211. **possess . . . fears**: convey fearful news. 217. **humours**: whims.

	To understand a law; to know the meaning	220
	Of dangerous majesty when perchance it frowns	
	More upon humour than advis'd respect.	
HUB.	Here is your hand and seal for what I did.	
K. JOHN.	O, when the last accompt 'twixt heaven and earth	
	Is to be made, then shall this hand and seal	225
	Witness against us to damnation!	
	How oft the sight of means to do ill deeds	
	Make deeds ill done! Hadst not thou been by,	
	A fellow by the hand of nature mark'd,	
	Quoted, and sign'd to do a deed of shame,	230
	This murther had not come into my mind;	
	But, taking note of thy abhorr'd aspect,	
	Finding thee fit for bloody villany,	
	Apt, liable to be employ'd in danger,	
	I faintly broke with thee of Arthur's death;	235
	And thou, to be endeared to a king,	
	Made it no conscience to destroy a prince.	
HUB.	My lord—	
K. JOHN.	Hadst thou but shook thy head or made a pause	
	When I spake darkly what I purposed,	240
	Or turn'd an eye of doubt upon my face,	
	As bid me tell my tale in express words,	
	Deep shame had struck me dumb, made me break off,	
	And those thy fears might have wrought fears in me.	
	But thou didst understand me by my signs	245
	And didst in signs again parley with sin;	
	Yea, without stop, didst let thy heart consent,	
	And consequently thy rude hand to act	
	The deed which both our tongues held vile to name.	
	Out of my sight, and never see me more!	250
	My nobles leave me, and my state is brav'd,	
	Even at my gates, with ranks of foreign pow'rs.	
	Nay, in the body of this fleshly land,	
	This kingdom, this confine of blood and breath,	
	Hostility and civil tumult reigns	255
	Between my conscience and my cousin's death.	

---

219. **winking**: disregarding. 222. **humour**: mood; caprice. 227. **ill**: evil. 228. **ill**: badly. 229–230. **mark'd . . . sign'd**: obviously destined. 232. **abhorr'd aspect**: hideous face. 235. **faintly**: hesitantly. 235. **broke with**: mentioned. 240. **spake darkly**: vaguely implied. 251. **brav'd**: challenged. 253. **fleshly land**: human body as a microcosmic kingdom; a little world in itself. 256. **cousin's**: kinsman's.

HUB.	Arm you against your other enemies;
	I'll make a peace between your soul and you.
	Young Arthur is alive. This hand of mine
	Is yet a maiden and an innocent hand,	260
	Not painted with the crimson spots of blood.
	Within this bosom never ent'red yet
	The dreadful motion of a murderous thought;
	And you have slander'd nature in my form,
	Which, howsoever rude exteriorly,	265
	Is yet the cover of a fairer mind
	Than to be butcher of an innocent child.

K. JOHN.	Doth Arthur live? O, haste thee to the peers!
	Throw this report on their incensed rage
	And make them tame to their obedience!	270
	Forgive the comment that my passion made
	Upon thy feature; for my rage was blind,
	And foul imaginary eyes of blood
	Presented thee more hideous than thou art.
	O, answer not! but to my closet bring	275
	The angry lords with all expedient haste!
	I conjure thee but slowly; run more fast. *Exeunt.*

SCENE III. [*Before the castle.*] †

Enter Arthur on the walls,
[disguised as a shipboy].

| ARTH. | The wall is high, and yet will I leap down.‡ |
| | Good ground, be pitiful and hurt me not! |

---

260. **maiden:** untainted. 265. **rude:** ugly. 270. **tame:** submissive. 275. **closet:** chamber.

---

† In the wake of his death, Arthur is hailed by the English nobility as a kind of departed saint. For example, the Bastard exclaims that "The life, the right, and truth of all this realm / Is fled to heaven" (151–152). What do you make of such hyperbole? Does this unusual expression of emotion stem from the fact that Arthur is not a teenager but a mere boy in Shakespeare's play? It seems that the others—Salisbury, Bigot, and the Bastard—come dangerously close to committing violence against Hubert when, in fact, Hubert (as the audience knows) has already spared Arthur from John's cruel sentence. How would you represent the tense exchanges between men in this scene?

‡ Imagine three different ways in which a director might credibly stage Arthur's leap of faith—one that, ironically, leads directly to the boy's death. What constitutes "believability" in this scene? Does it depend on the perceived height of the battlements from which he leaps—"The wall is high, and yet I will leap down" (1)—or does our sense of realism depend on the graphic display of his injuries? Some critics have suggested that Arthur's leap is actually a suicide—"As good to die and go, as die and stay" (8). How would you approach this scene as a director?

There's few or none do know me; if they did,
This shipboy's semblance hath disguis'd me quite.
I am afraid, and yet I'll venture it.   5
If I get down and do not break my limbs,
I'll find a thousand shifts to get away.
As good to die and go, as die and stay.   [*Leaps down.*]
O me! my uncle's spirit is in these stones.
Heaven take my soul, and England keep my bones!   *Dies.*   10

Enter Pembroke, Salisbury, and Bigot.

SAL.   Lords, I will meet him at Saint Edmundsbury.
It is our safety, and we must embrace
This gentle offer of the perilous time.

PEM.   Who brought that letter from the Cardinal?

SAL.   The Count Melun, a noble lord of France,   15
Whose private with me of the Dauphin's love
Is much more general than these lines import.

BIG.   To-morrow morning let us meet him then.

SAL.   Or rather then set forward; for 'twill be
Two long days' journey, lords, or ere we meet.   20

Enter Bastard.

BAST.   Once more to-day well met, distemper'd lords!
The King by me requests your presence straight.

SAL.   The King hath dispossess'd himself of us.
We will not line his thin bestained cloak
With our pure honours, nor attend the foot   25
That leaves the print of blood where'er it walks.
Return and tell him so. We know the worst.

BAST.   Whate'er you think, good words I think were best.

SAL.   Our griefs, and not our manners, reason now.

BAST.   But there is little reason in your grief.   30
Therefore 'twere reason you had manners now.

PEM.   Sir, sir, impatience hath his privilege.

BAST.   'Tis true—to hurt his master, no man else.

ACT 4, SCENE 3
4. **shipboy's semblance**: sailor's disguise. 4. **quite**: fully. 7. **shifts**: tricks; disguises (pun). 11. **him**: Louis, the Dauphin. 12. **embrace**: accept. 17. **general**: comprehensive. 20. **ere**: before. 21. **distemper'd**: vexed; disturbed. 22. **straight**: immediately. 24. **line**: act as a lining; reinforce. 29. **reason**: speak. 30. **grief**: grievances. 30. **reason**: logic; good sense. 31. **reason**: logical.

SAL.	This is the prison. What is he lies here?
PEM.	O death, made proud with pure and princely beauty! 35
	The earth had not a hole to hide this deed.
SAL.	Murther, as hating what himself hath done,
	Doth lay it open to urge on revenge.
BIG.	Or, when he doom'd this beauty to a grave,
	Found it too precious-princely for a grave. 40
SAL.	Sir Richard, what think you? Have you beheld,
	Or have you read or heard, or could you think?
	Or do you almost think, although you see,
	That you do see? Could thought, without this object,
	Form such another? This is the very top, 45
	The heighth, the crest, or crest unto the crest,
	Of murther's arms. This is the bloodiest shame,
	The wildest savagery, the vilest stroke
	That ever wall-ey'd wrath or staring rage
	Presented to the tears of soft remorse. 50
PEM.	All murthers past do stand excus'd in this;
	And this, so sole and so unmatchable,
	Shall give a holiness, a purity,
	To the yet unbegotten sin of times,
	And prove a deadly bloodshed but a jest, 55
	Exampled by this heinous spectacle.
BAST.	It is a damned and a bloody work,
	The graceless action of a heavy hand,
	If that it be the work of any hand.
SAL.	If that it be the work of any hand? 60
	We had a kind of light what would ensue.
	It is the shameful work of Hubert's hand,
	The practice and the purpose of the King;
	From whose obedience I forbid my soul,
	Kneeling before this ruin of sweet life, 65
	And breathing to his breathless excellence
	The incense of a vow, a holy vow,
	Never to taste the pleasures of the world,
	Never to be infected with delight

---

40. **grave**: princes were buried in tombs not graves. 47. **arms**: coat of arms; family crest. 49. **wall-ey'd**: glaring eyes. 50. **remorse**: compassion, pity. 54. **times**: the future. 56. **Exampled by**: compared to. 58. **graceless**: evil. 58. **heavy**: wicked. 61. **light**: inkling. 63. **practice**: crafty plot. 69. **infected**: affected and thus diseased.

	Nor conversant with ease and idleness,	70
	Till I have set a glory to this hand
	By giving it the worship of revenge.
PEM., BIG.	Our souls religiously confirm thy words.

Enter Hubert.

HUB.	Lords, I am hot with haste in seeking you.
	Arthur doth live; the King hath sent for you.	75
SAL.	O, he is bold, and blushes not at death.
	Avaunt, thou hateful villain, get thee gone!
HUB.	I am no villain.
SAL.	Must I rob the law? [*Draws.*]
BAST.	Your sword is bright, sir; put it up again.	80
SAL.	Not till I sheathe it in a murtherer's skin.
HUB.	Stand back, Lord Salisbury! stand back, I say!
	By heaven, I think my sword's as sharp as yours. [*Draws.*]
	I would not have you, lord, forget yourself
	Nor tempt the danger of my true defence,	85
	Lest I, by marking of your rage, forget
	Your worth, your greatness, and nobility.
BIG.	Out, dunghill! Dar'st thou brave a nobleman?
HUB.	Not for my life; but yet I dare defend
	My innocent life against an emperor.	90
SAL.	Thou art a murtherer.
HUB.	Do not prove me so.
	Yet I am none! Whose tongue soe'er speaks false,
	Not truly speaks; who speaks not truly, lies.
PEM.	Cut him to pieces!	95
BAST.	Keep the peace, I say.
SAL.	Stand by, or I shall gall you, Faulconbridge.
BAST.	Thou wert better gall the devil, Salisbury.
	If thou but frown on me, or stir thy foot,
	Or teach thy hasty spleen to do me shame,	100
	I'll strike thee dead. Put up thy sword betime,

71. **glory**: splendor. 72. **worship**: honor. 76. **death**: murder. 77. **Avaunt**: be gone. 85. **true defence**: honest cause; skill as a swordsman. 86. **marking of**: taking note, striking out. 88. **dunghill**: pile of refuse. 92. **prove me so**: don't test me. 97. **Stand by**: step aside. 97. **gall**: harm.

	Or I'll so maul you and your toasting iron	
	That you shall think the devil is come from hell.	
BIG.	What wilt thou do, renowned Faulconbridge?	
	Second a villain and a murtherer?	105
HUB.	Lord Bigot. I am none.	
BIG.	Who kill'd this prince?	
HUB.	'Tis not an hour since I left him well.	
	I honour'd him, I lov'd him, and will weep	
	My date of life out for his sweet live's loss.	110
SAL.	Trust not those cunning waters of his eyes,	
	For villainy is not without such rheum;	
	And he, long traded in it, makes it seem	
	Like rivers of remorse and innocency.	
	Away with me, all you whose souls abhor	115
	Th' uncleanly savours of a slaughterhouse,	
	For I am stifled with this smell of sin.	
BIG.	Away toward Bury, to the Dauphin there!	
PEM.	There, tell the King, he may inquire us out. *Exeunt Lords.*	
BAST.	Here's a good world! Knew you of this fair work?	120
	Beyond the infinite and boundless reach	
	Of mercy, if thou didst this deed of death,	
	Art thou damn'd, Hubert.	
HUB.	Do but hear me, sir!	
BAST.	Ha! I'll tell thee what.	125
	Thou'rt damn'd as black—nay, nothing is so black!	
	Thou art more deep damn'd than Prince Lucifer.	
	There is not yet so ugly a fiend of hell	
	As thou shalt be, if thou didst kill this child.	
HUB.	Upon my soul—	130
BAST.	If thou didst but consent	
	To this most cruel act, do but despair;	
	And if thou want'st a cord, the smallest thread	
	That ever spider twisted from her womb	
	Will serve to strangle thee; a rush will be a beam	135
	To hang thee on. Or wouldst thou drown thyself,	
	Put but a little water in a spoon,	

105. **Second**: assist. 110. **date**: span. 112. **rheum**: tears. 113. **long traded**: experienced. 132. **despair**: give up all hope. 133. **cord**: hope to hang himself. 135. **rush**: a reed.

	And it shall be as all the ocean,	
	Enough to stifle such a villain up.	
	I do suspect thee very grievously.	140
Hub.	If I in act, consent, or sin of thought	
	Be guilty of the stealing that sweet breath	
	Which was embounded in this beauteous clay,	
	Let hell want pains enough to torture me!	
	I left him well.	145
Bast.	Go, bear him in thine arms.	
	I am amaz'd, methinks, and lose my way	
	Among the thorns and dangers of this world.	
	How easy dost thou take all England up!	
	From forth this morsel of dead royalty	150
	The life, the right, and truth of all this realm	
	Is fled to heaven; and England now is left	
	To tug and scamble, and to part by th' teeth	
	The unowed interest of proud-swelling state.	
	Now for the bare-pick'd bone of majesty	155
	Doth dogged war bristle his angry crest	
	And snarleth in the gentle eyes of peace.	
	Now powers from home and discontents at home	
	Meet in one line; and vast confusion waits,	
	As doth a raven on a sick-fall'n beast,	160
	The imminent decay of wrested pomp.	
	Now happy he whose cloak and cincture can	
	Hold out this tempest! Bear away that child	
	And follow me with speed. I'll to the King.	
	A thousand businesses are brief in hand,	165
	And heaven itself doth frown upon the land. *Exeunt.*	

---

143. **embounded . . . clay**: enclosed in the body. 147. **amaz'd**: stunned. 149. **all England**: Prince Arthur, rightful king of England. 153. **scamble**: struggle; scramble. 154. **unowed interest**: not rightfully owned. 156. **dogged**: savage; bestial. 158. **from home**: foreign. 158. **discontents**: malcontents. 161. **wrested pomp**: seized nobility; usurped the throne. 162. **cincture**: belt. 165. **brief in hand**: work needing to be done.

ACT V

SCENE I. [*King John's Palace.*]

Enter King John and Pandulph, Attendants.

K. JOHN.   [*Gives the crown*] Thus have I yielded up into your hand
The circle of my glory.

PAND.   Take again
From this my hand, as holding of the Pope
Your sovereign greatness and authority.
[*Gives back the crown.*]   5

K. JOHN.   Now keep your holy word: go meet the French,
And from his Holiness use all your power
To stop their marches fore we are inflam'd.
Our discontented counties do revolt;
Our people quarrel with obedience,   10
Swearing allegiance and the love of soul
To stranger blood, to foreign royalty.
This inundation of mistemp'red humour
Rests by you only to be qualified.
Then pause not; for the present time's so sick   15
That present med'cine must be minist'red
Or overthrow incurable ensues.

PAND.   It was my breath that blew this tempest up,
Upon your stubborn usage of the Pope;
But since you are a gentle convertite,   20
My tongue shall hush again this storm of war
And make fair weather in your blust'ring land.
On this Ascension Day, remember well,
Upon your oath of service to the Pope,
Go I to make the French lay down their arms.   *Exit.*   25

K. JOHN.   Is this Ascension Day? Did not the prophet
Say that before Ascension Day at noon
My crown I should give off? Even so I have.
I did suppose it should be on constraint;
But (heav'n be thank'd!) it is but voluntary.   30

ACT 5, SCENE 1
2. **circle**: crown. 4. **of**: from. 8. **fore**: before. 9. **counties**: districts; shires. 11. **love of soul**: deepest soul.
12. **stranger**: foreign. 13. **inundation . . . humour**: flood of unbalanced dispositions. 14. **qualified**:
cured. 16. **present . . . minist'red**: medicine must be administered at once. 17. **overthrow incurable**:
death will follow. 19. **Upon**: because of. 20. **convertite**: convert. 28. **give off**: give up.

Enter Bastard.

BAST.   All Kent hath yielded; nothing there holds out
            But Dover Castle. London hath receiv'd,
            Like a kind host, the Dauphin and his powers.
            Your nobles will not hear you, but are gone
            To offer service to your enemy;   35
            And wild amazement hurries up and down
            The little number of your doubtful friends.

K. JOHN. Would not my lords return to me again
            After they heard young Arthur was alive?

BAST.   They found him dead and cast into the streets—   40
            An empty casket where the jewel of life
            By some damn'd hand was robb'd and ta'en away.

K. JOHN. That villain Hubert told me he did live.

BAST.   So, on my soul, he did, for aught he knew.
            But wherefore do you droop? Why look you sad?   45
            Be great in act, as you have been in thought.
            Let not the world see fear and sad distrust
            Govern the motion of a kingly eye.
            Be stirring as the time; be fire with fire;
            Threaten the threat'ner and outface the brow   50
            Of bragging horror. So shall inferior eyes,
            That borrow their behaviours from the great,
            Grow great by your example and put on
            The dauntless spirit of resolution.
            Away, and glister like the god of war   55
            When he intendeth to become the field.
            Show boldness and aspiring confidence.
            What, shall they seek the lion in his den,
            And fright him there? and make him tremble there?
            O, let it not be said! Forage, and run   60
            To meet displeasure farther from the doors
            And grapple with him ere he come so nigh.

K. JOHN. The legate of the Pope hath been with me,
            And I have made a happy peace with him,
            And he hath promis'd to dismiss the powers   65
            Led by the Dauphin.

---

36. **amazement:** confusion. 37. **doubtful:** untrustworthy; uncertain; fearful. 41. **casket:** jewel box. 41. **jewel of life:** the soul. 49. **Be stirring as the time:** be as active as the time demands. 50–51. **outface ... horrors:** defy the face of terror. 52. **borrow ... from the great:** imitate the great. 55. **glister:** shine. 56. **become:** grace. 58. **lion:** King John. 60. **Forage:** seek the enemy. 64. **happy:** fortunate.

BAST.

O inglorious league!
Shall we, upon the footing of our land,
Send fair-play orders and make compromise,
Insinuation, parley, and base truce   70
To arms invasive? Shall a beardless boy,
A cock'red silken wanton, brave our fields
And flesh his spirit in a warlike soil,
Mocking the air with colours idly spread,
And find no check? Let us, my liege, to arms.   75
Perchance the Cardinal cannot make your peace;
Or if he do, let it at least be said
They saw we had a purpose of defence.

K. JOHN.

Have thou the ordering of this present time.†

BAST.

Away, then, with good courage! Yet I know   80
Our party may well meet a prouder foe.   *Exeunt.*

SCENE II. [*Near St. Edmundsbury.*
The Dauphin's camp.]

Enter, in arms, Dauphin, Salisbury,
Melun, Pembroke, Bigot, Soldiers.

DAU.

My Lord Melun, let this be copied out
And keep it safe for our remembrance.
Return the precedent to these lords again,
That, having our fair order written down,
Both they and we, perusing o'er these notes,   5
May know wherefore we took the sacrament
And keep our faiths firm and inviolable.

---

68. **upon the footing**: standing on our land. 69. **fair-play orders**: rules of chivalry. 70. **Insinuation**: ingratiation. 72. **cock'red**: pampered. 72. **wanton**: unruly. 72. **brave**: challenge. 73. **flesh**: initiate bloodshed. 74. **idly**: madly, carelessly. 75. **check**: resistance, rebuke. 80. **Yet**: still. 81. **prouder**: braver; stronger.

ACT 5, SCENE 2
3. **precedent**: original from which a copy is made. 4. **fair order**: appropriate agreement. 6. **wherefore . . . sacrament**: agreement sealed by taking holy communion.

---

†   King John and the Bastard are alone when John assigns him "the ordering of this present time," a line implying advancement, though the Bastard's response does not indicate any personal expectations. How is the exchange presented in the BBC production? How might an actor wordlessly portray anticipation? In other places in the BBC version, for example, the Bastard licks his lips when the opportunity to pursue "gain" presents itself. What stage business would you insert here?

SAL.   Upon our sides it never shall be broken.
       And, noble Dauphin, albeit we swear
       A voluntary zeal, an unurg'd faith,   10
       To your proceedings, yet believe me, Prince,
       I am not glad that such a sore of time
       Should seek a plaster by contemn'd revolt
       And heal the inveterate canker of one wound
       By making many. O, it grieves my soul   15
       That I must draw this metal from my side
       To be a widow-maker! O, and there
       Where honourable rescue and defence
       Cries out upon the name of Salisbury!
       But such is the infection of the time   20
       That, for the health and physic of our right,
       We cannot deal but with the very hand
       Of stern injustice and confusèd wrong.
       And is't not pity, O my grieved friends,
       That we, the sons and children of this isle,   25
       Were born to see so sad an hour as this,
       Wherein we step after a stranger, march
       Upon her gentle bosom, and fill up
       Her enemies' ranks (I must withdraw and weep
       Upon the spot of this enforced cause)   30
       To grace the gentry of a land remote
       And follow unacquainted colours here?
       What, here? O nation, that thou couldst remove!
       That Neptune's arms, who clippeth thee about,
       Would bear thee from the knowledge of thyself   35
       And gripple thee unto a pagan shore,
       Where these two Christian armies might combine
       The blood of malice in a vein of league,
       And not to spend it so unneighbourly!

DAU.   A noble temper dost thou show in this,   40
       And great affections wrestling in thy bosom
       Doth make an earthquake of nobility.
       O, what a noble combat hast thou fought
       Between compulsion and a brave respect!

10. **unurg'd**: unforced oath; freely made. 13. **plaster**: salve. 13. **contemn'd**: despised. 14. **inveterate canker**: chronic sore. 16. **metal**: weapon; sword. 19. **Cries out upon**: shouts against. 21. **physic**: cure. 22. **deal**: proceed; act. 30. **spot**: shame. 31. **grace**: honor. 33: **remove**: leave; vacate. 34. **clippeth**: embraces. 35. **bear thee from**: transport you. 36. **gripple**: grapple; fasten. 38. **vein of league**: manner of amity. 40. **temper**: attitude. 41. **affections**: feelings; emotion. 44. **compulsion**: compelling circumstances. 44. **brave respect**: worthy of duty.

Let me wipe off this honourable dew   45
That silverly doth progress on thy cheeks.
My heart hath melted at a lady's tears,
Being an ordinary inundation;
But this effusion of such manly drops,
This show'r, blown up by tempest of the soul,   50
Startles mine eyes and makes me more amaz'd
Than had I seen the vaulty top of heaven
Figur'd quite o'er with burning meteors.
Lift up thy brow, renowned Salisbury,
And with a great heart heave away this storm.   55
Commend these waters to those baby eyes
That never saw the giant world enrag'd,
Nor met with fortune other than at feasts,
Full of warm blood, of mirth, of gossiping.
Come, come! for thou shalt thrust thy hand as deep   60
Into the purse of rich prosperity
As Lewis himself. So, nobles, shall you all
That knit your sinews to the strength of mine.

                    Enter Pandulph.

And even there, methinks an angel spake.
Look where the holy legate comes apace,   65
To give us warrant from the hand of heaven
And on our actions set the name of right
With holy breath.

PAND.   Hail, noble Prince of France!
The next is this: King John hath reconcil'd   70
Himself to Rome; his spirit is come in,
That so stood out against the holy Church,
The great metropolis and see of Rome.
Therefore thy threat'ning colours now wind up
And tame the savage spirit of wild war,   75
That, like a lion fostered up at hand,
It may lie gently at the foot of peace
And be no further harmful than in show.

DAU.   Your Grace shall pardon me, I will not back.
I am too high-born to be propertied,   80

---

53. **Figur'd**: adorned. 56. **Commend**: hand over. 59. **warm blood**: good feeling. 64. **angel spake**: possible pun on coin. 67. **set**: seal. 71. **come in**: yielded; submitted. 74. **colours**: flags. 74. **wind up**: fold up. 79. **shall**: directive, spoken emphatically. 80. **propertied**: treated as a piece of property.

To be a secondary at control,
Or useful servingman and instrument
To any sovereign state throughout the world.
Your breath first kindled the dead coal of wars
Between this chastis'd kingdom and myself   85
And brought in matter that should feed this fire;
And now 'tis far too huge to be blown out
With that same weak wind which enkindled it.
You taught me how to know the face of right,
Acquainted me with interest to this land,   90
Yea, thrust this enterprise into my heart;
And come ye now to tell me John hath made
His peace with Rome? What is that peace to me?
I, by the honour of my marriage bed,
After young Arthur claim this land for mine;   95
And, now it is half conquer'd, must I back
Because that John hath made his peace with Rome?
Am I Rome's slave? What penny hath Rome borne,
What men provided, what munition sent
To underprop this action? Is't not I   100
That undergo this charge? Who else but I,
And such as to my claim are liable,
Sweat in this business and maintain this war?
Have I not heard these islanders shout out
"*Vive le roi!*" as I have bank'd their towns?   105
Have I not here the best cards for the game
To win this easy match, play'd for a crown?
And shall I now give o'er the yielded set?
No, no! on my soul, it never shall be said!

PAND.   You look but on the outside of this work.   110

DAU.   Outside or inside, I will not return
Till my attempt so much be glorified
As to my ample hope was promised
Before I drew this gallant head of war,
And cull'd these fiery spirits from the world   115
To outlook conquest, and to win renown
Even in the jaws of danger and of death.   [*Trumpet sounds.*]
What lusty trumpet thus doth summon us?

---

81. **secondary**: not in control. 86. **matter**: fuel. 90. **interest**: right; claim. 101. **charge**: cost. 102. **such as**: those who are my followers. 105. **bank'd**: passed by. 108. **yielded**: conceded. 114. **drew . . . head of war**: assembled troops. 115. **cull'd**: chose. 116. **outlook**: outface; defy. 118. **lusty**: vigorous.

Enter Bastard, [attended].

BAST.   According to the fair play of the world,
         Let me have audience. I am sent to speak.   120
         My holy Lord of Milan, from the King
         I come to learn how you have dealt for him;
         And as you answer, I do know the scope
         And warrant limited unto my tongue.

PAND.   The Dauphin is too wilful-opposite   125
         And will not temporize with my entreaties.
         He flatly says he'll not lay down his arms.

BAST.   By all the blood that ever fury breath'd,
         The youth says well! Now hear our English King,
         For thus his royalty doth speak in me: 130
         He is prepar'd—and reason too he should;
         This apish and unmannerly approach,
         This harness'd masque and unadvised revel,
         This unhair'd sauciness and boyish troop,
         The King doth smile at, and is well prepar'd   135
         To whip this dwarfish war, these pygmy arms,
         From out the circle of his territories.
         That hand which had the strength, even at your door,
         To cudgel you and make you take the hatch,
         To dive like buckets in concealed wells,   140
         To crouch in litter of your stable planks,
         To lie like pawns lock'd up in chests and trunks,
         To hug with swine, to seek sweet safety out
         In vaults and prisons, and to thrill and shake
         Even at the crying of your nation's crow,   145
         Thinking his voice an armed Englishman—
         Shall that victorious hand be feebled here
         That in your chambers gave you chastisement?
         No! Know the gallant monarch is in arms
         And like an eagle o'er his aery tow'rs   150
         To souse annoyance that comes near his nest.
         And you degenerate, you ingrate revolts,

119. **fair play:** code of chivalry; honorable conduct. 120. **sent to speak:** ready to confer. 123. **as:** depending on your answer. 124. **limited:** prescribed. 125. **wilful-opposite:** stubbornly hostile. 126. **temporize:** negotiate; compromise. 132. **apish:** foolish. 133. **harness'd masque:** armed stage play. 133. **unadvised revel:** fool-hearty festivity. 134. **unhair'd sauciness:** beardless insolence. 137. **circle:** bounds; compass. 139. **hatch:** lower part of a divided door (crawl under or jump over). 141. **litter:** straw used to cover an animal pen. 141. **planks:** flooring. 142. **pawns:** pawned or forfeited. 143. **hug:** sleep. 145. **crow:** rooster. 150. **aery tow'rs:** nest. 151. **souse:** swoop upon, beat off.

You bloody Neroes, ripping up the womb
Of your dear Mother England, blush for shame!
For your own ladies, and pale-visag'd maids,   155
Like Amazons, come tripping after drums,
Their thimbles into armèd gauntlets change,
Their needs to lances, and their gentle hearts
To fierce and bloody inclination.

DAU.   There end thy brave, and turn thy face in peace.   160
We grant thou canst outscold us. Fare thee well.
We hold our time too precious to be spent
With such a brabbler.

PAND.   Give me leave to speak.

BAST.   No, I will speak.   165

DAU.   We will attend to neither.
Strike up the drums, and let the tongue of war
Plead for our interest and our being here.

BAST.   Indeed, your drums, being beaten, will cry out;
And so shall you, being beaten. Do but start   170
An echo with the clamour of thy drum,
And even at hand a drum is ready brac'd
That shall reverberate all, as loud as thine.
Sound but another, and another shall,
As loud as thine, rattle the welkin's ear   175
And mock the deep-mouth'd thunder; for at hand
(Not trusting to this halting legate here,
Whom he hath us'd rather for sport than need)
Is warlike John; and in his forehead sits
A bare-ribb'd death, whose office is this day   180
To feast upon whole thousands of the French.

DAU.   Strike up our drums to find this danger out.

BAST.   And thou shalt find it, Dauphin; do not doubt.   *Exeunt.*

---

153. **Neroes**: Emperor Nero. 156. **Amazons**: female warriors. 158. **needs**: needles. 159. **inclination**: temperament. 160. **brave**: bravado; boast. 161. **outscold**: out rail; out quarrel. 163. **brabbler**: braggart. 166. **attend**: listen. 173. **brac'd**: stretched. 175. **welkin's**: world's. 176. **deep-mouth'd**: loud. 177. **halting**: faltering. 180. **bare-ribb'd**: like a skeleton. 180. **office**: service; role.

SCENE III. [*Near Saint Edmundsbury. A field of battle.*]

Alarums. Enter [King] John and Hubert.

K. JOHN.	How goes the day with us? O, tell me, Hubert.
HUB.	Badly, I fear. How fares your Majesty?
K. JOHN.	This fever that hath troubled me so long
	Lies heavy on me. O, my heart is sick!

Enter a Messenger.

MESS.	My lord, your valiant kinsman, Faulconbridge,	5
	Desires your Majesty to leave the field	
	And send him word by me which way you go.	
K. JOHN.	Tell him toward Swinstead, to the abbey there.	
MESS.	Be of good comfort; for the great supply	
	That was expected by the Dauphin here	10
	Are wrack'd three nights ago on Goodwin Sands.	
	This news was brought to Richard but even now.	
	The French fight coldly, and retire themselves.	
K. JOHN.	Ay me, this tyrant fever burns me up	
	And will not let me welcome this good news!	15
	Set on toward Swinstead. To my litter straight.	
	Weakness possesseth me, and I am faint. *Exeunt.*	

SCENE IV. [*Another part of the field.*]

Enter Salisbury, Pembroke, and Bigot.

SAL.	I did not think the King so stor'd with friends.	
PEM.	Up once again! put spirit in the French.	
	If they miscarry, we miscarry too.	
SAL.	That misbegotten devil, Faulconbridge,	
	In spite of spite, alone upholds the day.	5
PEM.	They say King John, sore sick, hath left the field.	

ACT 5, SCENE 3
8. **Swinstead**: misnomer for Swineshead Abby, where John dies in the play (historically, however, he dies in Newark Castle). 9. **supply**: reinforcements. 11. **wrack'd**: shipwrecked. 11. **Goodwin Sands**: dangerous sandbar near Kent. 13. **coldly**: without sprit. 14. **tyrant**: pitiless fever.

ACT 5, SCENE 4
5. **In spite of spite**: despite everything.

Enter Melun, wounded.

MEL.	Lead me to the revolts of England here.
SAL.	When we were happy we had other names.
PEM.	It is the Count Melun.
SAL.	Wounded to death.

10

MEL.   Fly, noble English; you are bought and sold!
Unthread the rude eye of rebellion
And welcome home again discarded faith.
Seek out King John, and fall before his feet;
For if the French be lords of this loud day,   15
He means to recompense the pains you take
By cutting off your heads. Thus hath he sworn,
And I with him, and many moe with me,
Upon the altar at Saint Edmundsbury,
Even on that altar where we swore to you   20
Dear amity and everlasting love.

SAL.   May this be possible? May this be true?

MEL.   Have I not hideous death within my view,
Retaining but a quantity of life,
Which bleeds away, even as a form of wax   25
Resolveth from his figure 'gainst the fire?
What in the world should make me now deceive,
Since I must lose the use of all deceit?
Why should I then be false, since it is true
That I must die here, and live hence, by truth?   30
I say again, if Lewis do win the day,
He is forsworn if e'er those eyes of yours
Behold another day break in the East;
But even this night, whose black contagious breath
Already smokes about the burning crest   35
Of the old, feeble, and day-wearied sun—
Even this ill night, your breathing shall expire,
Paying the fine of rated treachery
Even with a treacherous fine of all your lives,
If Lewis by your assistance win the day.   40

---

7. **revolts**: malcontents. 8. **When . . . names**: we weren't called rebels when we were doing well. 11. **bought and sold**: betrayed. 12. **Unthread . . . eye**: withdraw from rebellion, as when an eye of a needle is unthreaded. 18. **moe**: more. 24. **quantity**: small amount. 25. **form of wax**: Witches were sometimes thought to destroy their enemies by sticking needles into their wax images. 30. **live hence, by truth**: go to heaven by being truthful. 32. **forsworn**: perjured. 35. **smokes**: spread like mist. 37. **fine**: penalty. 38. **rated**: assessed.

Commend me to one Hubert, with your king.
The love of him, and this respect besides,
For that my grandsire was an Englishman,
Awakes my conscience to confess all this.
In lieu whereof I pray you bear me hence   45
From forth the noise and rumour of the field,
Where I may think the remnant of my thoughts
In peace, and part this body and my soul
With contemplation and devout desires.

SAL. We do believe thee; and beshrew my soul   50
But I do love the favour and the form
Of this most fair occasion, by the which
We will untread the steps of damnèd flight
And, like a bated and retired flood,
Leaving our rankness and irregular course,   55
Stoop low within those bounds we have o'er-look'd
And calmly run on in obedience
Even to our ocean, to our great King John.
My arm shall give thee help to bear thee hence,
For I do see the cruel pangs of death   60
Right in thine eye. Away, my friends! New flight!
And happy newness, that intends old right!
                    Exeunt, [leading off Melun].

SCENE V. [*The French camp.*]

Enter Dauphin and his Train.

DAU. The sun of heaven, methought, was loath to set,
But stay'd and made the western welkin blush,
When English measure backward their own ground
In faint retire. O, bravely came we off
When with a volley of our needless shot,   5
After such bloody toil, we bid good night

42. **respect**: consideration. 43. **For that**: because. 45. **In lieu whereof**: in payment for. 46. **rumour**: confusion. 50. **beshrew**: evil befall. 51. **But I do love**: if I don't love. 51. **favour**: appearance. 51. **form**: shape. 53. **untread**: retrace. 53. **flight**: desertion; rebellion. 54. **bated**: abated. 55. **rankness**: rebellious. 56. **o'er-looked**: overflowed. 61. **Right**: clearly. 62. **happy**: promising. 62. **intends old right**: proceeds to our past allegiance.
ACT 5, SCENE 5
2. **welkin**: sky. 3. **measure**: walk. 4. **faint retire**: half-hearted retreat. 4. **bravely**: splendidly.

And wound our tott'ring colours clearly up,
Last in the field and almost lords of it!

Enter a Messenger.

MESS.   Where is my prince, the Dauphin?

DAU.   Here. What news?   10

MESS.   The Count Melun is slain. The English lords
By his persuasion are again fall'n off,
And your supply, which you have wish'd so long,
Are cast away and sunk on Goodwin Sands.

DAU.   Ah, foul shrewd news! Beshrew thy very heart!   15
I did not think to be so sad to-night
As this hath made me. Who was he that said
King John did fly an hour or two before
The stumbling night did part our weary pow'rs?

MESS.   Whoever spoke it, it is true, my lord.   20

DAU.   Well; keep good quarter and good care to-night.
The day shall not be up so soon as I
To try the fair adventure of to-morrow.   *Exeunt.*

SCENE VI. *[An open place near Swinstead Abbey.]*

Enter Bastard and Hubert, severally.

HUB.   Who's there? Speak, ho! speak quickly, or I shoot!

BAST.   A friend. What art thou?

HUB.   Of the part of England.

BAST.   Whither dost thou go?

HUB.   What's that to thee? Why may not I demand   5
Of thine affairs as well as thou of mine?

BAST.   Hubert, I think.

HUB.   Thou hast a perfect thought.
I will upon all hazards well believe

---

7. **tott'ring**: wavering. 7. **clearly**: freely. 12. **fall'n off**: rebellious. 13. **supply**: reinforcements; relief.
15. **shrewd**: hard. 15. **Beshrew**: curse. 19. **stumbling**: causing one to stumble. 21. **quarter**: watch. 23.
fair adventure: good fortune.
ACT 5, SCENE 6
3. **of the part**: on England's side. 9. **upon all hazards**: despite the risks.

	Thou art my friend that know'st my tongue so well.	10
	Who art thou?	
BAST.	Who thou wilt; and if thou please,	
	Thou mayst befriend me so much as to think	
	I come one way of the Plantagenets.	
HUB.	Unkind remembrance! thou and eyeless night	15
	Have done me shame. Brave soldier, pardon me	
	That any accent breaking from thy tongue	
	Should scape the true acquaintance of mine ear.	
BAST.	Come, come! Sans compliment, what news abroad?	
HUB.	Why, here walk I in the black brow of night	20
	To find you out.	
BAST.	Brief then! and what's the news?	
HUB.	O my sweet sir, news fitting to the night,	
	Black, fearful, comfortless, and horrible.	
BAST.	Show me the very wound of this ill news.	25
	I am no woman; I'll not swound at it.	
HUB.	The King, I fear, is poison'd by a monk.	
	I left him almost speechless, and broke out	
	To acquaint you with this evil, that you might	
	The better arm you to the sudden time	30
	Than if you had at leisure known of this.	
BAST.	How did he take it? Who did taste to him?	
HUB.	A monk, I tell you, a resolved villain,	
	Whose bowels suddenly burst out. The King	
	Yet speaks and peradventure may recover.	35
BAST.	Who didst thou leave to tend his Majesty?	
HUB.	Why, know you not? The lords are all come back,†	
	And brought Prince Henry in their company,	
	At whose request the King hath pardon'd them,	
	And they are all about his Majesty.	40

---

15. **eyeless night**: impenetrable darkness. 16. **done me shame**: shamed me. 17. **accent**: sound. 19. **Sans**: without. 19. **compliment**: ceremony. 26. **swound**: faint. 28. **broke out**: hastened; rushed. 32. **Who did taste**: who tasted the food. 33. **resolved**: committed. 35. **peradventure**: perhaps.

---

†   Hubert tells the Bastard that Prince Henry has arrived and is giving commands. The first two lines of the Bastard's reply (41–42) seem to be a prayerful aside, to be heard only by the audience. Do those lines imply personal disappointment? What might the Bastard do in the interim, between his short aside and his reply to Hubert, to show his true emotions to the audience? How does the BBC production interpret this brief exchange?

BAST.   Withhold thine indignation, mighty heaven,
         And tempt us not to bear above our power!
         I'll tell thee, Hubert, half my power this night,
         Passing these flats, are taken by the tide;
         These Lincoln Washes have devoured them;   45
         Myself, well mounted, hardly have escap'd.
         Away before! conduct me to the King;
         I doubt he will be dead or ere I come.   *Exeunt.*

SCENE VII. [*The orchard of Swinstead Abbey.*]†‡

Enter Prince Henry, Salisbury, and Bigot.

HEN.   It is too late. The life of all his blood
         Is touch'd corruptibly; and his pure brain
         (Which some suppose the soul's frail dwelling house)
         Doth, by the idle comments that it makes,
         Foretell the ending of mortality.   5

Enter Pembroke.

PEM.   His Highness yet doth speak, and holds belief
         That, being brought into the open air,
         It would allay the burning quality
         Of that fell poison which assaileth him.

HEN.   Let him be brought into the orchard here.   [*Exit Bigot.*] 10
         Doth he still rage?

PEM.   He is more patient
         Than when you left him. Even now he sung.

---

42. **power**: soldier; army. 44. **flats**: coastal flat land. 45. **Lincoln Washes**: flooded lowlands.
ACT 5, SCENE 7
2. **touch'd corruptibly**: so infected as to become rotten and decomposed. 2. **pure**: clear; lucid. 4. **idle**: mad; incoherent. 5. **mortality**: life. 9. **fell**: deadly. 11. **rage**: rave.

---

†   In the BBC production, Henry and Arthur look like brothers, with Henry appearing to be the older of the two. At first, however, their uncanny likeness might lead us to check the cast list to determine if both roles are being played by a single actor. Is there an advantage in doubling these parts? What kind of message does such a decision presage? Is Arthur "reborn" in the figure of the future King Henry III?

‡   Contrast the death scenes in the BBC's *King John* and in Beerbohm Tree's silent film. Why would Beerbohm Tree set the scene indoors, in what appears to be a throne room? Does this setting add or detract from the setting in Shakespeare's play? What other choices might a director consider?

HEN.	O vanity of sickness! Fierce extremes
	In their continuance will not feel themselves. 15
	Death, having prey'd upon the outward parts,
	Leaves them insensible; and his siege is now
	Against the mind, the which he pricks and wounds
	With many legions of strange fantasies,
	Which, in their throng and press to that last hold, 20
	Confound themselves. 'Tis strange that death should sing!
	I am the cygnet to this pale faint swan
	Who chants a doleful hymn to his own death
	And from the organ-pipe of frailty sings
	His soul and body to their lasting rest. 25
SAL.	Be of good comfort, Prince; for you are born
	To set a form upon that indigest
	Which he hath left so shapeless and so rude.

[King] John brought in [by Attendants,
Bigot accompanying him].

K. JOHN.	Ay, marry, now my soul hath elbow room.
	It would not out at windows nor at doors. 30
	There is so hot a summer in my bosom
	That all my bowels crumble up to dust.
	I am a scribbled form drawn with a pen
	Upon a parchment, and against this fire
	Do I shrink up. 35
HEN.	How fares your Majesty?
K. JOHN.	Poison'd, ill fare! dead, forsook, cast off!
	And none of you will bid the winter come
	To thrust his icy fingers in my maw,
	Nor let my kingdom's rivers take their course 40
	Through my burn'd bosom, nor entreat the North
	To make his bleak winds kiss my parched lips
	And comfort me with cold. I do not ask you much;
	I beg cold comfort; and you are so strait
	And so ingrateful you deny me that. 45
HEN.	O that there were some virtue in my tears
	That might relieve you!

---

17. **his**: death's. 22. **cygnet**: young swan. 27. **set a form**: give coherence. 27. **indigest**: confused mass. 37. **ill fare**: 1) bad fortune; 2) bad food. 39. **maw**: stomach. 43. **cold comfort**: 1) poor comfort; 2) cold to ease pain. 44. **strait**: stringy. 46. **virtue**: healing power.

K. JOHN.	The salt in them is hot.

K. JOHN. The salt in them is hot.
   Within me is a hell, and there the poison
   Is, as a fiend, confin'd to tyrannize   50
   On unreprievable condemned blood.

Enter Bastard.

BAST. O, I am scalded with my violent motion
   And spleen of speed to see your Majesty!

K. JOHN. O cousin, thou art come to set mine eye!
   The tackle of my heart is crack'd and burnt,   55
   And all the shrouds wherewith my life should sail
   Are turned to one thread, one little hair.
   My heart hath one poor string to stay it by,
   Which holds but till thy news be utterèd;
   And then all this thou seest is but a clod,   60
   And module of confounded royalty.

BAST. The Dauphin is preparing hitherward,
   Where God he knows how we shall answer him;
   For in a night the best part of my pow'r,
   As I upon advantage did remove,   65
   Were in the Washes all unwarily
   Devoured by the unexpected flood. *[King John dies.]*

SAL. You breathe these dead news in as dead an ear.
   My liege! my lord! But now a king, now thus!

HEN. Even so must I run on, and even so stop.   70
   What surety of the world, what hope, what stay,
   When this was now a king, and now is clay?

BAST. Art thou gone so? I do but stay behind
   To do the office for thee of revenge,
   And then my soul shall wait on thee to heaven,   75
   As it on earth hath been thy servant still.
   Now, now, you stars that move in your right spheres,
   Where be your pow'rs? Show now your mended faiths,
   And instantly return with me again
   To push destruction and perpetual shame   80
   Out of the weak door of our fainting land.

---

51. **blood**: life. 53. **spleen**: eagerness. 54. **set**: close in death. 55. **tackle**: rigging (nautical). 56. **shrouds**: sail ropes. 61. **confounded**: ruined. 68. **dead news**: deadly news. 71. **surety**: certainty. 76. **still**: away. 76. **stars . . . spheres**: In the Ptolemaic system each star moved harmonically around Earth as the center of the universe. Correspondingly, the court moved around the king as its center.

Straight let us seek, or straight we shall be sought.
The Dauphin rages at our very heels.

SAL.   It seems you know not, then, so much as we.
The Cardinal Pandulph is within at rest,   85
Who half an hour since came from the Dauphin,
And brings from him such offers of our peace
As we with honour and respect may take,
With purpose presently to leave this war.

BAST.   He will the rather do it when he sees   90
Ourselves well sinewed to our defence.

SAL.   Nay, it is in a manner done already;
For many carriages he hath dispatch'd
To the seaside, and put his cause and quarrel
To the disposing of the Cardinal;   95
With whom yourself, myself, and other lords,
If you think meet, this afternoon will post
To consummate this business happily.

BAST.   Let it be so; and you, my noble Prince,
With other princes that may best be spar'd,   100
Shall wait upon your father's funeral.

HEN.   At Worcester must his body be interr'd,
For so he will'd it.

BAST.   Thither shall it then;
And happily may your sweet self put on   105
The lineal state and glory of the land!
To whom with all submission, on my knee,
I do bequeath my faithful services
And true subjection everlastingly.

SAL.   And the like tender of our love we make,   110
To rest without a spot for evermore.

HEN.   I have a kind soul that would give you thanks,
And knows not how to do it but with tears.

BAST.   O, let us pay the time but needful woe,†
Since it hath been beforehand with our griefs.   115

---

†   Shakespeare commonly assigns a play's closing lines to the highest-ranking official. Why does he
give these lines to the Bastard and not to Prince Henry? In some productions, this speech is delivered as an aside spoken only to the audience. And since there are other characters present, the
camera might close in tightly here to frame only the Bastard, thus giving the illusion of a soliloquy, whereas in a stage production, the Bastard would walk away from the other characters and
toward the downstage space to address the audience directly. Is it possible, however, that

This England never did, nor never shall,
Lie at the proud foot of a conqueror
But when it first did help to wound itself.
Now these her princes are come home again,
Come the three corners of the world in arms,   120
And we shall shock them. Naught shall make us rue
If England to itself do rest but true.   *Exeunt.*

Shakespeare intended for the Bastard's speech to be a motivational address to Prince Henry—or perhaps to all those present on stage? How are these closing moments interpreted in the BBC film?

PLOT OUTLINE OF *KING JOHN*

Act 1.1.   The French Ambassador Chatillon demands that King John relinquish his claim to England and to some territories in France and that he acknowledge his nephew Prince Arthur as the rightful heir. John refuses and threatens war. The Faulconbridge brothers, Philip and Robert, ask King John to mediate their inheritance dispute. Robert claims that because his older brother Philip is a bastard their father had disinherited him. King John rules that Philip's inheritance is good but offers him a place at court, since Philip closely resemble King Richard the Lionhearted. Philip accepts, is knighted Sir Richard Plantagenet, and vows his allegiance to King John and his mother, Queen Elinor. Philip's mother suddenly arrives and privately confesses to her son that his true father was indeed King Richard; Philip proudly acknowledges his paternity and exonerates his mother of any wrongdoing.

Act 2.1.   King Philip of France, his son Prince Lewis, Lady Constance, her son Prince Arthur, and the Duke of Austria (wearing the lion's skin he had taken from Richard the Lionhearted) all assemble before the gates of Angiers. Austria promises to uphold Arthur's claims in England and France. Chatillon announces the unexpected arrival of the English army, including John, his niece Blanch, Queen Elinor, and the Bastard. Both the King of France and King John proclaim suzerainty over Angiers and both demand entry, which the town refuses until one of them can prove entitlement. The Bastard then proposes that the two armies combine to attack the town; but before this can happen, one of the citizens shrewdly suggests that a marriage between Prince Lewis and John's niece Blanch could bring about lasting peace. The idea is enthusiastically received by almost everyone except the Bastard, who closes the scene with a bitter soliloquy on human weakness and self-interest (commodity).

Act 3.1. Lady Constance is outraged when she learns that France has shifted allegiance from her son Arthur to King John. She berates France for breaking his promise of support and is inconsolable. Cardinal Pandulph, the papal legate, arrives and chastises King John for not accepting the new Archbishop of Canterbury. John boldly defies the Cardinal and is summarily excommunicated. Moreover, Cardinal Pandulph orders France to reopen the war. But France is torn between his new allegiance to England and his obligation to Rome—until the Cardinal reminds him that King John is now a heretic. Blanch, whose marriage binds her to France, laments her now having a divided allegiance. The scene ends with the two kings exchanging insults.

Act 3.2. The Bastard has killed Austria and enters with his head. King John has taken Arthur and commits him to Hubert's care. John is concerned for his mother but the Bastard assures him that she is safe.

Act 3.3. King John leaves his mother in France, sends the Bastard to gather money from the Church in England, and commissions Hubert to kill Arthur.

Act 3.4. France is concerned about the war but Pandulph consoles him; Constance grieves over Arthur's capture and is inconsolable. Pandulph reassures the Dauphin by telling him that John will almost certainly kill Arthur and that in doing so he will lose the support of his people. The Dauphin's marriage to Blanch will strengthen his claim to the English throne.

Act 4.1. Hubert intends to follow his instructions to blind and kill Arthur but the boy's pleas dissuade him, and Hubert decides to deceive the King.

Act 4.2. King John has staged a second coronation, which his barons perceive as weakening rather than strengthening his positon. Hearing that Arthur has died and believing that the King is responsible, the barons accuse John and leave the court angrily, determined to desert him. The news is brought that Prince Lewis' army has landed and that both Queen Elinor and Constance have died, within three days of each other. Then a soothsayer predicts that the King will lose his crown on Ascension Day, to which John summarily condemns the man to death on that day. Hubert reports that Arthur is actually alive and John sends him posthaste to the barons.

Act 4.3. Arthur accidentally dies trying to escape; Pembroke, Bigot, and Salisbury find the body and promise to avenge the boy's death. The Bastard charges Hubert with Arthur's death but is finally persuaded of his innocence.

Act 5.1. King John gives in to the Pope's authority and relinquishes his crown to Pandulph, who returns it to him, as the Pope's subject. John realizes that the soothsayer had told the truth and learns that his barons have joined with the French. Dispirited, he turns everything over to the Bastard, giving him "the ordering of this present time" (79).

Act 5.2. The English barons go over to the French. But Pandulph tells the Dauphin that John has returned to the Church and orders him to cease his war; the Dauphin, however, refuses to make peace. And so the Bastard, in John's name, declares that his king is ready for battle.

Act 5.3. John becomes ill with fever and is taken to Swinstead Abbey.

Act 5.4. The defected barons learn from Melun that the Dauphin plans to kill them if the French win the war, and so they return to King John.

Act 5.5. The Dauphin rejoices in thinking that he is winning but then discovers that the English barons have returned to their king and that he has lost his reinforcements.

Act 5.6. Hubert reports to the Bastard that John has been poisoned by a monk and is dying and that the King's nine-year-old son Prince Henry is in the company of the returning barons. The Bastard in turn reports that half his army has been lost in the Wash.

Act 5.7. Young Prince Henry orders that his dying father be brought into a nearby orchard. The Bastard arrives just in time to close King John's eyes, to learn that Pandulph has brought an offer of peace from the French, and to swear faithful service to his new King—King Henry III.

Genealogy of *King John*

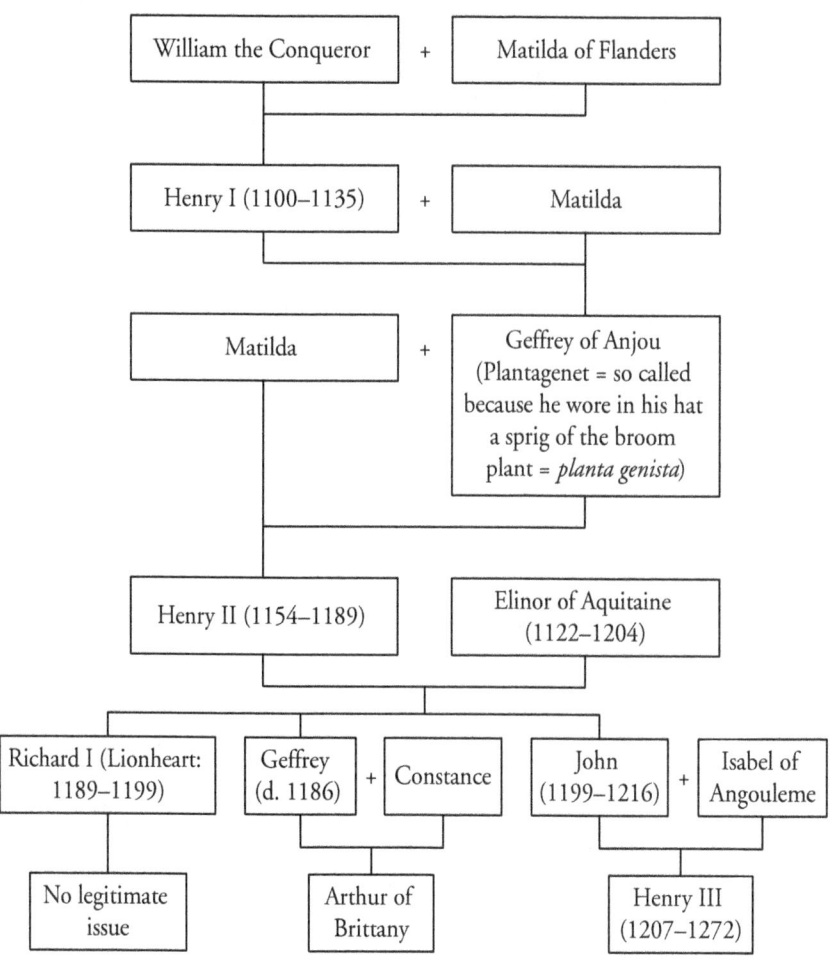

How to Read *King John*
as Performance

Shakespeare's plays take shape in the theater of the mind, constantly inviting us to envision our own version of what is on the page. But when it comes to the stage or screen, our perspective is circumscribed on some level by directors, who make decisions with respect to the blocking of a scene, an actor's intonation, the insertion of stage business, the dramatic use of lighting, and other narrative mechanisms. In the theater, there is no camera to direct the audience's gaze, so the eye creates "camera angles" from which to view the action. In cinema, this freedom is less available to the viewer, as the director predetermines our perspective, to a large degree, through shot composition. But imagine, for a moment, that you are directing *King John* for the stage or screen: What would your version look like?

How, for example, would you go about creating an "establishing shot" of King John in the opening scene? On the page, John initially strikes us as a strong figure who is unintimidated by the French threats. In response to Chatillon's haughtiness, demanding that John "take [his] king's defiance from [his] mouth" (1.1.21), John replies:

> Bear mine to him, and so depart in peace.
> Be thou as lightning in the eyes of France;
> For ere though canst report I will be there,
> The thunder of my cannon shall be heard. (1.1.23–26)

Whether spoken in rage or whispered in reason, John's words project the image of a decisive and confident king. He even seems capable of royal largess, bidding the English to provide Chatillon with "honourable conduct" home. (1.1.29).

As we have seen, few—if any—productions of the play have adopted a flattering approach to John. You may recall from the introduction that David Giles' production opens with an image of John slumped in his chair wielding a goblet of wine. In *The Lion in Winter*, John has a secondary role as a classic teenage loser and malcontent, who lacks any defense except to stammer, "But I am father's favorite." *Ironheart*'s depiction of John, by contrast, tells the story of a psychopath who revels in chopping off limbs at every conceivable opportunity. And, of course, in the Disney classic *Robin Hood*, John is the usurping prince who claims Richard's throne while he is at war; but John's ferocity is mitigated by the fact that he is depicted as a cartoonish lion who sleeps with the gold he pilfers from his people. These are just a few of the multiple perspectives from which John is, by turns, infantile, insane, ignorant, and—as suggested by his reliance on alcohol in Giles' production—addicted to power and its privileges.

The introduction discusses the singular importance of rhetoric for Shakespeare and his audience. On several occasions in the play, Shakespeare is testing rhetorical strategies by having a character, such as the Bastard, serve as an on-stage audience. In 3.1, for example, the Bastard listens intently to an expression used by Constance to insult Austria as a coward: "Thou wear a lion's hide? Doff it for shame, / And hang a calve's-skin on those recreant limbs" (3.1.131–132). The Bastard picks up the second half of Constance's phrase, "And hang a calve's-skin on those recreant limbs" and, throughout the remainder of the scene, he repeats the insult four times to Austria's face. Is the Bastard mocking Constance's rhetoric or is he taking up the gauntlet on her behalf? A more ambiguous use of this phrase follows when Austria exclaims: "King Philip, listen to the Cardinal" (3.1.202) to which the Bastard replies "And hang a calve's-skin on his recreant limbs" (3.1.203). In this case, "his" could be referring to either King Philip or Cardinal Pandulph. What "stage business" might you insert at this point to clarify which character the Bastard imputes for cowardice? Perhaps the Bastard looks one of the characters in the eye; or maybe the ambiguity is purposeful—indeed, a broader rebuke of the anti-English triumvirate forged between Austria, Philip, and Pandulph. But what, we must also ask, is the Bastard's function in this scene more generally? Is he like a chorus, occupying a formal, distant, and staid position on stage? Or is he more of a trickster figure—one who moves seamlessly between the upstage and downstage space to cultivate a rapport with the audience and comment on key events? Consider how these contrasting narrative modes would make for two very different productions.

When reading *King John* for performance, another crucial consideration is the treatment of the female characters. One significant omission from the text of Shakespeare's play is an answer to the question: What ever happens to Blanch? We can guess from her final speech that she will be (and already is) a victim of collateral damage in the wars between England and France. You may remember that in Marie Aberg's production, Blanch stays on stage for the remainder of the play, acting as a ghostly, silent chorus. Silences are important in Shakespeare; if you were to keep Blanch on stage as a mute observer of the action, then what kind of nonverbal cues—gestures and facial expressions—would you have her use to tell her literally unspeakable story? Conversely, if Blanch exits the play as expected in 3.1, can you imagine an "after story" for her character? The opposite of a backstory, an after story is an imaginative construction of a given character's future—a projection of possibilities that lie beyond the parameters of the narrative proper. Does Blanch, like Constance, struggle with her sanity as the war between her husband and her uncle waxes bloodier? Unlike Blanch, Constance delivers what is always a potentially show-stopping speech at the end of 3.3, when she chides both Cardinal Pandulph and King Philip for their complicity in the imminent death of her son Arthur. In her recollection of the 2012 production of *King John* at The Blackfriars Playhouse in Staunton, Virginia, Jane Wells considers the importance of nonverbal signs in the cultivation of sympathy, noting that

> The production was quite aware of how sympathy for characters is established and used on-stage cues and pauses to direct audiences to the potential sympathy in lines. Of particular note was the production's handling of Constance's act 3, scene 3 lamentation on the death of Arthur. The production, like the play text, was at first at pains to treat her grief as histrionics through hostility and impatience with her lengthy speeches. But by the point of her "fond of grief" speech, the production suddenly turned distance to intimacy. Through pacing of her speech and through pauses and on-stage reaction, Allison Glenzer's Constance is able to achieve a kind of tragic grandeur. She accomplishes in one concentrated scene the same move from repulsion to pathos that Queen Margaret does over the course of *Richard III*.[1]

Performances of this dramatic magnitude may explain why Shakespeare eliminates both Constance and Elinor in a matter of lines (4.2.121–126), when, in fact, three years separated their deaths. Indeed, in following the narrative arc between Elinor's vituperous wrath and Constance's elegiac refrains, there can be little doubt that these two women threaten to overshadow the men's war with women's grief. Like Mercutio in *Romeo and Juliet*, Constance and Elinor's lives end abruptly and without ceremony, and the void left in their wake is tangible.

But what happens when all we can do is listen to a performance? Try the following experiment in learning how to "see" with your *ears*. Close your eyes and listen to the Arkangel recording of Constance's "mad scene"; close them again and listen to the same scene in Giles' BBC film. Think about how the elements of voice— pitch, tempo, texture, and tone—lead us to conjure different images of what a particular actor looks like, as well as invite us to formulate impressions of the character's psychological disposition. What if Constance has a "shrill" voice? When coupled with the potential for melodrama, such an inflection could strain the audience's capacity for pathos, particularly if Constance's potential for hysteria is played up. Perhaps a balance can be struck through musical underscoring, a process in which

---

1. This synopsis was provided through private email correspondence, 8/4/2014.

sound effects are employed to heighten our emotional response to the story. If you were to compose a theme song for Constance's mourning, what kind of music would you employ to elicit greater pathos from the audience? Or is there an argument to be made for allowing her words to speak for themselves?

As mentioned in the introduction, in David Giles' BBC television adaptation, Arthur's death is so artificially staged that the audience nearly finds itself rooting for the poor child to die. The wall, which is perhaps five feet high but shot from a "God's eye" perspective to heighten the depth perception, is comprised of what appears to be a series of stacked cardboard bricks. The scene is totally unbelievable and drastically reduces the empathy that audiences typically experience. On the other hand, Josie Rourke's production rendered the death of Arthur so excruciatingly real that horror completely negated the pathos demanded by this scene. Surely there is a happy medium to be found between verisimilitude and metaphor? Ironically, one of the most profound and believable treatments of Arthur's leap from the tower is the Arkangel recording of *King John*. In this auditory performance, the "off-screen" sound of Arthur panting indicates that he is running toward the audience from somewhere in the distance. The closer he gets, the gasps become louder until at last he arrives, we presume, at the edge of the wall. Hanging on Arthur's every word, we would be hard-pressed *not* to be moved by the boy's entreaty to the stones: "be pitiful and hurt me not" (4.3.2)—especially as he musters the courage to say "I am afraid, and yet I'll venture it" (4.3.5). When Arthur jumps, it takes several seconds for the thump to occur, encouraging the audience to "see" just how high the tower walls are—an effect created simply by the silence that separates the boy's hopeful leap from his tragic landing.

Shakespeare's history plays are parables about power and its abuses, and in this context, it is especially significant who delivers the play's final lines; typically, this character is positioned to be the heir apparent. *King John* may be the only Shakespeare play in which the final lines are championed by an "other"—the Bastard—rather than Prince Henry, for example, who is John's true heir. Consider the play's final scene, 5.7, with Salisbury, Prince Henry, and, ostensibly, the dying John onstage with the Bastard. Imagine the thoughts of these characters; try composing inner-monologues for all of them. What, in particular, might the Bastard be thinking, knowing that his Plantagenet aspirations have just been dashed by the appearance of the Prince? In the film segment from Beerbohm Tree's *King John*, the scene features Pembroke, Bigot, and Prince Henry all standing by rather awkwardly as John suffers his death throes. If you were directing this scene back in 1899, would you have inserted an explanatory title card here? Would you indicate what any of the onlookers are thinking or feeling as the king dies before their eyes? Are they apprehensive? Ambitious? Happy that John is dead?

The blocking of this scene is also important, for there is room here—at least potentially—for tension between John's two "heirs": Prince Henry and the Bastard. Although the Bastard promises to "bequeath [his] faithful services / And true subjection everlastingly" to the young Henry III (5.7.108–109), one can't help but wonder how he feels about returning from the wars only to kneel to a nine-year-old boy. But the Bastard is given his due when he is awarded the play's final speech:

> This England never did, nor never shall,
> Lie at the proud foot of a conqueror,
> But when it first did help to wound itself.
> Now these her princes are come home again,
> Come the three corners of the world in arms,
> And we shall shock them. Nought shall make us rue
> If England to itself do rest but true. (5.7.116–122)

Typically, the blocking of this scene would distinguish the highest-ranking character through his central or elevated position on stage. The question is: Do the Bastard's words trump Prince Henry's rank? Certainly the Bastard's rousing display of patriotism should accord him a unique place on the stage; but would you go so far as to have the Bastard occupy center stage? If so, then how would you block this scene in a way that would satisfy the strategic interests of both parties? According to the theory of the "king's two bodies," we might, on the one hand, view the Bastard as the heir apparent to the divine spirit of kingship that John never possessed; on the other hand, we might consider the fact that the prince is John's natural heir who returns, presumably, to assume the throne as the king's physical, mortal body. Blocking can either maximize, minimize, or resolve the tensions between characters; what approach would you adopt?

There are, of course, many other considerations when imagining *King John*'s final scene. For example, could the Bastard's speech be performed as a soliloquy for the audience's ears only, aided by dramatic key lighting (in film) or spotlighting (in the theater) that would leave the other characters quite literally in shadow? Or does the Bastard intend to engage the other characters on stage who, like the audience, are seeking a moral exemplum from him? Unlike Shakespeare's other history plays, *King John* has no sequel (or, for that matter, a prequel). Whose story do you imagine would be the focus of *The (After)Life and Death of King John*? Would it revolve around the further adventures of the Bastard—the play's most appealing character—or would it give pride of place to the reign of Henry III, who ruled for the next fifty-six years?

Perhaps the sequel to *King John* is really our own commodity-obsessed society, in which corporations are kings, the barons are CEOs, and we are, collectively, the heir apparent to a global culture that is defined not by honorable precepts but by profit margins. But art is never entirely without optimism, and it is safe to say that, whatever lesson audiences go in search of, Shakespeare, as Gregory Doran reminds us, "just somehow provides."

TOPICS FOR DISCUSSION AND
FURTHER STUDY OF *KING JOHN*

Critical Issues

1. Do you find any changes, good or ill, in King John's character as the play progresses? Can you plot the stages in the progression? King John has only one soliloquy and it is only two lines long. Can you find it? Can you imagine three different ways to deliver these lines?
2. Early in the play (1.1.40–43), Elinor utters a brief aside to John, warning him that he must possess the throne strongly rather than relying on his right—"or else," she claims, "it must go wrong with you and me." Does this sound like a veiled threat to you? If John fails her in this regard, then what do you think the repercussions will be for him? Does Elinor control him as much as she thinks she does?
3. In the "romantic" exchange between the two "lovers," Blanch and the Dauphin (2.1.505–529), Shakespeare uses the Bastard's cynical rejoinders to make fun of the Dauphin's bad Petrarchan love poetry (2.1.513–518)—a process that Shakespeare famously repeats in *Romeo and Juliet* with the help of Mercutio. What does this type of meta-poetic commentary—of Shakespeare commenting on his own (and others') poetry—tell us about Shakespeare's confidence as a writer at the very beginning of his career? After all, it takes a certain degree of self-confidence to lampoon the very poetic devices he demonstrates and extols.
4. Blanch has a small role in *King John*, yet Shakespeare must have thought it important enough to give her one of the play's few soliloquies. Analyze the rhetorical moves that she makes in her speech to highlight the madness of her wedding day.

5. The Cardinal and the French King both accuse Constance of being melodramatic. Do you agree with them at all? If so, are there specific points in her lamentations where you find her bordering on hysteria?

6. What do you think about the fact that the Pope's emissary, Cardinal Pandulph, is an expert in Machiavellian rhetoric?

7. What advantages—practical or thematic—are there to having a single actor play the parts of both Prince Arthur and Prince Henry?

8. If you were to produce a modern-era version of *King John*, how might you translate the political and religious dimensions of the play for contemporary audiences?

9. Shakespeare and his audience were keenly interested in finding parallels and analogues between King John's reign and the reign of their own Queen Elizabeth. What can we learn from *King John* about our own time?

Performance Issues

1. Leonard Rossiter was a famous comic actor when he played King John in the BBC film production. What effect do you suppose this "intertextuality" has upon those audiences who know Rossiter's backstory? Can you imagine a particular comic actor whom you could take seriously in this role? Ideally, who would you cast as King John?

2. Read the Bastard's soliloquy on commodity, beginning "Mad world! mad kings!" (2.1.571) and think about several ways in which it might be delivered. Does the meaning of "commodity" change according to the various performance choices? Does this famous soliloquy in any way foreshadow the Bastard's change of heart later in the play, when he is no longer obsessed with self-promotion but concerned only for the wellbeing of the State?

3. In the BBC film, the citizens of Angiers stand upon the walls of their city to watch the opposing armies and their two kings square off below them. How would you direct this scene? In a sense, the spokesperson for the citizens of Angiers is an internal director, just as the citizens themselves are the internal audience: How would you show the unspoken reactions of the citizens to the "drama" they are watching?

4. There is a stage direction in the text for Queen Elinor to take Prince Arthur aside (3.3.19), while King John draws Herbert away to plan Arthur's death. In the BBC film production, the camera captures her expression at precisely that moment: What do you see in her face? Is she calculating and vicious? Or do her maternal instincts kick in and lead her to pity and comfort Arthur? Which "child"—John or Arthur—does she appear to favor at this moment? Consider having several people watch that moment with you and compare your responses.

5. We have seen how performances of Arthur's death can be completely unbelievable (the "cardboard" castle), as well as too believable (in the case of Josie Rourke's graphic rendering). Could these dissatisfying extremes be avoided by a more abstract interpretation of Arthur's fall? For example, what could you do with lighting that could convey the same outcome? What are the advantages of approaches that are less realistic but more artistic?
6. Near the middle of the play, King John says, "I am burn'd up with inflaming wrath" (3.1.350) and King Philip replies that "[t]hy rage shall burn thee . . . To ashes" (354–355). Do you see any ironic foreshadowing here, pointing to the end of the play when John starts feeling pain "burning" within him and finally describes himself as a "parchment" held "against this fire" (5.7.34)? In the Arkangel recording, for example, a fire crackles in the background whenever the characters are outdoors. What motifs, visual or audible, might you use to impress this foreshadowing upon your audience?
7. What can we learn about King John from watching other imaginative approaches to his persona in *Ironclad*, *The Lion in Winter*, and even Disney's *Robin Hood*?

KING JOHN BIBLIOGRAPHY AND FILMOGRAPHY

Recent Historical Studies

Carpenter, David. *Magna Carta*. London and New York: Penguin, 2015.

Holt, J. C. *Magna Carta*. Cambridge: Cambridge University Press, 2015.

Knight, Stephen. *Robin Hood: A Mythic Biography*. Ithaca: Cornell University Press, 2003.

Levin, Carole. *Propaganda in the English Reformation: Heroic and Villainous Images of King John*. Studies in British History 11. Lewiston and Queenston: Mellen, 1988.

Critical Collections

Brown, Jane K. *The Persistence of Allegory: Drama and Neoclassicism from Shakespeare to Wagner*. Philadelphia: University of Pennsylvania Press, 2007.

Includes discussion and tables showing Shakespeare's use of allegory throughout his plays but with special emphasis upon *King John*.

Candido, Joseph, ed. *King John: The Critical Tradition*. London and Atlantic Highlands, NJ: Athlone, 1996.

Reprints excerpts from key critical essays from 1790 to 1919, with an introductory survey of scholarship up to 1990.

Curren-Aquino, Deborah T. *King John: New Perspectives*. Newark: University of Delaware Press, 1989.

Prints twelve outstanding essays, plus a performance history and selective bibliography.

Shirley, Frances A. *King John and* Henry VIII: *Critical Essays.* New York and London: Garland, 1988.
      Reprints some of the most important essays from 1770 to 1982.

Selected Essays and Articles

Some of these are in the anthologies above, as indicated.

Anderson, Thomas. "Legitimation, Name, and All Is Gone: Bastardy and Bureaucracy in Shakespeare's *King John.*" *Journal for Early Modern Cultural Studies* 4.2 (Fall/Winter 2004): 35–61.
      Examines "a developing bureaucratic body politic in *King John*" in which "bastardy and illegitimacy are critical, a priori conditions for growth."
Bonjour, Adrien. "The Road to Swinstead Abbey: A Study of the Sense and Structure of *King John.*" *ELH* 18.4 (December 1951): 253–274.
      Argues that the play's coherence derives from the "dynamic representation of two closely connected characters [John and the Bastard] whose evolution curves are, in their very contrast, almost perfectly symmetrical."
Calderwood, James L. "Commodity and Honour in *King John.*" *University of Toronto Quarterly* 29 (1960): 341–356. Reprinted in Frances Shirley, King John *and* Henry VIII: *Critical Essays,* 127–144.
      Finds that the play's thematic coherence derives from the juxtaposition of self-interest and concern for the public good.
Champion, Larry S. "'Confound their skill in covetousness': The Ambivalent Perspective of Shakespeare's King John." *Tennessee Studies in Literature* 24 (1979): 36–55.
      Shows that the "thematic organization and arrangement of scenes" compel us to see the play from "various angles," thereby impressing upon us its thematic ambiguity.
Goodland, Katharine. *Female Mourning and Tragedy in Medieval and Renaissance English Drama: From the Raising of Lazarus to King Lear.* Burlington, VT: Ashgate, 2006. 119–133.
      Explores Constance's "performance of mourning" that, in turn, "prob[es] the tensions and contradictions of late sixteenth-century England's construction of female mourning, a construction that embodies the cultural trauma of the Reformation in England."

Groves, Beatrice. "'I am not he shall build the Lord a house': Religious Imagery and the Succession to the English Throne in *King John*." In *Texts and Traditions: Religious Imagery in Shakespeare 1592–1604*, edited by Beatrice Groves, 89–120. Oxford: Clarendon Press, 2007.

> "In *King John* majesty has not lost its sacredness, but John has lost his majesty. . . . *King John* shares with the New Testament and the [medieval] mystery plays a radical social agenda in which true royalty belongs to the dispossessed" (120).

Manheim, Michael. "The Four Voices of the Bastard." In Deborah T. Curren-Aquino, *King John: New Perspectives*. 126–135.

> Shows that the Bastard's three soliloquies reveal a character increasingly reflective of the "political pragmatism" of Shakespeare's time.

Piese, A. J. "King John: Changing Perspectives." *The Cambridge Companion to Shakespeare's History Plays*, edited by Michael Hattaway, 126–140. Cambridge: Cambridge University Press, 2002.

> Explores alternative views of history and competing ideas of "legitimacy" through the eyes of Elinor, Constance, Arthur, and the Bastard.

Waith, Eugene M. "King John and the Drama of History." *Shakespeare Quarterly* 29 (1978): 192–211. In Frances Shirley, King John *and* Henry VIII: *Critical Essays*, 31–50.

> Brilliant survey of the play's many productions and of the responses of audiences over the centuries.

Weimann, Robert. "Mingling Vice and 'Worthiness' in *King John*." *Shakespeare Studies* 27 (1999): 109–133.

> Argues that *King John* is a highly experimental play in which Shakespeare creates characters that challenge culturally dominant definitions of worth and value.

Filmography for *King John*

Ironclad (2011). Dir. Jonathan English. 120 minutes. VIP Medionfonds 4 Production. DVD release: 2011.

> A siege film depicting the battle between King John and his barons.

King John (1899). Dir. Sir Herbert Beerbohm Tree. Approximately 77 seconds. DVD release: 2000. Part of the compilation "Silent Shakespeare." Featuring *King John* (Britain, 1899), *The Tempest* (Britain, 1908), *A Midsummer Night's Dream* (US, 1909), *King Lear* (Italy, 1910), *Twelfth Night* (US, 1910), *The Merchant of Venice* (Italy, 1910), and *Richard III* (Britain, 1911).

King John (1984). Dir. David Giles. 120 minutes. Produced by the BBC and Time-Life Films. DVD release: December 2000. Part of *The Complete Dramatic Works of William Shakespeare.*

The Lion in Winter (1968). Dir. Anthony Harvey. 145 minutes. Conboy Productions. DVD release: 2001.

Henry II and Elinor of Aquitaine battle over their sons' competing claims to the throne.

Robin Hood (1973). Dir. Wolfgang Reitherman. 83 minutes. Walt Disney Productions. DVD release: 2013, 40th Anniversary Edition.

An animated feature in which Robin Hood, along with Little John and his Merry Men, outwit Prince John and restore Richard the Lionhearted to the throne.

Sound Recordings for *King John*

King John (2014). 147 minutes. Blackstone Audio. DVD release: 2014.

Part of the Complete Arkangel Shakespeare, with Michael Feast as the king, Michael Maloney as the Bastard, and Eileen Atkins as Constance.

William Shakespeare

THE FAMOUS HISTORY OF THE LIFE OF KING HENRY THE EIGHTH

Editor
Jane Wells
Muskingum University

INTRODUCTION TO THE
KITTREDGE EDITION OF *HENRY VIII*

The Famous History of the Life of King Henry the Eighth was first printed in the Folio of 1623, which is therefore the sole authority for the text.

The date of composition must be shortly before June 29, 1613, for on that day, during a performance of *Henry VIII*, then a new play, the Globe Theatre caught fire from the cannon salute that marks the king's approach (1.4.49) and was burned down. Sir Henry Wotton gave a lively account of the accident in a letter to his nephew Sir Edmund Bacon written a few days later (July 2):

> Now, to let matters of state sleep, I will entertain you at the present
> with what has happened this week at the Bank's side. The King's
> players had a new play, called *All Is True*, representing some principal
> pieces of the reign of Henry VIII, which was set forth with many
> extraordinary circumstances of pomp and majesty, even to the mat-
> ting of the stage; the Knights of the Order with their Georges and
> garters, the Guards with their embroidered coats, and the like: suffi-
> cient in truth within a while to make greatness very familiar, if not
> ridiculous. Now, King Henry making a masque at the Cardinal Wol-
> sey's house, and certain chambers being shot off at his entry, some of
> the paper, or other stuff, wherewith one of them was stopped, did
> light on the thatch, where being thought at first but an idle smoke,
> and their eyes more attentive to the show, it kindled inwardly, and
> ran round like a train, consuming within less than an hour the whole
> house to the very grounds. This was the fatal period of that virtuous
> fabric, wherein yet nothing did perish but wood and straw, and a few
> forsaken cloaks; only one man had his breeches set on fire, that would
> perhaps have broiled him, if he had not by the benefit of a provident
> wit put it out with bottle ale.

That the "new play" that Wotton mentions was *Henry VIII*—though he gives it a different title—is certain, not only from his description but from other testimony. Thus Thomas Lorkin, in a letter written on June 30, says that the fire occurred "yesterday, while Burbage's company were acting at the Globe the play of *Henry VIII*, and there shooting off certain chambers [i.e., short cannon, standing upright] in way of triumph." *All Is True* was doubtless an alternative title. The prologue of *Henry VIII* insists that the play is "our chosen truth," and a contemporary ballad "upon the pittifal burneing of the Globe playhowse" has "all this is true" in the refrain. The style and metre of the Shakespearean part of the drama accord with a late date.

That the greater part of *Henry VIII* is not Shakespeare's is certain. His share, except for a possible touch now and then, seems to comprise only scenes 1 and 2 of act 1, scenes 3 and 4 of act 2, the first 203 lines of scene 2 in act 3, and scene 1 in act 5. The rest is proved—to all intents and purposes—by style and manner, and especially by meter, to be the work of John Fletcher, though no direct evidence connects his name with the play. Such evidence, however, does exist for his association with Shakespeare in *The Two Noble Kinsmen*, which must be of about the same date. The allotment gives Fletcher the two most famous passages in the drama—Wolsey's farewell to greatness and his advice to Cromwell (3.2.351–372, 428–457). But Shakespeare can spare them, and they are not beyond Fletcher's powers. There is no reason to detect a third hand (Beaumont or another) in the play or to ascribe the Shakespearean scenes to Massinger.

That some of Shakespeare's scenes (5.1, for instance) have been touched up by Fletcher is of course possible. Whether there was intimate collaboration, or whether Fletcher completed an unfinished Shakespearean play, cannot be determined by any tests beyond those of editorial imagination. What Fletcher did, however, he must have done by Shakespeare's authority, for *Henry VIII* was prepared for Shakespeare's company, and it was accepted by his partners—Heminge and Condell—as sufficiently his to be included in their edition, the Folio of 1623.

For history, the authors went to Holinshed's *Chronicle*. For the Cranmer episode (5.1–3), however, both Shakespeare and Fletcher, whether they worked in concert or not, had recourse to Foxe's *Book of Martyrs*, phrases from which appear frequently in the text of both. Henry's remark in 5.3.174–176, for example, simply versifies Foxe's words: "It came into a common prouerbe: 'Do vnto my Lord of Canterbury displeasure or a shrewed turne, and then you may be sure to haue him your frend whiles he lyueth.'" Queen Katherine's speech at the Blackfriars trial (2.4.13–57) is versified from Holinshed with very little change. At least two lines of the blank verse are taken word for word from the prose chronicle. The whole may be compared with Hermione's defense in *The Winter's Tale* (3.2).

Chronology is sacrificed, as usual, to dramatic convenience, but without doing violence to the title *All Is True*. Thus Queen Katherine's petition in behalf of the commons overwhelmed by the sixth-part tax (1.2) comes immediately after the arrest of Buckingham (1.1) and before his trial and conviction (2.1). In fact, he was arrested in April 1521, and convicted on May 13, 1521; whereas the exaction of "the sixth part of every man's substance" was not decreed until 1525. Wolsey died in 1530; Elizabeth was born in 1533; Queen Katherine died in 1536. In the play, Queen Katherine's death precedes Elizabeth's birth, and Wolsey's death is told to the queen just before her own takes place. The accusation of Cranmer before the council (5.3) was not until after 1540 (probably in 1544). In the play, however, it precedes the christening of Elizabeth (1533).

In 1605 was published a play by Samuel Rowley entitled *When you see me, You know me. Or the famous Chronicle Historie of King Henry the eight, with the birth and vertuous life of Edward Prince of Wales.* It was probably known to the authors of *Henry VIII*, but they owe it nothing. Had they borrowed from this random-roaming play, their procedure would have merited what Rowley makes Patch, the cardinal's fool, say to Will Sommers: "Wee haue but little wit betweene vs already, and so we should haue none at all!"

—George Lyman Kittredge

INTRODUCTION TO THE
FOCUS EDITION OF *HENRY VIII*

In the story we often tell about his career, Shakespeare, the greatest poet and playwright ever to have written in English, went out with a flourish. In 1611, Shakespeare penned *The Tempest*—a tour de force of poetry, action, and spectacle that showcased and thematized the power of theater and that, more directly than any other play, probed the issues of what it means to be human. Here was Shakespeare, still at the height of power, reluctantly letting go of the art he made and that, in many respects, made him. If ever there were a couplet as fit to close a career as a play, "As you from crimes would pardon'd be / Let your indulgence set me free" would be that couplet.

The reality of Shakespeare's departure is neither as definitive nor as dramatic. His exit was more staggered. After *The Tempest*, Shakespeare wrote two plays that strike us as profoundly different in many ways: *The Two Noble Kinsmen* and a history play referred to by a contemporary account as *All Is True*, which was published in 1623 in the Folio collection of Shakespeare's work as *The Famous History of the Life of King Henry the Eighth* (hereafter *Henry VIII*). *The Two Noble Kinsmen* is distinct because it was not principally Shakespeare's work but a collaboration with John Fletcher, who replaced Shakespeare as the main playwright for their acting company The King's Men and who is noted for his many collaborations with fellow playwright Francis Beaumont. Like another likely collaboration, *Pericles*, *The Two Noble Kinsmen* was excluded from the first collected works of Shakespeare's plays published in 1623 by two of the shareholding actors in The King's Men.

As is the case with *The Two Noble Kinsmen*, *Henry VIII* is an unusual play for Shakespeare's late career, which was already marked by a shift from tragedies (*Antony and Cleopatra* and *Coriolanus)* to romances (*The Tempest, Pericles, The Winter's Tale*). In 1613, Shakespeare returned to writing history plays, a genre that he had not visited in the fourteen years since completing *Henry V*. In the 1590s, histories were surprisingly Shakespeare's go-to dramatic form. He wrote nine of them, compared to eight (or maybe nine) comedies and only three tragedies.

Additionally, as with *The Two Noble Kinsmen*, a number of critics and editors have believed *Henry VIII* is also a collaboration with John Fletcher. Not only do many of these critics think his authorship shared, some credit Shakespeare as the author of only a minority of scenes: 1.1, 1.2, 2.3, 2.4, 3.2.1–203, and 5.1. These, it turns out, contain the most memorable scenes and speeches, and, were it not for that fact, the play might seem the product of another playwright in which Shakespeare also had a hand instead of a work in which he had equal footing.

The Play and Its Structure

As a history play, *Henry VIII* is distinct from the nine other history plays among which the shareholders in his company who published his play group it. While military conflicts, foreign and civil, frame those plays, *Henry VIII* is almost entirely concerned with non-martial domestic affairs—the workings of his marriages and the maneuvers of his privy council. And when the play does move to foreign affairs, as it does with the intervention of the Cardinal, those issues have roots in Henry's domestic, household concerns.

The historical scope of the play covers the following events from Henry's reign:

1. Henry's encounters and compact with the French king at the Field of the Cloth of Gold.
2. The Duke of Buckingham's fall as orchestrated by the scheming Cardinal Wolsey.
3. Henry's misgivings over the legitimacy of his marriage to Queen Katherine, her refusal to endure trial, and her appeal to Rome as judge.
4. Henry's meeting with and eventual marriage to Anne Bullen (or Boleyn, as she is known historically) as well as her coronation.
5. Cardinal Wolsey's own fall based on his avarice and opposition to the King's marriage to Anne.
6. Queen Katherine's poignant dying speech and vision of her own beatification.
7. The rise of Archbishop Cranmer, whose Protestant leanings make him the object of the privy council's attack.
8. The King's reassertion of control over the maneuvers of his council.
9. The christening of Princess Elizabeth and Cranmer's prophecy of her rise to greatness as the "maiden phoenix."

Interspersed among these nine events or episodes is an equally impressive series of seven masques and pageants (or royal displays). These include the masque of the rustic shepherd's at Wolsey's feast (1.4), Buckingham's escort after his arraignment (2.1), the assembly of judges at Katherine's trial (2.4), the procession of dignitaries at Anne's coronation (4.1), Katherine's deathbed vision of the white-robed "spirits of peace" (4.2), the council assembled to arraign Archbishop Cranmer (5.2), and the retinue of local and court officials at Princess Elizabeth's christening (5.4). These pageants come together to make *Henry VIII* by far the most visually focused and impressive of all Shakespeare's works.

The play adds to the pageants and episodes the gossiping dialogue of two anonymous gentlemen who twice appear to relate action that takes place off stage in regard to Buckingham's trial, Anne's coronation, and Queen Katherine's fate, and to comment, chorus-like, on the action and on rumors of the King and his first wife. These gentlemen provide an important secondary perspective and even help level the general historical tilt of the play, often suggesting alternative motives for the action of key figures.

As this list suggests, rather than presenting an overarching focus (such as war between internal factions in *Henry IV* or with external ones in *Henry V*), the material of this play unfolds as a sequence of episodes that are tied together by theme more than by plot. Some critics have been less than generous about *Henry VIII*'s episodic nature. Seventeenth-century diarist and man-about-town Samuel Pepys is one. Having seen and reported on twelve Restoration productions of Shakespeare plays, Pepys is at once one of our best and worst historical sources of Shakespeare's plays, often dismissing them in very few words. Seeing *Henry VIII* on January 1, 1663, Pepys reports being "dissatisfied" that the play is such a gallimaufry: "It is so simple a thing made up of a great many patches, that, besides the shows and procession in it, there is nothing in the world good or well done" (qtd. in Odell, 179).

But the play does have a trajectory and course, albeit a quiet one. The end of the play would make it appear that its main conflict concerns Henry's difficulty contending with the machinations of Wolsey and those on his council. An early part of the play has set viewers up for such a resolution. Norfolk observes of Wolsey's schemes, "The King will know him one day," and indeed he does (2.2.17). The play's climax (or the closest thing to it) occurs when Henry finally rises above the manipulation and schemes of an independent and self-serving council. His renewed ascendancy occurs both physically—he gains the upper hand spying on them from the seating gallery above the back of the stage, which serves as a peephole for his surveillance—and politically—he reasserts dominion over the council that acted independently of him. In 5.2, he rebukes his council ("I had thought I had had men of some understanding / And wisdom of my Council") and orders the end of their deadly political squabbles ("Be friends for shame, my lords!"). However, to the extent that this plot thread has been woven, it has been done subtly and softly, rather than conspicuously.

The Authorship Question

Although in retrospect Shakespeare might appear to have ended his career on a quiet note, *Henry VIII* or *All Is True* made as much noise as any other Shakespeare play. In fact, it was the only play of Shakespeare that literally brought down the house. In a letter to Sir Edmund Bacon, dated July 2, 1613, Sir Henry Wotton famously recounts how "certain Canons being shot off" during the performance "did light upon the thatch" roof of the Globe Theatre. "[W]ithin less than an hour," Wotton reports, the fire consumed "the whole house to the very grounds." The Globe, it turns out, was the only casualty of the fire; the only other near one was a man who "had his breeches set on fire." This man might have been "broiled," "if he had not by the benefit of a provident wit put it out with bottle ale."

Although the near-comical account of the Globe's razing is the most memorable feature here, Wotton's letter is in many ways among the most important contemporary documents of any Shakespeare play. Wotton's designation of *All Is True* as "a new play" provides clear evidence that the play was composed sometime in early 1613. The letter is detailed enough even to offer the exact moment in the play that the fire started: "Now, King Henry making a masque at the Cardinal Wolsey's house." He also provides a very accurate description of the play's episodic content as "representing some principal pieces in the reign of Henry VIII" and details of its production, "which was set forth with many extraordinary circumstances of pomp and majesty, even to the matting of the stage." Finally, he offers a critique or an analysis of the effect of the play's presentation whereby the pageants provided within were "sufficient in truth within a while to make greatness very familiar, if not ridiculous."

Wotton, however, was not actually present at the play, and his absence makes his critique less authoritative. Still, his assessment that the play either "makes greatness" of the prominent historical figures "very familiar" or reduces them to being "ridiculous" is a startling pronouncement on how *Henry VIII* treats its subject and raises the central questions audiences and critics seem to ask about it: What is this play and just what indeed are Shakespeare (and Fletcher) up to in it? Although this question may be asked of any play, *Henry VIII* courts it more insistently than most other Shakespeare plays.

We can start with the question of authorship. Whether or not the play is a collaboration is itself an issue. When the shareholders in The King's Men assembled Shakespeare's collected works, they saw this play as enough of Shakespeare's to warrant its inclusion among the other plays he authored. Two other Shakespearean works were left out: *The Two Noble Kinsmen* and *Pericles*. However, it is impossible to know whether they were omitted for reasons of their shared authorship or for some other reason. Although 18th-century editors had noticed stylistic inconsistencies in the play, in 1850 James Spedding presented the first detailed argument for shared authorship between Shakespeare and Fletcher (Foakes, xvii). He was the first to divide the scenes as listed above, and, although others have modified his divisions, they have generally held among those who see the authorship as shared. Spedding and many others following him based their arguments on internal inconsistencies of language and prosody. Among these inconsistencies, critics find features characteristic of Fletcher's writing. Many sections use feminine endings— or lines of iambic pentameter that end in an unstressed eleventh syllable (Foakes, xviii). Some scenes of extreme pathos use falling rhythms, or lines of poetry where the stress falls on the first syllable of a metrical foot, rather than the second, as is customary for iambic pentameter (Foakes, xviii). On top of these features choices in contractions and pronouns distinguish the two hands. In those sections believed to be Shakespeare's, "them" and "you" predominate, while the Fletcher ones use "'em" and "ye" (Foakes, xix).

Other critics have objected (sometimes passionately) to the argument that *Henry VIII* is a collaboration. Hugh M. Richmond not only thinks the play is solely Shakespeare's, he also believes it trumps his more highly respected "last" play *The Tempest* in an important way: "Rather than *The Tempest*, this play is truly Shakespeare's artistic testament, for it shows how far he is from retreating into artistic passivity" (12). Those who argue for Shakespeare's sole authorship have shown that no tangible stylistic distinction holds up under intense scrutiny, and that many of the features allegedly belonging to Fletcher are also characteristic of Shakespeare's late work. This breakdown has led some critics to the compromise position that the play is principally Shakespeare's work modified here and there by Fletcher's hand.

Still, in the realm of intangible distinctions, it is difficult to ignore stylistic and even character differences such as the ones that take place with Katherine in 2.4 and 3.1. The following speeches—both by Katherine and both on the subject of her marriage fidelity—can easily strike readers and audiences as profoundly different. The first of these comes from the scene where Katherine offers her passionate and stalwart refusal to subject herself to the panel of judges assembled by the King and Wolsey.

> Heaven witness
> I have been to you a true and humble wife,
> At all times to your will conformable,
> Ever in fear to kindle your dislike,
> Yea, subject to your countenance—glad or sorry
> As I saw it inclin'd. When was the hour
> I ever contradicted your desire
> Or made it not mine too? Or which of your friends
> Have I not strove to love, although I knew
> He were mine enemy? (2.4.20–29)

This next example occurs in Katherine's response to Wolsey and Cardinal Campeius when they ask to interview her in private.

> There's nothing I have done yet, o' my conscience,
> Deserves a corner. Would all other women
> Could speak this with as free a soul as I do!
> My lords, I care not (so much I am happy
> Above a number) if my actions
> Were tried by ev'ry tongue, ev'ry eye saw 'em,
> Envy and base opinion set against 'em,
> I know my life so even. (2.1.30–37)

The difference between style registers to the hearing. It is marked by distinction in cadence and structure, as well as by the use of contractions that differ radically from one scene to the next. The most reasonable set of conclusions is that the play has more than one author, that Shakespeare wrote a stylistically desultory play in which he capriciously shifts from one way of writing to another, or that other hands (transcribers or print-in-house compositors) intervened to the extent that the text was significantly less consistent than other plays in the Folio collection.

Not only is the style different between these scenes, but Katherine's character also seems to undergo changes. In 2.4, her stalwart refusal to participate in the trial of her marriage provides one of the most confident representations of women in any of Shakespeare's plays. She exercises resolute strength under the guise of womanly deference. In 3.1, though, she comes across as genuinely naïve of her pivotal importance as queen. As a matter of fact, she seems to have almost forgotten what happened in the scene before when she asks,

> What can be their business
> With me, a poor weak woman, fall'n from favor?
> I do not like their coming. Now I think on't,
> They should be good men, their affairs as righteous;
> But all hoods make not monks. (3.1.19–23)

Although it is possible that her demureness is merely rhetorical, she is alone (or practically so) at this point, and she has no need to feign ignorance as to why the cardinals have sought her out. In the end whether the play belongs to Shakespeare alone or to a pair of authors is a difficult and vexing question, but one that makes little difference in how we experience its content in reading or performance.

Sources

As with many other of Shakespeare's history plays, *Henry VIII* draws its materials principally from Raphael Holinshed's *Chronicles of England, Scotland, and Ireland* (1587 edition). A study of history plays from the 1590s shows that Shakespeare's goal in writing this genre was never simply to transmit historical fact. Although he rarely falsifies historical record, Shakespeare regularly exercises poetic license, selecting, arranging, and compressing historical events to achieve greater dramatic intensity and to emphasize themes.

In addition to these changes, Shakespeare even creates historical events to the extent that they help him flesh out character, plot, and theme. *Henry VIII*, however, makes quite different claims for historical veracity, in its title and its prologue, both of which promise a kind of truth. And in many places, *Henry VIII* follows Holinshed very closely, at times merely versifying his prose. Yet, despite this claim of authenticity, in practice Shakespeare adapts and alters history in his typical ways. Some of these alterations are minor. For example, at the opening of the play Shakespeare has Buckingham tell Norfolk "an untimely ague" prevented his participation in the Field of the Cloth of Gold, when in fact he was in attendance. By inventing Buckingham's absence, Shakespeare provides the opportunity for Norfolk's exposition on the events and for the two of them to criticize the crushing extravagance of the affair. Occasionally, Shakespeare's alterations are more substantive, such as when he changes participants in historical events to suit his larger dramatic needs. In Shakespeare's version, Wolsey's fall occurs in part because he accidentally submits to the King's request for certain "papers of state" an inventory of "the piles of wealth he has accumulated / To his own portion" (3.2.121, 107–108). In Holinshed's version, this episode actually involves the wealthy Bishop Thomas Ruthall, who sends his inventory not to the King but to Wolsey, who uses it to "bring the bishop into the King's disgrace" (Bullough, 453).

Henry VIII also compresses and inverts historical events to increase dramatic effect. Kittredge's introduction lists the inversions and compressions in summary fashion:

> [Buckingham was] arrested in April 1521, and convicted on May 13, 1521; whereas the exaction of "the sixth part of every man's substance" was not decreed until 1525. Wolsey died in 1530; Elizabeth was born in 1533; Queen Katherine died in 1536. In the play, Queen Katherine's death precedes Elizabeth's birth, and Wolsey's death is told to the queen just before her own takes place. The accusation of Cranmer before the council (5.3) was not until after 1540 (probably in 1544). In the play, however, it precedes the christening of Elizabeth (1533).

Most of what we might call deviations actually embellish and develop character in a way that we have come to expect a work of dramatic fiction to operate. Shakespeare's Queen Katherine more trenchantly defies Cardinal Wolsey and is more demure in her self-effacement than Holinshed's. The chronicle is for the most part silent on Anne's personality, while Shakespeare makes her decidedly modest and kind to the queen's plight.

While the majority of the play's events come from Holinshed's *Chronicles,* Shakespeare mines other sources as well. Although it is not a direct source of material per se, Samuel Rowley's history play *When You See Me, You Know Me* (published in 1605 and reprinted in 1613) may have been highly influential on *Henry VIII.* Shakespeare does not so much borrow material or events in the way he does from Holinshed's *Chronicles* as much as write a play that responds to the structure and tenor of Rowley's work. The play purports to be a "famous chronicle historie of king Henry the eight," and, like Shakespeare's play, it culminates in the birth of an heir—in this case, Prince Edward, who later becomes King Edward VI (1548–1553). The portrait of Henry here is notably gruff and surly, and his frequent use of the exclamation "Ha!" may have influenced Shakespeare's King Henry's use of the same. In contrast with the prologue's claim in *Henry VIII* to show "things / The bear a weighty and a serious brow" (1–2), *When You See Me, You Know Me* presents a romping comedy featuring the frolics of Henry's court jester Will Sommers and a clown called Patch. When Shakespeare's prologue cautions those who wish "to hear a merry, bawdy play, / A noise of targets, or to see a fellow / In a long motley coat" (14–16), the speaker may allude to Rowley's play, although fools and battles were common in other plays. If Rowley's work was a negative inspiration for Shakespeare, this fact provides a possible explanation for Wotton's reported title *All Is True*: instead of making a general truth claim, Shakespeare's play might be making a pointed one by proposing to correct the misrepresentations of history in Rowley's play.

Shakespeare's most significant source besides Holinshed is John Foxe's *Acts and Monuments of Martyrs* (1583). More commonly known as *Foxe's Book of Martyrs,* this work, enormously popular in Shakespeare's day, recounted the lives and deaths of notable figures who defended emerging Protestantism and died doing so. This source provides accounts of Cranmer's narrow escape from trial by the malicious council and of the King's triumph over them, a feat that provides the culminating tension of act 5. Shakespeare's departure from Holinshed's to Foxe's work reinforces the new direction the play is taking in act 5, away from chronicle and toward compliment to Henry and to Protestantism. And, by the end of the play, Shakespeare has left history, whether disinterested or biased, altogether. The episode of Elizabeth's christening and Cranmer's political prophecy is obviously a fiction invented to suit the dramatic ends of the play.

The Question of Purpose

What those ends are precisely is not evident. One theory of the play holds that *Henry VIII* is an occasional piece—that is, one written to celebrate an occasion. In this case, the event is the marriage of King James I's daughter Elizabeth in February 1613 to Prince Frederick, Elector Palatine of Germany. The union is significant in large part because Germany was the most powerful Protestant nation on the continent, the birthplace of Martin Luther, whose name Wolsey evokes in the insulting epithet he attaches to Anne—"a spleeny Lutheran." The joining of the English princess with the future German ruler would certainly have been looked on as strengthening English Protestantism both from within the realm and from the outside, where it still contended with the threat of invasion by Spain. Thomas Heywood's epithalamium (or marriage poem) *A Marriage Triumph* honoring Frederick and Elizabeth expressly makes this point: "Behold that Prince, the Empire's prime Elector / Of the religious Protestant's protector" (qtd. in Foakes, xxx).

This reading certainly helps make sense of another significant element of the play, the sequence of pageants and royal displays that permeate it. This heightened visual component firmly aligns the play with the masque tradition. Masques are similar to plays but are better considered extravagant artistic spectacles of poetry, dialogue, costume, scenery, and movement. The main reason for their single-occasion existence is to pay compliment to a monarch or other noble figure. In *Henry VIII*, Wolsey's feast actually features a masque of Shepherds in which the King himself takes part. This masque appears at first to reverse the tradition because the King seems to be paying compliment to his subject, the cardinal. However, the cardinal, extemporaneously perhaps, rights the inversion when he chooses the King from among the disguised shepherds and gives up his place under the canopy of state to its rightful owner. *Henry VIII*, therefore, borrows heavily from the masque tradition to pay compliment to the princess as champion, protector, and future hope of English Protestant ascendancy. The main problem with this theory is that among the significant catalogue of festivities surrounding this royal nuptial no record exists for *Henry VIII*'s performance, although records for six other plays performed by Shakespeare's company do (Foakes, xxx). The lack of historical record does not necessarily disqualify the play as a paean to Frederick and Elizabeth. Shakespeare could have easily capitalized on the fervor surrounding the wedding to create a play of this nature, one that outlived the event that inspired it and transcended the one-off function of most masques. Even so, the more significant problem with this explanation is that while the element of compliment to Henry, to the former Queen Elizabeth, and to King James is certainly part of the play, *Henry VIII* is a far more subtle and complex play than this reading as mere compliment suggests.

Few plays of Shakespeare announce their theme and purpose as directly as *Henry VIII*. The prologue promises the audience an accurate, serious, true rendition of the history of Henry VIII, assuring those who "give / Their money out of hope they may believe" of the ability to "find truth too" (7–9). The "truth" he promises is a sad one that will please the wise—"the first and happiest hearers of the town" (24)—and elicit pity at the spectacle—"Such noble scenes that draw to the eye to flow, / We now present" (4–5). Truth is a preoccupation in the play, in word and in deed. *Henry VIII*'s twenty-one instances of the word are the most of any Shakespeare play, outnumbering the second most by five and being far above most other plays. Additionally, a number of key scenes in the play pivot on the issue and question of what is truth. Is Wolsey or Buckingham telling the truth about his loyalty to the King? Is Henry's marriage to Queen Katherine legitimate? Can Katherine get an honest trial as a "stranger" in England? Is Archbishop's Cranmer's religion a true one?

As is clear from this list, the definition of "truth" in the play divides equally between "authenticity of a claim" and "loyalty such as that belonging to a subject or a spouse." In the early part of the play, when Katherine complains to her husband of discontent among subjects under Wolsey's heavy taxations, she distinguishes the loyalty of the agitators by saying they are of "true condition," and not inborn malcontents or rebels. At many points in the play, the ideas of truth as "verity" and "loyalty" converge. The veracity of the surveyor's account of Buckingham will determine whether or not Buckingham himself is faithful (or true) to the king. In her pretrial negotiations, the closest to a defense that Katherine offers to the question of whether her marriage to the King is legitimate (and therefore true) is her own truth or loyalty as his wife: "Heaven witness / I have been a true and humble wife / At all times to your will conformable" (2.4.20–22). To Katherine's refusal of him as a valid judge by accusing him of being "not a friend to truth," Wolsey's response is to claim damage to his own truth, and he appeals to the King as able to wound (or punish) his "falsehood" as much as she has done his truth. At this point, so enmeshed are its meanings, it is no longer clear whether Wolsey's "truth" refers to his honesty or his loyalty.

Athwart the prologue's contention, *Henry VIII* does not give viewers an uncomplicated portrayal of truth. From the opening the play presents scenes that bring into question the truth of the history being reported. The first scene is an instance of this tension between representation and truth. It begins with what might itself be called a representation of history in which the Duke of Norfolk recounts for the absent Buckingham the lavish ceremonies at the Field of the Cloth of Gold. These, Norfolk claims, provided "the view of earthly glory" (1.1.14) and contained men who performed deeds "beyond thought's compass" (1.1.36). Buckingham's reply is understandably skeptical: "O, you go far!" (1.1.38). The significance of the opening dialogue in terms of the prologue's claim bears emphasis. The play opens with a representation of history, and the account's veracity is immediately brought into question. And it turns out that Norfolk is going too far, but not in the flattering form of exaggeration that Buckingham contends. Norfolk's description prefaces his complaint against the extravagance of the spectacle, one that he names a "vanity" that has impoverished the future offspring of the nobility who funded it. Additionally, the entire purpose of ceremonies of the Field of the Cloth of Gold—that is, the peace between England and France—endures no longer than the ceremonies themselves. In the end, the truth reveals history itself merely to be show. The prologue's pledge to yield truth runs into another problem in the play because it assumes that truth is objective and discoverable. But the play seems to resist such facile notions of truth. In the culminating event of the play, both Cranmer and his opponent, the Archbishop Gardiner, who charges Cranmer with sectarianism, appeal to the truth as the foundation of their claims. In matters of religious doctrine, both appeal equally to truth as their guide. In response to the King's warning of the factions plotting against him, Cranmer says, "The good I stand on is my truth and honesty" (5.1.122). His accuser, Archbishop Gardiner, calls Cranmer's truth "a painted gloss" of "words and weakness" (5.3.71,72). For Gardiner, Cranmer's truth is like the Field of the Cloth of Gold to Norfolk—a mere dazzling show. However, the opposite is also the case; the truth often needs to be ferried away and hidden. As the two gentlemen discuss rumors of the King and Anne, one reminds the other that their speech is indiscreet: "We are too open here to argue this. / Let's think in private more" (2.1.168–169). If the gentlemen's caution is any indication, the play gestures toward the possibility of truth without offering it in its fully realized form.

In fact, the pathos of the play exists in the extent to which truth is either beyond the control of any one character or it proves futile to that character's situation. Buckingham and Katherine both understand quite well that the truth of their situation has little bearing on their outcomes. Even before he is confronted with news of his surveyor's perfidious testimony (whether the surveyor is also perjurious is not made clear), Buckingham observes of his arrest, "It will help me nothing / To plead mine innocence, for that dye is on me / Which makes my whit'st part black" (1.1.207–209). And Katherine knows her context as a "stranger" in England means that her appeals to truth will fall on unfriendly ears. She asks the cardinals in her private interview, "Can you think, lords, / That any Englishman dare give me counsel?" (3.1.82–83). Henry's maturation at the end of the play centers on just such a discovery of the inefficacy of truth. In a rather tortured sentence, he tells the worried but stalwart Cranmer, "and not ever / The justice and the truth o' th' question carries / The due o' th' verdict with it" (5.1.129–131), meaning that the truth of an issue before a jury does not always receive the verdict it deserves (a line the irony of which is lost on Henry). As monarch, Henry is the one person who can help bring truth and verdict together, and, as his encounter with Gardiner near the end shows, even he must go to extraordinary lengths of surveillance to achieve such a union.

If truth is fluid rather than stable, multiple rather than singular, subjective rather than essential, this condition may serve the play's other goal of bringing forth tears more effectively than a one-dimensional truth might. For, as is characteristic of his plays, Shakespeare does not present any figure in the play whose behavior, situation, or end forbids and repels sympathy. Largely, what produces sympathy for Buckingham, Katherine, to a certain extent Anne, and, yes, even Wolsey is that they are in one way or another the victims of a truth that is beyond their control. With the first two, the tragedy is that the truth is subject to the manipulation of Wolsey or (per-haps) the King. With Wolsey, this lack of control comes about when truth emerges despite his best effort to conceal it. His downfall occurs when the inventory of his vast estate and letters that contravene Henry's interest in divorcing Anne both, by work of some "cross devil," fall into the King's possession (3.2.214).

The character of the King presents probably the greatest challenge in the play. Tied as Shakespeare was to the historical accounts of Henry as well as to the politi-cal necessity of not presenting a revered King and the father of the beloved late Queen Elizabeth in an unflattering light, Shakespeare's task of representing Henry's issues is quite delicate, and may in part be responsible for the sense that the play belongs more to Wolsey, Katherine, and Cranmer than it does to the King. The specific question Shakespeare faces is how he can dramatize the King's predicament without having him appear complicit, negligent, or naïve. Such is the danger in the opening scene when on discovering Wolsey's having levied one-sixth of the posses-sions to fund his proposed wars in France, the King demands, "Taxation? / Wherein? And what taxation?" (1.2.37–38). Plus, under the King's unwary rule, Wolsey car-ries out his machinations against Buckingham and promotes himself over the other nobility. Additionally, the King's progress from controlled to controlling over the course of the play, implies that he was to a certain extent complacent and naïve.

Henry VIII applies the same delicacy to the king's divorce from Katherine. Her arraignment is surprisingly notable because Henry, and not Katherine, is the one giving fifty-five lines of extemporaneous testimony on how his "conscience first received a tenderness, / Scruple, and prick" (2.4.167–168) in the matter of his mar-riage. The play, however, does not allow Henry's passionate defense to be the only words on issue. Before the King utters his account, Lord Chamberlain has voiced it and Lord Suffolk has denied it:

> *Cham.*   It seems the marriage with his brother's wife
> Has crept too near his conscience.
>
> *Suf.*   No, his conscience
> Has crept too near another lady. (2.2.12–14)

The response of the characters, however, is not to investigate the truth of the mat-ter, but to deflect it onto Wolsey. "This is the Cardinal's doing," Norfolk says, add-ing the epithet, "the King-Cardinal" (2.2.15).

The play extends a similar ambiguity to Anne. Like Henry's speech on his scru-ple, her dialogue is a model of properness. She is kind and generous toward Kath-erine's ordeal and abnegating of her own potential to be queen. She tells her old servant gentlewoman, "By my troth and maidenhead, I would not be a queen" (2.3.23–24). The old lady provides a foil to Anne's assumed modesty: "Beshrew me, I would, / And venture maidenhead for't! And so would you / For all this spice of hypocrisy" (2.3.24–26). As with the king's motive in divorce, the truth of Anne's ambition is never disclosed.

Even Wolsey's situation turns out not to be beyond pity. At the trough of his downfall, Lord Chamberlain advises the gloating Surrey, "Press not a falling man too far" (3.2.333). After his death, Katherine summarizes quite accurately the play's presentation of Wolsey as "a man / Of an unbounded stomach, ever ranking / Himself with princes" (4.2.33–35). Her usher Griffith turns her accusation of princely ambition into a kind of royal largesse, stating that though he was "unsatisfied in getting / (Which was a sin), yet in bestowing, madam, / He was most princely" (4.2.54–56). Shakespeare places the endorsement for Griffith's moderate appraisal in the mouth of the woman Wolsey most wounded, who appeals to the honesty and truth of his judgment:

> After my death I wish no other herald,
> No other speaker of my living actions
> To keep mine honor from corruption,
> But such an honest chronicler as Griffith.
> Whom I most hated living, thou hast made me,
> With thy religious truth and modesty,
> Now, in his ashes, honor. Peace be with him! (4.2.69–75)

These portraits make it clear that an ambiguous, elusive, and sophisticated truth is perhaps at the heart of human pathos. Henry may be all the more sympathetic because he is both conflicted morally and deeply lustful. Anne may be concerned for the welfare of her queen and cryptically ambitious as well. And Wolsey's ambition might have beneficial qualities that forbid easy condemnation of it.

Production History and Reception

Productions of *Henry VIII* have since the beginning and by design been elaborate. As the stage directions make clear, among Shakespeare's works, the play has no rivals. Beyond all other Shakespeare plays, *Henry VIII* is uniquely concerned with historical realism, with presenting "the very persons" of Tudor England "as they were living," the prologue suggests.

Given the relative obscurity of *Henry VIII* among casual readers today, it is surprisingly by one measure that the play might be called Shakespeare's most popular. It is the only play for which there exists a performance history without large gaps stretching all the way back to the Restoration of 1660—when Charles II reopened theaters after an eighteen-year closure due to war and policy, and when theater history became easier to track—to present day. Among defenders, this performance continuity is proffered as evidence for the play's quality. Yet, regardless of how "good" *Henry VIII* happens to be, it proved unusually equipped to withstand the same vagaries of 17th- and 18th-century theatrical tastes that caused theater companies to ignore certain plays or rewrite them to suit public sensibilities (Nahum Tate's 18th-century rewrite of *King Lear* with a happy ending is the most notorious of these adaptations).

During the Restoration, *Henry VIII* was very popular. Despite his displeasure at the play's "patches," Samuel Pepys reported that he went to the play because it was "cried up" (Pepys' Diary, January 1, 1663/1664). For the record, Pepys did attend the play a second time in 1668 and records that he was "mightily pleased better than [he] expected." According to John Downs, Sir William Davenant's December 1663 production of the play, starring Thomas Betterington as Henry, ran for "15 days together with general applause" (Downs, 24). Hugh Richmond and others have suggested that *Henry VIII*'s historical realism might have been behind its success during the Restoration. This realism worked very well with the turn to stage development and scene design. In the age of theater preceding it, plays often featured elaborate costumes, but the scenery they used was minimal, performing as they did on the almost bare stage. The Restoration, however, began offering more elaborate set designs. Richmond claims that directors such as Sir William Davenant extended "to the dressing of the whole stage what Shakespeare had begun with the uniquely elaborate, historically accurate stage directions for the pageantry and costuming of *Henry VIII*" (30).

In the 18th century, the play's popularity continued while its production evolved. According to the tabulations of George Winchester Stone, Jr., the play was performed at least 154 times, a figure that is comparable to staples such as *Macbeth* and *1 Henry IV* (181). In that century, production turned away from presenting Henry as the central focus and toward making Queen Katherine appear a moral casualty of the men in the play. This new focus owed very much to the powerful depiction of Katherine's character by the famous actress Sarah Siddons. According to Richmond, this shift to the "moral pre-eminence of Katherine's role . . . proved central to the play's recovery as serious drama" (39). Additionally, Richmond holds, her performance "permanently altered modern perceptions of the theatrical balance in the play" (46). No longer was King Henry the presumed center of sympathy, but emotion was distributed equally between him and his wife.

Nineteenth-century theater intensified the focus on historical realism that existed since the play's inception. Charles Kean's 1855 production moved beyond recreating scenery that was historically accurate in general and toward reproducing and imitating actual historical artifacts and sites. Using drawings contemporary to the play's setting, Kean's company recreated both the old palace yard and the council chambers of Westminster, a chimney-piece designed by Hans Holbein, and tapestries for the queen's chamber. Kean went so far as to make a moving panorama of London as it existed during Henry VIII's reign (Richmond, 36).

Twentieth-century productions have gone even further to outdo and sometimes subvert the fascination earlier representations had with authentic setting. Take, for example, Herbert Beerbohm Tree's 1911 Stratford-upon-Avon production. In terms of costumes, scenery, and personnel, it may be the most sumptuous version of a Shakespeare play ever produced (McMullan, 33). In all, 172 actors trod luxurious carpets surrounded by velvet and gold tapestries and overhung with opulent fan vaulting (at least in Wolsey's masque at York Palace). At 254 performances over eight months, its theater run was the longest to date of any Shakespeare play in England (McMullan, 36–37).

Despite this auspicious beginning, *Henry VIII*'s popularity decreased over the 20th century, and modern readers enter Shakespeare in this environment. In a century where no artistic pieties went unchallenged, it is not surprising that *Henry VIII*'s obsession with authenticity fell under the axe. As a reminder of all theater's ultimate fictional nature, Thomas Gray's 1931 production often used cardboard cutouts in place of humans, including one for the infant Elizabeth (McMullan, 39). And Tyrone Guthrie's production at Stratford, Ontario, was deliberately whimsical and irreverent. While these productions were challenging tradition in one way, they were preserving it in another by restoring to the stage scenes that in earlier eras were often left out.

Changing tastes have not meant that *Henry VIII* is not performed regularly. All major Shakespeare companies include it in their rotations (in 2009 two major companies performed it, a rarity for any play), and the play continues to provide challenges and opportunities for directors.

Henry VIII on Film

In a basic way it is not surprising that no major film of *Henry VIII* has been produced. Although no Shakespeare play may properly be called obscure, for the general populace today, *Henry VIII* ranks with *Timon of Athens*, *Pericles*, and *King John* as one of his least well-known plays. When we think of Shakespearean film, we think of marquis-worthy blockbusters all in capital letters: *HAMLET, ROMEO AND JULIET, HENRY V*, and *MACBETH*. Shakespearean film since the 1990s has given us notable exceptions: Julie Taymor's *Titus* (1999), Kenneth Branagh's *Love's Labours Lost* (2000) and Ralph Fiennes *Coriolanus* (2012), among the most little-known of Shakespeare's tragedies (but one well worthy of filmic treatment).

Surprisingly, *Henry VIII* was one of the first Shakespeare plays to be recorded on film. In 1911, Beerbohm Tree and noted entrepreneur W. G. Barker filmed five scenes from his elaborate stage production of the play. Technological limits meant that these scenes were recorded without sound (Richmond, 70). Still, this work had an immediate impact on film, and over the next few months F. R. Benson began recording several Stratford-upon-Avon stage productions (Richmond, 70). Although (as required by contract) all copies of this film were destroyed six weeks after its production, historians of British film recognize both the film's significance as the first major production in that country and its quality as being at the time "one of the finest picture plays ever produced" (Robert Ball, qtd. in Richmond, 71).

The only feature-length production of *Henry VIII* is Kevin Billington's 1978 small-screen television version that was made as part of the BBC's ambitious filming of the complete plays of Shakespeare. In terms of film technique, Billington's film is among the finest of the first season and the series as a whole. Although he does not pursue the visual possibilities of epic-scale scenery, he is able to use his medium to convey grandeur in a different way and to capture historical authenticity beyond that which the stage had previously attempted. Both of these he achieves by locating the film at Leeds Castle, which, although not a site in the play, was a favorite haunt of King Henry. Scenes shot within the castle and on its grounds give the film a grandeur of a different kind than that of extravagant stage productions. The film allows for characters to be framed in large spaces of dignity rather than small gilded ones.

Billington, however, does not use space only or primarily to convey grandeur. For Billington space is thematic, and he uses it to tease out issues of public and private that are latent in the play's text, employing techniques that film offers and that theater does not. In the play, from a certain perspective, Henry's scruples and concerns bring the issues of his most private life (his marriage to his wife and his potency in securing a male heir) out in the open. In the play, Henry's anxiety over public exposure is evident when he silences the rumors of his concerns of his marriage. Close-up shots of characters allow lines to be whispered or spoken *sotto voce* to suggest secrecy and privacy. When the unnamed gentlemen gossip at the procession following Anne's (Barbara Kellerman) coronation, extreme close-ups give a leering and voyeuristic effect to their dialogue: "Our King has all the Indies in his arms, / And more, and richer, when he strains that lady. / I cannot blame his conscience" (4.1.45–47).

In other scenes, Billington even uses this close-up technique to transfer dialogue from public to private. Early in the play, after the queen (Claire Bloom) has confronted the King with complaint about Wolsey's heavy taxation, the King (John Stride) counsels Cardinal Wolsey (Timothy West) privately rather castigating him publicly, even though they have not left the larger public space. The King quietly tells Wolsey, "Things done well / And with a care exempt themselves from fear" (1.2.88–89), after he has descended from his place of state and is standing apart with Wolsey, out of the earshot of others.

Billington also uses space to emphasize the more noticeable surface-level issues of authority and power struggle in the play. Instances of these struggles are frequent in the film. A representative one occurs in the scene with the queen. Wolsey here is supposedly the one who is on the defense and in danger of incurring the wrath of the King because his taxation has stirred rebellion. In the play's text, Wolsey defends himself by deferring power and claiming, "I know but of a single part in aught / Pertains to th' state, and front but in that file / Where others tell steps with me" (1.2.41–43). Billington's use of camera positioning tells a story of power much different from this deferential claim. The camera trains closely on Wolsey's face and demotes the King to the background of the frame. This positioning leaves little doubt of who is really in control at this point.

The climax of the film version, in which Henry asserts his dominance over his council, makes a similar use of space to suggest positions of power. Instead of having Henry physically rise above the council in surveillance as he does in the play, the film presents his council seated at a long rectangular table where they revile Cranmer for his alleged heresy. Henry, who has supposedly been eavesdropping through the door, enters and confronts the seated council. This position is opposite the play's in which the King enters and "takes his seat." As the only one standing, Henry proceeds to walk around the table and upbraid Archbishop Gardiner and the others for their indecorous treatment of Cranmer: "I had thought I had had men of some understanding / And wisdom of my Council; but I find none" (5.2.135–136). By single-handedly surrounding his men as he speaks, Henry literally and figuratively circumscribes them and reins them back into his fold.

Billington's technique works to heighten the intrigue and intensity of this play and to make the whole more powerful than we might have at first imaged possible. And his highly effective production was low-budget and small-screen. It is fun to imagine the possibilities of a film with higher funding and a big-screen medium some three and a half decades removed from his work. For an enterprising director of Shakespearean film there may never be a better time. As he did in Shakespeare's day, the figure of Henry VIII draws general interest for his violent treatment of his wife and subjects and his larger-than-life personality. As one reviewer of a modern play on this subject puts it, "Henry VIII is probably the only figure, apart from Jesus Christ, of whom even the most truanting schoolchild will have heard" (Lawson). However, the tide is at the full for other reasons. Henry's presence in high and pop cultures is as active as it has been in quite some time. In 2007–2010, Showtime presented *The Tudors*, a popular, highly eroticized, and lovably tawdry fictional version of Henry VIII's story.

In the print medium, Hilary Mantel's two novels on Henry VIII, *Wolf Hall* (2009) and *Bring Up the Bodies* (2012), both won the Man Booker prize, the U.K.'s highest honor for fiction. Mike Poulton has successfully translated both of these works to the stage in productions by the Royal Shakespeare Company, first at Stratford-upon-Avon, then at Aldwych Theatre in London's West End (2014), and most recently on Broadway (2015). The plays, like the novel, alter traditional character representations. Wolsey is more sympathetic—the true servant of the king he claims to be—as much victim as perpetrator, and Cromwell's morality alters as he struggles to succeed in Henry's court, first to keep his head and, finally, to avenge Wolsey's downfall, the focal point of both plays. The novels and the plays are enormously popular. As noted in his review in *The Guardian*, Mark Lawson reports that the two plays broke records for a nonmusical production in the West End.

It would be easy to assume that the intrigue and concerns of Shakespeare are of a different order than the titillating images of *The Tudors* and the greater violence of Poulton's plays. However, the power of Shakespeare's play has been ignored too long. Even with a sizzling screen production, it is unlikely that *Henry VIII* will ever join the ranks of Shakespeare's household names. But that *Henry VIII* is not more part of the conversation is an omission that deprives viewers of true delights.

Jane Wells

The Famous History of the Life of King Henry the Eighth

Dramatis Personæ.

King Henry the Eighth.
Cardinal Wolsey.
Cardinal Campeius.
Capucius, Ambassador from the Emperor Charles V.
Cranmer, Archbishop of Canterbury.
Duke of Norfolk.
Duke of Buckingham.
Duke of Suffolk.
Earl of Surrey.
Lord Chamberlain.
Lord Chancellor.
Gardiner, King's Secretary, afterwards Bishop of Winchester.
Bishop of Lincoln.
Lord Abergavenny.
Lord Sandys (also styled *Sir William Sandys*).
Sir Henry Guildford.
Sir Thomas Lovell.
Sir Anthony Denny.
Sir Nicholas Vaux.
Cromwell, servant to *Wolsey.*
Secretaries to *Wolsey.*
Griffith, Gentleman Usher to *Queen Katherine.*
Three Gentlemen.
Doctor Butts, Physician to the *King.*
Garter King-at-Arms.
Surveyor to the *Duke of Buckingham.*
Brandon, and a Sergeant-at-Arms.
Doorkeeper of the Council Chamber.
Porter, and his Man.
Page to *Gardiner.*
A Crier.

Queen Katherine, wife to *King Henry,* afterwards divorced.
Anne Bullen, her Maid of Honor, afterwards Queen.
An Old Lady, friend to *Anne Bullen.*
Patience, woman to *Queen Katherine.*

Spirits.

Several Bishops, Lords, and Ladies in the Dumb Shows; Women attending upon
   the Queen; Scribes, Officers, Guards, and other Attendants.

SCENE. *London; Westminster; Kimbolton.*

THE PROLOGUE†

I come no more to make you laugh. Things now
That bear a weighty and a serious brow,
Sad, high, and working, full of state and woe,
Such noble scenes as draw the eye to flow,
We now present. Those that can pity, here   5
May (if they think it well) let fall a tear:
The subject will deserve it. Such as give
Their money out of hope they may believe,
May here find truth too. Those that come to see
Only a show or two and so agree   10
The play may pass—if they be still and willing,
I'll undertake may see away their shilling
Richly in two short hours. Only they
That come to hear a merry bawdy play,
A noise of targets, or to see a fellow   15
In a long motley coat guarded with yellow,
Will be deceiv'd. For, gentle hearers, know,
To rank our chosen truth with such a show
As fool and fight is, beside forfeiting
Our own brains and the opinion that we bring   20
To make that only true we now intend,
Will leave us never an understanding friend.
Therefore, for goodness sake, and as you are known
The first and happiest hearers of the town,
Be sad, as we would make ye. Think ye see   25
The very persons of our noble story
As they were living. Think you see them great,
And follow'd with the general throng, and sweat

PROLOGUE
2. **bear . . . brow**: have a serious face or countenance. 3. **Sad, high, and working**: serious, lofty, and emotionally stirring. **state**: dignified stateliness. 4. **draw**: cause to flow as in "draw water." 9. **truth**: alludes to the play's original title, *All Is True*. 11. **pass**: succeed or suffice. **still and willing**: focused and so inclined. 12. **see away**: spend. **shilling**: twelve pence (the minimum price of admission to the Globe was one pence; twelve pence could purchase more expensive seats). 15. **targets**: small shields. 16. **long motley coat**: i.e., a fool's garment. **guarded**: trimmed. 17. **deceiv'd**: let down. 18. **rank**: classify or associate. 20–21. **opinion . . . intend**: self-respect (opinion) based on our conviction only to present the truth. 22. **understanding friend**: comprehending audience (with a possible pun on the groundlings, who literally stood under or lower than the stage). 24. **first and happiest hearers**: the best and most successful audience. 25. **sad**: serious. 26. **very**: true or actual. 27. **great**: important.

---

†   In Kevin Billington's 1978 film production, the prologue speaks as a voiceover that frames the play.

Of thousand friends. Then, in a moment, see
How soon this mightiness meets misery.   30
And if you can be merry then, I'll say
A man may weep upon his wedding day.

ACT I

SCENE I. [*London. An antechamber in the Palace.*]

*Enter the Duke of Norfolk at one door;
at the other, the Duke of Buckingham
and the Lord Abergavenny.*

BUCK.   Good morrow and well met. How have ye done
Since last we saw in France?

NOR.   I thank your Grace:
Healthful, and ever since a fresh admirer
Of what I saw there.

BUCK.   An untimely ague
Stay'd me a prisoner in my chamber when   5
Those suns of glory, those two lights of men,
Met in the vale of Andren.

NOR.   'Twixt Guynes and Arde.
I was then present, saw them salute on horseback;
Beheld them when they lighted, how they clung
In their embracement, as they grew together;   10
Which had they, what four thron'd ones could have weigh'd
Such a compound one?

BUCK.   All the whole time
I was my chamber's prisoner.

NOR.   Then you lost
The view of earthly glory. Men might say,
Till this time pomp was single, but now married   15

ACT I, SCENE I
2. **saw**: met. 3. **fresh**: not yet jaded. 4. **ague**: fever. 5. **Stay'd**: kept. 5–7. **when . . . Andren**: Norwich refers to the famous encounter between Henry VIII and King Francis I of France at the Field of the Cloth of Gold near Calais at the Vale of Ardres. 7. **Arde**: Ardres. 9. **lighted**: dismounted from their horses for hand-to-hand battle. 10. **as**: as if. 11. **thron'd ones**: kings. **weigh'd**: equaled in greatness or literal weight. 12. **compound**: i.e., of the two kings.

To one above itself. Each following day
Became the next day's master, till the last
Made former wonders its. Today the French,
All clinquant, all in gold, like heathen gods,
Shone down the English; and to-morrow they   20
Made Britain India—every man that stood
Show'd like a mine. Their dwarfish pages were
As cherubins, all gilt. The madams too,
Not us'd to toil, did almost sweat to bear
The pride upon them, that their very labor   25
Was to them as a painting. Now this masque
Was cried incomparable; and th' ensuing night
Made it a fool and beggar. The two kings,
Equal in lustre, were now best, now worst,
As presence did present them—him in eye   30
Still him in praise; and being present both,
'Twas said they saw but one, and no discerner
Durst wag his tongue in censure. When these suns
(For so they phrase 'em) by their heralds challeng'd
The noble spirits to arms, they did perform   35
Beyond thought's compass, that former fabulous story,
Being now seen possible enough, got credit,
That Bevis was believ'd.

BUCK.   O, you go far!

NOR.   As I belong to worship and affect
In honor honesty, the tract of ev'ry thing   40
Would by a good discourser lose some life
Which action's self was tongue to. All was royal.
To the disposing of it naught rebell'd;

16–18. **Each . . . its**: Every day was filled with greater pomp than the one before until the last, which possessed all the wonders of the previous days. 19. **clinquant**: glittering. 21. **India**: appear as India, fabled for its mines of gold. 22. **Show'd**: appeared. 23 **cherubins, all gilt**: cherubim in churches were sometimes covered in gold. **madams**: noble women. 25. **pride**: ostentatious clothing. 25–26. **labor . . . painting**: the exertion serves the same role as cosmetics. 26. **masque**: a formal-scripted pageant performed for nobility and often by it. 27. **cried**: acclaimed. 27–28. **th' ensuing . . . it**: the next night's masque (in comparison). 30. **As presence . . . them**: depending on which one was visible at the time. 30–31. **him in eye . . . praise**: The king in view continued to receive praise as long as he remained there. 32. **discerner**: observer. 33. **censure**: judgment (of one king over the other). 33–35. **When . . . arms**: The crowning event of the ceremony was a joust between Henry and Francis. 36. **thought's compass**: the limits of the imagination. 36–37. **that . . . credit**: That former story (*Bevis of Hampton*, a 14th-century romance) that seemed mere fable before it became credible (based on the feats of the two kings). 38. **go far**: exaggerate. 39. **belong to**: deserve. 39–40. **affect . . . honesty**: purport myself to be honest. 40–42. **the tract . . . to**: The telling of these events even by a good storyteller would (contrary to Buckingham's implication) actually pale in comparison to what the events themselves would have told.

Order gave each thing view. The office did
Distinctly his full function.

BUCK.   Who did guide—   45
I mean, who set the body and the limbs
Of this great sport together, as you guess?

NOR.   One, certes, that promises no element
In such a business.

BUCK.   I pray you, who, my lord?

NOR.   All this was ord'red by the good discretion   50
Of the right reverend Cardinal of York.

BUCK.   The devil speed him! No man's pie is freed
From his ambitious finger. What had he
To do in these fierce vanities? I wonder
That such a keech can with his very bulk   55
Take up the rays o' th' beneficial sun
And keep it from the earth.

NOR.   Surely, sir,
There's in him stuff that puts him to these ends;
For, being not propp'd by ancestry, whose grace
Chalks successors their way, nor call'd upon   60
For high feats done to th' crown, neither allied
To eminent assistants, but spiderlike
Out of his self-drawing web, 'a gives us note
The force of his own merit makes his way—
A gift that heaven gives for him, which buys   65
A place next to the King.

ABER.   I cannot tell
What heaven hath given him. Let some graver eye
Pierce into that; but I can see his pride
Peep through each part of him. Whence has he that?
If not from hell, the devil is a niggard,   70
Or has given all before and he begins

43. To . . . rebell'd: Nothing interfered with the proper execution of the day's events. 44–45. The office . . . function: Each of the officials performed his job competently. 46–47. set the body and the limbs / Of: i.e., orchestrated. 48. certes: assuredly. 48–49. promises no element / In: does not belong in. 51. Cardinal of York: Cardinal Wolsey. 52. The devil speed him!: a curse—may the devil make him prosper. pie: worldly allotment. 55. keech: roll of animal fat. 55–57. can . . . earth: The implication is that Wolsey does not deserve his honor and interferes with Henry's ["th' beneficial sun"] proper role. 58. puts . . . ends: spurs him to put on these shows. 60. Chalks successors: shows descendants. 61. to: for. 63. self-drawing: i.e., a web he has drawn himself. a . . . note: to hear him tell it. 69. Whence: from where. 70. niggard: miser. 71. he: Wolsey.

A new hell in himself.

BUCK.   Why the devil,
Upon this French going out, took he upon him
(Without the privity o' th' King) t' appoint
Who should attend on him? He makes up the file   75
Of all the gentry; for the most part such
To whom as great a charge as little honour
He meant to lay upon; and his own letter,
The Honorable Board of Council out,
Must fetch him in the papers.

ABER.   I do know   80
Kinsmen of mine, three at the least, that have
By this so sicken'd their estates that never
They shall abound as formerly.

BUCK.   O, many
Have broke their backs with laying manors on 'em
For this great journey. What did this vanity   85
But minister communication of
A most poor issue?

NOR.   Grievingly I think
The peace between the French and us not values
The cost that did conclude it.

BUCK.   Every man,
After the hideous storm that follow'd, was   90
A thing inspir'd, and, not consulting, broke
Into a general prophecy—that this tempest,
Dashing the garment of this peace, aboded
The sudden breach on't.

NOR.   Which is budded out;
For France hath flaw'd the league and hath attach'd   95
Our merchants' goods at Bordeaux.

---

73. **going out**: excursion. 74. **the privity . . . King**: having informed the king. 75. **file**: list. 76–78. **for . . . upon**: To most of the gentlemen Wolsey charged a fee for participating in the event proportional to the lack of honor he gave them in his list. 78–80. **and . . . papers**: And without the consent of the Honorable Board of Council, Wolsey's own letter compels compliance from the nobles he lists. 82. **sicken'd**: diminished. 84. **broke . . . manors**: proverbial for impoverishment (many of the nobles sold or mortgaged their property to fund this excursion). 85–87: **What . . . issue?**: What did this opulent display do except serve to show its lack of productive results or the poverty it caused (poor issue)? 88. **not values**: is not worth. 90. **hideous storm** (according to Holinshed, a storm that interrupted the festivities was taken as a bad omen). 93. **aboded**: boded. 94. **on't**: of it. **budded out**: already sprung. 95. **flaw'd**: broken. **attach'd**: confiscated.

ABER.   Is it therefore
          Th' ambassador is silenc'd?

NOR.   Marry is't!

ABER.   A proper title of a peace, and purchas'd
          At a superfluous rate!

BUCK.   Why, all this business
          Our reverend Cardinal carried.

NOR.   Like it your Grace,   100
          The state takes notice of the private difference
          Betwixt you and the Cardinal. I advise you
          (And take it from a heart that wishes towards you
          Honor and plenteous safety) that you read
          The Cardinal's malice and his potency   105
          Together; to consider further, that
          What his high hatred would effect wants not
          A minister in his power. You know his nature,
          That he's revengeful; and I know his sword
          Hath a sharp edge; it's long, and 't may be said   110
          It reaches far, and where 'twill not extend,
          Thither he darts it. Bosom up my counsel;
          You'll find it wholesome. Lo, where comes that rock
          That I advise your shunning.

              *Enter Cardinal Wolsey, the purse borne before
              him, certain of the Guard, and two Secretaries
              with papers. The Cardinal in his passage fixeth
              his eye on Buckingham, and Buckingham on
              him, both full of disdain.*

CARD.   The Duke of Buckingham's surveyor? Ha!   115
          Where's his examination?

SECR.   Here, so please you.

CARD.   Is he in person ready?

SECR.   Ay, please your Grace.

CARD.   Well, we shall then know more, and Buckingham
          Shall lessen this big look.   *Exeunt Cardinal and his Train.*

---

97. **Th' ambassador is silence'd?**: To retaliate, the English arrested the French ambassador. **Marry**: by the Virgin Mary (an oath). 98. **A proper . . . peace**: said ironically. 99. **superfluous**: excessive. 100. **carried**: carried out. **Like it**: may it please. 101. **state**: counsel. **private difference**: personal animosity. 104. **read**: heed. 107–108. **wants . . . power**: does not lack a means of carrying it out. 112. **Bosom up my counsel**: take it to heart. 114. s.d. *purse*: in which is contained the great seal of his position as Lord Chancellor. 115. **surveyor**: overseer of Buckingham's estate. 116. **examination**: court deposition. 119. **big look**: proud glare.

BUCK.	This butcher's cur is venom-mouth'd, and I 120
	Have not the power to muzzle him; therefore best
	Not wake him in his slumber. A beggar's book
	Outworths a noble's blood.
NOR.	What, are you chaf'd?
	Ask God for temp'rance. That's th' appliance only
	Which your disease requires.
BUCK.	I read in's looks 125
	Matter against me, and his eye revil'd
	Me as his abject object. At this instant
	He bores me with some trick. He's gone to th' King.
	I'll follow and outstare him.
NOR.	Stay, my lord,
	And let your reason with your choler question 130
	What 'tis you go about. To climb steep hills
	Requires slow pace at first. Anger is like
	A full hot horse, who being allow'd his way,
	Self-mettle tires him. Not a man in England
	Can advise me like you. Be to yourself 135
	As you would to your friend.
BUCK.	I'll to the King
	And from a mouth of honor quite cry down
	This Ipswich fellow's insolence, or proclaim
	There's difference in no persons.
NOR.	Be advis'd.
	Heat not a furnace for your foe so hot 140
	That it do singe yourself. We may outrun
	By violent swiftness that which we run at,
	And lose by overrunning. Know you not
	The fire that mounts the liquor till 't run o'er
	In seeming to augment it wastes it? Be advis'd. 145
	I say again there is no English soul
	More stronger to direct you than yourself,
	If with the sap of reason you would quench,
	Or but allay, the fire of passion.

120. **butcher's cur**: Wolsey was the son of a butcher. 122. **book**: education (Wolsey was a reputable scholar). 123. **chaf'd**: angry. 124. **appliance**: medicine. 127. **abject object**: lowly spectacle. 128. **bores**: dupes; weakens. 130. **question**: dispute. 133. **full hot**: overexcited. 134. **Self-mettle**: self-motivated drive. 137. **from . . . honor**: using or making appeal to my nobility. 138. **Ipswich**: Wolsey's birthplace. 139. **difference in no persons**: distinctions in degree. 142. **run at**: intend to catch. 144. **mounts the liquor**: raises (by boiling) the liquid. 149. **but allay**: at least calm.

BUCK.   Sir,
            I am thankful to you, and I'll go along   150
            By your prescription. But this top-proud fellow—
            Whom from the flow of gall I name not, but
            From sincere motions, by intelligence,
            And proofs as clear as founts in July when
            We see each grain of gravel—I do know   155
            To be corrupt and treasonous.

NOR.   Say not treasonous.

BUCK.   To th' King I'll say't and make my vouch as strong
            As shore of rock. Attend. This holy fox,
            Or wolf, or both (for he is equal rav'nous
            As he is subtile, and as prone to mischief   160
            As able to perform't, his mind and place
            Infecting one another, yea, reciprocally),
            Only to show his pomp as well in France
            As here at home, suggests the King our master
            To this last costly treaty, th' interview   165
            That swallowed so much treasure and like a glass
            Did break i' th' wrenching.

NOR.   Faith, and so it did.

BUCK.   Pray give me favor, sir. This cunning Cardinal
            The articles o' th' combination drew
            As himself pleas'd; and they were ratified   170
            As he cried "Thus let be!" to as much end
            As give a crutch to th' dead. But our Count-Cardinal
            Has done this, and 'tis well; for worthy Wolsey
            (Who cannot err) he did it. Now this follows
            (Which, as I take it, is a kind of puppy   175
            To th' old dam, treason), Charles the Emperor,
            Under pretence to see the Queen his aunt
            (For 'twas indeed his color, but he came
            To whisper Wolsey), here makes visitation.
            His fears were that the interview betwixt   180

151: **top-proud**: supremely arrogant. 152: **from . . . not**: whom I do not call ["top-proud"] because of anger. 153. **intelligence**: informants. 154. **founts**: springs. 157. **vouch**: claim. 159. **equal**: equally. 161. **place**: high position. 164. **suggests**: prompts or tempts. 165. **th' interview**: the meeting between the kings. 167. **i' th' wrenching**: in the twisted handling. 168. **Pray. . . . favor**: Indulge me further. 169. **combination**: treaty. 171. **end**: purpose. 172. **Count-Cardinal**: i.e., because Wolsey presumes to act as a nobleman. 175–176. **a kind . . . dam**: a miniature or incipient form of its mother ("dam"). 176. **the Emperor**: i.e., of the Holy Roman Empire (Charles was not in favor of the alliance between English and French). 177. **Queen his aunt**: Henry's Queen Katherine was Charles's aunt. 178. **color**: excuse.

England and France might through their amity
Breed him some prejudice; for from this league
Peep'd harms that menac'd him. He privily
Deals with our Cardinal; and, as I trow—
Which I do well, for I am sure the Emperor   185
Paid ere he promis'd; whereby his suit was granted
Ere it was ask'd—but when the way was made,
And pav'd with gold, the Emperor thus desir'd,
That he would please to alter the King's course
And break the foresaid peace. Let the King know   190
(As soon he shall by me) that thus the Cardinal
Does buy and sell his honor as he pleases,
And for his own advantage.

NOR.   I am sorry
To hear this of him, and could wish he were
Something mistaken in't.

BUCK.   No, not a syllable.   195
I do pronounce him in that very shape
He shall appear in proof.

Enter Brandon, a Sergeant-at-Arms before
him, and two or three of the Guard.

BRAN.   Your office, sergeant; execute it.

SERG.   Sir,
My lord the Duke of Buckingham and Earl
Of Hereford, Stafford, and Northampton, I   200
Arrest thee of high treason, in the name
Of our most sovereign King.

BUCK.   Lo you, my lord,
The net has fall'n upon me! I shall perish
Under device and practice.

BRAN.   I am sorry
To see you ta'en from liberty, to look on   205
The business present. 'Tis his Highness' pleasure
You shall to th' Tower.

BUCK.   It will help me nothing
To plead mine innocence, for that dye is on me
Which makes my whit'st part black. The will of heav'n

---

183. **privily**: secretly. 184. **trow**: believe. 189. **he**: Wolsey. 192. **his**: the king's. 195. **Something**: partly. 197. **in proof**: when tested. 198. **office**: duty. 202. **Lo you**: look you (i.e., observe). 204. **device and practice**: stratagem and trick. 205. **to look on**: to witness. 206. **business present**: present business.

Be done in this and all things! I obey.   210
O my Lord Aberga'ny, fare you well!

BRAN.   Nay, he must bear you company. [*To Abergavenny*] The King
Is pleas'd you shall to th' Tower till you know
How he determines further.

ABER.   As the Duke said,
The will of heaven be done, and the King's pleasure   215
By me obey'd!

BRAN.   Here is a warrant from
The King t' attach Lord Montacute and the bodies
Of the Duke's confessor, John de la Car,
One Gilbert Peck, his chancellor—

BUCK.   So, so!
These are the limbs o' th' plot. No more, I hope.   220

BRAN.   A monk o' th' Chartreux.

BUCK.   O, Nicholas Hopkins?

BRAN.   He.

BUCK.   My surveyor is false. The o'er-great Cardinal[†]
Hath show'd him gold; my life is spann'd already.
I am the shadow of poor Buckingham,   225
Whose figure even this instant cloud puts on
By dark'ning my clear sun. My lord, farewell.   *Exeunt.*

SCENE II. [*London. The Council Chamber.*]

Cornets. Enter King Henry, leaning
on the Cardinal's shoulder, the Nobles,
and Sir Thomas Lovell [with others].
The Cardinal places himself under the
King's feet on his right side.

---

217. **t' attach**: to arrest. 218, 219. **John de la Car, Gilbert Peck**: These are the names given in Shakespeare's historical source—Holinshed—of those who testified against Buckingham. 221. **Chartreux**: the Carthusian Order. 224. **spann'd**: already measured out. 225–227. **I . . . sun**: I am merely the semblance of poor Buckingham, a shape created (put on) by this sudden dark image (cloud), which obscures my more true self.

---

† "My surveyor is false." Buckingham does not clarify if "false" means "untruthful" in his testimony or "unfaithful" to him for not preserving secrets.

KING.   My life itself, and the best heart of it,
         Thanks you for this great care. I stood i' th' level
         Of a full-charg'd confederacy, and give thanks
         To you that chok'd it. Let be call'd before us
         That gentleman of Buckingham's. In person   5
         I'll hear him his confessions justify,
         And point by point the treasons of his master
         He shall again relate.

         A noise within, crying "Room for the Queen!"
         Enter the Queen [Katherine], usher'd by the
         Dukes of Norfolk and Suffolk. She kneels. The
         King riseth from his state, takes her up, kisses
         and placeth her by him.

QUEEN.   Nay, we must longer kneel. I am a suitor.

KING.   Arise and take place by us. Half your suit   10
         Never name to us; you have half our power.
         The other moiety ere you ask is given.
         Repeat your will, and take it.

QUEEN.   Thank your Majesty.
         That you would love yourself, and in that love
         Not unconsidered leave your honour nor   15
         The dignity of your office, is the point
         Of my petition.

KING.   Lady mine, proceed.

QUEEN.   I am solicited, not by a few,
         And those of true condition, that your subjects
         Are in great grievance. There have been commissions 20
         Sent down among 'em, which hath flaw'd the heart
         Of all their loyalties; wherein, although,
         My good Lord Cardinal, they vent reproaches
         Most bitterly on you as putter-on
         Of these exactions, yet the King our master,   25
         Whose honor heaven shield from soil!—even he escapes not
         Language unmannerly; yea, such which breaks

ACT I, SCENE 2
1. **the best heart**: (obscure) the noblest spirit. 2. **level**: aim or weapon sights. 3. **full-charg'd**: fully loaded. 5. **That gentleman of Buckingham**: Buckingham's surveyor (whom Wolsey has persuaded to testify against his master). 6. **justify**: confirm. 8. s.d. **state**: throne. 12. **moiety**: half. 13. **Repeat your will**: speak your wish. 14. **love**: have care for; protect. 15. **leave**: lose. 19. **true condition**: loyal disposition. 20. **grievance**: distress. **commissions**: official papers authorizing an action (for taxes in this case). 24. **putter-on**: instigator. 25. **exactions**: taxes. 26. **soil**: blemish.

Kevin Billington's BBC production (1978) initially puts Cardinal Wolsey (Timothy West) in full control with Henry VIII (John Stride) in the background.

	The sides of loyalty and almost appears	
	In loud rebellion.	
NOR.	Not almost appears—	
	It doth appear! for, upon these taxations,	30
	The clothiers all, not able to maintain	
	The many to them 'longing, have put off	
	The spinsters, carders, fullers, weavers, who,	
	Unfit for other life, compell'd by hunger	
	And lack of other means, in desperate manner	35
	Daring th' event to th' teeth, are all in uproar,	
	And danger serves among them.	
KING.	Taxation?	
	Wherein? And what taxation? My Lord Cardinal,	
	You that are blam'd for it alike with us,	
	Know you of this taxation?	

---

33. **spinsters, carders, fullers**: all workers in the wool trade: those who spin the wool, comb it out, and beat it to make it fuller, respectively. 34. **life**: livelihood. 36. **Daring . . . teeth**: fearless of the outcome of their actions. 37. **danger serves**: danger to the king serves (in the military sense as having been enlisted).

CARD.   Please you, sir,   40
I know but of a single part in aught
Pertains to th' state, and front but in that file
Where others tell steps with me.

QUEEN.   No, my lord;
You know no more than others! But you frame
Things that are known alike, which are not wholesome   45
To those which would not know them and yet must
Perforce be their acquaintance. These exactions
(Whereof my sovereign would have note)—they are
Most pestilent to th' hearing; and, to bear 'em,
The back is sacrifice to th' load. They say   50
They are devis'd by you, or else you suffer
Too hard an exclamation.

KING.   Still exaction!
The nature of it? In what kind, let's know,
Is this exaction?

QUEEN.   I am much too venturous
In tempting of your patience, but am bold'ned   55
Under your promis'd pardon. The subject's grief
Comes through commissions, which compels from each
The sixth part of his substance, to be levied
Without delay; and the pretence for this
Is nam'd, your wars in France. This makes bold mouths.   60
Tongues spit their duties out, and cold hearts freeze
Allegiance in them. Their curses now
Live where their prayers did; and it's come to pass
This tractable obedience is a slave
To each incensed will. I would your Highness   65
Would give it quick consideration, for
There is no primer business.†

KING.   By my life,
This is against our pleasure.

41–43. **I know . . . me**: I merely know one part of anything our government carries out and am only in the most exposed position (the "front") in the military line where others march ("tell steps") with me. 44. **You . . . others!**: Said ironically. 44–47. **But . . . acquaintance**: But you make things that are known to the whole council, which are harmful to those members who would rather not know of them and are forced to enact them. 48. **note**: knowledge. 50. **The . . . load**: The load of them breaks the back. 52. **exclamation**: condemnation. 53. **In**: of. 56. **grief**: grievance. 58. **substance**: wealth. 64. **tractable**: easily influenced. 67. **primer**: more pressing. 68. **our**: the king speaks in the royal plural.

---

† How angry the king is here and how much of a threat Cardinal Wolsey feels from him are clearly performance choices.

CARD.   And for me,
            I have no further gone in this than by
            A single voice, and that not pass'd me but   70
            By learned approbation of the judges, If I am
            Traduc'd by ignorant tongues, which neither know
            My faculties nor person yet will be
            The chronicles of my doing, let me say
            'Tis but the fate of place and the rough brake   75
            That virtue must go through. We must not stint
            Our necessary actions in the fear
            To cope malicious censurers, which ever,†
            As rav'nous fishes, do a vessel follow
            That is new-trimm'd, but benefit no further   80
            Than vainly longing. What we oft do best,
            By sick interpreters (once weak ones) is
            Not ours, or not allow'd; what worst, as oft,
            Hitting a grosser quality, is cried up
            For our best action. If we shall stand still,   85
            In fear our motion will be mock'd or carp'd at,
            We should take root here where we sit, or sit
            State-statues only.

KING.   Things done well
            And with a care exempt themselves from fear;
            Things done without example, in their issue   90
            Are to be fear'd. Have you a precedent
            Of this commission? I believe, not any.
            We must not rend our subjects from our laws
            And stick them in our will. Sixth part of each?
            A trembling contribution! Why, we take   95
            From every tree lop, bark, and part o' th' timber;

69–70. I . . . voice: Wolsey's role in this business was only one voice in a unanimous vote. 70. me: by me. 72. Traduc'd: slandered. 73. faculties: personal qualities; disposition (*Oxford English Dictionary* 1b). 75. place: elevated rank. brake: thorny thicket. 78. cope: encounter (as in battle). 80. new-trimm'd: recently prepared for voyage. 80–81. benefit . . . longing: receive no reward other than desiring (Wolsey's overthrow) in vain. 82. sick: carping or deliberately perverse. 83. Not ours . . . allow'd: i.e., not credited to us or condemned. worst: we do worst. 84–85. cried . . . action: is extolled (ironically) as the action that most represents what we are capable of. 86. fear: fear that. 88. State-statues: useless figures of ruling. 90. example: precedent. issue: result. 93–94. We . . . will: i.e., we must not substitute our desire for legal precedent. 95. trembling: dreadful. 96. lop: the smaller branches.

---

†   The actor playing Wolsey can decide how concerned or secure he is when Queen Katherine accuses him of overreaching his power. In Billington's version, he is quite composed.

And though we leave it with a root, thus hack'd,
The air will drink the sap. To every county
Where this is question'd send our letters with
Free pardon to each man that has denied   100
The force of this commission. Pray look to't.
I put it to your care.

CARD.   [*Aside to the Secretary*] A word with you.
Let there be letters writ to every shire
Of the King's grace and pardon. The grieved commons
Hardly conceive of me. Let it be nois'd   105
That through our intercession this revokement
And pardon comes. I shall anon advise you
Further in the proceeding.   *Exit Secretary.*

Enter Surveyor.

QUEEN.   I am sorry that the Duke of Buckingham
Is run in your displeasure.

KING.   It grieves many.   110
The gentleman is learn'd and a most rare speaker,
To nature none more bound; his training such
That he may furnish and instruct great teachers
And never seek for aid out of himself. Yet see,
When these so noble benefits shall prove   115
Not well dispos'd, the mind growing once corrupt,
They turn to vicious forms, ten times more ugly
Than ever they were fair. This man so complete,
Who was enroll'd 'mongst wonders, and when we,
Almost with ravish'd list'ning, could not find   120
His hour of speech a minute—he, my lady,
Hath into monstrous habits put the graces
That once were his and is become as black
As if besmear'd in hell. Sit by us; you shall hear
(This was his gentleman in trust) of him   125
Things to strike honor sad. Bid him recount
The fore-recited practices, whereof
We cannot feel too little, hear too much.

98: **drink**: dry. 99. **question'd**: disputed. 101. **force**: legitimacy. 104. **grace**: mercy. 105. **conceive of**: have preconceptions of. **nois'd**: rumored. 107. **anon**: very soon. 110. **Is run in**: has brought on. 112. **To . . . bound**: no one is more indebted to nature's gifts. 114. **out of himself**: outside his own learning. **see**: consider. 116. **Not well dispos'd**: put to ill use. 118. **complete**: gifted. 120. **ravish'd**: captivated. 122. **habits**: clothing. 127. **practices**: conspiracies.

CARD.   Stand forth and with bold spirit relate what you,
             Most like a careful subject, have collected   130
             Out of the Duke of Buckingham.

KING.   Speak freely.

SURV.   First, it was usual with him—every day
             It would infect his speech—that if the King
             Should without issue die, he'll carry it so
             To make the sceptre his. These very words   135
             I've heard him utter to his son-in-law,
             Lord Aberga'ny, to whom by oath he menac'd
             Revenge upon the Cardinal.

CARD.   Please your Highness note
             His dangerous conception in this point.
             Not friended by his wish, to your high person   140
             His will is most malignant, and it stretches
             Beyond you to your friends.

QUEEN.   My learn'd Lord Cardinal,
             Deliver all with charity.

KING.   Speak on.
             How grounded he his title to the crown
             Upon our fail? To this point hast thou heard him   145
             At any time speak aught?

SURV.   He was brought to this
             By a vain prophecy of Nicholas Hopkins.

KING.   What was that Hopkins?

SURV.   Sir, a Chartreux friar,
             His confessor, who fed him every minute
             With words of sovereignty.

KING.   How know'st thou this?   150

SURV.   Not long before your Highness sped to France,
             The Duke being at the Rose, within the parish
             Saint Lawrence Poultney, did of me demand
             What was the speech among the Londoners
             Concerning the French journey. I replied   155

---

130. **careful**: dutiful to the king. 130. **collected**: gathered. 134. **issue**: heir. **carry**: manage. 139.
conception: thing conceived of or presumed. 140. **Not friended**: not content with. 141. **will**: desire.
143. **Deliver . . . , charity**: Everything you say should show the spirit of Christian love. 145. **fail**: failure
(in dying without successor). 150. **words of sovereignty**: promises of kingship. 152. **the Rose**: Buckingham's manor. 153. **Saint Lawrence Poultney**: a London church.

Men fear'd the French would prove perfidious,
To the King's danger. Presently the Duke
Said 'twas the fear indeed, and that he doubted
'Twould prove the verity of certain words
Spoke by a holy monk "that oft," says he,   160
"Hath sent to me, wishing me to permit
John de la Car, my chaplain, a choice hour
To hear from him a matter of some moment;
Whom after under the confession's seal
He solemnly had sworn that what he spoke   165
My chaplain to no creature living but
To me should utter, with demure confidence
This pausingly ensu'd: 'Neither the King nor 's heirs
(Tell you the Duke) shall prosper. Bid him strive
To gain the love o' th' commonalty. The Duke   170
Shall govern England.'"

QUEEN.   If I know you well,
You were the Duke's surveyor and lost your office
On the complaint o' th' tenants. Take good heed
You charge not in your spleen a noble person
And spoil your nobler soul. I say, take heed;   175
Yes, heartily beseech you.

KING.   Let him on.
Go forward.

SURV.   On my soul, I'll speak but truth.
I told my lord the Duke, by th' devil's illusions
The monk might be deceiv'd; and that 'twas dangerous for
       him
To ruminate on this so far until   180
It forg'd him some design, which, being believ'd,
It was much like to do. He answer'd 'Tush,
It can do me no damage!' adding further
That, had the King in his last sickness fail'd,
The Cardinal's and Sir Thomas Lovell's heads   185
Should have gone off.

KING.   Ha! What? so rank? Aha!
There's mischief in this man. Canst thou say further?

---

158. **doubted**: suspected; feared. 163: **moment**: urgency. 167. **demure**: serious; grave. 174. **spleen**: grudge. 176. **on**: continue. 181. **forg'd**: formed in. 182. **Tush**: a dismissive exclamation. 184. **fail'd**: expired.

SURV.   I can, my liege.

KING.   Proceed.

SURV.   Being at Greenwich,
After your Highness had reprov'd the Duke
About Sir William Bulmer—

KING.   I remember   190
Of such a time. Being my sworn servant,
The Duke retain'd him his. But on! What hence?

SURV.   "If," quoth he, "I for this had been committed,
As to the Tower I thought, I would have play'd
The part my father meant to act upon   195
Th' usurper Richard, who, being at Salisbury,
Made suit to come in's presence, which if granted,
As he made semblance of his duty, would
Have put his knife into him."

KING.   A giant traitor!

CARD.   Now, madam, may his Highness live in freedom,   200
And this man out of prison?

QUEEN.   God mend all!

KING.   There's something more would out of thee. What say'st?

SURV.   After "the Duke his father," with the "knife,"
He stretch'd him, and, with one hand on his dagger,
Another spread on 's breast, mounting his eyes,   205
He did discharge a horrible oath, whose tenor
Was, were he evil us'd, he would outgo
His father by as much as a performance
Does an irresolute purpose.

KING.   There's his period,
To sheathe his knife in us. He is attach'd.   210
Call him to present trial. If he may
Find mercy in the law, 'tis his; if none,
Let him not seek't of us. By day and night,
He's traitor to the height!   *Exeunt.*

---

192. **his**: as his. 195–196. **my father . . . Richard**: Buckingham's father intended to assassinate Richard III. 198. **semblance of**: a pretended show of. 205. **mounting**: lifting. 207. **evil us'd**: abused. 208–209. **performance . . . purpose**: an action does a wavering plan. 209. **period**: end point. 210. **attach'd**: arrested. 211. **present**: instant. 214. **to the height**: in the highest degree.

SCENE III. [*London. An antechamber in the Palace.*]

Enter Lord Chamberlain and Lord Sandys.

CHAM.   Is't possible the spells of France should juggle
Men into such strange mysteries?

SANDYS.   New customs,
Though they be never so ridiculous
(Nay, let 'em be unmanly), yet are follow'd.

CHAM.   As far as I see, all the good our English   5
Have got by the late voyage is but merely
A fit or two o' th' face; but they are shrewd ones;
For when they hold 'em, you would swear directly
Their very noses had been councilors
To Pepin or Clotharius, they keep state so.   10

SANDYS.   They have all new legs, and lame ones. One would take it,
That never saw 'em pace before, the spavin
Or springhalt reign'd among 'em.

CHAM.   Death, my lord!
Their clothes are after such a pagan cut to't
That sure th' have worn out Christendom.

Enter Sir Thomas Lovell.

                                        How now?   15
What news, Sir Thomas Lovell?

LOV.   Faith, my lord,
I hear of none but the new proclamation
That's clapp'd upon the court gate.

CHAM.   What is't for?

LOV.   The reformation of our travell'd gallants
That fill the court with quarrels, talk, and tailors.   20

ACT I, SCENE 3
1. **juggle**: enchant; beguile. 2. **mysteries**: i.e., of strange fashions ("mystery" continues the metaphors of occult religion). 6. **late voyage**: i.e., to France. 7. **fit . . . face**: a new way of holding the face, which the Lord Chamberlain likens to a paroxysm. 8. **'em**: i.e., their faces. 10. **Pepin or Clotharius**: legendary kings of France. **keep state**: presume a royal air. 11. **legs**: fashionable walks or bows of obeisance. 12–13. **spavin / Or springhalt**: both are diseases that afflict horses and mar walking. 13. **Death**: (an oath) "By God's Death." 14. **are . . . to't**: resemble Pagan fashion. 14. **worn out Christendom**: adorned themselves with and/or gone through all the fashions of Christian nations. 18. **clapp'd**: posted (resolutely so). 19. **travell'd gallants**: i.e., those who affect French mannerisms.

CHAM.   I'm glad 'tis there. Now I would pray our monsieurs
          To think an English courtier may be wise
          And never see the Louvre.

LOV.   They must either
          (For so run the conditions) leave those remnants
          Of fool and feather that they got in France,   25
          With all their honorable points of ignorance
          Pertaining thereunto—as fights and fireworks;
          Abusing better men than they can be,
          Out of a foreign wisdom—renouncing clean
          The faith they have in tennis and tall stockings,   30
          Short blist'red breeches, and those types of travel,
          And understand again like honest men,
          Or pack to their old playfellows. There, I take it,
          They may *cum privilegio* "oui" away
          The lag-end of their lewdness and be laugh'd at.   35

SANDYS.   'Tis time to give 'em physic, their diseases
          Are grown so catching.

CHAM.   What a loss our ladies
          Will have of these trim vanities!

LOV.   Ay, marry,
          There will be woe indeed, lords. The sly whoresons
          Have got a speeding trick to lay down ladies.   40
          A French song and a fiddle has no fellow.

SANDYS.   The devil fiddle 'em! I am glad they are going,
          For sure there's no converting of 'em. Now
          An honest country lord, as I am, beaten
          A long time out of play, may bring his plain-song   45
          And have an hour of hearing, and, by'r Lady,
          Held current music too.

CHAM.   Well said, Lord Sandys.
          Your colt's tooth is not cast yet.

---

23. **Louvre**: the French king's court. 25. **feather**: fashion. 26. **all . . . ignorance**: their ignorant mannerisms that they believe honorable. 27. **fireworks**: (possibly) whoring. 29. **renouncing**: refers back to
what the proclamation directs. **clean**: completely. 31. **blist'red**: puffy. 32. **understand**: adopt the
worldviews. 33. **pack to**: go back to. 34. *cum privilegio*: with immunity. **"oui"**: Kittredge follows the
second Folio edition of the play in choosing "wear"; the first Folio prints "wee" or "oui." 35. **lag-end . . .
lewdness**: the backside or latter part of their folly (with a possible bawdy meaning). 36. **physic**: medicine meant to purge. 38. **trim**: handsomely dressed; proper (used ironically). 40. **speeding**: foolproof.
41. **fellow**: equal. 43. **converting**: (returns to the conceit of paganism/Christianity). 44–45. **beaten . . .
play**: having long been vanquished as a wooer. 45. **plain-song**: single melody line.

SANDYS.   No, my lord,
    Nor shall not while I have a stump.

CHAM.   Sir Thomas,
    Whither were you a-going?

LOV.   To the Cardinal's.   50
    Your lordship is a guest too.

CHAM.   O, 'tis true.
    This night he makes a supper, and a great one,
    To many lords and ladies. There will be
    The beauty of this kingdom, I'll assure you.

LOV.   That churchman bears a bounteous mind indeed,   55
    A hand as fruitful as the land that feeds us;
    His dews fall everywhere.

CHAM.   No doubt he's noble.
    He had a black mouth that said other of him.

SANDYS.   He may, my lord; h'as wherewithal. In him
    Sparing would show a worse sin than ill doctrine.   60
    Men of his way should be most liberal;
    They are set here for examples.

CHAM.   True, they are so;
    But few now give so great ones. My barge stays;
    Your lordship shall along. Come, good Sir Thomas,
    We shall be late else; which I would not be,   65
    For I was spoke to, with Sir Henry Guildford,
    This night to be comptrollers.

SANDYS.   I am your lordship's.   *Exeunt.*

SCENE IV. [*Westminster. The
presence chamber in York Palace.*]

*Hautboys. A small table under a state for the
Cardinal, a longer table for the guests. Then
enter Anne Bullen and divers other Ladies and
Gentlemen, as guests at one door; at another
door enter Sir Henry Guildford.*

48. **colt's tooth**: youthful lust. **cast**: lost. 49. **stump**: tooth's stump (a bawdy suggestion). 52. **makes**: gives. 56. **fruitful**: lavish; generous. 58. **black**: foul or malicious. 59. **h'as**: he has. 60. **Sparing**: holding back; hoarding. **ill doctrine**: heresy. 61. **way**: vocation. 63. **ones**: examples. **stays**: awaits. 64. **along**: come along. 67. **comptrollers**: stewards, masters of ceremonies.

SIR H. GUILD.   Ladies, a general welcome from his Grace
                Salutes ye all. This night he dedicates
                To fair content and you. None here, he hopes,
                In all this noble bevy, has brought with her
                One care abroad. He would have all as merry   5
                As, first, good company, good wine, good welcome
                Can make good people.

                        Enter Lord Chamberlain,
                  Lord Sandys, and [Sir Thomas] Lovell.

                             O my lord, y'are tardy!
                The very thought of this fair company
                Clapp'd wings to me.

CHAM.   You are young, Sir Harry Guildford.

SANDYS.   Sir Thomas Lovell, had the Cardinal   10
                But half my lay thoughts in him, some of these
                Should find a running banquet, ere they rested,
                I think would better please 'em. By my life,
                They are a sweet society of fair ones.

LOV.   O that your lordship were but now confessor   15
                To one or two of these!

SANDYS.   I would I were.
                They should find easy penance.

LOV.   Faith, how easy?

SANDYS.   As easy as a down bed would afford it.

CHAM.   Sweet ladies, will it please you sit? Sir Harry,
                Place you that side; I'll take the charge of this.   20
                His Grace is ent'ring. Nay, you must not freeze!
                Two women plac'd together makes cold weather.
                My Lord Sandys, you are one will keep 'em waking.
                Pray sit between these ladies.

SANDYS.   By my faith,
                And thank your lordship. By your leave, sweet ladies.   25
                      [Seats himself between Anne
                       Bullen and another Lady.]

ACT 1, SCENE 4
s.d. **Hautboys**: an earlier type of oboe. **state**: canopy. **3. fair content**: mirth. 4. **bevy**: company of
ladies. 11. **lay**: secular, of the laity (with a bawdy meaning). 12. **running banquet**: a fast meal or one
that must be eaten while fleeing from lustful pursuit. 17. **Faith**: by faith (an oath). 20. **Place**: assign
seating. 23. **waking**: stimulated (with a bawdy suggestion).

	If I chance to talk a little wild, forgive me.	
	I had it from my father.	
ANNE B.	Was he mad, sir?	
SANDYS.	O, very mad, exceeding mad, in love too.	

        If I chance to talk a little wild, forgive me.
        I had it from my father.

ANNE B.   Was he mad, sir?

SANDYS.   O, very mad, exceeding mad, in love too.
        But he would bite none. Just as I do now,
        He would kiss you twenty with a breath.   [*Kisses her.*]

CHAM.   Well said, my lord.   30
        So, now y'are fairly seated. Gentlemen,
        The penance lies on you if these fair ladies
        Pass away frowning.

SANDYS.   For my little cure,
        Let me alone.

               Hautboys. Enter Cardinal Wolsey,
               [attended] and takes his state.

CARD.   Y'are welcome, my fair guests. That noble lady   35
        Or gentleman that is not freely merry
        Is not my friend. This to confirm my welcome;
        And to you all, good health.†   [*Drinks.*]

SANDYS.   Your Grace is noble.
        Let me have such a bowl may hold my thanks
        And save me so much talking.

CARD.   My Lord Sandys,   40
        I am beholding to you. Cheer your neighbours.
        Ladies, you are not merry. Gentlemen,
        Whose fault is this?

SANDYS.   The red wine first must rise
        In their fair cheeks, my lord; then we shall have 'em
        Talk us to silence.

ANNE B.   You are a merry gamester,   45
        My Lord Sandys.

SANDYS.   Yes, if I make my play.

---

30. **kiss you . . . breath**: kiss twenty women in one breath. 32. **penance**: need for penance. 33. **cure**: remedy; parish under care (cure) of a priest. 34. **Let me alone**: give me privacy. 39. **may**: able to. 41. **beholding**: indebted. 45. **gamester**: a sportive or playful person. 46. **make my play**: i.e., in cards and in sex.

---

†   "Your Grace is noble." The depiction of Wolsey's largesse in this scene offers a counterbalance to the general one offered thus far. This scene has given directors such as Sir Herbert Beerbohm Tree license to indulge the most sumptuous displays in the history of Shakespearean theater.

	Here's to your ladyship; and pledge it, madam,	
	For 'tis to such a thing—	
ANNE B.	You cannot show me.	
SANDYS.	I told your Grace they would talk anon.	
	[Drum and trumpet. Chambers discharg'd.]	
CARD.	What's that?	
CHAM.	Look out there, some of ye. [Exit a Servant.]	

CARD.   What warlike voice,   50
And to what end, is this? Nay, ladies, fear not.
By all the laws of war y'are privileg'd.

                    Enter a Servant.

CHAM.   How now? What is't?

SERV.   A noble troop of strangers,
For so they seem. Th' have left their barge and landed,
And hither make, as great ambassadors   55
From foreign princes.

CARD.   Good Lord Chamberlain,
Go, give 'em welcome; you can speak the French tongue;
And pray receive 'em nobly and conduct 'em
Into our presence, where this heaven of beauty
Shall shine at full upon them. Some attend him.   60
          [Exit Chamberlain, attended.]
          All rise, and tables remov'd.
You have now a broken banquet; but we'll mend it.
A good digestion to you all! and once more
I show'r a welcome on ye. Welcome all.

     Hautboys. Enter King and others, as Maskers,
     habited like shepherds, usher'd by the Lord
     Chamberlain. They pass directly before the
     Cardinal and gracefully salute him.
A noble company! What are their pleasures?

---

47. **pledge it**: vow it (through drink). 48. **You . . . me**: Anne responds to his bawdy use of "thing." 49. s.d. ***Chambers***: a small cannon (its firing at this point is thought to be responsible for the Globe Theatre's burning down in 1613). 52. **privileg'd**: i.e., protected. 54. **barge**: i.e., that has docked on the Thames River. 55. **as**: and appear to be. 59. **heaven of beauty**: the manor in general or the assembly of ladies. 63. s.d. ***Maskers***: Masques were elaborate dramatic spectacles or dialogue, movement, and costume, performed often by nobility and intended for the praise of a noble figure.

A disguised King Henry, one of the masked dancers with his back to the viewers, bows before Cardinal Wolsey, who is seated in his chair of state in the upper center of the frame.

CHAM.	Because they speak no English, thus they pray'd	65
	To tell your Grace: that, having heard by fame	
	Of this so noble and so fair assembly	
	This night to meet here, they could do no less	
	(Out of the great respect they bear to beauty)	
	But leave their flocks and, under your fair conduct,	70
	Crave leave to view these ladies and entreat	
	An hour of revels with 'em.	
CARD.	Say, Lord Chamberlain,	
	They have done my poor house grace; for which I pay 'em	
	A thousand thanks and pray 'em take their pleasures.	
	Choose ladies. King and Anne Bullen.	
KING.	The fairest hand I ever touch'd! O beauty,	75
	Till now I never knew thee! *Music. Dance.*	
CARD.	My lord!	
CHAM.	Your Grace?	

66. **fame**: rumor or report. 70. **conduct**: management. 71. **leave**: permission. 74. **pleasures**: choice in dancing partners.

CARD.   Pray tell 'em thus much from me:
            There should be one amongst 'em, by his person,
            More worthy this place than myself; to whom,
            If I but knew him, with my love and duty   80
            I would surrender it.

CHAM.   I will, my lord.   *Whisper [with the Maskers].*

CARD.   What say they?

CHAM.   Such a one they all confess
            There is indeed, which they would have your Grace
            Find out, and he will take it.

CARD.   Let me see then.   *[Comes from his state.]*
            By all your good leaves, gentlemen, here I'll make   85
            My royal choice.

KING.   *[Unmasks.]* Ye have found him, Cardinal.
            You hold a fair assembly. You do well, lord.
            You are a churchman, or, I'll tell you, Cardinal,
            I should judge now unhappily.

CARD.   I am glad
            Your Grace is grown so pleasant.

KING.   My Lord Chamberlain,   90
            Prithee come hither. What fair lady's that?

CHAM.   An't please your Grace, Sir Thomas Bullen's daughter,
            The Viscount Rochford, one of her Highness' women.

KING.   By heaven, she is a dainty one! Sweetheart,
            I were unmannerly to take you out   95
            And not to kiss you. *[Kisses her.]* A health, gentlemen!
            Let it go round.

CARD.   Sir Thomas Lovell, is the banquet ready
            I' th' privy chamber?

LOV.   Yes, my lord.

CARD.   Your Grace,
            I fear, with dancing is a little heated.   100

KING.   I fear, too much.

CARD.   There's fresher air, my lord,
            In the next chamber.

---

79. **this place**: i.e., Wolsey's official chair of state. 84. **Find out**: choose. **it**: the chair of state. 89. **unhappily**: with disfavor (at the ostentation). 92. **An't**: if it. 93. **women**: ladies in waiting. 95. **take you out**: i.e., for a dance. 96. **health**: Henry toasts.

KING.   Lead in your ladies, ev'ry one. Sweet partner,
         I must not yet forsake you. Let's be merry.
         Good my Lord Cardinal, I have half a dozen healths   105
         To drink to these fair ladies and a measure
         To lead 'em once again; and then let's dream
         Who's best in favor. Let the music knock it.

                                        Exeunt with Trumpets.

ACT II

SCENE I. [*Westminster. A street.*]

Enter two Gentlemen at several doors.

1. GENT.   Whither away so fast?

2. GENT.   O, God save ye!
            Ev'n to the Hall, to hear what shall become
            Of the great Duke of Buckingham.

1. GENT.   I'll save you
            That labor, sir. All's now done but the ceremony
            Of bringing back the prisoner.

2. GENT.   Were you there?   5

1. GENT.   Yes indeed was I.

2. GENT.   Pray speak what has happen'd.

1. GENT.   You may guess quickly what.

2. GENT.   Is he found guilty?

1. GENT.   Yes, truly is he, and condemn'd upon't.

2. GENT.   I am sorry for't.

1. GENT.   So are a number more.

2. GENT.   But pray how pass'd it?   10

1. GENT.   I'll tell you in a little. The great Duke
            Came to the bar; where to his accusations
            He pleaded still not guilty and alleg'd

---

106. **measure**: stately dance. 107. **dream**: dream about. 108. **best in favor**: most attractive. **knock it**: strike; begin.

ACT 2, SCENE 1
s.d. ***several***: separate. 2. **Hall**: Westminster (site of the trial). 10. **how pass'd it**: what took place. 12. **bar**: familiar name for the railing behind which prisoners sit. 13. **alleg'd**: offered.

Many sharp reasons to defeat the law.
The King's Attorney, on the contrary,   15
Urg'd on the examinations, proofs, confessions
Of divers witnesses, which the Duke desir'd
To have brought *viva voce* to his face;
At which appear'd against him his surveyor,
Sir Gilbert Peck his chancellor, and John Car,   20
Confessor to him, with that devil monk,
Hopkins, that made this mischief.

2. GENT.   That was he
That fed him with his prophecies.

1. GENT.   The same.
All these accus'd him strongly, which he fain
Would have flung from him, but indeed he could not;   25
And so his peers upon this evidence
Have found him guilty of high treason. Much
He spoke, and learnedly, for life, but all
Was either pitied in him or forgotten.

2. GENT.   After all this how did he bear himself?   30

1. GENT.   When he was brought again to th' bar to hear
His knell rung out, his judgment, he was stirr'd
With such an agony he sweat extremely
And something spoke in choler, ill and hasty;
But he fell to himself again and sweetly   35
In all the rest show'd a most noble patience.

2. GENT.   I do not think he fears death.

1. GENT.   Sure he does not;
He never was so womanish. The cause
He may a little grieve at.

2. GENT.   Certainly
The Cardinal is the end of this.

1. GENT.   'Tis likely   40
By all conjectures: first, Kildare's attainder,
Then Deputy of Ireland, who remov'd,

---

16. **examinations**: depositions. **proofs**: written statements. 18. *viva voce*: literally *with living mouth* or in person. 20. **Sir**: courteously applied to a priest. 24. **fain**: eagerly. 28–29. **all . . . forgotten**: his pleas either resulted in mere pity or were ignored. 32. **judgment**: condemnation. 33. **sweat**: sweated. 34. **choler**: anger. 35. **fell to**: recovered. 38. **cause**: motive. 40. **end of**: force behind. 41–44. **Kildare's . . . father**: According to Shakespeare's historical source, Wolsey had the Earl of Kildare arrested and his property confiscated (by attainder) and replaced him with Buckingham's son-in-law, effectively exiling Buckingham's ally. 42. **Deputy**: governor. **remov'd**: having been removed.

Earl Surrey was sent thither, and in haste too,
Lest he should help his father.

2. GENT.   That trick of state
Was a deep envious one.

1. GENT.   At his return   45
No doubt he will require it. This is noted
(And generally), whoever the King favors
The Cardinal instantly will find employment,
And far enough from court too.

2. GENT.   All the commons
Hate him perniciously and, o' my conscience,   50
Wish him ten fathom deep. This duke as much
They love and dote on, call him bounteous Buckingham,
The mirror of all courtesy—

Enter Buckingham from his arraignment;
Tipstaves before him; the axe with the edge
towards him; Halberds on each side;
accompanied with Sir Thomas Lovell, Sir
Nicholas Vaux, Sir William Sandys, and
common people, &c.

1. GENT.   Stay there, sir,
And see the noble ruin'd man you speak of.

2. GENT.   Let's stand close and behold him.

BUCK.   All good people,   55
You that thus far have come to pity me,
Hear what I say and then go home and lose me.
I have this day receiv'd a traitor's judgment
And by that name must die. Yet heaven bear witness,
And if I have a conscience, let it sink me   60
Even as the axe falls, if I be not faithful!
The law I bear no malice for my death:
'T has done, upon the premises, but justice.
But those that sought it I could wish more Christians.
Be what they will, I heartily forgive 'em.   65
Yet let 'em look they glory not in mischief
Nor build their evils on the graves of great men;

44. **trick of state**: political strategy. 45. **envious**: vindictive. 46. **he**: i.e., the earl of Surrey. **requite**: avenge. 47. **generally**: by the general populace. 50. **perniciously**: i.e., in a way that wishes him dead. 53. s.d. *Tipstaves*: bailiffs who carry long metal-tipped staves. *Halberds*: guards who carry halberdiers. 57. **lose**: forget. 60. **sink**: damn. 63. **premises**: evidence offered.

      For then my guiltless blood must cry against 'em.
      For further life in this world I ne'er hope,
      Nor will I sue, although the King have mercies   70
      More than I dare make faults. You few that lov'd me
      And dare be bold to weep for Buckingham,
      His noble friends and fellows, whom to leave
      Is only bitter to him, only dying,
      Go with me like good angels to my end;   75
      And, as the long divorce of steel falls on me,
      Make of your prayers one sweet sacrifice
      And lift my soul to heaven. Lead on, a God's name!

LOV.   I do beseech your Grace, for charity,
      If ever any malice in your heart   80
      Were hid against me, now to forgive me frankly.

BUCK.   Sir Thomas Lovell, I as free forgive you
      As I would be forgiven. I forgive all.
      There cannot be those numberless offences
      'Gainst me that I cannot take peace with. No black envy   85
      Shall mark my grave. Commend me to his Grace;
      And if he speak of Buckingham, pray tell him
      You met him half in heaven. My vows and prayers
      Yet are the King's and, till my soul forsake me,
      Shall cry for blessings on him. May he live   90
      Longer than I have time to tell his years!
      Ever belov'd and loving may his rule be!
      And when old time shall lead him to his end,
      Goodness and he fill up one monument!

LOV.   To th' waterside I must conduct your Grace;   95
      Then give my charge up to Sir Nicholas Vaux,
      Who undertakes you to your end.

VAUX.   Prepare there;
      The Duke is coming. See the barge be ready
      And fit it with such furniture as suits
      The greatness of his person.

BUCK.   Nay, Sir Nicholas,   100
      Let it alone. My state now will but mock me.

---

67. **build their evils**: forward their ill-gotten careers. 70. **sue**: pursue; request. 71. **make faults**: commit wrongs (in need of mercy). 73–74. **whom . . . him**: who is only bitter because he must leave (his dear friends). 74. **only dying**: dying alone. 76. **long divorce of steel**: the eternal separation of the executioner's axe. 78. **a**: in. 82. **free**: freely. 85. **take**: make. 89. **Yet**: still. 91. **tell**: count. 94. **monument**: tomb. 97. **undertakes**: conducts. 99. **furniture**: furnishings. 101. **state . . . mock**: actual situation will humiliate.

When I came hither, I was Lord High Constable
And Duke of Buckingham; now, poor Edward Bohun.
Yet I am richer than my base accusers,
That never knew what truth meant. I now seal it;   105
And with that blood will make 'em one day groan for't.
My noble father, Henry of Buckingham,
Who first rais'd head against usurping Richard,
Flying for succour to his servant Banister,
Being distress'd, was by that wretch betray'd   110
And without trial fell. God's peace be with him!
Henry the Seventh succeeding, truly pitying
My father's loss, like a most royal prince
Restor'd me to my honors and out of ruins
Made my name once more noble. Now his son,   115
Henry the Eighth, life, honor, name, and all
That made me happy, at one stroke has taken
For ever from the world. I had my trial,
And must needs say a noble one; which makes me
A little happier than my wretched father.   120
Yet thus far we are one in fortunes: both
Fell by our servants, by those men we lov'd most—
A most unnatural and faithless service!
Heaven has an end in all. Yet, you that hear me,
This from a dying man receive as certain: 125
Where you are liberal of your loves and counsels
Be sure you be not loose; for those you make friends
And give your hearts to, when they once perceive
The least rub in your fortunes, fall away
Like water from ye, never found again   130
But where they mean to sink ye. All good people,
Pray for me! I must now forsake ye. The last hour
Of my long weary life is come upon me.
Farewell!
And when you would say something that is sad,   135
Speak how I fell. I have done; and God forgive me!
                                   Exeunt Duke and Train.

---

103. **Bohun:** Shakespeare follows his source; Buckingham's actual name was Stafford. 105. **truth:** fidelity. **seal:** vouch or ratify (as one does an authentic document). 106. **will:** that will. 108. **rais'd head:** brought an army. **Richard:** Richard III. 111. **fell:** was executed. 120. **happier:** more fortunate. 124. **end:** purpose. 126. **liberal:** freely giving; open. 127. **loose:** lax; careless. 129. **rub:** slow down; an impediment (in bowling).

1. GENT.	O, this is full of pity! Sir, it calls,
	I fear, too many curses on their heads
	That were the authors.

2. GENT.   If the Duke be guiltless,
'Tis full of woe. Yet I can give you inkling   140
Of an ensuing evil, if it fall,
Greater than this.

1. GENT.   Good angels keep it from us!
What may it be? You do not doubt my faith, sir?

2. GENT. This secret is so weighty 'twill require
A strong faith to conceal it.

1. GENT.   Let me have it.   145
I do not talk much.

2. GENT.   I am confident.
You shall, sir. Did you not of late days hear
A buzzing of a separation
Between the King and Katherine?

1. GENT.   Yes, but it held not;
For when the King once heard it, out of anger   150
He sent command to the Lord Mayor straight
To stop the rumour and allay those tongues
That durst disperse it.

2. GENT.   But that slander, sir,
Is found a truth now; for it grows again
Fresher than e'er it was, and held for certain   155
The King will venture at it. Either the Cardinal,
Or some about him near, have out of malice
To the good Queen possess'd him with a scruple
That will undo her. To confirm this too,
Cardinal Campeius is arriv'd, and lately;   160
As all think, for this business.

1. GENT.   'Tis the Cardinal;
And merely to revenge him on the Emperor

---

143. **faith**: ability to keep a secret. 146. **confident**: i.e., in his trustworthiness. 148. **buzzing**: murmur; rumor. 149. **held not**: did not stick. 152. **allay**: restrain; subdue. 156. **venture**: risk (i.e., a separation). 158. **a scruple**: Here, concerning the legality of his marriage to Katherine. From a standpoint of strict Church law, Katherine's former marriage to Henry's deceased elder brother Arthur would have disqualified her for marriage with the king. They were allowed to marry only after getting special permission from the Pope. 160. **Cardinal Campeius**: Cardinal Lorenzo Cameggio who was sent from the Pope to consider the marriage question. 162. **the Emperor**: Charles V, Holy Roman Emperor and Katherine's nephew.

For not bestowing on him at his asking
The archbishopric of Toledo, this is purpos'd.

2. GENT.   I think you have hit the mark. But is't not cruel   165
That she should feel the smart of this? The Cardinal
Will have his will, and she must fall.

1. GENT.   'Tis woful.
We are too open here to argue this.
Let's think in private more.   *Exeunt.*

SCENE II. [*London. An antechamber in the Palace.*]

Enter Lord Chamberlain, reading this letter.

CHAM.   "My Lord,—The horses your lordship sent for, with all the
care I had, I saw well chosen, ridden, and furnish'd. They were
young and handsome and of the best breed in the North.
When they were ready to set out for London, a man of my
Lord Cardinal's by commission and main power took 'em
from me, with this reason—his master would be serv'd before
a subject, if not before the King; which stopp'd our mouths,
sir."   5
I fear he will indeed. Well, let him have them.
He will have all, I think.

*Enter to the Lord Chamberlain
the Dukes of Norfolk and Suffolk.*

NOR.   Well met, my Lord Chamberlain.

CHAM.   Good day to both your Graces.

SUF.   How is the King employ'd?

CHAM.   I left him private,   10
Full of sad thoughts and troubles.

NOR.   What's the cause?

CHAM.   It seems the marriage with his brother's wife
Has crept too near his conscience.

SUF.   No, his conscience
Has crept too near another lady.

---

166. **smart**: pain. 168. **open**: carelessly exposed.
ACT 2, SCENE 2
2. **ridden, and furnish'd**: trained and equipped. 3–4. **commission and main / power**: authorizing
documents and strength in general. 11. **sad**: serious.

Nor.   'Tis so.
         This is the Cardinal's doing, the King-Cardinal!   15
         That blind priest, like the eldest son of Fortune,
         Turns what he list. The King will know him one day.

Suf.   Pray God he do! He'll never know himself else.

Nor.   How holily he works in all his business
         And with what zeal! for, now he has crack'd the league   20
         Between us and the Emperor, the Queen's great nephew,
         He dives into the King's soul, and there scatters
         Dangers, doubts, wringing of the conscience,
         Fears, and despairs—and all these for his marriage.
         And out of all these to restore the King,   25
         He counsels a divorce, a loss of her
         That like a jewel has hung twenty years
         About his neck, yet never lost her lustre;
         Of her that loves him with that excellence
         That angels love good men with; even of her   30
         That, when the greatest stroke of fortune falls,
         Will bless the King—and is not this course pious?

Cham.   Heaven keep me from such counsel! 'Tis most true
         These news are everywhere, every tongue speaks 'em,
         And every true heart weeps for't. All that dare   35
         Look into these affairs see this main end—
         The French King's sister. Heaven will one day open
         The King's eyes that so long have slept upon
         This bold bad man.

Suf.   And free us from his slavery.

Nor.   We had need pray,   40
         And heartily, for our deliverance,
         Or this imperious man will work us all
         From princes into pages. All men's honors
         Lie like one lump before him, to be fashion'd
         Into what pitch he please.

Suf.   For me, my lords,   45
         I love him not, nor fear him. There's my creed.

---

16. **blind priest . . . Fortune**: Wolsey is depicted as the inheritor of the allegorical figure Fortune's blindness or indiscriminate dispensing of favors. 17. **list**: wishes. 19. **he**: Wolsey. 31. **stroke**: weapon's stroke. **falls**: i.e., on her. 32. **and . . . pious?**: asked ironically. 37. **French King's sister**: i.e., Wolsey intends for the king to marry the duchess of Alençon. 38. **slept upon**: been blinded to. 42. **work us**: transform us. 43. **pages**: servants. 45. **pitch**: height or stature. 46. **creed**: statement of religious position (here, a metaphor for general belief).

As I am made without him, so I'll stand,
If the King please. His curses and his blessings
Touch me alike; th' are breath I not believe in.
I knew him, and I know him; so I leave him   50
To him that made him proud, the Pope.

NOR.   Let's in
And with some other business put the King
From these sad thoughts that work too much upon him.
My lord, you'll bear us company?

CHAM.   Excuse me.
The King has sent me otherwise. Besides,   55
You'll find a most unfit time to disturb him.
Health to your lordships!

NOR.   Thanks, my good Lord Chamberlain.

*Exit Lord Chamberlain; and the King
draws the curtain and sits reading pensively.*

SUF.   How sad he looks! Sure he is much afflicted.

KING.   Who's there, ha?

NOR.   Pray God he be not angry.

KING.   Who's there, I say? How dare you thrust yourselves   60
Into my private meditations?
Who am I? ha?

NOR.   A gracious king, that pardons all offences
Malice ne'er meant. Our breach of duty this way
Is business of estate; in which we come   65
To know your royal pleasure.

KING.   Ye are too bold.
Go to! I'll make ye know your times of business.
Is this an hour for temporal affairs? ha?

*Enter [Cardinals] Wolsey and
Campeius with a commission.*

Who's there? My good Lord Cardinal? O my Wolsey,
The quiet of my wounded conscience!   70
Thou art a cure fit for a king. [*To Campeius*] You're welcome,
Most learned reverend sir, into our kingdom.

---

49. **breath**: mere words. 52. **put**: distract. 53. **sad**: serious. **63. gracious**: merciful. 64. **Malice ne'er
meant**: not done with malicious intent. 65. **business of estate**: state business. 67. **make . . . business**:
teach you to respect propriety. 68. **temporal**: secular, state business.

Use us and it. [*To Wolsey*] My good lord, have great care
I be not found a talker.

CARD.   Sir, you cannot.
I would your Grace would give us but an hour   75
Of private conference.

KING.   [*To Norfolk and Suffolk*] We are busy. Go.

NOR.   [*Aside to Suffolk*] This priest has no pride in him!

SUF.   [*Aside to Norfolk*] Not to speak of.
I would not be so sick though for his place.
But this cannot continue.

NOR.   [*Aside to Suffolk*] If it do,
I'll venture one have-at-him.

SUF.   [*Aside to Norfolk*] I another.   *Exeunt Norfolk and Suffolk.*   80

CARD.   Your Grace has given a precedent of wisdom
Above all princes in committing freely
Your scruple to the voice of Christendom.
Who can be angry now? What envy reach you?
The Spaniard, tied by blood and favor to her   85
Must now confess, if they have any goodness,
The trial just and noble. All the clerks
(I mean the learned ones) in Christian kingdoms
Have their free voices. Rome, the nurse of judgment,
Invited by your noble self, hath sent   90
One general tongue unto us, this good man,
This just and learned priest, Cardinal Campeius,
Whom once more I present unto your Highness.

KING.   And once more in mine arms I bid him welcome
And thank the holy conclave for their loves.   95
They have sent me such a man I would have wish'd for.

CAMP.   Your Grace must needs deserve all strangers' loves,
You are so noble. To your Highness' hand
I tender my commission; by whose virtue,
The Court of Rome commanding, you, my Lord   100

---

73. **Use . . . it**: we are at your service. 74. **not found a talker**: be guilty of saying but not showing hospitality. 77: **no pride in him**: said ironically. 78. **sick**: prideful. **for his place**: even if I had his power. 80. **have-at-him**: go at him; an attack. 81. **precedent**: a model. 83. **scruple**: doubt. **voice of Christendom**: the judgment of the Church. 84. **envy**: ill will. 85. **The Spaniard**: Even the Emperor Charles. **tied**: obliged. 87. **clerks**: clerics; scholars. 89. **Have their free voices**: may judge as they see fit. 91. **One general tongue**: one authorized to speak on Rome's behalf. 95: **holy conclave**: college of cardinals. 96. **such a man**: exactly the sort of man that. 97. **must needs**: necessarily. **strangers'**: foreigners'. 99. **tender**: offer.

Cardinal of York, are join'd with me their servant
In the unpartial judging of this business.

KING.   Two equal men. The Queen shall be acquainted
Forthwith for what you come. Where's Gardiner?

CARD.   I know your Majesty has always lov'd her   105
So dear in heart not to deny her that
A woman of less place might ask by law—
Scholars allow'd freely to argue for her.

KING.   Ay, and the best she shall have; and my favor
To him that does best. God forbid else. Cardinal,   110
Prithee call Gardiner to me, my new Secretary.
I find him a fit fellow.   [*Exit Wolsey.*]

Enter [*Wolsey, with*] *Gardiner.*

CARD.   [*Aside to Gardiner*] Give me your hand. Much joy and favor
to you!
You are the King's now.

GARD.   [*Aside to Wolsey*] But to be commanded
Forever by your Grace, whose hand has rais'd me.   115

KING.   Come hither, Gardiner.   *Walks and whispers.*

CAMP.   My Lord of York, was not one Doctor Pace
In this man's place before him?

CARD.   Yes, he was.

CAMP.   Was he not held a learned man?

CARD.   Yes, surely.

CAMP.   Believe me, there's an ill opinion spread then,   120
Even of yourself, Lord Cardinal.

CARD.   How? of me?

CAMP.   They will not stick to say you envied him,
And fearing he would rise (he was so virtuous),
Kept him a foreign man still, which so griev'd him
That he ran mad and died.

CARD.   Heav'n's peace be with him!   125
That's Christian care enough. For living murmurers
There's places of rebuke. He was a fool,

---

103. **equal**: alike; impartial. **acquainted**: informed. 104. **for what you**: with the reason that. **Gardiner**: presently Wolsey's secretary. 117. **Doctor Pace**: former secretary to the king, whose fate is explained. 122. **stick**: hesitate. 124. **a foreign man still**: continuously on missions abroad. 126. **murmurers**: fault-finders; detractors.

For he would needs be virtuous. That good fellow,
If I command him, follows my appointment.
I will have none so near else. Learn this, brother,   130
We live not to be grip'd by meaner persons.

KING.   Deliver this with modesty to th' Queen.   *Exit Gardiner.*
The most convenient place that I can think of
For such receipt of learning is Blackfriars.
There ye shall meet about this weighty business.   135
My Wolsey, see it furnish'd. O my lord,
Would it not grieve an able man to leave
So sweet a bedfellow? But, conscience, conscience!
O, 'tis a tender place! and I must leave her.   *Exeunt.*

SCENE III. [*London. An antechamber
in the Queen's apartments.*]

Enter Anne Bullen and an Old Lady.

ANNE B.   Not for that neither! Here's the pang that pinches:
His Highness having liv'd so long with her, and she
So good a lady that no tongue could ever
Pronounce dishonor of her—by my life,
She never knew harm-doing!—O, now, after   5
So many courses of the sun enthroned,
Still growing in a majesty and pomp, the which
To leave a thousandfold more bitter than
'Tis sweet at first t' acquire—after this process
To give her the avaunt, it is a pity   10
Would move a monster.

OLD L.   Hearts of most hard temper
Melt and lament for her.

ANNE B.   O, God's will! much better
She ne'er had known pomp. Though't be temporal,
Yet, if that quarrel, fortune, do divorce

---

128. **needs be**: felt it necessary to be. **good fellow**: Gardiner. 129. **appointment**: instructions. 131. **grip'd**: gripped; clutched at. **meaner**: lower. 132. **modesty**: gentleness. 134. **receipt of learning**: to receive this learned host. **Blackfriars**: a monastery in London. 137. **able**: potent; lusty.

ACT 2, SCENE 3
1. **Not ... neither**: Ann and the Old Lady are discussing the queen's ordeal. **pang that pinches**: pain that clings. 6. **courses of the sun**: years. 8. **To leave**: to give up is. 10. **the avaunt**: her packing orders. 11. **temper**: tempering, disposition. 13. **be temporal**: pomp is transitory. 14. **quarrel**: meddler; quarreler.

| | It from the bearer, 'tis a sufferance panging | 15 |
| | As soul and body's severing. | |

OLD L.   Alas, poor lady!
She's a stranger now again.

ANNE B.   So much the more
Must pity drop upon her. Verily
I swear 'tis better to be lowly born
And range with humble livers in content   20
Than to be perk'd up in a glist'ring grief
And wear a golden sorrow.

OLD L.   Our content
Is our best having.

ANNE B.   By my troth and maidenhead,
I would not be a queen.

OLD L.   Beshrew me, I would,
And venture maidenhead for't! And so would you,†   25
For all this spice of your hypocrisy.
You that have so fair parts of woman on you
Have, too, a woman's heart, which ever yet
Affected eminence, wealth, sovereignty;
Which, to say sooth, are blessings, and which gifts   30
(Saving your mincing) the capacity
Of your soft chiverel conscience would receive,
If you might please to stretch it.

ANNE B.   Nay, good troth!

OLD L.   Yes, troth, and troth! You would not be a queen?

ANNE B.   No, not for all the riches under heaven.   35

OLD L.   'Tis strange! A threepence bow'd would hire me,
Old as I am, to queen it. But I pray you,
What think you of a duchess? Have you limbs
To bear that load of title?

---

15. **panging**: painful. 17. **stranger**: foreigner. 20. **content**: contentment. 21. **perk'd up**: propped up; decked out. 23. **having**: possession. **maidenhead**: virginity. 24. **Beshrew me**: a mild curse. 26. **For**: despite. **spice**: perfume; aroma. 29. **Affected eminence**: aspired to importance. 30. **sooth**: truly. 31. **Saving your mincing**: in spite of your coyness. 32. **chiverel**: cheveril or kid leather (known for its pliancy). 36. **bow'd**: bent (and therefore of no value), with a possible pun on "bawd." See also bawdy puns on "queen" ("quean" or "whore").

---

† "and so would you, / For all this spice of your hypocrisy." Anne's character in this scene insists upon her integrity and pity for the queen. Billington's Anne is not above showing some pleasure at being singled out by the king.

ANNE B.	No, in truth.	
OLD L.	Then you are weakly made. Pluck off a little.	40
	I would not be a young count in your way	
	For more than blushing comes to. If your back	
	Cannot vouchsafe this burthen, 'tis too weak	
	Ever to get a boy.	
ANNE B.	How you do talk!	
	I swear again, I would not be a queen	45
	For all the world.	
OLD L.	In faith, for little England	
	You'ld venture an emballing. I myself	
	Would for Carnarvonshire, although there 'long'd	
	No more to th' crown but that. Lo, who comes here?	

Enter Lord Chamberlain.

CHAM.	Good morrow, ladies. What were't worth to know	50
	The secret of your conference?	
ANNE B.	My good lord,	
	Not your demand; it values not your asking.	
	Our mistress' sorrows we were pitying.	
CHAM.	It was a gentle business and becoming	
	The action of good women. There is hope	55
	All will be well.	
ANNE B.	Now I pray God, amen!	
CHAM.	You bear a gentle mind, and heav'nly blessings	
	Follow such creatures. That you may, fair lady,	
	Perceive I speak sincerely and high note's	
	Ta'en of your many virtues, the King's Majesty	60
	Commends his good opinion of you, and	
	Does purpose honor to you no less flowing	
	Than Marchioness of Pembroke; to which title	
	A thousand pound a year, annual support,	
	Out of his grace he adds.	

---

40. **Pluck off**: pull off (literally, remove her clothing; figuratively, her prudish pretense). 41. **be . . . way**: settle for being a count (ranked below a duke) in your situation. 42. **more . . . blushing**: for fear of the indiscretion I would commit in marrying nobly. 43. **vouchsafe**: carry; support. 44. **get**: 1) attract; 2) beget. 47. **emballing**: carrying the coronation orb (with an obvious bawdy meaning). 48. **Carnarvonshire**: a poor county in Wales. **'long'd**: belonged. 50. **What . . . know**: What would you charge for me to know? 52. **Not**: the subject is not even worth. **values not**: is worth less than. 61. **Commends**: prompts him to express. 62. **flowing**: abundant.

ANNE B.   I do not know   65
What kind of my obedience I should tender.
More than my all is nothing; nor my prayers
Are not words duly hallowed, nor my wishes
More worth than empty vanities. Yet prayers and wishes
Are all I can return. Beseech your lordship,   70
Vouchsafe to speak my thanks and my obedience,
As from a blushing handmaid, to his Highness;
Whose health and royalty I pray for.

CHAM.   Lady,
I shall not fail t' approve the fair conceit
The King hath of you. [*Aside*] I have perus'd her well.   75
Beauty and honour in her are so mingled
That they have caught the King; and who knows yet
But from this lady may proceed a gem
To lighten all this isle?—I'll to the King
And say I spoke with you.

ANNE B.   My honor'd lord!   *Exit Lord Chamberlain.*   80

OLD L.   Why, this it is! See, see!
I have been begging sixteen years in court
(Am yet a courtier beggarly) nor could
Come pat betwixt too early and too late
For any suit of pounds; and you (O fate!),   85
A very fresh fish here—fie, fie, fie upon
This compell'd fortune!—have your mouth fill'd up
Before you open it.

ANNE B.   This is strange to me.

OLD L.   How tastes it? Is it bitter? Forty pence, no.
There was a lady once ('tis an old story)   90
That would not be a queen, that would she not,
For all the mud in Egypt. Have you heard it?

ANNE B.   Come, you are pleasant.

OLD L.   With your theme I could
O'ermount the lark. The Marchioness of Pembroke?

---

67. **More than . . . nothing**: more than everything I have still amounts to nothing. 68. **duly hallowed**: sufficiently holy. 69. **empty vanities**: useless nothings. 70. **Beseech**: I plead with. 71. **Vouchsafe**: grant out of generosity. 74. **t' approve . . . conceit**: second the good estimation. 78. **proceed**: Anne will give birth to the future Queen Elizabeth I. 83. **beggarly**: "In the condition of a beggar" (*OED*, 1). 84. **pat**: more timely. 85. **suit of pounds**: plea for money. 87. **compell'd fortune**: forced good luck. 87–88. **have . . . it**: have gotten filled up (with treasure) without any request at all. 89. **Forty pence, no**: I'll wage forty pence it isn't. 92. **mud in Egypt**: wealth (mud is the source of Egypt's fertile land). 94. **O'ermount**: outsoar.

A thousand pounds a year, for pure respect?   95
No other obligation? By my life,
That promises moe thousands! Honor's train
Is longer than his foreskirt. By this time
I know your back will bear a duchess. Say,
Are you not stronger than you were?

ANNE B.   Good lady,   100
Make yourself mirth with your particular fancy
And leave me out on't. Would I had no being
If this salute my blood a jot! It faints me
To think what follows.
The Queen is comfortless, and we forgetful   105
In our long absence. Pray do not deliver
What here y'have heard to her.

OLD L.   What do you think me?   *Exeunt.*

SCENE IV. [*London. A hall in Blackfriars.*]

> *Trumpets, sennet, and cornets. Enter two*
> *Vergers, with short silver wands; next them,*
> *two Scribes, in the habit of Doctors; after them,*
> *the [Arch]bishop of Canterbury alone; after*
> *him, the Bishops of Lincoln, Ely, Rochester, and*
> *Saint Asaph; next them, with some small*
> *distance, follows a Gentleman bearing the*
> *purse, with the great seal, and a Cardinal's hat;*
> *then two Priests, bearing each a silver cross;*
> *then a Gentleman Usher bareheaded,*
> *accompanied with a Sergeant-at-Arms bearing*
> *a silver mace; then two Gentlemen bearing two*
> *great silver pillars; after them, side by side, the*
> *two Cardinals, [Wolsey and Campeius,] two*
> *Noblemen with the sword and mace. The King*
> *takes place under the cloth of state; the two*
> *Cardinals sit under him as Judges. The Queen*
> *takes place some distance from the King. The*

---

95. **for pure respect**: out of respect unrelated to sexual interest. 97. **moe**: more. 97–98. **Honor's . . . foreskirt**: Honors to follow (like the train of a robe) are much greater than the honors we've seen coming. 101. **particular fancy**: personal fantasy. 102. **on't**: of it. **had no being**: did not exist. 103. **salute . . . jot**: makes me the slightest bit excited ("salute": enlivens). **faints me**: makes me faint. 106. **deliver**: make known.

> *Bishops place themselves on each side the court,*
> *in manner of a consistory; below them, the*
> *Scribes. The Lords sit next the Bishops. The rest*
> *of the Attendants stand in convenient order*
> *about the stage.*

CARD. Whilst our commission from Rome is read,
Let silence be commanded.

KING.   What's the need?
It hath already publicly been read,
And on all sides th' authority allow'd.
You may then spare that time.

CARD.   Be't so. Proceed.   5

SCRIBE. Say, "Henry King of England, come into the court."

CRIER. Henry King of England, come into the court.

KING. Here.

SCRIBE. Say, "Katherine Queen of England, come into the court."

CRIER. Katherine Queen of England, come into the court.   10

> *The Queen makes no answer, rises out of her*
> *chair, goes about the court, comes to the King,*
> *and kneels at his feet; then speaks.*

QUEEN. Sir, I desire you do me right and justice†
And to bestow your pity on me; for
I am a most poor woman and a stranger,
Born out of your dominions, having here
No judge indifferent, nor no more assurance   15
Of equal friendship and proceeding. Alas, sir,
In what have I offended you? What cause
Hath my behaviour given to your displeasure
That thus you should proceed to put me off
And take your good grace from me? Heaven witness   20

ACT 2, SCENE 4
s.d. *sennet*: trumpet fanfare signaling a formal procession. *Vergers*: dignitaries who hold rods or other official symbols. *habit of Doctors*: i.e., wearing lawyers' black fur gowns and flat caps. *cloth of state*: royal canopy. *consistory*: ecclesiastical court. 1. **commission**: authoritative instructions. 4. **allow'd**: recognized. 13. **stranger**: foreigner. 15. **indifferent**: impartial. 16. **equal friendship and proceeding**: a fair representation and process. 19. **put me off**: i.e., divorce me.

---

† Katherine's lines in this scene are among the most powerful of any female character in Shake-speare, and some of the finest actors—Sarah Siddons and Peggy Ashcroft—have exulted in speaking her.

I have been to you a true and humble wife,
At all times to your will conformable,
Ever in fear to kindle your dislike,
Yea, subject to your countenance—glad or sorry
As I saw it inclin'd. When was the hour   25
I ever contradicted your desire
Or made it not mine too? Or which of your friends
Have I not strove to love, although I knew
He were mine enemy? What friend of mine
That had to him deriv'd your anger did I   30
Continue in my liking? nay, gave notice
He was from thence discharg'd? Sir, call to mind
That I have been your wife in this obedience
Upward of twenty years and have been blest
With many children by you. If in the course   35
And process of this time you can report,
And prove it too, against mine honor aught,
My bond to wedlock, or my love and duty,
Against your sacred person, in God's name
Turn me away, and let the foul'st contempt   40
Shut door upon me, and so give me up
To the sharp'st kind of justice. Please you, sir,
The King your father was reputed for
A prince most prudent, of an excellent
And unmatch'd wit and judgment. Ferdinand,   45
My father, King of Spain, was reckon'd one
The wisest prince that there had reign'd by many
A year before. It is not to be question'd
That they had gather'd a wise council to them
Of every realm, that did debate this business,   50
Who deem'd our marriage lawful. Wherefore I humbly
Beseech you, sir, to spare me till I may
Be by my friends in Spain advis'd, whose counsel
I will implore. If not, i' th' name of God,
Your pleasure be fulfill'd!

CARD.   You have here, lady   55
     (And of your choice), these reverend fathers, men
     Of singular integrity and learning,

---

22. **conformable**: compliant with. 24. **subject . . . countenance**: responsive to your moods. 30.
deriv'd: incurred. 34–35. **blest . . . you**: Of the five children Katherine bore, only Mary survived and
would later become queen, 1553–1558. 37. **against . . . aught**: anything against my fidelity in marriage.
39. **Against**: toward. 45. **wit**: wisdom; intelligence. 46–47. **reckon'd . . . wisest**: considered the very
wisest.

<blockquote>
Yea, the elect o' th' land, who are assembled
To plead your cause. It shall be therefore bootless
That longer you defer the court, as well   60
For your own quiet as to rectify
What is unsettled in the King.
</blockquote>

CAMP. His Grace
<blockquote>
Hath spoken well and justly. Therefore, madam,
It's fit this royal session do proceed
And that (without delay) their arguments   65
Be now produc'd and heard.
</blockquote>

QUEEN. Lord Cardinal,
<blockquote>To you I speak.</blockquote>

CARD. Your pleasure, madam?

QUEEN. Sir,
<blockquote>
I am about to weep; but, thinking that
We are a queen (or long have dream'd so), certain
The daughter of a king, my drops of tears   70
I'll turn to sparks of fire.
</blockquote>

CARD. Be patient yet.

QUEEN.
<blockquote>
I will, when you are humble; nay, before,
Or God will punish me. I do believe
(Induc'd by potent circumstances) that
You are mine enemy; and make my challenge   75
You shall not be my judge; for it is you
Have blown this coal betwixt my lord and me—
Which God's dew quench! Therefore I say again
I utterly abhor, yea, from my soul
Refuse you for my judge, whom yet once more   80
I hold my most malicious foe and think not
At all a friend to truth.
</blockquote>

CARD. I do profess
<blockquote>
You speak not like yourself, who ever yet
Have stood to charity and display'd th' effects
Of disposition gentle and of wisdom   85
</blockquote>

---

59. **bootless**: to no avail; profitless. 60. **defer the court**: attempt to delay the proceedings. 61. **quiet**: peace of mind. **rectify**: set right. 69. **certain**: certainly. 72. **before**: sooner than (implying never). 73. **Or**: else. 74. **Induc'd . . . circumstances**: persuaded by powerful facts at hand. 75. **make my challenge**: give my objection stating that. 77. **blown this coal**: caused this controversy. 79. **abhor**: Canon law's term for protest against. 82. **profess**: openly proclaim. 84. **stood to**: upheld; stood up for. 86. **O'ertopping**: exceeding. 87. **spleen**: ill will.

Queen Katherine (Claire Bloom) at trial appears stately and isolated at once.

O'ertopping woman's pow'r. Madam, you do me wrong.
I have no spleen against you, nor injustice
For you or any. How far I have proceeded,
Or how far further shall, is warranted
By a commission from the Consistory,   90
Yea, the whole Consistory of Rome. You charge me
That I have blown this coal. I do deny it.
The King is present. If it be known to him
That I gainsay my deed, how may he wound,
And worthily, my falsehood! Yea, as much   95
As you have done my truth. If he know
That I am free of your report, he knows
I am not of your wrong. Therefore in him
It lies to cure me, and the cure is to
Remove these thoughts from you; the which before   100

94. **gainsay my deed**: deny something I actually did. 95. **worthily**: justly. 96. **done**: i.e., wounded. 97. **free**: untouched. **report**: imputation. 98. **not . . . wrong**: untouched by the wrong you have done me. 99. **cure me**: i.e., heal me of the wound of your accusations. 100. **the which**: which, i.e., the thoughts.

His Highness shall speak in, I do beseech
You, gracious madam, to unthink your speaking
And to say so no more.

QUEEN.   My lord, my lord,
I am a simple woman, much too weak
T' oppose your cunning. Y'are meek and humble-mouth'd;   105
You sign your place and calling, in full seeming,
With meekness and humility; but your heart
Is cramm'd with arrogancy, spleen, and pride.
You have, by fortune and his Highness' favors,
Gone slightly o'er low steps and now are mounted   110
Where pow'rs are your retainers and your words
(Domestics to you) serve your will as't please
Yourself pronounce their office. I must tell you
You tender more your person's honor than
Your high profession spiritual; that again   115
I do refuse you for my judge and here,
Before you all, appeal unto the Pope,
To bring my whole cause fore his Holiness
And to be judg'd by him.
                    She curtsies to the King and offers to depart.

CAMP.   The Queen is obstinate,
Stubborn to justice, apt to accuse it, and   120
Disdainful to be tried by't. 'Tis not well.
She's going away.

KING.   Call her again.

CRIER.   Katherine Queen of England, come into the court.

GENT. USHER.   Madam, you are call'd back.

QUEEN.   What need you note it? Pray you keep your way.†   125
When you are call'd, return. Now the Lord help!
They vex me past my patience. Pray you pass on.
I will not tarry; no, nor ever more

---

101. **speak in**: pronounce upon. 106. **sign**: signify. **in full seeming**: fully in the way you appear. 110. **slightly**: with ease. **mounted**: established yourself. 111. **pow'rs . . . retainers**: noble men are your servants. 112. **Domestics**: household servants. 112–113: **serve . . . office**: do your bidding in any way you decide. 114. **tender . . . honor**: care more about your personal power. 120. **Stubborn**: resistant. 124. **you**: Here, Katherine addresses her attendants, who have obviously stopped departing from the room. 127. **pass on**: keep moving.

---

† The king is himself much moved by Katherine's lines, even though he is the cause of her displeasure.

Upon this business my appearance make
In any of their courts.   *Exeunt Queen and her Attendants.*

KING.   Go thy ways, Kate.   130
That man i' th' world who shall report he has
A better wife, let him in naught be trusted
For speaking false in that. Thou art, alone
(If thy rare qualities, sweet gentleness,
Thy meekness saintlike, wifelike government,   135
Obeying in commanding, and thy parts
Sovereign and pious else, could speak thee out)
The queen of earthly queens. She's noble born,
And like her true nobility she has
Carried herself towards me.

CARD.   Most gracious sir,   140
In humblest manner I require your Highness
That it shall please you to declare in hearing
Of all these ears (for where I am robb'd and bound,
There must I be unloos'd, although not there
At once and fully satisfied) whether ever I   145
Did broach this business to your Highness, or
Laid any scruple in your way which might
Induce you to the question on't, or ever
Have to you, but with thanks to God for such
A royal lady, spake one the least word that might   150
Be to the prejudice of her present state
Or touch of her good person.

KING.   My Lord Cardinal,
I do excuse you; yea, upon mine honour,
I free you from't. You are not to be taught
That you have many enemies that know not   155
Why they are so, but, like to village curs,
Bark when their fellows do. By some of these
The Queen is put in anger. Y'are excus'd.
But will you be more justified? You ever
Have wish'd the sleeping of this business; never   160

---

135. **government**: self-control. 136. **Obeying in commanding**: showing proper reverence to her station as a woman even while she dispenses sovereign orders. **parts**: qualities. 137. **could speak thee out**: could fully describe you (this predicate completes the "if" clause beginning at line 134). 140. **Carried**: Conducted. 141. **require**: request. 143. **robb'd and bound**: Wolsey is referring back to effects of the queen's accusation. 144–145. **although . . . satisfied**: Wolsey suggests that not even the king can fully restore his reputation. 148. **on't**: i.e., on the question of his marriage. 151. **prejudice**: harm. 152. **touch**: blemishing. 153. **excuse**: exculpate; free from accusation. 156. **curs**: dogs.

Desir'd it to be stirr'd; but oft have hind'red, oft,
The passages made toward it. On my honor,
I speak my good Lord Cardinal to this point,
And thus far clear him. Now, what mov'd me to't,
I will be bold with time and your attention.   165
Then mark th' inducement. Thus it came; give heed to't.
My conscience first receiv'd a tenderness,
Scruple, and prick on certain speeches utter'd
By th' Bishop of Bayonne, then French ambassador,
Who had been hither sent on the debating   170
A marriage 'twixt the Duke of Orleans and
Our daughter Mary. I' th' progress of this business,
Ere a determinate resolution, he
(I mean the Bishop) did require a respite
Wherein he might the King his lord advertise   175
Whether our daughter were legitimate,
Respecting this our marriage with the dowager,
Sometimes our brother's wife. This respite shook
The bosom of my conscience, enter'd me,
Yea, with a spitting power and made to tremble   180
The region of my breast, which forc'd such way
That many maz'd considerings did throng
And press'd in with this caution. First, methought
I stood not in the smile of heaven, who had
Commanded nature that my lady's womb,   185
If it conceiv'd a male child by me, should
Do no more offices of life to't than
The grave does to th' dead; for her male issue
Or died where they were made or shortly after
This world had air'd them. Hence I took a thought   190
This was a judgment on me, that my kingdom
(Well worthy the best heir o' th' world) should not
Be gladded in't by me. Then follows that
I weigh'd the danger which my realms stood in
By this my issue's fail, and that gave to me   195
Many a groaning throe. Thus hulling in

---

162. **passages**: proceedings. 163. **speak**: testify on behalf of. 167. **tenderness**: sore spot. 173. **determinate**: final. 175. **advertise**: consider (from Latin, "turn to"). 177. **dowager**: widow.: 178. **Sometimes**: formerly. 179. **bosom**: inmost part; the heart. 180. **spitting**: impaling (as on a "spit"). 182. **maz'd**: amazed; baffling. 183. **caution**: warning. 187. **offices**: favors; services. 189. **Or**: either. **where . . . made**: in the uterus. 190. **air'd them**: 1) brought them into public view; 2) given them air. 193. **Be gladded**: made glad. 195. **fail**: death. 196. **throe**: pain. **hulling**: drifting caused by force of the winds even when the sails are down.

The wild sea of my conscience, I did steer
Toward this remedy whereupon we are
Now present here together. That's to say
I meant to rectify my conscience, which   200
I then did feel full sick, and yet not well,
By all the reverend fathers of the land
And doctors learn'd. First I began in private
With you, my Lord of Lincoln. You remember
How under my oppression I did reek   205
When I first mov'd you.

B. LINC.   Very well, my liege.

KING.   I have spoke long. Be pleas'd yourself to say
How far you satisfied me.

B. LINC.   So please your Highness,
The question did at first so stagger me,
Bearing a state of mighty moment in't   210
And consequence of dread, that I committed
The daring'st counsel which I had to doubt
And did entreat your Highness to this course
Which you are running here.

KING.   I then mov'd you,
My Lord of Canterbury, and got your leave   215
To make this present summons. Unsolicited
I left no reverend person in this court,
But by particular consent proceeded
Under your hands and seals. Therefore go on;
For no dislike i' th' world against the person   220
Of the good Queen, but the sharp thorny points
Of my alleged reasons, drives this forward.
Prove but our marriage lawful, by my life
And kingly dignity, we are contented
To wear our mortal state to come with her,   225
Katherine our queen, before the primest creature
That's paragon'd o' th' world.

CAMP.   So please your Highness,
The Queen being absent, 'tis a needful fitness

---

201. **yet not**: still have not been made. 205. **How . . . reek**: how I sweated under this burden. 210. **mighty moment**: great importance. 211. **consequence of dread**: dreadful consequences. 211–212. **committed . . . doubt**: committed myself to the most extreme advice I feared. 216. **Unsolicited**: free of consultation. 219. **hands and seals**: signed approval. 225. **wear . . . come**: live the remainder of my life. 226. **primest**: most excellent. 227. **paragon'd**: served as a model of perfection. 228. **needful fitness**: only proper.

That we adjourn this court till further day.
Meanwhile must be an earnest motion   230
Made to the Queen to call back her appeal
She intends unto his Holiness.

KING.   [*Aside*] I may perceive
These Cardinals trifle with me. I abhor
This dilatory sloth and tricks of Rome.
My learn'd and well-beloved servant Cranmer,   235
Prithee return. With thy approach I know
My comfort comes along.—Break up the court.
I say, set on.   *Exeunt in manner as they enter'd.*

Act III

SCENE I. [*London. A room in the Queen's apartments.*]

Enter the Queen and her Women, as at work.

QUEEN.   Take thy lute, wench. My soul grows sad with troubles.
Sing, and disperse 'em if thou canst. Leave working.

Song.

Orpheus with his lute made trees
And the mountain tops that freeze
Bow themselves when he did sing.   5
To his music plants and flowers
Ever sprung, as sun and showers
There had made a lasting spring.

Everything that heard him play,
Even the billows of the sea,   10
Hung their heads, and then lay by.
In sweet music is such art
Killing care and grief of heart
Fall asleep, or hearing, die.

Enter a Gentleman.

---

230. **must be**: there must be. **motion**: request. 231. **call back**: retract. 235–236. **My . . . Prithee, return**: Henry is thinking aloud (apostrophizing) about his servant Cranmer, a Protestant who has been on the continent collecting learned opinions about the king's divorce. 238. **set on**: go forth.

ACT 3, SCENE I:
1. **wench**: here, a term of endearment. 2. **Leave**: cease. 3. **Orpheus**: superlatively skilled lute player of Greek mythology. 7. **as**: as if. 11. **lay by**: withdrew. 12–13. **such . . . care**: such skill in soothing worry.

QUEEN.	How now?	15

GENT. An't please your Grace, the two great Cardinals
Wait in the presence.

QUEEN.   Would they speak with me?

GENT. They will'd me say so, madam.

QUEEN.   Pray their Graces
To come near. [*Exit Gentleman*] What can be their business
With me, a poor weak woman, fall'n from favor?† 20
I do not like their coming. Now I think on't,
They should be good men, their affairs as righteous;
But all hoods make not monks.

Enter the two Cardinals,
Wolsey and Campeius.

CARD.   Peace to your Highness!

QUEEN. Your Graces find me here part of a housewife
(I would be all) against the worst may happen. 25
What are your pleasures with me, reverend lords?

CARD. May it please you, noble madam, to withdraw
Into your private chamber, we shall give you
The full cause of our coming.

QUEEN.   Speak it here.
There's nothing I have done yet, o' my conscience, 30
Deserves a corner. Would all other women
Could speak this with as free a soul as I do!
My lords, I care not (so much I am happy
Above a number) if my actions
Were tried by ev'ry tongue, ev'ry eye saw 'em, 35
Envy and base opinion set against 'em,
I know my life so even. If your business
Seek me out, and that way I am wife in,
Out with it boldly. Truth loves open dealing.

CARD. *Tanta est erga te mentis integritas, regina serenissima—* 40

---

15. **How now**: a statement of reproach. 17. **presence**: place for receiving guests. 22. **as**: likewise: 24. **part of**: in part. 25. **against**: in preparation for. 31. **Deserves a corner**: that needs a place to hide. 34. **a number**: most. 36. **Envy ... opinion**: envy and fault-finding. 37. **so even**: to be spotless. 39. **Seek ... in**: i.e., concerns my conduct as a wife. 40. *Tanta ... serenissima*: So great is my mind's integrity concerning you, most peaceful queen.

---

† "a poor weak woman, fall'n from favor?" More a question here than it was in the previous scene is how defeated the queen feels or how defiant she remains.

QUEEN.	O, good my lord, no Latin!

I am not such a truant since my coming
As not to know the language I have liv'd in.
A strange tongue makes my cause more strange, suspicious.
Pray speak in English. Here are some will thank you,   45
If you speak truth, for their poor mistress' sake.
Believe me, she has had much wrong. Lord Cardinal,
The willing'st sin I ever yet committed
May be absolv'd in English.

CARD.   Noble lady,
I am sorry my integrity should breed   50
(And service to his Majesty and you)
So deep suspicion where all faith was meant.
We come not by the way of accusation
To taint that honor every good tongue blesses,
Nor to betray you any way to sorrow—   55
You have too much, good lady—but to know
How you stand minded in the weighty difference
Between the King and you, and to deliver
(Like free and honest men) our just opinions
And comforts to your cause.

CAMP.   Most honor'd madam,   60
My Lord of York, out of his noble nature,
Zeal and obedience he still bore your Grace,
Forgetting (like a good man) your late censure
Both of his truth and him (which was too far),
Offers, as I do, in a sign of peace,   65
His service and his counsel.

QUEEN.   [Aside] To betray me.—
My lords, I thank you both for your good wills.
Ye speak like honest men (pray God ye prove so!).
But how to make ye suddenly an answer
In such a point of weight, so near mine honor   70
(More near my life, I fear), with my weak wit,
And to such men of gravity and learning,
In truth I know not. I was set at work
Among my maids, full little (God knows) looking
Either for such men or such business.   75

---

42. **my coming**: i.e., to England. 44. **strange**: foreign. 48. **willing'st**: most deliberate. 52. **all faith**: only loyalty to you. 55. **any**: in any. 57. **stand minded**: have resolved to believe. 59. **free**: candid. 62. **still bore**: still recognized. 63. **late**: recent. 64. **was**: went. 71. **wit**: intelligence. 73. **set**: seated.

For her sake that I have been—for I feel
The last fit of my greatness—good your Graces,
Let me have time and counsel for my cause.
Alas, I am a woman friendless, hopeless!

CARD.   Madam, you wrong the King's love with these fears.   80
Your hopes and friends are infinite.

QUEEN.   In England
But little for my profit. Can you think, lords,
That any Englishman dare give me counsel?
Or be a known friend 'gainst his highness' pleasure
(Though he be grown so desperate to be honest)   85
And live a subject? Nay forsooth, my friends,
They that must weigh out my afflictions,
They that my trust must grow to, live not here.
They are (as all my other comforts) far hence,
In mine own country, lords.

CAMP.   I would your Grace   90
Would leave your griefs and take my counsel.

QUEEN.   How, sir?

CAMP.   Put your main cause into the King's protection.
He's loving and most gracious. 'Twill be much
Both for your honor better and your cause;
For if the trial of the law o'ertake ye,   95
You'll part away disgrac'd.

CARD.   He tells you rightly.

QUEEN.   Ye tell me what ye wish for both—my ruin.
Is this your Christian counsel? Out upon ye!
Heaven is above all yet. There sits a judge
That no king can corrupt.

CAMP.   Your rage mistakes us.   100

QUEEN.   The more shame for ye! Holy men I thought ye,
Upon my soul, two reverend cardinal virtues;
But cardinal sins and hollow hearts I fear ye.

---

76. **For . . . been**: in honor of the queenly personage I was. 77. **fit**: a spell or episode (usually in illness). 82. **profit**: avail. 85. **desperate**: crazy (said cynically). 86. **live a subject**: escape death. **forsooth**: truly. 87. **weigh out**: measure; consider the gravity of. 88. **grow to**: become engrafted to. 93–94. **be . . . better**: be much better for your honor. 96. **part away**: leave. 97. **Ye . . . both**: You both tell me . . . 98. **Out upon**: a curse. 100. **mistakes**: causes you to misjudge. 102. **cardinal virtues**: With a pun on the Church office of cardinal. The cardinal virtues are prudence, justice, temperance, and fortitude, and they counter four of the cardinal (or "deadly") sins. 103. **cardinal sins**: with a possible pun on "cardinal" as "carnal."

Mend 'em for shame, my lords! Is this your comfort?
The cordial that ye bring a wretched lady?   105
A woman lost among ye, laugh'd at, scorn'd?
I will not wish ye half my miseries;
I have more charity. But say I warn'd ye.
Take heed, for heaven's sake take heed, lest at once
The burthen of my sorrows fall upon ye.   110

CARD.   Madam, this is a mere distraction.
You turn the good we offer into envy.

QUEEN. Ye turn me into nothing. Woe upon ye
And all such false professors! Would you have me
(If you have any justice, any pity,   115
If ye be anything but churchmen's habits)
Put my sick cause into his hands that hates me?
Alas, has banish'd me his bed already,
His love, too long ago! I am old, my lords,
And all the fellowship I hold now with him   120
Is only my obedience. What can happen
To me above this wretchedness? All your studies
Make me a curse like this!

CAMP.   Your fears are worse.

QUEEN. Have I liv'd thus long (let me speak myself,
Since virtue finds no friends) a wife, a true one?   125
A woman (I dare say, without vainglory)
Never yet branded with suspicion?
Have I with all my full affections
Still met the King? lov'd him next heav'n? obey'd him?
Been (out of fondness) superstitious to him?   130
Almost forgot my prayers to content him?
And am I thus rewarded? 'Tis not well, lords.
Bring me a constant woman to her husband,
One that ne'er dream'd a joy beyond his pleasure,
And to that woman (when she has done most)   135
Yet will I add an honor—a great patience.

---

105. **cordial**: restoring medicine. 106. **lost**: a number of possible senses apply: "confused," "abandoned," "damned." 109. **at once**: all at once. 111. **mere distraction**: utter madness. 112. **envy**: ill will. 114. **false professors**: i.e., They hypocritically "profess" faith they do not have. 116. **habits**: robes or vestments. 118. **me**: me from. 122. **above**: beyond. **studies**: efforts. 123. **a curse**: perhaps should read "accursed." 124. **speak**: defend; explain. 129. **Still**: continuously. 130. **fondness**: love (to the point of folly). **Been . . . superstitious**: idolized. 133. **constant woman**: a woman so constant (or loyal). 136. **add**: surpass her by.

CARD.   Madam, you wander from the good we aim at.

QUEEN.   My lord, I dare not make myself so guilty
              To give up willingly that noble title
              Your master wed me to. Nothing but death   140
              Shall e'er divorce my dignities.

CARD.   Pray hear me.

QUEEN.   Would I had never trod this English earth
              Or felt the flatteries that grow upon it!
              Ye have angels' faces, but heaven knows your hearts.
              What will become of me now, wretched lady?   145
              I am the most unhappy woman living.

              [*To her Women*] Alas, poor wenches, where are now your
                    fortunes?
              Shipwrack'd upon a kingdom where no pity,
              No friends, no hope, no kindred weep for me,
              Almost no grave allow'd me! Like the lily   150
              That once was mistress of the field and flourish'd,
              I'll hang my head and perish.

CARD.   If your Grace
              Could but be brought to know our ends are honest,
              You'ld feel more comfort. Why should we, good lady,
              Upon what cause, wrong you? Alas, our places,   155
              The way of our profession is against it.
              We are to cure such sorrows, not to sow 'em.
              For goodness sake, consider what you do;
              How you may hurt yourself, ay, utterly
              Grow from the King's acquaintance, by this carriage.   160
              The hearts of princes kiss obedience,
              So much they love it; but to stubborn spirits
              They swell and grow as terrible as storms.
              I know you have a gentle, noble temper,
              A soul as even as a calm. Pray think us   165
              Those we profess—peacemakers, friends, and servants.

CAMP.   Madam, you'll find it so. You wrong your virtues
              With these weak women's fears. A noble spirit,
              As yours was put into you, ever casts

---

137. **wander from**: misunderstand. 138. **make ... guilty**: implicitly concede my guilt. 141. **dignities**: titles. 153. **ends**: intentions. 155. **places**: dignity of office. 160. **Grow from**: estrange yourself from. **carriage**: course of action. 164. **temper**: make-up; temperament. 169. **As yours**: such as the one that.

Such doubts as false coin from it. The King loves you. 170
Beware you lose it not. For us, if you please
To trust us in your business, we are ready
To use our utmost studies in your service.

QUEEN. Do what ye will, my lords; and pray forgive me
If I have us'd myself unmannerly. 175
You know I am a woman, lacking wit
To make a seemly answer to such persons.
Pray do my service to his Majesty.
He has my heart yet and shall have my prayers
While I shall have my life. Come, reverend fathers, 180
Bestow your counsels on me. She now begs
That little thought, when she set footing here,
She should have bought her dignities so dear. *Exeunt.*

SCENE II. [*London. Antechamber to the King's apartment.*]

Enter the Duke of Norfolk, Duke of Suffolk,
Lord Surrey, and Lord Chamberlain.

NOR. If you will now unite in your complaints
And force them with a constancy, the Cardinal
Cannot stand under them. If you omit
The offer of this time, I cannot promise
But that you shall sustain moe new disgraces 5
With these you bear already.

SUR. I am joyful
To meet the least occasion that may give me
Remembrance of my father-in-law, the Duke,
To be reveng'd on him.

SUF. Which of the peers
Have uncontemn'd gone by him, or at least 10
Strangely neglected? When did he regard
The stamp of nobleness in any person
Out of himself?

170. **false**: counterfeit. 173. **studies**: efforts. 175. **us'ed**: behaved. 177. **seemly**: proper. 178. **do my service**: pay my respects. 182. **That**: who. 183. **so dear**: at so great a price.
ACT 3, SCENE 2
2. **force . . . constancy**: press persistently. 3–4. **omit . . . time**: pass up this opportunity. 5. **But**: except. **moe**: more. 8. **father-in-law**: Buckingham (Surrey has been in virtual exile in Ireland; see 2.2.40–45). 10–11. **uncontemn'd . . . neglected**: passed by him without open contempt or at least unexpected snubbing. 13. **Out of**: besides him.

CHAM.   My lords, you speak your pleasures.
        What he deserves of you and me I know.
        What we can do to him (though now the time   15
        Gives way to us) I much fear. If you cannot
        Bar his access to th' King, never attempt
        Anything on him; for he hath a witchcraft
        Over the King in's tongue.

NOR.   O, fear him not!
        His spell in that is out. The King hath found   20
        Matter against him that forever mars
        The honey of his language. No, he's settled
        (Not to come off) in his displeasure.

SUR.   Sir,
        I should be glad to hear such news as this
        Once every hour.

NOR.   Believe it, this is true.   25
        In the divorce his contrary proceedings
        Are all unfolded; wherein he appears
        As I would wish mine enemy.

SUR.   How came
        His practices to light?

SUF.   Most strangely.

SUR.   O, how? how?

SUF.   The Cardinal's letters to the Pope miscarried   30
        And came to th' eye o' th' King, wherein was read
        How that the Cardinal did entreat his Holiness
        To stay the judgment o' th' divorce; for if
        It did take place, "I do," quoth he, "perceive
        My king is tangled in affection to   35
        A creature of the Queen's, Lady Anne Bullen."

SUR.   Has the King this?

SUF.   Believe it.

SUR.   Will this work?

CHAM.   The King in this perceives him, how he coasts
        And hedges his own way. But in this point

---

16. **Gives way**: provides an opportunity. **fear**: doubt. 20. **out**: over. 22: **he's**: probably "the king is."
23. **come off**: desist. 26. **contrary proceedings**: duplicitous undertakings. 27. **unfolded**: exposed. 29.
practices: tricks; machinations. 30. **miscarried**: failed. 33. **stay**: halt or delay. 36. **creature**: underling;
servant. 38–39. **coasts / And hedges**: works by subterfuge to achieve (as if sneaking around coasts and
hedges).

| | All his tricks founder and he brings his physic | 40 |

All his tricks founder and he brings his physic 40
After his patient's death: the King already
Hath married the fair lady.

SUR.   Would he had!

SUF.   May you be happy in your wish, my lord!
For I profess you have it.

SUR.   Now all my joy
Trace the conjunction!

SUF.   My amen to't!

NOR.   All men's! 45

SUF.   There's order given for her coronation.
Marry, this is yet but young and may be left
To some ears unrecounted. But, my lords,
She is a gallant creature and complete
In mind and feature. I persuade me, from her 50
Will fall some blessing to this land which shall
In it be memoriz'd.

SUR.   But will the King
Digest this letter of the Cardinal's?
The Lord forbid!

NOR.   Marry amen!

SUF.   No, no!
There be moe wasps that buzz about his nose 55
Will make this sting the sooner. Cardinal Campeius
Is stol'n away to Rome, hath ta'en no leave,
Has left the cause o' th' King unhandled, and
Is posted as the agent of our Cardinal
To second all his plot. I do assure you 60
The King cried "Ha!" at this.

CHAM.   Now God incense him
And let him cry "Ha!" louder!

NOR.   But, my lord,
When returns Cranmer?

SUF.   He is return'd in his opinions, which
Have satisfied the King for his divorce, 65

40. **physic**: remedy. 45. **Trace**: "Follow" (*GLK*). 47. **young**: new. 48 **unrecounted**: untold. 49. **complete**: perfect. 50. **persuade me**: am persuaded. 52. **memoriz'd**: "ma[d]e memorable or glorious" (*GLK*). 53. **Digest**: stomach; endure. 59. **Is posted**: has hurried off. **agent**: accomplice. 64. **is . . . opinions**: has sent his opinions ahead his return.

Together with all famous colleges
Almost in Christendom. Shortly, I believe,
His second marriage shall be publish'd and
Her coronation. Katherine no more
Shall be call'd Queen, but Princess Dowager   70
And widow to Prince Arthur.

NOR.   This same Cranmer's
A worthy fellow and hath ta'en much pain
In the King's business.

SUF.   He has, and we shall see him
For it an archbishop.

NOR.   So I hear.

SUF.   'Tis so.

Enter [Cardinal] Wolsey and Cromwell.

The Cardinal!

NOR.   Observe, observe! He's moody.   75

CARD.   The packet, Cromwell—gave't you the King?

CROM.   To his own hand, in's bedchamber.

CARD.   Look'd he
O' th' inside of the papers?

CROM.   Presently
He did unseal them; and the first he view'd,
He did it with a serious mind; a heed   80
Was in his countenance. You he bade
Attend him here this morning.

CARD.   Is he ready
To come abroad?

CROM.   I think by this he is.

CARD.   Leave me awhile.   *Exit Cromwell.*
[*Aside*] It shall be to the Duchess of Alençon,   85
The French king's sister. He shall marry her.
Anne Bullen? No! I'll no Anne Bullens for him.
There's more in't than fair visage. Bullen?

---

68. **publish'd**: openly proclaimed. 74. **For it**: as a reward for it. 76. **packet**: i.e., of letters. 78. **Presently**: at once. 80. **heed**: serious or concerned appearance. 83. **abroad**: out of his private room. 84. **by this**: by now. 88. **fair visage**: a pretty face.

No, we'll no Bullens! Speedily I wish
To hear from Rome. The Marchioness of Pembroke?   90

NOR.   He's discontented.

SUF.   May be he hears the King
Does whet his anger to him.

SUR.   Sharp enough,
Lord, for thy justice!

CARD.   [*Aside*] The late Queen's gentlewoman, a knight's daughter,
To be her mistress' mistress? the Queen's queen?   95
This candle burns not clear. 'Tis I must snuff it.
Then out it goes! What though I know her virtuous
And well deserving? Yet I know her for
A spleeny Lutheran, and not wholesome to
Our cause that she should lie i' th' bosom of   100
Our hard-rul'd king. Again, there is sprung up
An heretic, an arch one—Cranmer, one
Hath crawl'd into the favor of the King
And is his oracle.

NOR.   He is vex'd at something.

Enter King, reading of a schedule, [and Lovell].

SUR.   I would 'twere something that would fret the string,   105
The master-cord on's heart!

SUF.   The King, the King!

KING.   What piles of wealth hath he accumulated
To his own portion! and what expense by th' hour
Seems to flow from him! How i' th' name of thrift
Does he rake this together?—Now, my lords,   110
Saw you the Cardinal?

NOR.   My lord, we have
Stood here observing him. Some strange commotion
Is in his brain. He bites his lip and starts,
Stops on a sudden, looks upon the ground,
Then lays his finger on his temple; straight   115
Springs out into fast gait, then stops again,

---

94. **late**: recent. 96. **snuff it**: trim the wick. 99. **spleeny Lutheran**: a contentious Protestant—follower of the beliefs of Martin Luther. 101. **hard-rul'd**: barely manageable. 104. **oracle**: an interpreter of God's will (in this case, on the divorce). 105–106. **fret . . . heart**: Picking up on Wolsey's being "vex'd," Norfolk wishes that something would "fret" or "cut through" the lifeline ("master-cord") of his heart. 106. **on's**: on his. 110. **rake this**: accumulate this wealth. 115. **straight**: at once. 116. **gait**: a walk.

Strikes his breast hard, and anon he casts
His eye against the moon. In most strange postures
We have seen him set himself.

KING.   It may well be;
There is a mutiny in's mind. This morning   120
Papers of state he sent me to peruse,
As I requir'd; and wot you what I found
There—on my conscience, put unwittingly?
Forsooth, an inventory, thus importing,
The several parcels of his plate, his treasure,   125
Rich stuffs and ornaments of household; which
I find at such proud rate that it outspeaks
Possession of a subject.

NOR.   It's heaven's will.
Some spirit put this paper in the packet
To bless your eye withal.

KING.   If we did think   130
His contemplation were above the earth
And fix'd on spiritual object, he should still
Dwell in his musings; but I am afraid
His thinkings are below the moon, not worth
His serious considering.

                    King takes his seat; whispers to
                    Lovell, who goes to the Cardinal.

CARD.   Heaven forgive me!   135
Ever God bless your Highness!

KING.   Good my lord,
You are full of heavenly stuff and bear the inventory
Of your best graces in your mind; the which
You were now running o'er. You have scarce time
To steal from spiritual leisure a brief span   140
To keep your earthly audit. Sure, in that
I deem you an ill husband, and am glad
To have you therein my companion.

---

122. **wot**: know. 124. **importing**: spelling out; signifying. 125. **several parcels**: the various collections.
plate: gold or silver (often formed into serving plates). 127. **proud**: high. 127–128. **outspeaks . . . subject**: speaks more loudly than a mere subject should. 130. **withal**: with. 132. **he
should still**: it would be proper that he continue to. 134. **below the moon**: are on earthly things. 137.
stuff: make-up; mettle or considerations. **bear**: suffer under the burden of. 140. **spiritual leisure**: A
difficult phrase given that the context suggests spiritual devotion and leisure is normally time away
from obligation. The king perhaps is being ironic. 142. **husband**: caretaker; manager (Henry puns on
the marital sense of the word in the next line when he equates Wolsey as his "companion").

CARD.   Sir,
　　　For holy offices I have a time; a time
　　　To think upon the part of business which   145
　　　I bear i' th' state; and nature does require
　　　Her times of preservation, which perforce
　　　I, her frail son, amongst my brethren mortal,
　　　Must give my tendance to.

KING.   You have said well.

CARD. And ever may your Highness yoke together   150
　　　(As I will lend you cause) my doing well
　　　With my well saying!

KING.   'Tis well said again,
　　　And 'tis a kind of good deed to say well;
　　　And yet words are no deeds. My father lov'd you;
　　　He said he did, and with his deed did crown   155
　　　His word upon you. Since I had my office,
　　　I have kept you next my heart; have not alone
　　　Employ'd you where high profits might come home,
　　　But par'd my present havings to bestow
　　　My bounties upon you.

CARD.   [Aside] What should this mean?   160

SUR.   [Aside] The Lord increase this business!

KING.   Have I not made you
　　　The prime man of the state? I pray you tell me
　　　If what I now pronounce you have found true;
　　　And if you may confess it, say withal
　　　If you are bound to us or no. What say you?   165

CARD. My sovereign, I confess your royal graces,
　　　Show'r'd on me daily, have been more than could
　　　My studied purposes requite, which went
　　　Beyond all man's endeavours. My endeavours
　　　Have ever come too short of my desires,   170
　　　Yet fil'd with my abilities. Mine own ends
　　　Have been mine so that evermore they pointed
　　　To th' good of your most sacred person and
　　　The profit of the state. For your great graces

---

147. **preservation**: i.e., of preserving life. 149. **give . . . to**: attend to. 155. **crown**: realize. 157. **next**: nearest. 159. **par'd . . . havings**: pared or reduced my own belongings. 162. **prime**: highest ranking (Lord Chancellor). 164. **withal**: besides. 168. **studied purposes requite**: dedicated efforts repay. 171. **fil'd with**: ranked with. **ends**: purposes; possessions. 172. **so that**: only insofar as.

Heap'd upon me (poor undeserver) I   175
Can nothing render but allegiant thanks,
My pray'rs to heaven for you, my loyalty,
Which ever has and ever shall be growing
Till death (that winter) kill it.

KING.   Fairly answer'd!
A loyal and obedient subject is   180
Therein illustrated. The honor of it
Does pay the act of it, as, i' th' contrary,
The foulness is the punishment. I presume
That, as my hand has open'd bounty to you,
My heart dropp'd love, my pow'r rain'd honor, more   185
On you than any, so your hand and heart,
Your brain, and every function of your power
Should, notwithstanding that your bond of duty,
As 'twere in love's particular, be more
To me, your friend, than any.

CARD.   I do profess   190
That for your Highness' good I ever labor'd
More than mine own; that am, have, and will be—
Though all the world should crack their duty to you
And throw it from their soul; though perils did
Abound as thick as thought could make 'em and   195
Appear in forms more horrid—yet my duty,
As doth a rock against the chiding flood,
Should the approach of this wild river break
And stand unshaken yours.

KING.   'Tis nobly spoken.
Take notice, lords, he has a loyal breast,   200
For you have seen him open't. Read o'er this;
                              [Gives him papers.]
And after, this; and then to breakfast with
What appetite you have.

                Exit King frowning upon the Cardinal.
                The Nobles throng after him, smiling
                        and whispering.

---

176. **allegiant**: loyal. 181. **Therein**: i.e., within your answer. **The . . . it**: the honor you receive from such loyalty. 183. **foulness**: disgrace. 184. **as**: to the same extent as. 188: **notwithstanding . . . duty**: outside your obligations as a priest. 189. **As . . . particular**: (a challenging phrase) as if they (i.e., Wolsey's functions) were in love's possession. 192. **have**: have been. 193. **crack**: break. 197. **chiding**: scolding; noisy. 198. **break**: stem; hold off.

CARD.   What should this mean?
            What sudden anger's this? How have I reap'd it?
            He parted frowning from me, as if ruin   205
            Leap'd from his eyes. So looks the chafèd lion
            Upon the daring huntsman that has gall'd him;
            Then makes him nothing. I must read this paper;
            I fear, the story of his anger. 'Tis so!
            This paper has undone me. 'Tis th' accompt   210
            Of all that world of wealth I have drawn together
            For mine own ends; indeed, to gain the popedom
            And fee my friends in Rome. O negligence
            Fit for a fool to fall by! What cross devil
            Made me put this main secret in the packet   215
            I sent the King? Is there no way to cure this?
            No new device to beat this from his brains?
            I know 'twill stir him strongly; yet I know
            A way, if it take right, in spite of fortune,
            Will bring me off again. What's this? "To th' Pope"?   220
            The letter (as I live!) with all the business
            I writ to's Holiness! Nay then, farewell!
            I have touch'd the highest point of all my greatness,
            And from that full meridian of my glory
            I haste now to my setting. I shall fall   225
            Like a bright exhalation in the evening,
            And no man see me more.

                    *Enter to Wolsey the Dukes of Norfolk
                    and Suffolk, the Earl of Surrey,
                    and the Lord Chamberlain.*

NOR.   Hear the King's pleasure, Cardinal, who commands you
            To render up the great seal presently
            Into our hands and to confine yourself   230
            To Asher House, my Lord of Winchester's,
            Till you hear further from his Highness.

CARD.   Stay.
            Where's your commission, lords? Words cannot carry
            Authority so weighty.

---

204. **reap'd**: incurred. 206. **chafèd**: angered. 207. **gall'd**: injured. 208. **Then . . . nothing**: before destroying the hunter. 210. **accompt**: account. 213. **fee**: secure through payment (perhaps "bribe"). 214. **cross**: "perverse" (*GLK*); thwarting. 217. **device**: strategy. 219. **take right**: succeed. 220. **bring me off**: restore me. 224. **meridian**: zenith; highest point. 226. **exhalation**: shooting star; meteor. 229. **presently**: without delay. 231. **Asher House**: Esher House, residence of the Bishop of Winchester. 233. **commission**: official warrant.

SUF.   Who dares cross 'em,
             Bearing the King's will from his mouth expressly?   235

CARD.   Till I find more than will or words to do it
             (I mean your malice), know, officious lords,
             I dare and must deny it. Now I feel
             Of what coarse metal ye are moulded—envy;
             How eagerly ye follow my disgraces,   240
             As if it fed ye! and how sleek and wanton
             Ye appear in everything may bring my ruin!
             Follow your envious courses, men of malice.
             You have Christian warrant for 'em, and no doubt
             In time will find their fit rewards. That seal   245
             You ask with such a violence, the King
             (Mine and your master) with his own hand gave me;
             Bade me enjoy it, with the place and honors,
             During my life, and to confirm his goodness
             Tied it by letters patents. Now who'll take it?   250

SUR.   The King, that gave it.

CARD.   It must be himself then.

SUR.   Thou art a proud traitor, priest.

CARD.   Proud lord, thou liest!
             Within these forty hours Surrey durst better[†]
             Have burnt that tongue than said so.

SUR.   Thy ambition
             (Thou scarlet sin) robb'd this bewailing land   255
             Of noble Buckingham, my father-in-law.
             The heads of all thy brother cardinals
             (With thee and all thy best parts bound together)
             Weigh'd not a hair of his. Plague of your policy!
             You sent me Deputy for Ireland;   260
             Far from his succour, from the King, from all

---

237. **officious**: Wolsey implies they presumptuously carry out their office. 239. **metal**: mettle. **envy**: malice. 241. **sleek and wanton**: fawning and ruthless. 244. **Christian warrant**: Christian justification (said sarcastically). 246. **ask**: request. 250. **tied**: authorized. **letters patent**: open letters meant to confer a privilege (*OED* "patent" adj., 1a). 255. **scarlet sin**: Surrey ties Wolsey's ambition to the color of his cardinal's habit. 258. **parts**: qualities (but with a nod to "body parts"). 259. **Weigh'd not**: were not worth. **Plague . . . policy!** A plague on your political scheming! 261. **his succour**: aiding him (in Buckingham's trial).

---

†   The cardinal seems to go through at least six of the seven stages of grief as he deals with the king's discovery of his schemes. The largest challenge is being credible in his penitence over a losing position he cherished so much.

That might have mercy on the fault thou gav'st him;
Whilst your great goodness, out of holy pity,
Absolv'd him with an axe.

CARD.   This, and all else
This talking lord can lay upon my credit,   265
I answer is most false. The Duke by law
Found his deserts. How innocent I was
From any private malice in his end,
His noble jury and foul cause can witness.
If I lov'd many words, lord, I should tell you   270
You have as little honesty as honor,
That in the way of loyalty and truth
Toward the King, my ever royal master,
Dare mate a sounder man than Surrey can be
And all that love his follies.

SUR.   By my soul,   275
Your long coat, priest, protects you! Thou shouldst feel
My sword i' th' lifeblood of thee else. My lords,
Can ye endure to hear this arrogance?
And from this fellow? If we live thus tamely,
To be thus jaded by a piece of scarlet,   280
Farewell nobility! let his Grace go forward
And dare us with his cap, like larks!

CARD.   All goodness
Is poison to thy stomach.

SUR.   Yes, that goodness
Of gleaning all the land's wealth into one,
Into your own hands, Cardinal, by extortion;   285
The goodness of your intercepted packets
You writ to th' Pope against the King. Your goodness,
Since you provoke me, shall be most notorious.
My Lord of Norfolk,—as you are truly noble,
As you respect the common good, the state   290
Of our despis'd nobility, our issues
(Who, if he live, will scarce be gentlemen),—
Produce the grand sum of his sins, the articles

---

262. **fault . . . him**: crime you accused him of. 264: **Absolv'd . . . axe**: freed him from sin by execution. 265. **credit**: reputation. 268. **From**: of. 269. **noble jury**: i.e., jury of nobility and peers. 274. **Dare
mate**: dare call myself the rival of. 276. **long coat**: i.e., the dignity of your cardinal's cassock. 279. **fellow**: a demeaning title for a cardinal. 280. **jaded**: daunted; made fools of. 282. **dare . . . like**: stupefy
us with his scarlet hat in the same way birds are with similar tricks. 284. **gleaning**: gathering. 291.
issues: sons. 292. **he**: Wolsey. 293: **articles**: list of crimes.

Collected from his life. I'll startle you
Worse than the sacring bell when the brown wench   295
Lay kissing in your arms, Lord Cardinal.

CARD.   How much, methinks, I could despise this man
But that I am bound in charity against it!

NOR.   Those articles, my lord, are in the King's hand;
But thus much—they are foul ones.

CARD.   So much fairer   300
And spotless shall mine innocence arise
When the King knows my truth.

SUR.   This cannot save you.
I thank my memory, I yet remember
Some of these articles, and out they shall!
Now if you can blush and cry "guilty," Cardinal,   305
You'll show a little honesty.

CARD.   Speak on, sir.
I dare your worst objections. If I blush,
It is to see a nobleman want manners.

SUR.   I had rather want those than my head. Have at you!
First, that without the King's assent or knowledge   310
You wrought to be a legate, by which power
You maim'd the jurisdiction of all bishops.

NOR.   Then, that in all you writ to Rome, or else
To foreign princes, *"Ego et Rex meus"*
Was still inscrib'd; in which you brought the King   315
To be your servant.

SUF.   Then, that without the knowledge
Either of King or Council, when you went
Ambassador to the Emperor, you made bold
To carry into Flanders the great seal.

SUR.   Item, you sent a large commission   320
To Gregory de Cassado to conclude,

---

295. **sacring bell**: the bell rung to call parishioners to prayer or communion (*OED* "sacring bell," 2). 295–296: **when . . . arms**: Surrey imagines a compromising scene in which Wolsey is in bed with a peasant girl. 299: **hand**: possession. 300. **thus much**: I can say this. 302. **truth**: fidelity. 304. **out they shall**: these are they. 307. **objections**: accusations. 308. **want**: lack. 309. **Have at you!**: a cry of attack. 311. **wrought**: schemed. **legate**: official representative to the Pope. 312. **maim'd the jurisdiction**: exceeded the authority. 314. *Ego et Rex meus*: Latin for "I and my king." (Surrey accuses Wolsey of demoting the king by the order of the names.) 315. **still**: consistently. 319. **To . . . seal**: Taking the seal out of England was forbidden. 320. **large**: fully empowered.

	Without the King's will or the state's allowance,	
	A league between his Highness and Ferrara.	
SUF.	That out of mere ambition you have caus'd	
	Your holy hat to be stamp'd on the King's coin.	325
SUR.	Then, that you have sent innumerable substance	
	(By what means got, I leave to your own conscience)	
	To furnish Rome and to prepare the ways	
	You have for dignities, to the mere undoing	
	Of all the kingdom. Many more there are,	330
	Which, since they are of you, and odious,	
	I will not taint my mouth with.	
CHAM.	O my lord,	
	Press not a falling man too far! 'Tis virtue.†	
	His faults lie open to the laws; let them,	
	Not you, correct him. My heart weeps to see him	335
	So little of his great self.	
SUR.	I forgive him.	
SUF.	Lord Cardinal, the King's further pleasure is—	
	Because all those things you have done of late	
	By your power legatine within this kingdom	
	Fall into th' compass of a præmunire—	340
	That therefore such a writ be sued against you,	
	To forfeit all your goods, lands, tenements,	
	Chattels, and whatsoever, and to be	
	Out of the King's protection. This is my charge.	
NOR.	And so we'll leave you to your meditations	345
	How to live better. For your stubborn answer	
	About the giving back the great seal to us,	
	The King shall know it, and (no doubt) shall thank you.	
	So fare you well, my little good Lord Cardinal.	

Exeunt all but Wolsey.

323. **Ferrara**: The Duke of Ferrara. 324. **mere**: pure; unconstrained. 326. **innumerable substance**: unimaginable wealth. 328–329: **To . . . dignities**: to purchase and ease the way for acquiring titles in Rome. 329. **mere**: total. 332. **with**: with them. 333. **virtue**: a virtue (not to). 339. **legatine**: as a legatine. 340. **fall . . . præmunire**: are subject to be considered præmunire, or the serious crime of appealing to foreign or papal authority in a matter that should be considered the jurisdiction of the English crown. 341. **sued**: prosecuted. 342. **tenements**: properties that yield income for a limited term. 343. **Chattles**: private possessions. 349. **little . . . Cardinal**: a play on the familiar address "Good Lord Cardinal."

† "Press not a falling man too far!" How much sympathy does the play take away from the lords to move the balance of pity toward the cardinal?

CARD.   So farewell to the little good you bear me!   350
             Farewell, a long farewell, to all my greatness!
             This is the state of man: to-day he puts forth
             The tender leaves of hopes; to-morrow blossoms
             And bears his blushing honors thick upon him;
             The third day comes a frost, a killing frost,   355
             And when he thinks, good easy man, full surely
             His greatness is a-ripening, nips his root,
             And then he falls, as I do. I have ventur'd,
             Like little wanton boys that swim on bladders,
             This many summers in a sea of glory;   360
             But far beyond my depth. My high-blown pride
             At length broke under me, and now has left me,
             Weary and old with service, to the mercy
             Of a rude stream that must forever hide me.
             Vain pomp and glory of this world, I hate ye!   365
             I feel my heart new open'd. O, how wretched
             Is that poor man that hangs on princes' favors!
             There is betwixt that smile we would aspire to,
             That sweet aspect of princes, and their ruin
             More pangs and fears than wars or women have;   370
             And when he falls, he falls like Lucifer,
             Never to hope again.

                        Enter Cromwell, standing amazed.

                             Why, how now, Cromwell!

CROM.   I have no power to speak, sir.

CARD.   What, amaz'd
             At my misfortunes? Can thy spirit wonder
             A great man should decline? Nay, an you weep,   375
             I am fall'n indeed.

CROM.   How does your Grace?

CARD.   Why, well;
             Never so truly happy, my good Cromwell.
             I know myself now, and I feel within me
             A peace above all earthly dignities,

---

354. **blushing**: shining. 356. **easy**: unsuspecting. 359. **wanton**: careless. **bladders**: floatation devices (made from animal bladders). 364. **rude stream**: rough current. 369. **their ruin**: the ruin that their smiles can cause or the ruin (end) of the smiles that grant favors. 371. **Lucifer**: In the Christian tradition, the archangel who rebelled against God and was forever cast into hell. 373. **amaz'd**: stunned. 375. **an**: if.

	A still and quiet conscience. The King has cur'd me—	380
	I humbly thank his Grace—and from these shoulders,	
	These ruin'd pillars, out of pity taken	
	A load would sink a navy—too much honor.	
	O 'tis a burden, Cromwell, 'tis a burden	
	Too heavy for a man that hopes for heaven!	385

CROM. I am glad your Grace has made that right use of it.

CARD. I hope I have. I am able now, methinks,
Out of a fortitude of soul I feel,
To endure more miseries and greater far
Than my weak-hearted enemies dare offer.   390
What news abroad?

CROM.   The heaviest and the worst
Is your displeasure with the King.

CARD.   God bless him!

CROM. The next is that Sir Thomas More is chosen
Lord Chancellor in your place.

CARD.   That's somewhat sudden.
But he's a learned man. May he continue   395
Long in his Highness' favor and do justice
For truth's sake and his conscience; that his bones,
When he has run his course and sleeps in blessings,
May have a tomb of orphans' tears wept on him!
What more?

CROM.   That Cranmer is return'd with welcome,   400
Install'd Lord Archbishop of Canterbury.

CARD. That's news indeed.

CROM.   Last, that the Lady Anne,
Whom the King hath in secrecy long married,
This day was view'd in open as his queen,
Going to chapel; and the voice is now   405
Only about her coronation.

CARD. There was the weight that pull'd me down. O Cromwell,
The King has gone beyond me! All my glories
In that one woman I have lost forever.
No sun shall ever usher forth mine honors   410
Or gild again the noble troops that waited

---

392. **displeasure:** fall into disgrace. 399. **tomb . . . him:** tomb composed of the copious tears of orphans
under his care. 405. **voice:** rumor. 408. **gone beyond:** overreached. 411. **troops:** followers; servants.

Upon my smiles. Go get thee from me, Cromwell!
I am a poor fall'n man, unworthy now
To be thy lord and master. Seek the King.
That sun, I pray, may never set! I have told him　　　　415
What and how true thou art. He will advance thee.
Some little memory of me will stir him
(I know his noble nature) not to let
Thy hopeful service perish too. Good Cromwell,
Neglect him not; make use now, and provide　　　　420
For thine own future safety.

CROM.　　　　　　　　　　O my lord,
Must I then leave you? Must I needs forgo
So good, so noble, and so true a master?
Bear witness, all that have not hearts of iron,
With what a sorrow Cromwell leaves his lord.　　　　425
The King shall have my service, but my pray'rs
Forever and forever shall be yours.

CARD.　　Cromwell, I did not think to shed a tear
In all my miseries; but thou hast forc'd me
(Out of thy honest truth) to play the woman.　　　　430
Let's dry our eyes; and thus far hear me, Cromwell,
And when I am forgotten, as I shall be,
And sleep in dull cold marble, where no mention
Of me more must be heard of, say I taught thee—
Say Wolsey, that once trod the ways of glory　　　　435
And sounded all the depths and shoals of honor,
Found thee a way (out of his wrack) to rise in—
A sure and safe one, though thy master miss'd it.
Mark but my fall and that that ruin'd me.
Cromwell, I charge thee, fling away ambition!　　　　440
By that sin fell the angels. How can man then
(The image of his Maker) hope to win by it?
Love thyself last. Cherish those hearts that hate thee;
Corruption wins not more than honesty.
Still in thy right hand carry gentle peace　　　　445
To silence envious tongues. Be just, and fear not.
Let all the ends thou aim'st at be thy country's,

---

419. **hopeful**: promising. 420. **make use**: i.e., be practical minded. 430. **play the woman**: i.e., by crying. 435–438. **Say . . . it**: Audiences would have been aware that Cromwell himself will later go to the block because of his own ambition. 436. **sounded**: plumbed or measured. **shoals**: shallow parts. 437. **wrack**: ruin. :442. **Maker**: i.e., of God. 445. **Still**: always.

Thy God's, and truth's. Then if thou fall'st, O Cromwell,
Thou fall'st a blessed martyr. Serve the King.
And prithee lead me in.   450
There take an inventory of all I have
To the last penny. 'Tis the King's. My robe,
And my integrity to heaven, is all
I dare now call mine own. O Cromwell, Cromwell!
Had I but serv'd my God with half the zeal   455
I serv'd my king, he would not in mine age
Have left me naked to mine enemies.

CROM.   Good sir, have patience.

CARD.   So I have. Farewell
The hopes of court! My hopes in heaven do dwell.   *Exeunt.*

ACT IV

SCENE I. [*A street in Westminster.*]

Enter two Gentlemen, meeting one another.

1. GENT.   Y'are well met once again.

2. GENT.   So are you.

1. GENT.   You come to take your stand here and behold
The Lady Anne pass from her coronation?

2. GENT.   'Tis all my business. At our last encounter
The Duke of Buckingham came from his trial.   5

1. GENT.   'Tis very true; but that time offer'd sorrow;
This, general joy.

2. GENT.   'Tis well. The citizens
I am sure have shown at full their royal minds—
As, let 'em have their rights, they are ever forward—
In celebration of this day with shows,   10
Pageants, and sights of honor.

---

452. **robe**: simple cleric's robe. 457. **naked**: utterly vulnerable.
ACT 4, SCENE 1
1. **well**: happily. 8. **royal minds**: loyalty to the king. 9. **let . . . rights**: to give them their due. **forward**:
eager; first in line.

1. GENT.   Never greater,
        Nor, I'll assure you, better taken, sir.

2. GENT.   May I be bold to ask what that contains,
        That paper in your hand?

1. GENT.   Yes. 'Tis the list
        Of those that claim their offices this day   15
        By custom of the coronation.
        The Duke of Suffolk is the first, and claims
        To be High Steward; next, the Duke of Norfolk,
        He to be Earl Marshal. You may read the rest.

2. GENT.   I thank you, sir. Had I not known those customs,   20
        I should have been beholding to your paper.
        But, I beseech you, what's become of Katherine,
        The Princess Dowager? How goes her business?

1. GENT.   That I can tell you too. The Archbishop
        Of Canterbury, accompanied with other   25
        Learned and reverend fathers of his order,
        Held a late court at Dunstable, six miles off
        From Ampthill, where the Princess lay, to which
        She was often cited by them, but appear'd not;
        And, to be short, for not appearance and   30
        The King's late scruple, by the main assent
        Of all these learned men she was divorc'd
        And the late marriage made of none effect;
        Since which she was remov'd to Kimbolton,
        Where she remains now sick.

2. GENT.   Alas, good lady!   [*Trumpets.*]†   35
        The trumpets sound. Stand close! The Queen is coming.
                                                Hautboys.

---

18. **High Steward**: managing official. 19. **Earl Marshal**: Another high state official who by custom was never lower than an Earl in rank (*OED*, 1). 21. **beholding**: beholden, a dependent on. 27. **Dunstable**: a town northwest of London. 29. **cited**: sent a summons. 30. **short**: brief. 31. **scruple**: doubt. **main assent**: general judgment ("assent" here is a legal term, *OED*, 2). 33. **late**: past. **made . . . effect**: voided. 34. **Kimbolton**: a castle in Huntingdonshire. 36. **close**: aside. 12. **better taken**: gratefully received.

---

† The procession of dignitaries from Anne's coronation provides an opportunity, like Wolsey's feast, for sumptuous display. The question for modern directors is how to get the most effect out of a scene where the main point is to look at people.

THE ORDER OF THE CORONATION

1. A lively flourish of trumpets.
2. Then two *Judges*.
3. *Lord Chancellor,* with purse and mace before him.
4. *Choristers* singing.   *Music.*
5. *Mayor of London,* bearing the mace. Then *Garter,* in his coat of arms, and on his head he wore a gilt copper crown.   36.6
6. *Marquess Dorset,* bearing a sceptre of gold, on his head a demi-coronal of gold. With him the *Earl of Surrey,* bearing the rod of silver with the dove, crowned with an earl's coronet. Collars of Esses.
7. *Duke of Suffolk,* in his robe of estate, his coronet on his head, bearing a long white wand, as High Steward. With him the *Duke of Norfolk,* with the rod of marshalship, a coronet on his head. Collars of Esses.   36.12
8. A canopy borne by four of the *Cinque Ports;* under it, the *Queen* in her robe, in her hair, richly adorned with pearl, crowned. On each side her the *Bishops of London* and *Winchester.*   36.15
9. The old *Duchess of Norfolk,* in a coronal of gold, wrought with flowers, bearing the *Queen's* train.
10. Certain *Ladies* or *Countesses,* with plain circlets of gold without flowers.   *Exeunt, first passing over the stage in order and state, and then a great flourish of trumpets.*

2. GENT.   A royal train, believe me. These I know.
            Who's that that bears the sceptre?

1. GENT.   Marquess Dorset;
            And that the Earl of Surrey with the rod.

2. GENT.   A bold brave gentleman. That should be   40
            The Duke of Suffolk.

1. GENT.   'Tis the same: High Steward.

2. GENT.   And that my Lord of Norfolk?

1. GENT.   Yes.

36.1. **flourish**: trumpet fanfare. 36.5. *Garter*: Garter King-at-Arms, official announcer or herald. 36.7. **demi-coronal**: Half crown. 36.9. **Collars of Esses**: gold chains of interlocking S's. 36.13. *Cinque Ports*: the barons of the five (cinque) major port towns in Southwest England (Hythe, Romney, Sandwich, Dover, Hastings). 37. **train**: procession.

Billington's Queen Anne (Barbara Kellerman) at her Coronation—satisfied and regal in her new role.

2. GENT.	[*Looks on the Queen*] Heaven bless thee!
	Thou hast the sweetest face I ever look'd on.
	Sir, as I have a soul, she is an angel!
	Our King has all the Indies in his arms,	45
	And more, and richer, when he strains that lady.
	I cannot blame his conscience.
1. GENT.	They that bear
	The cloth of honor over her are four Barons
	Of the Cinque Ports.
2. GENT.	Those men are happy, and so are all are near her.	50
	I take it, she that carries up the train
	Is that old noble lady, Duchess of Norfolk.
1. GENT.	It is, and all the rest are countesses.
2. GENT.	Their coronets say so. These are stars indeed,
	And sometimes falling ones.

45. **Indies**: India and America: known for luxuries and riches. 46. **strains**: embraces (with a possible bawdy sense). 50. **all**: all who.

An appreciative gentleman leers at the comely new Queen Anne.

| 1. GENT. | No more of that. [*Exit procession.*] | 55 |

Enter a third Gentleman.

God save you, sir! Where have you been broiling?

3. GENT.   Among the crowd i' th' Abbey, where a finger
Could not be wedg'd in more. I am stifled
With the mere rankness of their joy.

2. GENT.   You saw
The ceremony?

3. GENT.   That I did.

1. GENT.   How was it?   60

3. GENT.   Well worth the seeing.

2. GENT.   Good sir, speak it to us.

---

55. **falling ones**: the implication is 1) a bawdy reference to loss of chastity, and 2) a reminder of Buckingham and Wolsey's falls. 56. **broiling**: 1) battling; 2) mingling. 59. **mere rankness**: sheer 1) overgrowth; 2) foulness. 61. **speak**: describe.

3. GENT.   As well as I am able. The rich stream
              Of lords and ladies, having brought the Queen
              To a prepar'd place in the choir, fell off
              A distance from her, while her Grace sat down   65
              To rest awhile, some half an hour or so,
              In a rich chair of state, opposing freely
              The beauty of her person to the people.
              Believe me, sir, she is the goodliest woman
              That ever lay by man; which when the people   70
              Had the full view of, such a noise arose
              As the shrouds make at sea in a stiff tempest,
              As loud, and to as many tunes. Hats, cloaks
              (Doublets, I think) flew up; and had their faces
              Been loose, this day they had been lost. Such joy   75
              I never saw before. Great-bellied women
              That had not half a week to go, like rams
              In the old time of war, would shake the press
              And make 'em reel before 'em. No man living
              Could say "This is my wife" there, all were woven   80
              So strangely in one piece.

2. GENT.   But what follow'd?

3. GENT.   At length her Grace rose and with modest paces
              Came to the altar, where she kneel'd and saintlike
              Cast her fair eyes to heaven and pray'd devoutly;
              Then rose again and bow'd her to the people;   85
              When by the Archbishop of Canterbury
              She had all the royal makings of a queen;
              As holy oil, Edward Confessor's crown,
              The rod, and bird of peace, and all such emblems,
              Laid nobly on her; which perform'd, the choir   90
              With all the choicest music of the kingdom
              Together sung "Te Deum." So she parted
              And with the same full state pac'd back again
              To York Palace, where the feast is held.

1. GENT.   Sir,
              You must no more call it York Palace. That's past;   95
              For since the Cardinal fell that title's lost.
              'Tis now the King's, and call'd Whitehall.

---

64. **fell off**: withdrew. 67. **opposing freely**: openly revealing. 72. **shrouds**: sailing ropes or rigging. 74. **Doublets**: form-fitting jackets. 77. **rams**: battering rams. 78. **press**: crowd. 87. **royal makings**: ceremonial accoutrements. 91. **choicest music**: best musicians. 92. **Te Deum**: shortened Latin title of a thanksgiving hymn "We praise thee, O Lord." 93. **state**: procession.

3. GENT.	I know it; But 'tis so lately alter'd that the old name Is fresh about me.
2. GENT.	What two reverend bishops Were those that went on each side of the Queen?
3. GENT.	Stokesly and Gardiner; the one of Winchester, Newly preferr'd from the King's Secretary, The other, London.
2. GENT.	He of Winchester Is held no great good lover of the Archbishop's, The virtuous Cranmer.
3. GENT.	All the land knows that. However, yet there is no great breach. When it comes, Cranmer will find a friend will not shrink from him.
2. GENT.	Who may that be, I pray you?
3. GENT.	Thomas Cromwell, A man in much esteem with th' King, and truly A worthy friend. The King has made him Master O' th' Jewel House And one, already, of the Privy Council.
2. GENT.	He will deserve more.
3. GENT.	Yes, without all doubt. Come, gentlemen, ye shall go my way, which Is to th' court, and there ye shall be my guests. Something I can command. As I walk thither, I'll tell ye more.
BOTH.	You may command us, sir. *Exeunt.*

100

105

110

115

Scene II. [*Kimbolton.*]

Enter Katherine, Dowager, sick; led between
Griffith (her Gentleman Usher) and Patience
(her Woman).

GRIF.	How does your Grace?
KATH.	O Griffith, sick to death!

98. **lately**: recently. 102. **preferr'd**: promoted. 103. **He of Winchester**: Shakespeare reverses the titles: Gardiner is Bishop of Winchester; Stokesly of London. 107. **will not**: who will not. 116. **Something...command**: I have some clout (among the court).

My legs like loaden branches bow to th' earth,
Willing to leave their burthen. Reach a chair.
So. Now, methinks, I feel a little ease.
Didst thou not tell me, Griffith, as thou led'st me,   5
That the great child of honor, Cardinal Wolsey,
Was dead?

GRIF.   Yes, madam; but I think your Grace,
Out of the pain you suffer'd, gave no ear to't.

KATH.   Prithee, good Griffith, tell me how he died.
If well, he stepp'd before me happily   10
For my example.

GRIF.   Well, the voice goes, madam;
For after the stout Earl Northumberland
Arrested him at York and brought him forward,
As a man sorely tainted, to his answer,
He fell sick suddenly and grew so ill   15
He could not sit his mule.

KATH.   Alas, poor man!

GRIF.   At last, with easy roads, he came to Leicester,
Lodg'd in the abbey; where the reverend Abbot,
With all his covent, honorably receiv'd him;
To whom he gave these words: "O Father Abbot,   20
An old man, broken with the storms of state,
Is come to lay his weary bones among ye.
Give him a little earth for charity!"
So went to bed; where eagerly his sickness
Pursu'd him still; and three nights after this,   25
After the hour of eight, which he himself
Foretold should be his last, full of repentance,
Continual meditations, tears, and sorrows,
He gave his honors to the world again,
His blessed part to heaven, and slept in peace.   30

KATH.   So may he rest! His faults lie gently on him!
Yet thus far, Griffith, give me leave to speak him,
And yet with charity. He was a man
Of an unbounded stomach, ever ranking

ACT 4, SCENE 2
2. loaden: heavily loaded. 10. well: sanctified. happily: fittingly. 11. the voice goes: the report is. 14. tainted: disgraced. answer: arraignment or trial. 16. sit: stride. 17. with easy roads: taking the trip in short stages. 19. covent: convent; monastery. 23. little earth: small burial plot. 32. speak: describe. 34. stomach: 1) pride; 2) appetite (ambition).

Himself with princes; one that by suggestion   35
Tied all the kingdom. Simony was fair play;
His own opinion was his law. I' th' presence
He would say untruths, and be ever double
Both in his words and meaning. He was never
(But where he meant to ruin) pitiful.   40
His promises were, as he then was, mighty;
But his performance, as he is now, nothing.
Of his own body he was ill, and gave
The clergy ill example.

GRIF.   Noble madam,
Men's evil manners live in brass; their virtues   45
We write in water. May it please your Highness
To hear me speak his good now?

KATH.   Yes, good Griffith.
I were malicious else.

GRIF.   This Cardinal,
Though from an humble stock, undoubtedly
Was fashion'd to much honor from his cradle.   50
He was a scholar, and a ripe and good one;
Exceeding wise, fair-spoken, and persuading;
Lofty and sour to them that lov'd him not,
But to those men that sought him sweet as summer.
And though he were unsatisfied in getting   55
(Which was a sin), yet in bestowing, madam,
He was most princely. Ever witness for him
Those twins of learning that he rais'd in you,
Ipswich and Oxford; one of which fell with him,
Unwilling to outlive the good that did it;   60
The other, though unfinish'd, yet so famous,
So excellent in art, and still so rising,
That Christendom shall ever speak his virtue.
His overthrow heap'd happiness upon him;
For then, and not till then, he felt himself   65
And found the blessedness of being little.

---

35. **suggestion**: "wily insinuation" (*GLK*). 36. **Tied . . . kingdom**: kept the whole kingdom bound. **Simony**: selling church offices. 37. **I' th' presence**: in the king's official private chamber. 38. **double**: duplicitous. 40. **pitiful**: merciful. 43. **Of . . . body**: in the (sexual) conduct of his body. 50. **to**: to achieve. 53. **Lofty**: aloof. 55. **were . . . getting**: was utterly rapacious. 59. **Ipswich and Oxford**: Wolsey founded two colleges; the latter here survives as Christ Church, Oxford. 60. **good that did**: good man who made. 62. **art**: learning. **rising**: growing. 65. **felt**: understood. 66. **little**: humble.

And, to add greater honors to his age
Than man could give him, he died fearing God.

KATH.   After my death I wish no other herald,
No other speaker of my living actions   70
To keep mine honor from corruption,
But such an honest chronicler as Griffith.
Whom I most hated living, thou hast made me,
With thy religious truth and modesty,
Now, in his ashes, honor. Peace be with him!   75
[*To her servant*] Patience, be near me still, and set me lower.
I have not long to trouble thee. Good Griffith,
Cause the musicians play me that sad note
I nam'd my knell, whilst I sit meditating.
On that celestial harmony I go to. *Sad and solemn music.* 80

GRIF.   She is asleep. Good wench, let's sit down quiet
For fear we wake her. Softly, gentle Patience.†

The Vision.

*Enter, solemnly tripping one after another, six
personages clad in white robes, wearing on their
heads garlands of bays, and golden vizards on
their faces; branches of bays or palm in their
hands. They first congee unto her, then dance;
and, at certain changes, the first two hold a
spare garland over her head; at which the other
four make reverent curtsies. Then the two that
held the garland deliver the same to the other
next two, who observe the same order in their
changes and holding the garland over her head;
which done, they deliver the same garland to
the last two, who likewise observe the same
order; at which (as it were by inspiration) she
makes (in her sleep) signs of rejoicing and
holdeth up her hands to heaven. And so in their
dancing vanish, carrying the garland with
them.   The music continues.*

---

70. **living actions**: actions done during life. 73. **Whom**: the man whom. **living**: while he was alive.
74. **modesty**: humbleness; clemency (*OED*, 1). 78. **note**: song. 79. **knell**: death knell; song or sound of
dying. 82.s.d. **tripping**: moving lightly and gracefully. **bays**: laurels. **vizards**: masks. **congee**: bow
ceremoniously.

---

†   The scene of the personages robed in white crowning Katherine with garlands elevates the previous queen above the fray embroiling the others in the play.

KATH.	Spirits of peace, where are ye? Are ye all gone
	And leave me here in wretchedness behind ye?
GRIF.	Madam, we are here.
KATH.	It is not you I call for.	85
	Saw ye none enter since I slept?
GRIF.	None, madam.
KATH.	No? Saw you not even now a blessed troop
	Invite me to a banquet, whose bright faces
	Cast thousand beams upon me like the sun?
	They promis'd me eternal happiness	90
	And brought me garlands, Griffith, which I feel
	I am not worthy yet to wear. I shall, assuredly.
GRIF.	I am most joyful, madam, such good dreams
	Possess your fancy.
KATH.	Bid the music leave.
	They are harsh and heavy to me.

Music ceases.

PAT.	Do you note	95
	How much her Grace is alter'd on the sudden?
	How long her face is drawn? how pale she looks,
	And of an earthy color? Mark her eyes!
GRIF.	She is going, wench. Pray, pray!
PAT.	Heaven comfort her!

Enter a Messenger.

MESS.	An't like your Grace—
KATH.	You are a saucy fellow.	100
	Deserve we no more reverence?
GRIF.	You are to blame,
	Knowing she will not lose her wonted greatness,
	To use so rude behavior. Go to, kneel!
MESS.	I humbly do entreat your Highness' pardon.
	My haste made me unmannerly. There is staying	105
	A gentleman, sent from the King, to see you.

---

100. **An't like**: if it please (a greeting unfit for someone of Katherine's rank). 102. **lose**: give up. **wonted**: customary. 105. **staying**: waiting.

KATH.   Admit him entrance, Griffith. But this fellow
        Let me ne'er see again.   *Exit Messenger.*

                    Enter Lord Capucius.

                    If my sight fail not,
        You should be Lord Ambassador from the Emperor,
        My royal nephew, and your name Capucius.   110

CAP.   Madam, the same—your servant.

KATH.   O my lord,
        The times and titles now are alter'd strangely
        With me since first you knew me. But I pray you,
        What is your pleasure with me?

CAP.   Noble lady,
        First mine own service to your Grace; the next,   115
        The King's request that I would visit you,
        Who grieves much for your weakness and by me
        Sends you his princely commendations
        And heartily entreats you take good comfort.

KATH.   O my good lord, that comfort comes too late!   120
        'Tis like a pardon after execution.
        That gentle physic, given in time, had cur'd me;
        But now I am past all comforts here but prayers.
        How does his Highness?

CAP.   Madam, in good health.

KATH.   So may he ever do! and ever flourish   125
        When I shall dwell with worms, and my poor name
        Banish'd the kingdom! Patience, is that letter
        I caus'd you write yet sent away?

PAT.   No, madam.   [*Gives it to Katherine.*]

KATH.   Sir, I most humbly pray you to deliver
        This to my lord the King.

CAP.   Most willing, madam.   130

KATH.   In which I have commended to his goodness
        The model of our chaste loves, his young daughter—
        The dews of heaven fall thick in blessings on her!—
        Beseeching him to give her virtuous breeding—

---

134. **breeding**: rearing; upbringing. 109. **Emperor**: i.e., Charles V, Holy Roman Emperor. 115. **service**: obeisance. 122. **physic**: medicine. 130. **willing**: willingly. 132. **model**: image. **young daughter**: the Princess Mary, later queen (1553–1558).

	She is young and of a noble modest nature;	135
	I hope she will deserve well—and a little	
	To love her for her mother's sake, that lov'd him,	
	Heaven knows how dearly. My next poor petition	
	Is that his noble Grace would have some pity	
	Upon my wretched women, that so long	140
	Have follow'd both my fortunes faithfully;	
	Of which there is not one, I dare avow	
	(And now I should not lie), but will deserve,	
	For virtue and true beauty of the soul,	
	For honesty and decent carriage,	145
	A right good husband—let him be a noble;	
	And sure those men are happy that shall have 'em.	
	The last is for my men—they are the poorest	
	(But poverty could never draw 'em from me)—	
	That they may have their wages duly paid 'em,	150
	And something over to remember me by.	
	If heaven had pleas'd to have given me longer life	
	And able means, we had not parted thus.	
	These are the whole contents; and, good my lord,	
	By that you love the dearest in this world,	155
	As you wish Christian peace to souls departed,	
	Stand these poor people's friend and urge the King	
	To do me this last right.	

CAP.   By heaven, I will,
                  Or let me lose the fashion of a man!

KATH.   I thank you, honest lord. Remember me   160
                  In all humility unto his Highness.
                  Say his long trouble now is passing
                  Out of this world. Tell him in death I bless'd him,
                  For so I will. Mine eyes grow dim. Farewell,
                  My lord. Griffith, farewell. Nay, Patience,   165
                  You must not leave me yet. I must to bed;
                  Call in more women. When I am dead, good wench,
                  Let me be us'd with honor. Strew me over
                  With maiden flowers, that all the world may know

---

141. **both my**: my good and bad. 143. **now**: i.e., when she is dying and would not want to carry the sin into her death. 145. **honesty**: chastity. **carriage**: conduct. 147. **are happy**: will be fortunate. 151. **over**: extra. 153: **able**: adequate. 154. **contents**: i.e., of the king's letter. 159. **fashion**: shape (i.e., to match his deformed nature). 168. **us'd with honor**: treated with appropriate dignity. 169. **maiden flowers**: flowers appropriate for a virgin.

I was a chaste wife to my grave. Embalm me,   170
Then lay me forth. Although unqueen'd, yet like
A queen, and daughter to a king, inter me.
I can no more.   *Exeunt, leading Katherine.*

ACT V

SCENE I. [*London. A gallery in the Palace.*]

Enter Gardiner, Bishop of Winchester,
a Page with a torch before him,
met by Sir Thomas Lovell.

GARD.   It's one o'clock, boy, is't not?

BOY.   It hath struck.

GARD.   These should be hours for necessities,
Not for delights; times to repair our nature
With comforting repose, and not for us
To waste these times. Good hour of night, Sir Thomas!   5
Whither so late?

LOV.   Came you from the King, my lord?

GARD.   I did, Sir Thomas, and left him at primero
With the Duke of Suffolk.

LOV.   I must to him too,
Before he go to bed. I'll take my leave.

GARD.   Not yet, Sir Thomas Lovell. What's the matter?   10
It seems you are in haste. An if there be
No great offence belongs to't, give your friend
Some touch of your late business. Affairs that walk
(As they say spirits do) at midnight have
In them a wilder nature than the business   15
That seeks dispatch by day.

LOV.   My lord, I love you,
And durst commend a secret to your ear

---

171. **forth**: out to be buried. 173. **can no more**: am out of strength.
6. **Whither**: Where are you going? 7. **primero**: a card game. 11. **An if**: and if. 12. **No great . . . to't**:
nothing inappropriate about it. 13. **touch**: hint. 16. **dispatch**: carrying out. 17. **commend**: entrust.

Much weightier than this work. The Queen's in labor,
They say in great extremity, and fear'd
She'll with the labor end.

GARD.   The fruit she goes with   20
I pray for heartily, that it may find
Good time, and live; but for the stock, Sir Thomas,
I wish it grubb'd up now.

LOV.   Methinks I could
Cry the amen; and yet my conscience says
She's a good creature, and, sweet lady, does   25
Deserve our better wishes.

GARD.   But, sir, sir!
Hear me, Sir Thomas! Y'are a gentleman
Of mine own way. I know you wise, religious;
And let me tell you it will ne'er be well—
'Twill not, Sir Thomas Lovell, take't of me—   30
Till Cranmer, Cromwell, her two hands, and she
Sleep in their graves.

LOV.   Now, sir, you speak of two
The most remark'd i' th' kingdom. As for Cromwell,
Beside that of the Jewel House, is made Master
O' th' Rolls and the King's Secretary; further, sir,   35
Stands in the gap and trade of moe preferments,
With which the time will load him. Th' Archbishop
Is the King's hand and tongue; and who dare speak
One syllable against him?

GARD.   Yes, yes, Sir Thomas,
There are that dare, and I myself have ventur'd   40
To speak my mind of him; and indeed this day
(Sir I may tell it you, I think) I have
Incens'd the lords o' th' Council that he is
(For so I know he is, they know he is)
A most arch-heretic, a pestilence   45
That does infect the land; with which they mov'd

---

18. **this work**: my other work. 19. **extremity**: distress. **fear'd**: it is feared that. 20. **fruit . . . with**: child she bears. 22. **Good time**: good fortune. **stock**: i.e., the trunk bearing the fruit. 23. **grubb'd up**: uprooted (Gardiner disapproves of Anne's Protestant leanings). 24. **Cry the amen**: agree. 28. **way**: religious leaning. 33. **remark'd**: esteemed; "noted, notable" (*OED*, 1). 34–35. **Master / O' th' Rolls**: supervisor of the king's patents, grants, and charters. 36. **Stands . . . preferments**: He is opportunistically situated in the open road ("trade") for receiving more ("moe") promotions. 37. **time**: present moment or course of events. 43. **Incens'd**: incense, "inflame with the idea" (*GLK*). 46. **with . . . mov'd**: moved by this idea.

	Have broken with the King, who hath so far	
	Given ear to our complaint—of his great grace	
	And princely care, foreseeing those fell mischiefs	
	Our reasons laid before him—hath commanded	50
	To-morrow morning to the Council board	
	He be convented. He's a rank weed, Sir Thomas,	
	And we must root him out. From your affairs	
	I hinder you too long. Good night, Sir Thomas.	
LOV.	Many good nights, my lord! I rest your servant.	

Exeunt Gardiner and Page.   55

Enter King and Suffolk.

KING.	Charles, I will play no more to-night;	
	My mind's not on't; you are too hard for me.	
SUF.	Sir, I did never win of you before.	
KING.	But little, Charles,	
	Nor shall not when my fancy's on my play.	60
	Now, Lovell, from the Queen what is the news?	
LOV.	I could not personally deliver to her	
	What you commanded me, but by her woman	
	I sent your message, who return'd her thanks	
	In the great'st humbleness and desir'd your Highness	65
	Most heartily to pray for her.	
KING.	What say'st thou? Ha?	
	To pray for her? What, is she crying out?	
LOV.	So said her woman, and that her suff'rance made	
	Almost each pang a death.	
KING.	Alas, good lady!	
SUF.	God safely quit her of her burthen and	70
	With gentle travail, to the gladding of	
	Your Highness with an heir!	
KING.	'Tis midnight, Charles.	
	Prithee to bed, and in thy pray'rs remember	
	Th' estate of my poor queen. Leave me alone,	
	For I must think of that which company	75
	Would not be friendly to.	

---

47. **broken with**: informed. 49. **fell**: "fierce, cruel, savage" (*GLK*). 52. **convented**: summoned. **rank**: 55. **rest**: remain. 58. **win of**: win against (at cards). 60. **fancy's**: mind is focused. 68. **suff'rance**: suffering. 70. **quit**: relieve. 71. **travail**: labor. **gladding**: gladdening. 74. **estate**: condition.

SUF.	I wish your Highness A quiet night and my good mistress will Remember in my prayers.
KING.	Charles, good night. *Exit Suffolk.*

Enter Sir Anthony Denny.

	Well, sir, what follows?
DEN.	Sir, I have brought my lord the Archbishop, 80 As you commanded me.
KING.	Ha? Canterbury?
DEN.	Ay, my good lord.
KING.	'Tis true. Where is he, Denny?
DEN.	He attends your Highness' pleasure.
KING.	Bring him to us. *[Exit Denny.]*
LOV.	*[Aside]* This is about that which the Bishop spake. I am happily come hither. 85

Enter Cranmer and Denny.

KING.	Avoid the gallery. (*Lovell seems to stay.*) Ha! I have said. Be gone. What!

Exeunt Lovell and Denny.

CRAN.	*[Aside]* I am fearful. Wherefore frowns he thus? 'Tis his aspect of terror. All's not well.
KING.	How now, my lord? You do desire to know Wherefore I sent for you?
CRAN.	*[Kneels]* It is my duty 90 T' attend your Highness' pleasure.†
KING.	Pray you arise, My good and gracious Lord of Canterbury. Come, you and I must walk a turn together. I have news to tell you. Come, come, give me your hand. Ah, my good lord, I grieve at what I speak 95

77. **will**: I will. 84. **about . . . spake**: i.e., Gardiner's accusation that Cranmer is a heretic. 86. **Avoid**: leave. 87. **Wherefore**: for what reason. 88. **aspect of terror**: face of rage. 93. **turn**: spell; a short time.

† The king in this scene is in some ways a new king, as the dialogue suggests. The challenge of performance is to define and project that newness in the scene.

And am right sorry to repeat what follows.
I have, and most unwillingly, of late
Heard many grievous—I do say, my lord,
Grievous complaints of you; which, being consider'd,
Have mov'd us and our Council that you shall   100
This morning come before us; where I know
You cannot with such freedom purge yourself
But that, till further trial in those charges
Which will require your answer, you must take
Your patience to you and be well contented   105
To make your house our Tow'r. You a brother of us,
It fits we thus proceed, or else no witness
Would come against you.

CRAN.   I humbly thank your Highness,
And am right glad to catch this good occasion
Most throughly to be winnowed where my chaff   110
And corn shall fly asunder; for I know
There's none stands under more calumnious tongues
Than I myself, poor man.

KING.   Stand up, good Canterbury.
Thy truth and thy integrity is rooted
In us, thy friend. Give me thy hand, stand up.
                     [*Cranmer rises.*] 115
Prithee let's walk. Now by my holidame,
What manner of man are you? My lord, I look'd
You would have given me your petition that
I should have ta'en some pains to bring together
Yourself and your accusers and to have heard you 120
Without indurance further.

CRAN.   Most dread liege,
The good I stand on is my truth and honesty.
If they shall fail, I with mine enemies
Will triumph o'er my person, which I weigh not,
Being of those virtues vacant. I fear nothing   125
What can be said against me.

---

102. **with such freedom purge**: with ease exculpate. 106. **brother of us**: an intimate; a member of the privy council. 107. **fits**: is fitting. 110. **throughly**: thoroughly. 110–111. **to . . . asunder**: to be tested so that my good qualities ("corn" or grain) can be separated from my ill-formed ideas ("chaff"). 112. **stands under**: is subjected to. **calumnious**: slandering. 116. **by my holidame**: by my holy-dame (a mild oath). 117. **look'd**: expected. 121. **indurance**: imprisonment. 123. **they**: i.e., truth and honesty. **with mine**: in conjunction. 124. **triumph o'er**: joy in the vanquishing of. **weigh**: value. 125. **fear nothing**: do not fear.

KING.   Know you not
How your state stands i' th' world, with the whole world?
Your enemies are many and not small; their practices
Must bear the same proportion; and not ever
The justice and the truth o' th' question carries   130
The due o' th' verdict with it. At what ease
Might corrupt minds procure knaves as corrupt
To swear against you! Such things have been done.
You are potently oppos'd, and with a malice
Of as great size. Ween you of better luck,   135
I mean in perjur'd witness, than your Master,
Whose minister you are, whiles here he liv'd
Upon this naughty earth? Go to, go to!
You take a precipice for no leap of danger
And woo your own destruction.

CRAN.   God and your Majesty   140
Protect mine innocence, or I fall into
The trap is laid for me!

KING.   Be of good cheer.
They shall no more prevail than we give way to.
Keep comfort to you, and this morning see
You do appear before them. If they shall chance,   145
In charging you with matters, to commit you,
The best persuasions to the contrary
Fail not to use, and with what vehemency
Th' occasion shall instruct you. If entreaties
Will render you no remedy, this ring   150
Deliver them and your appeal to us
There make before them. Look, the good man weeps!
He's honest, on mine honor. God's blest Mother!
I swear he is true-hearted, and a soul
None better in my kingdom. Get you gone   155
And do as I have bid you.   [*Exit Cranmer.*]
                          He has strangled
His language in his tears.

---

128. **not small**: important; significant. **practices**: schemes; acts. 129–131. **ever . . . with**: Not always
("ever") does the justice and truth of a matter result ("carries") in a verdict that is due it. 131. **At**: with.
132. **procure knaves**: hire scoundrels. 135. **Ween you of**: are you expecting. 136. **your Master**: i.e.,
Jesus Christ, against whom false witnesses testified. 138. **Go to**: a reproach. 142. **trap**: trap that. 143.
we . . . to: than I permit. 146. **commit**: i.e., to prison. 151. **to us**: to me.

Enter Old Lady.

GENT.   (*Within*) Come back! What mean you?

OLD L.   I'll not come back. The tidings that I bring
Will make my boldness manners. Now good angels
Fly o'er thy royal head and shade thy person   160
Under their blessed wings!

KING.   Now by thy looks
I guess thy message. Is the Queen deliver'd?
Say ay, and of a boy.

OLD L.   Ay, ay, my liege!
And of a lovely boy. The God of heaven
Both now and ever bless her! 'Tis a girl   165
Promises boys hereafter. Sir, your queen
Desires your visitation, and to be
Acquainted with this stranger. 'Tis as like you
As cherry is to cherry.

KING.   Lovell!

[Enter Lovell.]

LOV.   Sir?

KING.   Give her an hundred marks. I'll to the Queen. *Exit.*   170

OLD L.   An hundred marks? By this light, I'll ha' more!
An ordinary groom is for such payment.
I will have more or scold it out of him.
Said I for this the girl was like to him?
I will have more or else unsay 't, and now,   175
While it is hot, I'll put it to the issue.   *Exeunt.*

---

159. **make . . . manners**: turn my presumption ("boldness," a breach of protocol in approaching the king) into good manners. 166. **Promises boys hereafter**: who sets the stage for boys to be born. 170. **an hundred marks**: about sixty-six pounds (not a small sum). 172: **groom**: male servant. 174. **for**: that. 176. **put it to**: doggedly pursue.

SCENE II. [*Lobby before the Council Chamber.*]

[*Pursuivants and others in waiting.*]
Enter Cranmer, Archbishop of Canterbury.

CRAN.   I hope I am not too late; and yet the gentleman
That was sent to me from the Council pray'd me
To make great haste. All fast? What means this? Ho!
Who waits there? Sure you know me?

Enter Keeper.

KEEP.   Yes, my lord.
But yet I cannot help you.

CRAN.   Why?   5

KEEP.   Your Grace must wait till you be call'd for.

Enter Doctor Butts.

CRAN.   So.

BUTTS.   [*Aside*] This is a piece of malice. I am glad
I came this way so happily. The King
Shall understand it presently.   *Exit.*

CRAN.   'Tis Butts,
The King's physician. As he pass'd along,   10
How earnestly he cast his eyes upon me!
Pray heaven he sound not my disgrace! For certain,
This is of purpose laid by some that hate me
(God turn their hearts! I never sought their malice)
To quench mine honor. They would shame to make me   15
Wait else at door, a fellow councillor,
'Mong boys, grooms, and lackeys. But their pleasures
Must be fulfill'd, and I attend with patience.

Enter the King and Butts at a window above.

BUTTS.   I'll show your Grace the strangest sight—

KING.   What's that, Butts?

BUTTS.   I think your Highness saw this many a day.   20

KING.   Body o' me, where is it?

ACT 5, SCENE 2
s.d. **Pursuivants**: servants to heralds. 3. **All fast**: i.e., he is locked out of the room. 4. **Sure**: I am sure. 8 **happily**: luckily. 9. **presently**: immediately. 12. **sound**: discover; find. 13. **of . . . laid**: designed as a trap. 21. **Body o' me**: by my own body.

BUTTS.   There, my lord:
The high promotion of his Grace of Canterbury,
Who holds his state at door 'mongst pursuivants,
Pages, and footboys.

KING.   Ha? 'Tis he indeed.
Is this the honor they do one another?   25
'Tis well there's one above 'em yet. I had thought
They had parted so much honesty among 'em—
At least, good manners—as not thus to suffer
A man of his place and so near our favor
To dance attendance on their lordships' pleasures,   30
And at the door too, like a post with packets.
By holy Mary, Butts, there's knavery!
Let 'em alone, and draw the curtain close.
We shall hear more anon.   [*Exeunt.*]

SCENE III. [*The Council Chamber.*]

A Council table brought in, with chairs and
stools, and placed under the state. Enter Lord
Chancellor, places himself at the upper end of
the table on the left hand, a seat being left void
above him, as for Canterbury's seat. Duke of
Suffolk, Duke of Norfolk, Surrey, Lord
Chamberlain, Gardiner seat themselves in
order on each side; Cromwell at lower end, as
Secretary. [Keeper at the door.]

CHAN.   Speak to the business, Master Secretary.
Why are we met in Council?

CROM.   Please your Honors,
The chief cause concerns his Grace of Canterbury.

GARD.   Has he had knowledge of it?

CROM.   Yes.

---

23. **Who . . . state**: who is reduced to preserving his dignity. 26. **one above**: i.e., God (?) or the king (who is also literally placed above the council). 27. **parted so much**: shared enough. 30. **dance attendance**: to wait as if an obsequious servant (*OED* "dance," 5). 31. **post with packets**: messenger with mail.

ACT 5, SCENE 3
s.d. **Lord Chancellor**: Historically, Thomas More, who was famously executed for refusing to endorse the king's divorce. He is not named in the play.

NOR.	Who waits there?
KEEP.	Without, my noble lords?
GARD.	Yes.
KEEP.	My Lord Archbishop, 5
	And has done half an hour to know your pleasures.
CHAN.	Let him come in.
KEEP.	Your Grace may enter now.
	Cranmer approaches the Council table.
CHAN.	My good Lord Archbishop, I'm very sorry
	To sit here at this present and behold
	That chair stand empty; but we all are men, 10
	In our own natures frail and capable
	Of our flesh; few are angels; out of which frailty
	And want of wisdom, you, that best should teach us,
	Have misdemean'd yourself, and not a little:
	Toward the King first, then his laws, in filling 15
	The whole realm by your teaching and your chaplains
	(For so we are inform'd) with new opinions,
	Divers and dangerous; which are heresies,
	And, not reform'd, may prove pernicious.
GARD.	Which reformation must be sudden too, 20
	My noble lords; for those that tame wild horses
	Pace 'em not in their hands to make 'em gentle,
	But stop their mouths with stubborn bits and spur 'em
	Till they obey the manage. If we suffer,
	Out of our easiness and childish pity 25
	To one man's honor, this contagious sickness,
	Farewell all physic! And what follows then?
	Commotions, uproars, with a general taint
	Of the whole state, as of late days our neighbours,
	The upper Germany, can dearly witness, 30
	Yet freshly pitied in our memories.
CRAN.	My good lords, hitherto, in all the progress
	Both of my life and office, I have labor'd,

5. **Without**: outside. 10. **That chair**: i.e., his own chair. 11–12. **capable . . . flesh**: subject to the weakness of the flesh. 13. **want**: lack. 14. **Misdemean'd yourself**: committed misconduct. 17. **opinions**: religious beliefs. 18. **Divers**: various. 19. **pernicious**: deadly. 22. **Pace 'em . . . hands**: do not train them (lead them through "paces") with their hands alone. 24. **manage**: handling; manage. **suffer**: permit. 25. **easiness**: permissiveness; indolence. 27. **physic**: cures. 28. **taint**: tainting. 29–30. **of late . . . witness**: alludes to recent uprisings in Germany—e.g., the Peasants War of the 1520s and the Anabapists' massacre.

And with no little study, that my teaching
And the strong course of my authority   35
Might go one way, and safely; and the end
Was ever to do well; nor is there living
(I speak it with a single heart, my lords)
A man that more detests, more stirs against,
Both in his private conscience and his place,   40
Defacers of a public peace than I do.
Pray heaven the King may never find a heart
With less allegiance in it! Men that make
Envy and crooked malice nourishment
Dare bite the best. I do beseech your lordships   45
That in this case of justice my accusers,
Be what they will, may stand forth face to face
And freely urge against me.

SUF.   Nay, my lord,
That cannot be. You are a Councillor,
And by that virtue no man dare accuse you.   50

GARD.   My lord, because we have business of more moment,
We will be short with you. 'Tis his Highness' pleasure
And our consent, for better trial of you,
From hence you be committed to the Tower,
Where, being but a private man again,   55
You shall know many dare accuse you boldly,
More than, I fear, you are provided for.

CRAN.   Ah, my good Lord of Winchester, I thank you.
You are always my good friend. If your will pass,
I shall both find your lordship judge and juror,   60
You are so merciful. I see your end—
'Tis my undoing. Love and meekness, lord,
Become a churchman better than ambition;
Win straying souls with modesty again,
Cast none away. That I shall clear myself,   65
Lay all the weight ye can upon my patience,
I make as little doubt as you do conscience
In doing daily wrongs. I could say more,
But reverence to your calling makes me modest.

---

34. **study**: diligence. 38. **a single heart**: integrity. 39. **stirs**: fights. 40. **place**: official function. 45. **bite**: feed on; get nourishment from. 48. **urge**: i.e., their accusations. 50. **by that virtue**: by virtue of being a councilor. 59. **your will pass**: you get what you wish for. 64. **with modesty**: by showing restraint. 67. **make**: have.

GARD.   My lord, my lord, you are a sectary!   70
        That's the plain truth. Your painted gloss discovers,
        To men that understand you, words and weakness.

CROM.   My Lord of Winchester, you are a little,
        By your good favor, too sharp. Men so noble,
        However faulty, yet should find respect   75
        For what they have been. 'Tis a cruelty
        To load a falling man.

GARD.   Good Master Secretary,
        I cry your Honor mercy. You may worst
        Of all this table say so.

CROM.   Why, my lord?

GARD.   Do not I know you for a favorer   80
        Of this new sect? Ye are not sound.

CROM.   Not sound?

GARD.   Not sound, I say.

CROM.   Would you were half so honest!
        Men's prayers then would seek you, not their fears.

GARD.   I shall remember this bold language.

CROM.   Do.
        Remember your bold life too.

CHAN.   This is too much.   85
        Forbear for shame, my lords.

GARD.   I have done.

CROM.   And I.

CHAN.   Then thus for you, my lord: it stands agreed,
        I take it, by all voices, that forthwith
        You be convey'd to th' Tower a prisoner,
        There to remain till the King's further pleasure   90
        Be known unto us. Are you all agreed, lords?

ALL.   We are.

CRAN.   Is there no other way of mercy
        But I must needs to th' Tower, my lords?

---

70. **sectary**: an adherent of heretical Protestant beliefs. 71. **painted gloss**: deceptive resplendence or interpretation (of scripture). **discovers**: reveals. 72. **words**: i.e., empty words. 75. **find**: merit. 77. **load**: weight down. 78. **may worst**: are the least qualified. 81. **sound**: i.e., in beliefs. 84. **bold**: impudent. 93. **needs**: by force go.

GARD.   What other
          Would you expect? You are strangely troublesome.
          Let some o' th' guard be ready there!

                          Enter the Guard.

CRAN.   For me?   95
          Must I go like a traitor thither?

GARD.   Receive him
          And see him safe i' th' Tower.

CRAN.   Stay, good my lords,
          I have a little yet to say. Look there, my lords.   [*Shows ring.*]
          By virtue of that ring I take my cause
          Out of the gripes of cruel men and give it   100
          To a most noble judge, the King my master.

CHAN.   This is the King's ring.

SUR.   'Tis no counterfeit.

SUF.   'Tis the right ring, by heav'n! I told ye all,
          When we first put this dangerous stone a-rolling,
          'Twould fall upon ourselves.

NOR.   Do you think, my lords,   105
          The King will suffer but the little finger
          Of this man to be vex'd?

CHAN.   'Tis now too certain.
          How much more is his life in value with him!
          Would I were fairly out on't!

CROM.   My mind gave me,
          In seeking tales and informations   110
          Against this man—whose honesty the devil
          And his disciples only envy at—
          Ye blew the fire that burns ye. Now have at ye!

                  Enter King, frowning on them; takes his seat.

GARD.   Dread sovereign, how much are we bound to heaven
          In daily thanks, that gave us such a prince,   115
          Not only good and wise but most religious;
          One that in all obedience makes the Church

---

100. **gripes**: grip; control. 106. **suffer**: permit. 108. **in value with him**: worth to the king. 109. **fairly out on't**: safely free from this affair. **gave**: forewarned; presented misgivings (*OED*, 22). 110. **tales and informations**: rumors and imputation. 113. **have at ye**: a cry of attack, here meaning, "you asked for it."

The chief aim of his honor, and, to strengthen
That holy duty, out of dear respect,
His royal self in judgment comes to hear   120
The cause betwixt her and this great offender.

KING.   You were ever good at sudden commendations,
Bishop of Winchester. But know I come not
To hear such flattery now, and in my presence.
They are too thin and bare to hide offences.   125
To me you cannot reach you play the spaniel
And think with wagging of your tongue to win me.
But whatsoe'er thou tak'st me for, I'm sure
Thou hast a cruel nature and a bloody.
[*To Cranmer*] Good man, sit down. Now let me see the
    proudest,   130
He that dares most, but wag his finger at thee.
By all that's holy, he had better starve
Than but once think this place becomes thee not.

SUR.   May it please your Grace—

KING.   No, sir, it does not please me.
I had thought I had had men of some understanding   135
And wisdom of my Council; but I find none.
Was it discretion, lords, to let this man,
This good man (few of you deserve that title),
This honest man, wait like a lousy footboy
At chamber door? And one as great as you are?   140
Why, what a shame was this! Did my commission
Bid ye so far forget yourselves? I gave ye
Power as he was a Councillor to try him,
Not as a groom. There's some of ye, I see,
More out of malice than integrity,   145
Would try him to the utmost, had ye mean;
Which ye shall never have while I live.

CHAN.   Thus far,
My most dread sovereign, may it like your Grace
To let my tongue excuse all. What was purpos'd
Concerning his imprisonment was rather   150

---

119. **dear respect**: concerned conscience. 122. **sudden commendations**: improvising flattery. 125: **They**: the commendations. 126. **reach**: scope or jurisdiction. 130–131. **proudest, / He**: The Folio version of the play omits the comma. In that case, "He" would work as a noun meaning "man." As punctuated here "proudest" is a noun, which "He" renames. 133. **this place**: i.e., next to the king. 136. **of**: on. 137. **discretion**: sound judgment. 146. **mean**: means; power.

(If there be faith in men) meant for his trial
And fair purgation to the world than malice,
I'm sure, in me.

KING.   Well, well, my lords, respect him.
Take him, and use him well; he's worthy of it.
I will say thus much for him—if a prince   155
May be beholding to a subject, I
Am for his love and service so to him.
Make me no more ado, but all embrace him.
Be friends for shame, my lords! My Lord of Canterbury,
I have a suit which you must not deny me.   160
That is, a fair young maid that yet wants baptism,
You must be godfather and answer for her.

CRAN.   The greatest monarch now alive may glory
In such an honor. How may I deserve it
That am a poor and humble subject to you?   165

KING.   Come, come, my lord, you'd spare your spoons! You shall
       have
Two noble partners with you, the old Duchess of Norfolk
And Lady Marquess Dorset. Will these please you?
Once more, my Lord of Winchester, I charge you
Embrace and love this man.

GARD.   With a true heart   170
And brother's love I do it.

CRAN.   And let heaven
Witness how dear I hold this confirmation.

KING.   Good man, those joyful tears show thy true heart.
The common voice I see is verified
Of thee, which says thus: "Do my Lord of Canterbury   175
A shrewd turn, and he's your friend for ever."
Come, lords, we trifle time away. I long
To have this young one made a Christian.
As I have made ye one, lords, one remain;
So I grow stronger, you more honor gain.   *Exeunt.*   180

---

152. **fair purgation**: proper exculpation or freeing from guilt. 154. **use**: treat. 156. **beholding**: indebted.
161. **yet wants**: still needs. 166. **spare your spoons**: The king teasingly accuses Cranmer of hesitating
because he is too cheap to buy a christening gift for Princess Elizabeth. 174. **voice**: report. 176. **shrewd
turn**: an injury.

SCENE IV. [*The Palace Yard.*]

Noise and tumult within.
Enter Porter and his Man.

PORT.   You'll leave your noise anon, ye rascals! Do you take the court
        for Parish Garden?
        Ye rude slaves, leave your gaping!
        [*One (Within).*] Good Master Porter, I belong to th' larder.

PORT.   Belong to th' gallows and be hang'd, ye rogue! Is this a place
        to roar in? Fetch me a dozen crabtree staves, and strong ones.
        These are but switches to 'em. I'll scratch your heads. You
        must be seeing christenings! Do you look for ale and cakes
        here, you rude rascals?   6

MAN.   Pray, sir, be patient! 'Tis as much impossible,
        Unless we sweep 'em from the door with cannons,
        To scatter 'em as 'tis to make 'em sleep
        On May Day morning, which will never be.   10
        We may as well push against Powl's as stir 'em.

PORT.   How got they in, and be hang'd?

MAN.   Alas, I know not. How gets the tide in?
        As much as one sound cudgel of four foot
        (You see the poor remainder) could distribute,   15
        I made no spare, sir.

PORT.   You did nothing, sir.

MAN.   I am not Samson, nor Sir Guy, nor Colebrand,
        To mow 'em down before me; but if I spar'd any
        That had a head to hit, either young or old,
        He or she, cuckold or cuckold-maker,   20
        Let me ne'er hope to see a chine again;
        And that I would not for a cow, God save her!
        [(*Within*)] Do you hear, Master Porter?

ACT 5, SCENE 4
1. **leave**: cease. **anon**: at once. **Parish Garden**: Paris Garden: a bear-baiting arena near the Globe. 2.
gaping: yelping; shouting. 3. **belong ... larder**: Am I servant in the king's food pantry? 5. **These ...
'em**: The cudgels I'm using now are mere switches compared to the crabtree staves I will use against
you. 6. **Do ... here**: i.e., you're here only for free treats and beer. 10. **May Day**: a celebration of spring
in which celebrants rose before dawn. 11. **Powl's**: St. Paul's Cathedral. 12. **be hang'd**: a curse. 16.
made no spare: did not hold back. 17. **Sir ... Colebrand**: In popular English romance, Sir Guy of
Warwick slew Colebrand, a Danish giant. 20. **He or she**: man or woman. **cuckold**: a man whose wife
is unfaithful. 21. **Let ... chine**: I never want to see another backbone (presumably because he has been
beating so many revelers on their backs).

PORT.   I shall be with you presently, good Master Puppy!
—Keep the door close, sirrah.

MAN.   What would you have me do?   25

PORT.   What should you do but knock 'em down by th' dozens? Is
this Moorfields to muster in? Or have we some strange Indian
with the great tool come to court, the women so besiege us?
Bless me, what a fry of fornication is at door! On my Christian
conscience, this one christening will beget a thousand; here
will be father, godfather, and all together.   29

MAN.   The spoons will be the bigger, sir. There is a fellow somewhat
near the door; he should be a brazier by his face, for, o' my
conscience, twenty of the dogdays now reign in's nose. All that
stand about him are under the Line; they need no other penance. That firedrake did I hit three times on the head, and
three times was his nose discharged against me. He stands
there like a mortar-piece to blow us. There was a haberdasher's
wife of small wit near him, that rail'd upon me till her pink'd
porringer fell off her head, for kindling such a combustion in
the state. I miss'd the meteor once and hit that woman, who
cried out "Clubs!" when I might see from far some forty trun-
cheoners draw to her succor, which were the hope o' th'
Strond, where she was quartered. They fell on; I made good
my place. At length they came to th' broomstaff to me. I
defied 'em still; when suddenly a file of boys behind 'em, loose
shot, deliver'd such a show'r of pebbles that I was fain to draw
mine honor in and let 'em win the work. The devil was
amongst 'em, I think surely.   40

---

26. **Moorfields**: fields outside of London is which military exercises ("musters") were held. 27. **tool**: penis. 28. **fry of fornication**: swarm of sexually aroused people. 30. **spoons**: christening gifts. 31. **brazier**: a brass-forger, who worked in extreme heat. **dogdays**: considered summer's hottest days. 32. **under the Line**: i.e., of the equator (in tropical heat). **need**: should be required to do. **firedrake**: fiery dragon. 33. **discharged**: i.e., like a weapon is fired. **mortar-piece**: small cannon. 34. **blow us**: 1) fire at us; 2) blow us up. **haberdasher**: hat-maker or seller. 34–35. **pink'd / porringer**: a small, form-fitting cap with pinking (small holes cut) in it. 35. **kindling . . . combustion**: fueling such a disturbance. **meteor**: i.e., the man previously mentioned. 36. **"Clubs!"**: A cry to rally apprentices to riot. **truncheon-ers**: men bearing clubs. 37. **succor**: aid. **hope of th' Strond**: most noble men of the Strand (a shopping district). **fell on**: attacked. 38. **made good**: defended. **came . . . broomstaff**: came near enough to fight with sticks. 39. **file**: row. **loose shot**: sharpshooters that are detached from (i.e., "loose") a company. **fain**: forced. 40. **work**: fortification.

PORT.   These are the youths that thunder at a playhouse and fight for[†]
bitten apples; that no audience but the tribulation of Tower
Hill or the limbs of Limehouse, their dear brothers, are able
to endure. I have some of 'em in *Limbo Patrum*, and there they
are like to dance these three days, besides the running banquet
of two beadles that is to come.   44

Enter Lord Chamberlain.

CHAM.   Mercy o' me, what a multitude are here!
They grow still too; from all parts they are coming
As if we kept a fair here! Where are these porters,
These lazy knaves? Y'have made a fine hand, fellows!
There's a trim rabble let in. Are all these
Your faithful friends o' th' suburbs? We shall have   50
Great store of room, no doubt, left for the ladies
When they pass back from the christening.

PORT.   An't please your Honor,
We are but men; and what so many may do,
Not being torn a-pieces, we have done.
An army cannot rule 'em.

CHAM.   As I live,   55
If the King blame me for't, I'll lay ye all
By th' heels, and suddenly, and on your heads
Clap round fines for neglect. Y'are lazy knaves,
And here ye lie baiting of bombards when
Ye should do service. Hark! the trumpets sound;   60
Th'are come already from the christening.
Go break among the press and find a way out
To let the troop pass fairly, or I'll find
A Marshalsea shall hold ye play these two months.

---

41. **fight . . . apples**: quarrel over half-eaten fruit. 42. **tribulation . . . Hill**: gangs from Tower Hill
(where executions were held). **limbs of Limehouse**: offshoots, progeny of Limehouse (a rough dock-
area). 43. **have . . . *Limbo Patrum***: have sent some of them to prison, named for the place in the
Catholic Hell that held the souls of the unbaptized. **dance**: wait idly. 44. **running banquet**: refers to
a public beating by those officers in charge of punishment ("beadles"). 48. **made . . . hand**: done fine
work (said sarcastically). 49. **trim**: first-rate. 50. **suburbs**: the area outside the authority of London's
power, considered an unruly place. 51. **store**: supply. 52. **An't**: if it. 55. **rule**: control. 56–57. **lay . . .
heels**: clasp your feet in the stocks. 59. **Clap round**: impose large. 60. **baiting of bombards**: a challenging phrase; perhaps, drinking with drunkards (here named "bombards" for the leather containers
that hold liquor). 62. **among the press**: through the crowd. 64. **Marshalsea**: a prison near the Globe
Theatre. **hold ye play**: restrain you from entertainment.

---

†   "These are the youths that thunder at a playhouse . . ." The final scene balances two moods—the
headiness of the revelers at Princess Elizabeth's christening with the solemnity of Cranmer's
prophecy.

PORT.   Make way there for the Princess!

MAN.   You great fellow,   65
              Stand close up, or I'll make your head ache!

PORT.   You i' th' chamblet,
              Get up o' th' rail. I'll peck you o'er the pales else!   *Exeunt.*

SCENE V. [*The Palace.*]

Enter Trumpets, sounding; then two Aldermen,
Lord Mayor, Garter, Cranmer, Duke of Norfolk
with his Marshal's staff, Duke of Suffolk, two
Noblemen bearing great standing bowls for the
christening gifts; then four Noblemen bearing a
canopy, under which the Duchess of Norfolk,
godmother, bearing the child richly habited in a
mantle, &c. train borne by a Lady; then follows
the Marchioness Dorset, the other godmother,
and Ladies. The troop pass once about the stage,
and Garter speaks.

GART.   Heaven, from thy endless goodness send prosperous life, long,
             and ever happy, to the high and mighty Princess of England,
             Elizabeth!

                        Flourish. Enter King and Guard.

CRAN.   [*Kneels*] And to your royal Grace and the good Queen!
             My noble partners and myself thus pray
             All comfort, joy, in this most gracious lady,   5
             Heaven ever laid up to make parents happy,
             May hourly fall upon ye!

KING.   Thank you, good Lord Archbishop:
             What is her name?

CRAN.   Elizabeth.

KING.   Stand up, lord.
             [*Cranmer rises. The King kisses the child.*]

---

67. **chamblet**: camblet—a fine fabric made from silk and camel hair (*OED* 1). 68. **peck**: heave. **pales**:
railing.
ACT 5, SCENE 5:
s.d. *Garter*: Garter King-at-Arms, the primary herald. ***standing bowls***: bowls that have stands.
habited: attired. 6. **Heaven**: that Heaven.

With this kiss take my blessing. God protect thee!
Into whose hand I give thy life.

CRAN.   Amen.   10

KING.   My noble gossips, y'have been too prodigal.
I thank ye heartily. So shall this lady,
When she has so much English.

CRAN.   Let me speak, sir,
For heaven now bids me; and the words I utter
Let none think flattery, for they'll find 'em truth.   15
This royal infant—heaven still move about her!—
Though in her cradle, yet now promises
Upon this land a thousand thousand blessings,
Which time shall bring to ripeness. She shall be
(But few now living can behold that goodness)   20
A pattern to all princes living with her
And all that shall succeed. Saba was never
More covetous of wisdom and fair virtue
Than this pure soul shall be. All princely graces
That mold up such a mighty piece as this is,   25
With all the virtues that attend the good,
Shall still be doubled on her. Truth shall nurse her,
Holy and heavenly thoughts still counsel her.
She shall be lov'd and fear'd. Her own shall bless her;
Her foes shake like a field of beaten corn   30
And hang their heads with sorrow. Good grows with her.
In her days every man shall eat in safety
Under his own vine what he plants, and sing
The merry songs of peace to all his neighbors.
God shall be truly known, and those about her   35
From her shall read the perfect ways of honor
And by those claim their greatness, not by blood.
Nor shall this peace sleep with her; but as when
The bird of wonder dies, the maiden phœnix,
Her ashes new create another heir   40
As great in admiration as herself,

---

11. **gossips**: God sibs' (siblings)—how parents refer to the godparents of their children. **prodigal**: i.e., in bestowing gifts. 16. **heaven still**: may Heaven always. 21. **A pattern**: an exemplary model. 22. **Saba**: the queen of Sheba, who, according to Biblical account, sought wisdom from King Solomon. 25. **mold up**: compose. 29. **own**: subjects. 30. **beaten corn**: wind-swept grain. 35. **God . . . known**: the right religious understanding will win out. **about her**: i.e., her court. 36. **read**: learn. 37. **blood**: noble birth. 38. **sleep**: i.e., when she dies. 39. **phœnix**: a mythical bird that was reborn from its ashes after it died. 41. **admiration**: creating wonder.

So shall she leave her blessedness to one
(When heaven shall call her from this cloud of darkness)
Who from the sacred ashes of her honor
Shall starlike rise, as great in fame as she was,   45
And so stand fix'd. Peace, plenty, love, truth, terror,
That were the servants to this chosen infant,
Shall then be his and like a vine grow to him.
Wherever the bright sun of heaven shall shine,
His honor and the greatness of his name   50
Shall be, and make new nations. He shall flourish
And like a mountain cedar reach his branches
To all the plains about him. Our children's children
Shall see this, and bless heaven.

KING.   Thou speakest wonders.

CRAN.   She shall be, to the happiness of England,   55
An aged princess; many days shall see her,
And yet no day without a deed to crown it.
Would I had known no more! But she must die—
She must, the saints must have her—yet a virgin,
A most unspotted lily, shall she pass   60
To th' ground, and all the world shall mourn her.

KING.   O Lord Archbishop,
Thou hast made me now a man! Never before
This happy child did I get anything.
This oracle of comfort has so pleas'd me   65
That when I am in heaven I shall desire
To see what this child does, and praise my Maker.
I thank ye all. To you, my good Lord Mayor,
And your good brethren I am much beholding.
I have receiv'd much honor by your presence,   70
And ye shall find me thankful. Lead the way, lords.
Ye must all see the Queen, and she must thank ye;
She will be sick else. This day no man think
'Has business at his house; for all shall stay.
This little one shall make it Holy-day. *Exeunt.*   75

---

43. **cloud of darkness**: mortal existence, where things are but half-understood. 46. **fix'd**: immovable (as a star). **terror**: rightful ability to create respect. 57. **deed**: act of virtue. 64. **get**: beget. 69. **beholding**: beholden. 73. **sick**: unhappy; less than satisfied. 74. **stay**: i.e., here to celebrate. 75. **Holy-day**: holiday.

THE EPILOGUE

'Tis ten to one this play can never please
All that are here. Some come to take their ease
And sleep an act or two; but those, we fear,
W'have frighted with our trumpets; so, 'tis clear,
They'll say 'tis naught; others, to hear the city   5
Abus'd extremely, and to cry "That's witty!"
Which we have not done neither; that, I fear,
All the expected good w'are like to hear
For this play at this time, is only in
The merciful construction of good women;   10
For such a one we show'd 'em. If they smile
And say 'twill do, I know within a while
All the best men are ours; for 'tis ill hap,
If they hold when their ladies bid 'em clap.

EPILOGUE:
5. **naught**: trivial; worthless. 5–6. **the city / Abus'd**: the manners of the citizens be satirized (as they were in popular plays called city comedies). 7. **that**: so that. 8. **good**: praise. 10. **construction**: instruction; representation. 11. **one**: which woman is the model of goodness is not evident. **they**: i.e., the women. 13. **are ours**: will approve. **ill hap**: bad luck. 14. **hold**: hold back.

Plot Outline of *Henry VIII*

Prologue. An unnamed Prologue comes on stage to announce that the play will tell the sober history of Henry VIII. He exalts this sincere subject matter above plays that present battles and the antics of fools. In place of those, he offers the truth of history and the promise of tears at the downfall of the mighty.

Act 1.1. The Duke of Norfolk tells the Duke of Buckingham of the splendid pageantry he missed at the important meeting between King Henry of England and the French king at the Field of the Cloth of Gold. The discussion then turns to Cardinal Wolsey's presumption in orchestrating the event and the onus he places on the lords for funding it. They find some solace in the failure because it is reported that the French have already broken their treaty with the English. Buckingham tells of his plan to expose Wolsey's alleged treachery to the King, while Wolsey, in the meantime, has already acted against Buckingham, and the scene ends with Buckingham's arrest for treason.

Act 1.2. The queen implores King Henry on behalf of subjects oppressed by a heavy one-sixth taxation and implicates Wolsey as the chief architect of this tax scheme. Ignorant of the tax, the King is incensed against Wolsey who denies having a greater part than the rest of the council and claims to have only been going along with the general vote. The King admonishes Wolsey, but all is well in the end. The talk then turns to Buckingham, and Wolsey introduces the duke's disgraced surveyor who testifies against his former employer. At the end of the scene, the King determines to bring Buckingham to trial.

Act 1.3. Lord Sandys and Lord Chamberlain express their pleasure with the proclamation barring French fashion and believe that their English manners will be more successful with ladies than they had been of late.

Act 1.4. At Wolsey's York Palace, Sandys and Chamberlain disport with Anne Bullen until the cardinal arrives to begin his lavish festivities. His servant announces the arrival of masked foreign revelers, who later reveal themselves as the King and his retainers. The King then dances with Anne Bullen and shows her great favor before they move in to dinner.

Act 2.1.   Two anonymous gentlemen recount the trial of Buckingham and the process that led up to his being found guilty of treason and, like Buckingham before, they blame the cardinal for his downfall. Buckingham enters on the way to execution and laments the lack of Christian charity in those who urged the case against him, but he graciously accepts the verdict and proclaims the trial to have been fair. The scene ends with the gentlemen secretly discussing the King's recent scruple about his marriage to his current wife over the fact that she was once married to his older brother Arthur.

Act 2.2.   Lord Chamberlain, who has been in private conference with the King, meets Suffolk and Norfolk and reports the King's turmoil over his current marriage. They are seeking the King's counsel on a different matter and blame Wolsey for having set this turmoil in the King's conscience. When the two encounter the King, he impatiently dismisses them. In the King's process of doing so, Wolsey arrives with Cardinal Campeius from Rome. The King is happy to see them as he believes they will help him out of his difficulty. Near the end of the scene, the King calls for his new secretary Gardiner, who was formerly employed by Wolsey and expresses loyalty to his old master. The scene ends with the King announcing that they shall hear his case at Blackfriars.

Act 2.3.   Anne Bullen and her Old Lady servant discuss the queen's plight. Anne claims she would not be queen for anything, and her servant accuses her of hypocrisy. Chamberlain enters and informs Anne that the King has bestowed upon her the title of Marchioness of Pembroke and an income of a thousand pounds a year, all undeniable signs of the King's favor toward her.

Act 2.4.   At this court proceeding, the queen contends that she has always been a faithful wife and a true subject to her husband. When she is urged to have the marriage issue heard, Katherine reviles Wolsey for having set the King on in this matter and refuses to allow him for her judge. She demands to have her case heard by the Pope, then exits the room. Once she has gone, the King exonerates Wolsey for the queen's accusation and explains the rise of his doubt. The visiting cardinal says that he cannot pass judgement unless Katherine changes her mind about the suit to Rome, and the King (in an aside) accuses him of stalling.

Act 3.1.   The queen sits working with her ladies in her chamber. The two cardinals urge her to hear their counsel and to trust the matter to the

King's care. The queen argues that no one in England will give her counsel and that she does not trust the cardinals. She appeals to hear weakness as a woman and, at the end of the scene, relents and requests the cardinals' counsel in the matter.

Act 3.2. Norway, Suffolk, Surrey, and Chamberlain discuss the King's recent discovery of Wolsey's vast inventory of wealth and that same cardinal's treasonous attempt to thwart the King's divorce. Cromwell and Wolsey enter and discuss the King's plans to marry Anne Bullen, to his great consternation as he objects to the King's marrying a "spleeny Lutheran." The others exit. The King joins Wolsey and reveals through letters than he has discovered Wolsey's infidelity to him. The lords reenter and upbraid Wolsey, demanding his seal to return to the King. Wolsey remains indignant. Cromwell enters with news that Henry has named Thomas Cranmer as Wolsey's successor and has married Anne Bullen in secret.

Act 4.1. At the new queen's coronation, the two gentlemen from act 1 now discuss the fate of Katherine. These same gentlemen provide additional commentary on the train of dignitaries that accompany the coronation, and gush upon seeing Anne's beauty.

Act 4.2. Katherine, ailing and moribund, rails against Wolsey. Griffith, her gentleman usher, gives a more measured estimation of the former cardinal in which he weighs his generosity against his avarice. Katherine, now Princess Dowager, falls asleep and is treated to a beatific vision of six dancing personages in white robes who hold garlands above her head. When she awakens, her nephew Capucius enters with commendation from the King, and she replies asking favor that her daughter and her servants be taken care of. She ends the scene in a way indicating that death is imminent.

Act 5.1. Bishop Gardiner speaks with Lovell about the new queen's labor and explains how he has incensed the council against Archbishop Cranmer for his Protestant religious leanings. The King enters and is soon met by Cranmer whom he warns of the enemies conspiring against him, and to whom, after sounding his fidelity to his views, he gives his ring as evidence of his support. Anne's old lady servant enters to announce the birth of the infant Elizabeth and pursues the King in hope of a larger reward for her role as messenger.

Act 5.2. Cranmer arrives at the council's chamber but is unceremoniously denied entrance by the keeper. Butts shows the King to a place of surveillance so that the two can look on the scene below.

Act 5.3. Gardiner and the other lords admit Cranmer and proceed to inform him that he has incurred the King's displeasure for his sectarian beliefs. As the guard goes to arrest Cranmer, he shows them the King's ring.

The King enters at that moment and upbraids the councilors for their treatment and instructs them to "embrace and love" Cranmer.

Act 5.4.   In the palace yard outside Princess Elizabeth's christening, enthusiasts and revelers press to enter and celebrate. The folksy Porter chastises his man for not keeping the revelers at bay. After the man gives a lengthy comic defense, Lord Chamberlain enters and worries himself about the size of the crowd that has been admitted.

Act 5.5.   The christening procession of dignitaries emerges from the palace. Cranmer, who has officiated, prophesies peace and prosperity during the reign of Elizabeth, who, as a Maiden Phoenix, will be reborn as James, a monarch as great as her. The play ends with the King inviting all in the crowd to stay and celebrate.

Epilogue.   The epilogue concedes that the play will not please all. Those who do take pleasure will mainly be the "merciful" women, whom the epilogue instructs to urge their men to applaud in order to avoid the bad luck of disagreeing with women.

GENEALOGY OF *HENRY VIII*

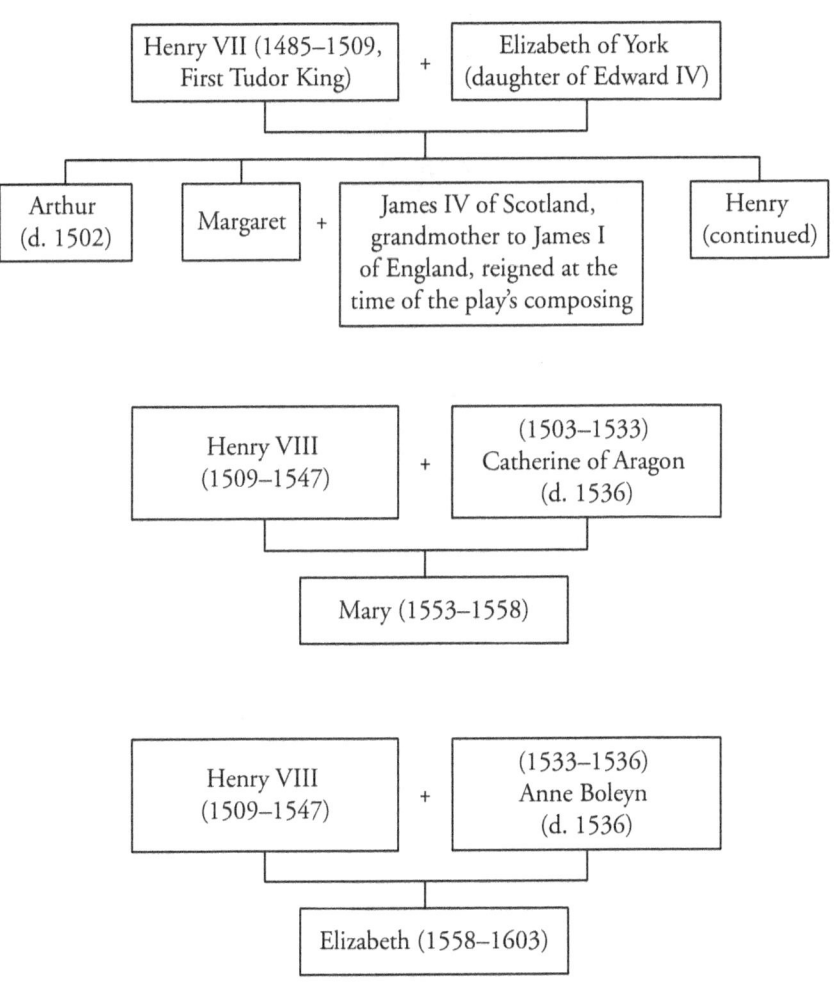

How to Read *Henry VIII* as Performance

In an important way *Henry VIII* is almost unique. No Shakespeare play other than *Henry V* makes demands on the actors and audiences as bold as *Henry VIII*. The Prologue of the play instructs the audience to identify the characters in the play with the actual historical personages: "Think ye see / The very persons of our noble story / As they were living" (25–27). The requirement strains the imaginative capacity of audience and actors alike. To a certain extent, Shakespeare has made it easier for this identification of characters with real people if not actual personages to take place. He has drawn realistic-speaking characters facing real-world dramas of life, marriage, love, and religion.

For actors, one of the main draws of the play has been the role of Queen Katherine, the focus of so much emotional energy. Readers have no trouble imagining the indignation she feels at having her marriage and royalty challenged, and the play prompts them to feel it. Still, the degree of tragedy that she is facing is greater because the play takes great pain to emphasize its undeserved nature. Katherine is a princess of Spain, royal even without her marriage to Henry. Her sense of injury intensifies the power of lines such as these she speaks to Wolsey before the court:

> Sir,
> I am about to weep; but, thinking that
> We are a queen (or long have dream'd so), certain
> The daughter of a king, my drops of tears
> I'll turn to sparks of fire. (2.4.67–71)

The combination of injury and outrage in such lines places Katherine between water and fire. And it requires the actor playing her both to generate and restrain energy for a cause that would justify a much angrier outburst. Given the pathos and power of Katherine's situation, it is little wonder that some actors have pursued her role to the point of obsession. One of the most famous actors of the mid-20th century,

Peggy Ashcroft was known for having considered herself the owner of Katherine's part and would often attempt to introduce dialogue from historical accounts of her that was not part of the original play. Clearly, she took the Prologue's charge seriously.

Although the primary challenge of performing Katherine is finding an actor with skills large enough to fill her personality, with Anne Bullen the actor and reader must apply a finer sense of detail and subtlety in analyzing her character and representation. Considering Katherine's plight, Anne may demur at the idea of being queen, but the old lady serving her suggests her hesitancy is mere coyness. In Kevin Billington's film version, the facial expressions of Barbara Kellerman's Anne show undeniable excitement at the prospect of being queen, and her bearing in the procession after she is crowned is one of clear pride in her new title. However, the play's text is mainly opaque about which version of her is ultimately more truthful. Anne is certainly capable of being coy and gamesome in her encounters. At Cardinal Wolsey's feast, she endures bawdy humor and even engages in it with Sandys. However, her engagement with his risqué language is as resistant as it is inviting. In his boast about his ability to goad women into speaking, Sandys makes reference to offering a pledge, which he is suggestively using to mean his genitalia: "Yes, if I make my play. / Here's to your ladyship; and pledge it, madam, / For 'tis such a thing" (1.2.46–48). Anne cuts him off in a way that acknowledges his reference while denying him the ability to make it fully: "You cannot show me," Anne says of his "thing." Although Anne clearly knows the games of court and her role in them, whether and how much she enjoys these games is not clear, and the production can decide to what extent it wants to emphasize or obscure her attitude.

Henry's character raises specific questions in a similar way to Anne's. Because the king does not have a soliloquy in which he unfolds a deep interior character or set of motives, audiences must measure his claims against those of others who observe him. Additionally, how actors represent or readers perceive Henry makes a difference in whether we judge him as negligent of his kingdom's management and lustful for a new queen or genuinely afflicted with scruples of conscience and hoodwinked only by the most skillful politicians. Henry clearly finds Anne supremely pretty; "O beauty, / Till now I never knew thee!" (1.4.75–76) he tells Anne on singling her out for the dance. And in his only aside, Henry shows that he is aware of political maneuvering. When Cardinal Campeius acknowledges Katherine's right to appeal to the Pope, Henry infers, "I may perceive / These Cardinals trifle with me. I abhor / This dilatory sloth and tricks of Rome" (2.4.232–234). Although Henry clearly has preferences that drive him, the extent to which his dealings are duplicitous is never revealed.

Wolsey's performance has to be particularly accomplished. His repentance once he is brought down is instant and audience sympathy for him depends on finding it believable. Whether or not he attains sympathy in his downfall that he could not at his height depends entirely on how credibly he performs his speech's beginning: "Farewell, a long farewell, to all my greatness" (3.2.351). In so many ways, Wolsey's speech is consistently gracious in defeat. Yet his conclusion about this fate does not apply seamlessly to his situation. In it, he resorts to seeing himself as a pawn of kings, an estimation that differs from the one others have of the relationship between Henry and him. He states, "O, how wretched is that poor man that hangs on princes' favors" (3.2.367). His choice of the phrase "poor man" to explain or analogize his own condition conflicts on a primary level with the reality of his existence. For although Wolsey may be subject to the king's favors, he could not by any stretch be considered poor. In fact, the inventory of his own princely wealth is in part what leads to his undoing. If he identifies himself with the "poor man" in his aphorism, then we must wonder how much we can believe the reason he tells Cromwell that he is happy after his fall: "I know myself now" (3.2.378). Still, he is loving and avuncular to Cromwell, giving him sound advice on ambition. In the end, the Cardinal cuts an ambivalent figure, risking a self-pity that can undo the pathos he potentially achieves. Actors playing him get to decide how much of that risk to take.

One of the main challenges for modern audiences is appreciating the special kind of spectacle in the play's processions and pageants. This play is filled with scenes of royal display in which the main point is for the audience to look on noble assemblies. Beyond the spectacle, little happens in these moments. This lack of action in scenes such as the procession after Anne's coronation might strike audiences today as odd and even alienating. However, sumptuous displays of royalty of the kind represented in the play would have been rarities for Renaissance audiences. When on the rare occasions royalty went on progress through the streets of London, throngs descended upon them to view the royal display and observers wrote detailed accounts of the display. Audiences attending *Henry VIII* would have gotten to see an imitation of events that normally generated excitement for spectators.

In our day, those performing the play must face the challenge of making these scenes familiar for modern audiences. The more extravagant productions have attempted to let the spectacle itself connect audience with pageantry. But there seems to be a sense that, in an age of easily accessible images of royalty, such sumptuous displays are not enough. Billington's 1978 film version provides an example of one way for directors and actors to address these challenges. As Anne and her extensive retinue exit the church after the ceremony, the gentlemen who describe the scene are not just gawking and excited but excited in particular ways. The first is with their eagerness to show knowledge of the participants, and so lend themselves cachet. In view of the procession, gentleman two eagerly exclaims, "A royal train, believe me. These I know" (4.1.37). On viewing the queen, his excitement is more lewd even when his lines sound respectful. In Billington's production, the declaration he makes as a lead-up to his lines about not blaming the king's conscience— "Sir, as I have a soul, she is an angel!" (4.1.44)—is spoken enviously and lustfully.

The ending of the play presents another important issue of performance. After Henry reasserts dominion over his council, the play dramatizes Londoners' rowdy excitement at Princess Elizabeth's christening and Cranmer's prophecy of her rise as the "maiden Phoenix." This material has struck some directors as so superfluous that they have omitted it from their productions. However, cutting out these scenes has an impact on the tone and focus of the play. If these scenes are cut, then the play focuses squarely on Henry. If the material is included, the play looks at Henry in order to look beyond him. It becomes about the future as well as about the past.

Such a tension is in many ways behind so many of the issues of performance in this or any other Shakespeare play. Is the focus on the play itself, or does it look beyond, to the audience in the present moment? The most satisfying productions are those that find a way to do what *Henry VIII* does so well: look to the past in order to help us understand ourselves.

TOPICS FOR DISCUSSION AND
FURTHER STUDY OF *HENRY VIII*

1. How does the play treat the question of Buckingham's guilt for his crime of treason of which his peers convict him? Where and to what extent does the text support his claim for innocence?

2. What kind of king is Henry, especially when you consider that Wolsey has been conducting ignoble practices under his rule and he falls in love with a woman not his wife? How does the play make attempts to exonerate or impugn him for his actions (or lack thereof)? Is he more sympathetic than pathetic?

3. Henry claims his desire for a divorce from Katherine is based on what he calls a scruple of conscience over having married a woman who was previously married to his brother (by Church law, such a remarriage is technically incest). How credible are his claims of a gnawing conscience? Where does the play support or undermine them?

4. How does the play characterize Anne Bullen in regard to her being singled out as a favorite by Henry? Point to passages that help audiences understand the extent of her involvement or ambition.

5. Many stage productions cut out the last scenes of act 5, ending after the King's reemergence as leader over his council. To what extent do you find this practice defensible? How might excluding the christening and prophecy alter the meaning of the play?

6. Many critics and editors believe *Henry VIII* to be a collaboration between William Shakespeare and fellow playwright John Fletcher; some even publish the play under both names. Are there places in the play where you believe the writing style is different enough to suggest two authors? What difference do you think it makes in terms of understanding or reception if you consider it a multi-authored play?

7. Although Shakespeare's acting company listed the play under the title *The Famous History of the Life of King Henry the Eighth* in their collection of plays

published six years after Shakespeare's death, an account of its performance in 1613 names the play by the title *All Is True*. Which title would you name the play, and why would you choose one over the other?

8. The play is called *Henry VIII*, but it presents questions about which character might be called the central focus in the play. Is there a character who you believe the play promotes to central focus? Or, if not, what do you think the purpose might be of not presenting a character as the protagonist?

9. For the more advanced student, consider the role of religion in the play. In the age the play was written, England was a Protestant nation. Although the play does not make an issue of it per se, Henry's divorce from Katherine was the pivotal event that thrust England into Protestantism. Some critics have even called *Henry VIII* a kind of Protestant propaganda. Does the play have particular bias for Protestantism and/or against Catholicism?

10. For the more advanced student, check out Volume 4 of Geoffrey Bullough's *Narrative and Dramatic Sources of Shakespeare* from your library. This work contains excerpts from Shakespeare's historical sources (Holinshed's *Chronicles* and Fox's *Acts and Monuments*) and the play *When You See Me, You Know Me* to which the Prologue likely refers. Using that source, examine and consider how Shakespeare uses and alters history in the writing of this play—adding features, speeches, and motives. How do Shakespeare's authorial choices create meaning out of history?

Performance Questions

11. How sympathetic would you make the performance of Buckingham at the beginning of the play? Does the Cardinal wrong him, or has he merely discovered his guilt?

12. In 3.1, Katherine has retired to her chambers after refusing to participate in the trial. Here, Katherine claims surprise at the attention from the two cardinals and describes herself as "a poor weak woman, fall'n from favor." In performance, would you present Katherine the way she describes herself in this scene, or would you do it in some other way?

13. How would you present Anne Bullen in the play? Would you have her played as a woman sympathic to Katherine and reluctant to take up the role of queen herself? Or would you make her delighted to be singled out by the King?

14. The play contains numerous pageants and other royal displays, the purpose of which is in part for the audience to admire royalty. How might you envision staging such a display? With an unlimited budget? Or with no money?

15. A challenge of this play is accepting two instant reversals: Wolsey's repentance from the lavish life he has just lost, and Katherine's forgiveness of Wolsey at the instigation of Griffith. How would you present these moments? If

you believe them to be sincere, how might you have them acted to make them credible?

16. If Henry has changed by the end of the play, how has he done so? And how might you convey his change in a production of your own?

HENRY VIII BIBLIOGRAPHY
AND FILMOGRAPHY

Ball, Robert Hamilton. "The Shakespeare Film as Record: Sir Herbert Beerbohm Tree." *Shakespeare Quarterly* 3.3 (1952): 227–236.

This article cites the value of film as evidence of stage history and recounts cinema's shaky start through the experiences of Beerbohm Tree. A large part of this article is dedicated to the filming of a handful of scenes from Beerbohm Tree's *Henry VIII*, one of the first films of a Shakespeare play and one of the first to shoot scenes on site rather than in theater. The destruction of all copies of Beerbohm Tree's film (as was stipulated by contract) leads Ball to suggest a method of investigation that searches both for film and for interviews of those still living who were associated with the film's making.

Bliss, Lee. "The Wheel of Fortune and the Maiden Phoenix of Shakespeare's *King Henry the Eighth*." *ELH* 42.1 (1975): 1–25.

Often cited as a seminal work in the serious critical investigation of the play, Bliss' work contests ideas that Henry VIII is a "misled youth" or the play is a study of his maturation as king (2). The end, Bliss suggests, shows us the "moral complexity" of the "'historical' political world" and how King Henry's own "shadowy existence" generates "alarming shifts in its perspective on character and action" (3). The article is dedicated to showing how shifts in perspective mean that "truth" is very difficult to locate at any moment in the play. The play's end prophecy of the infant Elizabeth as the maiden Phoenix highlights the cyclical nature of fortune and looks hopefully to her transcendence over the political shifts shown in the play.

Bosman, Anston, "Seeing Tears: Truth and Sense in *All Is True*." *Shakespeare Quarterly* 50.4 (1999): 459–476.

Bosman takes up questions of the nature of truth, but focuses his study on the relationship between "vision and truth" in the play. Bosman compares and notes the supremacy of visual over auditory and scripted evidence for establishing truth. Tears provide the most concentrated example of the association between vision and truth, serving as they do as "subject and object" of establishing truth—as "tears that see and tears that are seen" (473).

Bullough, Geoffrey. *Narrative and Dramatic Sources of Shakespeare.* Vol. 4. *Later English History Plays.* London: Routledge and Kegan Paul, 1962.

This excellent resource excerpts relevant passages from the primary sources from which Shakespeare derived his history of *Henry VIII* and the play's events and from sources to which he responded. Included in Bullough's work are extensive passages from Raphael Holindshed's *Third Volume of the Chronicles of England, Scotland, and Ireland* (1587, 2nd edition), John Fox's *Acts and Monuments of Martyrs* (1583 edition), and Samuel Rowley's popular play on Henry VIII, *When You See Me, You Know Me* (1605).

Carney, Jo Eldridge. "Queenship in Shakespeare's *Henry VIII*: The Issue of Issue." In *Political Rhetoric, Power, and Renaissance Women*, edited by Carol Levin and Patricia A. Sullivan, 188–202. Albany: State University of New York Press, 1995.

Carney argues that as much as *Henry VIII* is about kingship, the play is also "presenting what it means to be queen, and illustrating the nature and limitations of the role" (190). For Shakespeare's play, Carney holds that for queens the "capacity for" childbearing is "much more important" than their fitness to reign (190). So much of Henry's attraction to Anne, and of the play's depiction of her, rests on her procreative potential for bearing offspring, particularly a male heir.

Cox, John. "*Henry VIII* and the Masque." *ELH* 45.3 (1978): 390–409.

In taking up the question of elements of court masque in *Henry VIII*, Cox explains them in terms of Shakespeare's development as a dramatist and argues that the play is "an experiment in adapting the principles of the court masque to the dramatic tradition of the public theatre" (391). The principles of the masque, for Cox, not only exist as elements in the play, but they permeate its structure. Chief among these is the notion that the masque is designed to a "full display of royal power," and the plot of *Henry VIII* continuously moves in the direction of this display (396). Far from simply reproducing a masque, the play shows Shakespeare's typically assimilative mind at work, "combining and recombining traditions in a way that transforms them" (406).

Downs, John. *Roscius Anglicanus.* London: H, Playford, 1708.

Downs' work provides a history of the theater in late 17th-century London from one of its early practicioners.

Foakes, R. A. "Introduction." Shakespeare, William. *King Henry VIII*, edited by R. A. Foakes (1968). Arden edition. London: Methuen, 1984.

See description under Shakespeare, William, below.

Kyle, Chris R. *"Henry VIII or All Is True*: Shakespeare's Favorite Play." In *How to Do Things with Shakespeare*, edited by Laurie Maguire, 82–100. Malden, MA: Blackwell, 2008.

This chapter reads *Henry VIII* to read as history contemporary to its date of composition as opposed to the dates of history covered by its plot. Kyle primarily compares Wolsey's influence as a favorite of King Henry to the influence of favorites in the court of King James. Kyle ultimately sees the play as a "commentary on contemporary politics and on the role of faction and courtly intrigue" (96).

Lawson, Mark. *"Wolf Hall* and *Bring Up the Bodies*: A Familiar Tale Infused with Thrilling Originality of Storytelling." *The Guardian*, May 18, 2014, http://www.theguardian.com/stage/2014/may/18/wolf-hall-bring-up-the-bodies-review-mantel-aldwych-theatre.

McMullan, Gordan. "Introduction." Shakespeare, William, and John Fletcher. *King Henry VIII*, edited by Gordon McMullan. Arden edition. London: Thompson Learning, 2000.

See description under Shakespeare, William, below.

O'Connor, Newman Kelly. *"Henry VIII* at Shakespeare's Globe and the Folger Theatre." *The Shakespeare Newsletter* 60.3 (2010/2011): 83–84, 100, 119.

This review article discusses two recent productions of *Henry VIII* at major venues and serves to supplement Richmond's book, which covers performance through the mid-1990s. It also shows the versatility of *Henry VIII* in production.

Odell, George C. D. *Shakespeare—From Betterton to Irving* (1920). 2 Vols. Bronx, NY: Benjamin Blom, 1963.

Odell covers the history of staging Shakespeare plays from the 17th century through the end of the 19th century. Odell offers important information on staging, reception, actors, and venues of *Henry VIII*.

Patterson, Annabel. *"All Is True*: Negotiating the Past in *Henry VIII*." In *Elizabethan Theater: Essays in Honor of S. Schoenbaum*, edited by R. B. Parker and S. P. Zitner, 147–166. Newark: University of Delaware Press, 1996.

Patterson suggests that instead of trying to present true history in the play, Shakespeare's use of deliberately unhistorical elements and his choice in subject help "explain, in historical terms, why historical objectivity was . . . hard to come by" (147). Part of her argument is that the seminal historical passages that Shakespeare uses from Holindshed's 1587 edition of his *Chronicles* are themselves collaborations and even interpolations placed in the work by other historians. Patterson states Shakespeare in the end "saw himself as merely one of a series of collaborators in a never-ending process of history writing" (161).

Richards, Jennifer. "Shakespeare and the Politics of Co-authorship." In *Shakespeare and Early Modern Political Thought*, edited by David Armitage, Conal Condren, and Andrew Fitzmaurice, 176–194. Cambridge, UK: Cambridge University Press, 2009.

Richards' chapter disputes the notion that *Henry VIII* is a disjointed and unsuccessful collaboration between Shakespeare and John Fletcher and suggests instead that the work is a careful collaboration and one in which Fletcher takes the lead. She argues the play is Fletcher's defense of "honesty," which she claims the play distinguishes from "truth." Honesty at the time the play was written could mean verity, but it also meant "moderation." And the play does not just display moderation in the characters, it also expects it from the audience in the way they judge the actions of them.

Richmond, Hugh M. *King Henry VIII*. Manchester, UK: Manchester University Press, 1994.

This history from the Shakespeare in Performance series (Eds. J. R. Mulryne and J. C. Bulman) provides an in-depth study of the extensive history of a play that, as it reminds us, is the only play of Shakespeare's to be performed continuously since it was written. Richmond focuses specifically on trends in historical reception that come out of performance—for example, the shifts from early insincere performances to sincere renditions with Katherine as the moral center of the work, and ultimately to the pursuit of historical realism and responses to it that characterize performances of the 19th century up to those today.

Shakespeare, William. *King Henry VIII*, edited by R. A. Foakes (1968). Arden edition. London: Methuen, 1984.

This second-series Arden edition of the play is a scholarly one, written for graduate students and professors. Foakes' introduction to his edition has been especially influential in its compelling argument for Shakespeare as the sole author of the work with Fletcher as an editor after the fact.

Shakespeare, William, and John Fletcher. *King Henry VIII*, edited by Gordon McMullan. Arden edition. London: Thompson Learning, 2000.

This third-series Arden edition (a scholarly one, written for graduate students and professors) offers the most up-to-date analysis of the arguments about co-authorship in the play and reads the debate in light of the desire to prop up Shakespeare as the preeminent English playwright.

Stone, George Winchester. "The Making of the Repertory." In *The London Theatre World 1660–1800*, edited by Robert D. Hume. Carbondale: Southern Illinois University Press, 1980.

This important study provides data on the number of times Shakespeare's plays were performed in London in the Restoration and 18th century.

Filmography

The Famous History of the Life of King Henry the Eighth (1978). Dir. Kevin Billington. Produced by BBC and Time Life Films. With John Stride (King Henry VIII), Claire Bloom (Katherine), Timothy West (Cardinal Wolsey), Barbara Kellerman (Anne Bullen), and Ronald Pickup (Archbishop Cranmer).

This made-for-television production of the play is shot on location (as opposed to in-studio) as part of the BBC's ambitious project to produce all of Shakespeare's plays over the course of seven seasons. This, the last play of the first season, is regarded as one of the finest in the whole series in terms of its use of film technique. In this case Billington uses film to establish intimacy, secrecy, and alienation (when necessary), and so intensify the political intrigue of the play.

Sir Herbert Beerbohm Tree (1908). Producer W. G. Barker. Ealing Studios.

This silent-film version of five scenes from *Henry VIII* is not available for viewing. It was highly influential on British film, and started a trend of filming stage productions. As stipulated by contract, all twelve copies of this play were destroyed after six weeks.

TIMELINE FOR *KING JOHN* AND *HENRY VIII*

King John	Reigned as king of England from 1199 to 1216.
1167	Born December 24, son of King Henry II and Eleanor of Aquitaine.
1189	Richard named Arthur of Brittany as heir to the English throne.
1192	King Richard returning from the Holy Land was captured and imprisoned by the duke of Austria and held for ransom. The ransom was paid and Richard was released on February 4, 1194.
1199, April 6	King Richard the Lionhearted died and John succeeded him to the throne of England. May 27: the coronation of King John.
1200	King John married Isabelle of Angouleme on August 24, 1200. They had five children: Henry (who became King Henry III); Richard, Earl of Cornwall; Joan of England; Isabella of England; and Eleanor of England.
1202, April 28	John forfeited Aquitaine, Poitou, and Anjou to King Philip II of France.
1203, April 3	John probably involved in the murder of Arthur.
1205	John entered dispute with Pope Innocent III.
1209	John excommunicated because of his opposition to Stephen Langton, chosen as archbishop of Canterbury by Pope Innocent III. The excommunication was lifted when John agreed to the wishes of the Pope.
1212	King John imposed taxes on the Barons in his attempts to regain the lost lands of Aquitaine, Poitou, and Anjou.
1214, July 27	Defeat at the Battle of Bovines; King John forced to accept an unfavorable peace with France.

1215, June 15	The English barons forced John to sign the Great Charter (Latin name: Magna Carta). Omitted from Shakespeare's play.
1215–1217	First Barons War: Rebel barons supported the son of Philip II, king of France, Prince Louis (Louis VIII).
1216, May 21	Louis invaded England and marches to London where he received support and is proclaimed king of England, although not actually crowned. King John escapes to Winchester. October 19: King John dies at Newark and is buried in Worcester Cathedral. October 28: the barons turned against Louis and gave their support to King John's nine-year-old son, Henry, who then became King Henry III of England.
1455–1485	Wars of the Roses. Dynastical wars between the houses of Lancaster and York, concluding with the Battle of Bosworth Field, where Henry, earl of Richmond, killed Richard III and established the Tudor dynasty, becoming Henry VII (d. 1509). The succeeding members of the House of Tudor were Henry VIII (1509–1547), Edward VI (1547–1553), Mary I (1553–1558), and Elizabeth I (1558–1603).
1466–1536	Erasmus, Desiderius: *Teaching at Oxford*. Wrote *In Praise of Folly* (1509, Latin), *On Copia* (1512), and *Education of a Christian Prince* (1516), an early courtesy book or "behavior manual," a genre that was very popular throughout the period.
1469–1527	Niccolo Machiavelli: *The Prince* (Rome, 1532), written in 1513. The Machiavel was an important stage figure. One type was a comic contriver, the other a more serious politician, doing whatever is necessary for success, as Cardinal Pandulph does in *King John*; some are even villains, such as King John or King Claudius in *Hamlet*.
1473–1530	Thomas Wolsey named cardinal in the Catholic Church and lord chancellor under Henry VIII.
1485–1636	Katherine of Aragon, first wife of Henry VIII, queen of England (1509–1533); after, Princess Dowager of Wales.
1489–1556	Thomas Cranmer, archbishop of Canterbury under Henry VIII and leader of the Protestant Reformation in England.

King Henry VIII	Reigned as king of England from 1509 to 1547.
1491	Born June 28.
1501–1536	Anne Boleyn (Bullen in the play), wife of Henry VIII and queen of England (1533–1536).
1517	Martin Luther (1483–1546) posted ninety-five theses in Wittenberg, initiating the Protestant Reformation.
1528	Baldessare Castiglione (1478–1529): *The Book of the Courtier* (Trans. Sir Thomas Hoby, 1561), an important courtesy manual defining the ideal gentleman.
1547	Death of Henry VIII.
1553–1558	Reign of Mary Tudor (b. 1516). Mary restored Catholicism to England.
1554–1586	Philip Sidney, *Apology for Poetry* (1595), defends poets and playwrights as seers.
1557	John Shakespeare married Mary Arden.
1558–1603	Reign of Elizabeth I (b. 1533). Elizabeth established the Protestant National Church of England.
1559	*The Mirror for Magistrates*, induction by Thomas Sackville. Shows dangers of ambition in high places and by implication the general danger of ambition. Influenced by Giovanni Boccaccio's *De Casibus Virorum Illustrium* (see above).
1564	William Shakespeare born; christened April 26 (d. April 23, 1616). Christopher Marlowe born (d. 1593). Wrote *Tamburlaine* (c. 1587) and *Doctor Faustus* (c. 1592)—two plays that ultimately punish ambition. The latter play is about a young man who, like Hamlet, is a Wittenberg scholar. Marlowe's work greatly influenced Shakespeare, as did the work of Thomas Kyd and Robert Greene.
1567	Red Lion Playhouse: first public playhouse.
c. 1568	Richard Burbage born (d. 1619). Great tragedian, and a shareholder with Shakespeare in The Lord Chamberlain's Men, later The King's Men.
1576	The Theatre, long thought to be the first public theater, built by James Burbage and his sons Richard and Cuthbert; located outside of London in Finnesbury Field. Other theaters, such as the Rose, followed.
1582	William Shakespeare married Anne Hathaway (November).
1583	Birth of Shakespeare's daughter, Susanna (baptized May 26).
1585	Birth of Shakespeare's son Hamnet and daughter Judith (baptized February 2).

1587	Mary Queen of Scots beheaded (b. 1542).
1588	Defeat of the Spanish Armada.
c. 1589	*Titus Andronicus*, Shakespeare's first revenge tragedy.
1592	Robert Greene's *A Groat's Worth of Wit Bought with a Million of Repentance* refers to Shakespeare as an "upstart crow" (plagiarist). The publisher, Henry Chettle, later apologized.
c. 1592	*Richard III*.
1592–1594	Plague years; theaters closed. Shakespeare composed many of his sonnets.
1593	Publication of *Venus and Adonis*, dedicated to Henry Wriothesley, third earl of Southampton, Shakespeare's patron.
1594	Publication of *The Rape of Lucrece*, also dedicated to the Earl of Southampton. William Shakespeare and Richard Burbage become shareholders in The Lord Chamberlain's Men.
1594–1595	*Romeo and Juliet*; c. 1595, *A Midsummer Night's Dream*.
1595–1597	*King John*, first published in the Folio of 1623.
1595–1596	*Richard II*; c. 1596–1597, *The Merchant of Venice* and *Henry IV, Part I*.
1596	Burial of Shakespeare's only son, Hamnet, August 11 in Stratford.—Shakespeare's family granted a coat of arms, making Shakespeare officially a "gentleman."
1597	Shakespeare bought New Place (May 4), the second largest house in Stratford.
1598–1599	*Much Ado about Nothing*; 1598–1600: *As You Like It*; 1599: *Henry V* and *Julius Caesar*.
1599	The opening of the Globe Theatre, built with lumber salvaged from The Theatre, demolished when lease expired. *Julius Caesar* probably the first of Shakespeare's plays to be staged at the Globe.
1599–1601	*Hamlet*.
1601	Death of John Shakespeare.
1603	Death of Queen Elizabeth. James VI of Scotland (b. 1566) becomes James I of England. The Lord Chamberlain's Men becomes The King's Men.
1603–1604	*Othello*; 1604–1605: *King Lear*.
1606–1607	*Macbeth, Antony*, and *Cleopatra*.
1608	Death of Mary Arden. John Milton born (d. 1674). Milton writes the dedication to the second Folio of 1632.

1608–1609	Shakespeare's company took possession of Blackfriars Playhouse.
1609	Shakespeare's sonnets published by Thomas Thorpe.
c. 1611	*The Tempest*. Shakespeare retired to Stratford.
1613	The Globe destroyed by fire during a performance of *Henry VIII*; rebuilt 1614.
1616	Judith Shakespeare married Thomas Quiney. Shakespeare writes his will. Death of William Shakespeare. Death of Cervantes (b. 1547).
1617	Ben Jonson named Poet Laureate.
1623	Publication of the first Folio. Jonson wrote dedicatory verses.
1625	Death of King James I. Charles I crowned king (beheaded: 1649; monarchy restored: 1660, with King Charles II).
1632	Publication of the second Folio. Milton wrote dedicatory verses.
1642	Closing of the theaters by the Puritans.